ESPIONAGE
Spies and Secrets

Richard M. Bennett

Foreword by James Bamford

Preface by David Shayler

To my wonderful late mother, Florence, eccentric journalist and more, and to my daughter Katie who has helped me greatly and moreover put up with me during the writing of this book. Not forgetting my editor at Virgin, Paul Copperwaite, who claims, probably correctly, that he has been a tower of strength.

This paperback edition published in Great Britain in 2003 by
Virgin Books Ltd
Thames Wharf Studios
Rainville Road
London W6 9HA

First published in 2002 by Virgin Books Ltd

A catalogue record for this book is available
from the British Library.

ISBN 0 7535 0830 3

Typeset by Phoenix Photosetting, Chatham, Kent

Printed and bound by Mackays of Chatham, Kent

PREFACE

On Wednesday, 13 February 2002 the population of United States was asked to place itself in the highest state of vigilance and to expect terrorist activity of an unspecified nature. An appeal like this would have been unimaginable before 11 September 2001. In exactly what way the Americans were expected to be extra-cautious was left unspecified: military-style attack? Further hijack attempts of the kind that have already produced such horrific results? Bioterrorism?

When I joined the security services in 1991, the world was a very different place. Just two years previously, the Cold War had come to an end after Eastern Bloc governments had been overthrown by popular revolution. Then, while I was undergoing recruitment into the secret state, the Red Army refused to fire on its citizens as they protested at a counter-coup by the Soviet old guard which had seen Russian Confederate President, Mikhail Gorbachev held under house arrest. A few years beforehand, both events would have been unthinkable. Indeed, when both events happened, they didn't just surprise and amaze the British public, they also astounded the British intelligence agencies. So when I walked into the MI5 building on Grosvenor Street on 11 November 1991 for my first day in the service, the threat from Soviet communism and its adherents had disappeared. In other words, the main threat to the UK's national security, which had pre-occupied MI5 and MI6 since World War I, was finally over. What were MI5, MI6 and GCHQ to do with their 10,000+ full-time staff?

Of course, the Security Service – to give it its proper Whitehall title – still had to deal with threats from international terrorist groups and the regimes which sponsored them, as happened in the Gulf in 1991. At the same time, the break up of the Soviet Union made this work more difficult. For the first time, terrorists and their sponsors *potentially* had access to the know-how, technology and materials to build WMDs as they are known in the jargon (weapons of mass destruction or nuclear, chemical and biological warheads). Counter-proliferation – the term given to the thwarting of this threat – therefore grew during the 1990s, leading to seemingly contradictory intelligence relationships with countries like Pakistan and Turkey. On the one hand, Britain shared information about Islamic extremist terrorism with the agencies of these countries; on the other, it spied on the self-same agencies to assess their WMD capability.

But counter-terrorism mainly meant monitoring the civil war in Northern Ireland, which we rather quaintly refer to on the British mainland as 'The Troubles'. With its communist enemy 'defeated', MI5 successfully lobbied government to take over lead responsibility for investigating the Provisional IRA on the British mainland. In October 1992, MI5 began its new role. There were many individual successes and record numbers of IRA members arrested, tried and convicted. There were, though, too many institutional failures – the Bishopsgate attack, for instance, which saw one death and 350 million pounds of damage to the City.

The successes against terrorism are noteworthy for two reasons. One, T2A did not resort to internment, intimidation, assassination or torture to get its results: it worked within the law, arresting suspects and putting them on trial. Two, working within the law to bring suspects to trial laid the seeds for the Good Friday agreement, which has brought some kind of peace – albeit an uneasy one – to the Province for the first time in over 30 years. The remaining rump of Irish Republican terrorism in the form of the Real IRA has neither the support, nor the discipline, nor the ordnance to carry out a serious, prolonged 'armed struggle'.

The main job of the intelligence services in the years to come will concentrate on the conflict created by Israeli's occupation of the West Bank and the Gaza Strip, which has been the subject of a UN condemnation since Israel invaded in 1967. Imagine if the religious sectarianism of Northern Ireland had spilled over into international conflict. Imagine if it had begun to rip the fabric of geopolitics apart. Imagine if it had led to the state openly killing terrorist suspects and innocent bystanders. In the case of Northern Ireland terrorism, it was bad enough that a parochial dispute between Catholics and Protestants, which had long been settled on the mainland, kept spilling over into mainstream British life. It is frightening to think that the Middle East conflict over a tiny piece of land does not just spill over into international affairs but has come to wholly dominate the issue of world peace and stability.

The world of course responded very differently when Iraqi tanks rolled into Kuwait in 1991. The UN condemned Iraq but backed its words with actions and Iraq was quickly defeated in the ensuing Gulf War.

It has yet to be established just how many innocent civilians died as a result of the recent US and UK invasion of Afghanistan, prompted by intelligence – rather than any convincing evidence – indicating that Osama bin Laden was responsible for the barbaric attack on the US. Although America has argued it acted in self-defence, I believe history will more accurately judge the US's response to be naked Wild West-style revenge. In this spirit, George W. Bush did say that Osama bin Laden was wanted 'Dead or Alive'. No terrorist conflict has ever been resolved by resorting to violence. Look at Bloody Sunday, Londonderry, 1972 or Israeli's current policy of 'pinpoint prevention', its euphemistic term used to justify the extra-judicial execution of 'suspected terrorists' and – by Israel's own admission – innocent bystanders. Or the violent relationship between the UK/US and Libya from 1984 to 1996, in which many innocent people died on both sides. These include individuals like WPC Yvonne Fletcher and Colonel Gaddafi's adopted two year old daughter; the 270 who were murdered in the Lockerbie attack; and the many civilians reportedly murdered in the 1986 bombing of Tripoli and an attempt to assassinate Colonel Gaddafi in March 1996.

Terror begets terror. It simply leads to the deaths of more innocent people on both sides. Although some commentators have tried to claim that the recent bombing of Afghanistan was a success, the mission failed to achieve its objectives: neither Osama bin Laden nor Mullah Omar, the leader of the Taliban, has been apprehended. Around the same time, Al-Qa'ida activist, Richard Reid, come close to murdering another couple of hundred innocent people in a planned suicide attack on a transatlantic jet. After Afghanistan, there could be many more Richard Reids.

Meanwhile George W. Bush is pumping 48 billion dollars into his war on the 'axis of evil'. Part of this money is to be spent on a new federal agency known as the Information Awareness Office. Its main function will be to harvest the information shared between citizens of the United States by phone, email and all manner of telecommunications. In 2000, Parliament passed the Regulation of Investigatory Powers Act, giving the UK intelligence agencies the power to glean personal information like records of telephone numbers dialled to and from your phone; websites surfed; and email sent and received, without a warrant. In other words, Big Brother is listening to you, and the first casualty of the war on terrorism is perhaps not truth but personal privacy.

In the face of criticism from the EU and some degree of cheerleading from the British Government, the Americans have made it plain that they're willing to go it alone, if necessary, in their pursuit not just of terrorists but of those that arm them. 'I think the President has made it clear that if it comes to a choice between action to protect the American people, without allies or [with] allies but no action, we'll go without allies,' says Richard Perle, Assistant Secretary of Defense from 1981 to 1987. Meanwhile the remnants of Al-Qa'ida remain scattered to the four winds, hell-bent on humiliating the US again. Unless there is some original thinking on the part of our leaders and the intelligence agencies who advise them, an Iron Curtain will descend between the Western and Islamic worlds as the prelude to a Second Cold War. In the same way that technology made World War II more violent and more horrific than the 'war to end all wars', the conflict of the 21st century Cold War will see terrorists becoming ever more sophisticated and ever more deadly.

In January 2002, Britain's BBC1 explored this nightmare scenario. It transmitted *Smallpox 2002: Silent Weapon* – a mock-documentary featuring real news personnel. It tells in retrospect how Britain has become the victim of an attack involving this deadly virus brought over unwittingly by, in their scenario, an airline passenger flying from New York to London. This is the unimaginably chilling scenario that modern intelligence agencies must face. It seems a long way from shadowy brush contacts between men in trenchcoats on Berlin street corners, monitored by equally shadowy looking characters in unmarked builders' vans listening to reel-to-reel tape recorders. Yet, that was still the de facto nature of intelligence work when I joined just eleven short years ago.

Information is power and good intelligence – secret information – is the key to winning any conflict. We're living in a world in which it is absolutely vital not just to be informed but to be reliably informed. You'll find within this book a wealth of facts about the fields of espionage and counter-terrorism past and present which have never been made available in one publication before. The book will make a valid and timely contribution to an ongoing process: to demystify the murky world of intelligence and to ensure that the services provide the protection we have a right to expect. There are more people than ever who would like to see information democratised in this way. When I was a journalist on *The Sunday Times* in the early nineties, there were occasions when I'd have been glad to have been able to pull a book like this off the shelf.

David Shayler
London 2002

FOREWORD

In the days following the 11 September 2001 terrorist attacks on New York and Washington, amid the endless news accounts of how such a thing could happen and what the Bush administration was planning in response, a new lexicon began emerging. The very next day *The New York Times* noted, 'obtaining "humint" as the Central Intelligence Agency likes to call it, has been dismayingly difficult'. *The Washington Post* later told of the US efforts to compile intelligence on Afghan terrorist camps through 'signals intelligence' and 'satellite imagery'. Other articles spoke of collecting 'sigint' and 'imint', spying with the help of such systems as 'carnivore' and 'echelon', and how organisations like Al-Qa'ida may still have 'sleepers' hidden in the US.

Overnight, ratings-hungry network news organisations were forced to switch from exploiting bloody shark attacks and missing interns to discussing the vulnerabilities of pilotless spy planes, and the pros and cons of satellite espionage versus clandestine operations. Both for the journalists in the field and the audience at home, the sudden switch was jarring and the learning curve steep. Thus the need for a comprehensive encyclopedia of espionage.

Richard M. Bennett's timely new book, *Espionage: An Encyclopedia of Spies and Secrets*, fills that need. In it he not only defines the language of spying, he also presents comprehensive outlines of the intelligence services belonging to the major countries of the world today, and biographical sketches of the key players, past and present.

In addition to being a useful companion to the news of the day – and the never-ending flow of spy novels – many of the entries are simply fun to read. A 'blind date' in spy-speak, Bennett notes, in a meeting between an intelligence officer and an agent at a time and place of the agents choosing. Not always a good idea, he points out. 'These are potentially dangerous,' says Bennett, 'as the officer could be set up for capture or an attempt be made to "turn" him.' A 'bridge agent', on the other hand, is not a spy who hangs out on the Golden Gate but one 'who acts as a courier or go-between from a case officer to an agent in a denied area'. Even experienced journalists often fail to understand the key difference between an intelligence 'case officer' – such as a career employee of the CIA's Clandestine Service – and an 'agent', usually a local who has agreed to pass secrets on to the case officer. Here again, Bennett offers a useful explanation of the important distinction.

The need to understand the definitions and nuances of espionage will certainly grow in importance. The 'war on terrorism', announced with fanfare but lacking an end-date, will likely go on for years, if not decades; a sort of perpetual conflict. Clearly leading the charge is the US Intelligence Community. Officers from the CIA's Clandestine Service were the first ones into Afghanistan, even before the September attacks, and the first American killed in the fighting also came from their ranks. At the same time, the role of the CIA has gone beyond simply collecting intelligence to operating guided missile-armed drones used to kill suspected enemy forces.

To a large extent, the war in Afghanistan has become a testing ground for every new intelligence innovation to come along over the years. And in contrast to the cave-to-cave fighting taking place on the ground, the spy community is using futuristic technology in order to attempt to locate suspected terrorists. This includes multi-billion-dollar eavesdropping and imaging satellites, high-altitude unmanned aircraft, listening posts in Pakistan and Afghanistan, and massive supercomputers to sort through millions of phone calls and bits of data. All this will require billions of additional dollars for the spy world, leading to more technology and more clandestine operations.

In previous wars, intelligence was a support function but today it has become a frontline force in itself. This is especially true when it comes to cyberwarfare – also known as information operations – a speciality of the supersecret National Security Agency. The agency has been preparing for years to use the networks of communications channels, encircling the earth like a fuzzy ball of knitting, to wreak electronic havoc on our enemies. While seldom used in the past, it may become an important weapon as the countries drawn into the conflict grow in sophistication.

Thus, being well informed in this new war will require knowing far more than what a B-52 is or how a howitzer operates. Richard Bennett's new book serves as a good primer for anyone seeking to decipher the growing dialogue of spy-talk taking place on television and in the newspapers. It is also simply nice to know the difference between a 'swallow' and a 'raven'!

James Bamford
Bestselling author of *The Puzzle Palace* and *Body of Secrets*

A

ABEL, Col. Rudolf Ivanovich (born William Fisher, Emil R. Goldfus/'Mark', 1903–71)   KGB officer operating in the USA during the 1950s and exchanged for U-2 pilot Francis Gary Powers in February 1962 some five years after his conviction and imprisonment for 30 years as a Soviet master spy. The KGB's top intelligence officer in the US (1948–57), Abel moved freely about the US from his base in New York, supervising a vast network of Soviet spies until he was finally exposed by one of his own colleagues. Even after Abel was arrested, the details of his espionage activities were never fully understood and most of the agents he controlled were never identified. Abel died on 16 November 1971, and was buried without fanfare. So little notice was taken of his passing that news of his death did not reach the West until the following year.

ABWEHR   (Amtes Ausland/Abwehr Intelligence Section OKW) In February 1938 the Reich War Ministry was abolished and a new overall Armed Forces authority, known as the High Command of the Armed Forces – Oberkommando der Wehrmacht or OKW took its place. The Abwehr was the OKW's intelligence agency and its responsibilities covered the full spectrum of intelligence activities. They ranged from making reconnaissance flights over Poland and England prior to the Polish campaign to the prevention of sabotage and subversion and indeed operating very active sabotage organisations behind the enemy front.

The Abwehr achieved a number of striking successes in their operations against the Allies. OPERATION NORTH POLE started with the arrest of two Dutch underground agents infiltrated from England. The Abwehr succeeded in contacting the agents' British HQ, and passing themselves off as being the agents. For two years the Germans maintained this deception, capturing successive waves of agents as soon as they landed on the continent.

Admiral Canaris, during the first years of the war, had laid great stress on good relations with the SS and the necessity for close co-operation with the SS. But the Abwher department was abolished by Himmler in February 1944, and its operations were integrated into the SS intelligence service to destroy what had become a hotbed for dissent against the Fuhrer. The Abwehr was in fact the centre of the July 1944 conspiracy to assassinate Hitler, in the wake of which Admiral Canaris was hanged on 9 April 1945, hours before Allied forces entered the area.

ACCESS   The ability through the possession of appropriate security clearances to obtain classified information.

ACCOMMODATION ADDRESS   A 'safe' address – not overtly associated with intelligence activities – used by an agent to communicate with the intelligence service.

ACOUSTIC INTELLIGENCE   ACINT intelligence derived from the collection and processing of acoustic data, especially the noise 'signatures' of warships and underwater weapons detected by sonar.

ACTION OFFICER   The case officer designated to perform an operational act during a clandestine operation especially in a hostile area.

AERIAL ESPIONAGE   US surveillance aircraft aren't the only ones spying over the borders of other nations. With varying levels of sophistication, dozens of countries operate aircraft to monitor their neighbours. Due to advances in technology, outfitting a standard plane with antennae and other surveillance equipment offers a relatively affordable alternative to launching expensive spy satellites. While the USA collects electronic and communications signals from virtually every corner of the globe, most countries tend to focus on their near neighbours.

Chinese operations include the turboprop EY-8, a modified version of a Soviet aircraft that is designed to detect land- and ship-based radar emitters. China's principal focus is regional targets such as Vietnam, S Korea, N Korea, Japan, Indonesia and the Philippines, as well as US military operations in the area. But China's aircraft and those of other countries, for that matter, are not thought to be shadowing the borders of the US mainland.

Russia's airborne surveillance capability has deteriorated markedly since the end of the Cold War. Russia still carefully watches the USA, although it no longer flies electronic warfare aircraft along the US coast. The Russians still fly regular surveillance flights in the Baltic Sea to monitor events in Poland, Sweden, Germany and Denmark, and occasional flights in the Barents Sea towards N Norway, in the Sea of

Japan to watch both N Korea and Japan, and along its borders with China.

US operations during the Cold War: the USA had to come to terms with the true number of airmen who did not return from more than 10,000 spy flights over the Soviet Union. Figures compiled after the collapse of Communism in Russia allowed a far more comprehensive picture to be created and it then appeared that at least 138 US aircrew were lost during the 1950s and 60s. The revelations stemming from close examination of Soviet records indicates that the USA tended to cover up when aircraft were shot down and their crews captured. The Department of Defence would simply write off the loss and give alternative explanations to the families. A Pentagon team, Task Force Russia, sifted documents in the early 1990s and discovered that 24 aircrew were known to have died; the other 114 were unaccounted for. Some may indeed have been held for up to twenty years in Soviet camps. Abandoned by Washington and thought dead by their families, these men would have had all hope extinguished, but there is no suggestion that any captured US aircrew survived beyond the mid 1980s. The Soviet Union wasn't the only Communist State to shoot down US spy aircraft, both Cuba and China certainly claimed successes. China in particular was responsible for the loss of a Constellation over the Sea of Japan, with 19 aircrew on board.

See also J-STARS; RIVET JOINT; SR-71 SENIOR CROWN; U-2

AFSA US Air Force Security Agency.

AGEE, Philip Burnett Franklin (1936–) Former CIA case officer in Latin America – a major 'whistleblower' who has written and broadcast widely about alleged abuse of power and dirty tricks carried out by the CIA particularly within Latin America.

AGENT A person acting under control of an intelligence or security service to obtain or help obtain information for intelligence purposes. A person, usually a foreign national who has been recruited by a staff officer from an intelligence service to perform clandestine activities.

AGENT IN PLACE Someone who remains in the current position while acting under the direction of a hostile intelligence service in order to obtain information.

AGENT PROVOCATEUR An agent who instigates incriminating overt acts by individuals or groups whom the security services already have under surveillance in order to discredit them further.

AGER US Navy designation for passive intelligence collection vessels. The letters AGER indicate miscellaneous auxiliary (AG) and environmental research (ER). An example being the USS Pueblo (AGER-2) captured by N Korea in 1968.

AGTR Similar to the AGER programme, the TR referring to technical research, an example being the USS *Liberty* (AGTR-5) attacked by Israel in 1967.

AIA Air Intelligence Agency (part of USAF).

AIR AMERICA A CIA proprietary company, which provided air support during the secret war in Laos. It has since been sold. This was an outwardly normal American commercial airline that was, however, covertly operated by the CIA to support its operations throughout SE Asia. It had evolved from a little known organisation; Civil Air Transport or CAT, which had been formed in 1946 to support US covert operations in mainland China. At its peak during the Vietnam War (1961–75) Air America was to operate the world's largest fleet of commercial aircraft. Its pilots were usually ex-military personnel and flew a wide variety of aircraft in support of CIA operations. This sometimes involved activities of great secrecy and not a little danger, transporting agents across national borders. One specialist group of CIA pilots flew secret reconnaissance missions out of Thailand using both the U-2 and SR-71. Air America would be sold after the end of the Vietnam War to continue simply as a small-scale air charter company.

AIR PROPRIETARIES Airlines established by an intelligence agency that are ostensibly private enterprises. They are employed by the agency to carry out clandestine operations, often in addition to their commercial cover with their affiliation to an intelligence organisation kept secret.

AJAX US codename for joint SIS (MI6) and CIA operation in 1953 to overthrow the Prime Minister of Iran, Dr Mohammed Mossadegh. The British codename for the operation was BOOT.

AKBAR, Jelial-Ud-Din Mohammed (1542–1605) The greatest of all the Mogul emperors, Akbar's empire extended from Kashmir in the north to Ahmedabad in the south, and to Dacca in the east at its greatest. He courageously moved his empire away from fanatical Mohammedanism to a greater level of universal toleration and to ensure his survival built one the world's first national intelligence services which included a degree of genuine security surveillance of dissident elements. Akbar had some 4,000 agents and built up networks of spies in neighbouring countries. Many foreign visitors, including Britain's Sir John Hawkins, were greatly impressed with Akbar's ideas.

ALBANIA *Sigurimi (State Security Service):* this service was severely downsized and restructured with the assistance of the CIA following the final overthrow of the Communist regime in Tirana. It provided cover for a number of supposedly secret CIA and NSA listening sites at Durres, Tirana and Shkoder intercepting Serbian communications. These bases also provided training and logistic support for Muslim terrorist groups in the Serbian province of Kosovo both before and during the campaign in 1999.

National Intelligence Service (NIS): believed to be an independent but quite small intelligence service tasked mainly with keeping track of anti-Government exiles abroad.

ALGERIA Coordination de la Sécurité du Territoire (CST) and Département de Recherche et Sécurité (DRS) The Algerian internal security services have faced enormous problems in recent years dealing with the vicious Islamic revolt; there are, however, well-founded suspicions that the CST & DRS have been behind a number of the atrocities themselves.

ALL SOURCE INTELLIGENCE Intelligence based on all available information including OPEN SOURCE (OSINT).

AMAN The Intelligence Corps of the Israeli Defence Forces (IDF).

AMES, Aldrich (1941–) Former CIA employee who was arrested in 1994 for having committed espionage as an agent of the KGB and SVR (1985–94). Ames eventually pleaded guilty to the charges. Ames had worked in the CIA's office that handled clandestine operations around the word and had done incalculable damage to Western interests and he was found to have disclosed about 100 undercover operations and 30 Western agents.

Although the money he made from spying allowed him to live extravagantly, his lifestyle had failed to arouse the suspicions of his CIA colleagues or those responsible for internal security. Changes have been made within the Agency to ensure that much closer attention is paid to unaccountable changes in both lifestyle and behaviour patterns, even among senior officers.

ANDRÉ, Major John (1751–80)   Major André of the 54th Foot regiment was a courageous British officer during the rebellion against the Crown by British subjects in America, popularly known as the American War of Independence. André was a man of considerable integrity who had been a popular Adjutant General in the New York garrison and was chosen as the ideal officer to negotiate with Benedict Arnold when he made an offer to surrender his rebel forces in 1780. André was provided with a pass in the name of John Anderson, but when challenged by a rebel patrol he admitted he was an Officer of the Crown and offered a bribe of 100 guineas to be allowed to go free. He was arrested, tried and hanged as a spy at Tappan on 2 October 1780. A deal of sympathy was extended to this honourable young officer who could not bring himself to lie when challenged and there was a widespread demand for his reprieve by the rebellious British settlers, but it was turned down. Until the new state had finally won its freedom, the lands of N America still belonged to the Crown of England. Therefore it can be argued that André could not be a spy in his own country, but that matters little today, save that a touch of mercy might not have gone amiss in the midst of a bloody conflict.

ANDROPOV, Yuri Vladimirovich (1914–84)   Andropov was named a counsellor at the Soviet Embassy in Budapest and wormed his way to the ambassadorship just in time to witness the Hungarian uprising in 1956. Andropov succeeded in luring the leaders of the Hungarian uprising to a so-called conciliatory meeting and then had them all arrested and later executed. It was the lure of this promise that they would be given safe conduct to the West. Moreover, along with General Ivan Serov he oversaw the wholesale slaughter of the remaining rebels by the Soviet Divisions that entered Budapest. Such ruthlessness was appreciated by the brutal Soviet leadership who were to promote him to higher positions. He was appointed Chairman of the KGB in 1967 and was responsible for an accelerated Soviet espionage effort around the world, particularly in Europe and the USA. Scores of talented spies were inserted over the next few years and indeed the London Rezident controlled so many officers that as many as 105 Soviet intelligence personnel were expelled from the Soviet Embassy in 1971 without completely destroying either the KGB or GRU networks operating in the UK.

A firm believer in disinformation, Andropov upgraded the KGB department responsible for spreading disinformation, retitling it Directorate A. At the time he stated: 'The political role of the USSR must be supported abroad by the dissemination of false news and provocative information.' Much of Andropov's modern espionage ideas were culled, it was reported, from the British traitor and SIS spy, Kim Philby, who worked closely with the Officer Training Directorate of the KGB in Moscow. When Andropov became President of the USSR he continued to promote a self-image of being cultured and sophisticated, compared with his 'peasant' predecessors. He was nevertheless little different from any other Soviet dictator. He remained a die-hard Communist to his death in February 1984; however, he left one lasting and outstanding legacy to his nation and the world, for he had actively promoted Mikhail Gorbachev as a future Soviet leader and this led directly to the destruction of everything he had fought for throughout his life.

ANGEL   Slang used by intelligence officers for a member of an opposing service.

ANGLETON, James Jesus (1917–87)   A leading CIA (1941–80) counter-intelligence specialist and a noted 'hardliner', Angleton believed strongly that the Soviet intelligence apparatus had successfully penetrated both MI5 and the CIA. Angleton began his career in espionage in the wartime OSS. During his time in Italy both before and after the end of the war, Angleton developed a deep relationship with leaders of the Jewish underground who later became senior officers in Israel's secret service, the Mossad. Because of these ties, he entered the CIA with the clear understanding that he would head the Israeli desk. In Angleton the Israel Intelligence Service found a firm friend and was to receive much help in intelligence gathering. Most of Angleton's efforts, however, were directed at counter-intelligence. He would spend endless hours studying every detail concerning a suspect. On the international front, Angleton became obsessed with the KGB and constantly highlighted its activities. What had really convinced him that there was a Soviet 'mole' or even 'moles' inside this organisation were the claims made by a Soviet defector, Antoli Golytsin. This former KGB spy, who was once described as a charming con artist, insisted that a Soviet spy worked right in the heart of the HQ at Langley, Virginia. Angleton was the only senior CIA officer who really took Goltsin seriously. He spent 13 years (1961–74), doggedly pursuing this mole in vain.

Becoming something of an institution at the CIA, his authority was unchallenged. He walked into director Allen Dulles's office unannounced at any time. When Richard Helms took over from Dulles he permitted Angleton to continue to operate autonomously, utilising an enormous budget. All of this came to an end when William Colby became Director of the CIA. Colby thought little of Angleton's counter-intelligence activities, believing them to be a waste of money, effort and time. Both men had disliked each other since their days together in the OSS and in December 1974 Colby relieved Angleton of his duties with the Israeli desk and counter-intelligence. Colby allowed Angleton to stay on with the CIA as a consultant following his dismissal, but expected that Angleton's demotion would cause him to resign. When Angleton hung on, Colby leaked a story that Angleton was spying on American agents by opening CIA mail. Believing that there was a plot against him, he finally resigned. He made no secret of his dislike for Colby, telling associates that the DCI had irreparably damaged the CIA by revealing its secrets to the Church Commission and by eventually dismantling the counter-intelligence branch. A point not lost on present-day CIA Directors when looking back on the millionaire mole in their midst, Aldrich Ames, who effectively proved that although Angleton had become paranoid and divisive, there had been more than a grain of truth in his beliefs.

ARCOS AFFAIR   Diplomatic incident created by the presence of a Soviet spy ring which operated as part of the Soviet trade delegation with offices in London with the All Russia Cooperative Society Ltd (ARCOS). In May 1927 the operation was closed down following a raid by some 150 Metropolitan police and MI5 officers.

ARGENTINA   *CNI National Intelligence Centre*: a co-ordination and intelligence analysis organisation with only a limited operational ability; it was created in 1972 and is governed by a secret Presidential decree.

SIDE State Intelligence Secretary: responsible for foreign intelligence, counter-intelligence and internal security. It is the most important service in the Argentinian intelligence community. Originally established in 1946, it became the SIDE in 1956. It has gained an appalling reputation for human rights abuse involving rape, torture, illegal imprisonment and murder. Indeed many of its senior personnel have committed crimes against humanity on a par with anything seen in the Balkans during the 1990s.

National Direction of Internal Intelligence: a weak co-ordination intelligence unit responsible for domestic security within the Ministry of Interior. Established only in the mid 1990s.

J-2 Intelligence, Joint Staff of the Armed Forces: this department controls the *G-2 Army Intelligence* and a *CRIM Military Intelligence Collection Centre* originally called Intelligence Battalion 601 (Batallón de

Inteligencia 601). This unit was deeply involved in domestic intelligence and played a major part in the Military Dictatorship's so called 'dirty war'. The gross violation of human rights during that period 1976–83 in which thousands were murdered or disappeared.

ARMENIA KGB. After the break-up of the Soviet Union in 1991, the local KGB organisation and much of its staff were transferred to the newly independent Armenia. It still includes a number of officers who maintain covert links with Moscow and the new FSB.

ARTIST An artist trained in forgery working for the CIA's Technical Service.

ASA US Army Security Agency (1945–77).

ASSASSINATION Despite being a 'no-word' in polite circles, assassination has been an active policy of many intelligence agencies for most of the 20th century. The OSS, CIA, KGB and its predecessors, SOE and SIS (MI6), the French, Israeli, Indonesian and most Arab services among others have retained this ultimate sanction on occasions, as a threat, as an act of revenge or as part of much larger clandestine operations such as the CIA's OPERATION PHOENIX in Vietnam. This resulted in the elimination of over 30,000 Communist cadre, the KGB had its variation of SMERSH, while the SIS or its effective executive arm the SAS are 'open minded' about the subject.

The murder of VIPs by intelligence officers either from their own or from a foreign service is certainly not unknown. Indeed in the War on Terrorism declared by the US Government following the attacks on Washington, DC and New York on 11 September 2001 the threat of 'executive action' against the heads of terrorist movements cannot be ruled out. A list of assassination plots instigated or planned by the CIA amply demonstrates both the longevity and breadth of US interest in the subject. These include the bombing of Iraq on 26 June 1993 in what appeared to be a direct attempt to kill Saddam Hussein in retaliation for an alleged Iraqi plot to assassinate former President George Bush in Kuwait. 'It was essential,' said President Clinton, 'to send a message to those who engage in state-sponsored terrorism ... and to affirm the expectation of civilised behaviour among nations'. The list of prominent foreign individuals whose assassination was considered by the USA since the end of WWII is considerable.

However, there is ample evidence that the CIA lied to the US Senate. An example being the dispatch of two CIA officers, both with criminal backgrounds, to the Congo to murder Patrice Lumumba. In autumn

1960, Allen Dulles had directly issued the contract to be carried out within three months. Later the CIA sent Joseph Schneider, a scientific and technology officer, to the Congo carrying 'lethal biological material' (i.e. a deadly virus) in a diplomatic bag specifically to be used to murder the Congolese leader. The CIA Africa Division chief recommended a person who 'will dutifully undertake appropriate action for its execution without pangs of conscience'. Luckily for the US, Belgian and probably British resources assassinated Lumumba before the US plan could be 'executed'.

There was a lot of talk about language at the meetings of the Church Committee. CIA officers testified that phrases such as 'getting rid of Castro' were only figures of speech; they just wanted him out of the way, not dead and buried. It was a kind of shorthand, reflecting the determined spirit of the time. Perhaps they talked about 'eliminating' Castro, or even 'knocking him off', but they intended only to replace or remove him, not literally get rid of him. A handful of former CIA officials – notably Richard Bissell, William Harvey, Justin O'Donnell, Richard Helms – admitted that talk of getting rid of Castro or Lumumba meant just that in one or two instances, but when they really meant 'get rid of', they sometimes used a circumlocution or euphemism instead. In particular, they testified, conversations with high government officials, and especially any that might have occurred with the very highest government official, were deliberately opaque, allusive, and indirect, using 'rather general terms', in Bissell's phrase.

The Church Committee reported that it had discovered at least eight separate plots against Castro of varying seriousness, ranging from an attempt to give him a poisoned wet suit for scuba diving to a more determined effort, through agents recruited by the Mafia, to poison his food.

The idea of assassination itself did not seem to trouble CIA officials who testified to the Church Committee. The wisdom of the undertaking was something else again. It was stupid, foolish, ridiculous and unworkable; at worst a crime or at best a blunder. Everyone had his own adjective, none of them flattering. The best they could muster by way of justification was 'the climate of the time', the Kennedys' hysteria on the subject of Castro, the eager willingness of the Cubans who were recruited seriatim to do the job. But all the same, they shook their heads in dismay. More than anything else, it seemed to be the sheer difficulty of assassination, that is, of a genuinely secret assassination that left them wondering.

But on the question of presidential authority, there is no such equanimity. One exception said that no one in the CIA doubted for a minute that Eisenhower and Kennedy 'jolly well knew', but others, more closely involved, did more than simply squirm in their chairs. Several different men, in fact, showed dramatic signs of psychological stress in discussing this point.

In his testimony before the Church Committee, Helms more than once revealed an uncharacteristic degree of irritation with the committee's insistent return to the question of authority. He was being as clear as he could: 'the Kennedys wanted Castro out of there, the CIA did not go off on its own in these matters, the Agency was only trying to do its job. What more could he say? Senator, how can you be so goddamned dumb? This isn't the kind of thing you put in writing.'

Despite all the evidence gathered by the Church Committee, it never found anything like an order to kill Castro in writing, and it never found a witness who would confess explicitly that he had received such an order. The committee's response to the incomplete record was to leave the question of authority hanging. Must we do the same? Lacking a smoking gun in the form of an incriminatory document or personal testimony, we can reach no firm conclusion, but at the same time the available evidence leans heavily towards a finding that the Kennedys did, in fact, authorise the CIA to make an attempt on Castro's life. After the Church Committee issued its assassination report on 20 November 1975 they confirmed, at least to their own satisfaction, that the CIA had never actually executed, i.e. pulled the trigger, the murder of a *'foreign leader'*, with the emphasis added on both the words *foreign* and *leader*. In the case of Fidel Castro, it wasn't for want of trying!

Nor does this list, published widely in the USA, include a number of assassinations in various parts of the world carried out by anti-Castro Cubans employed by the CIA. Or those carried out probably at the behest of Western intelligence or the tens of thousands who have been directly killed in operations like PHOENIX, who were foreign, but not *'leaders'*.

The list includes, so far: 1949 – Kim Koo, Korean opposition leader; 1950s – Chou En-lai, PM of China, several attempts on his life; 1951 – Kim Il Sung, Premier of N Korea; 1953 – Mohammed Mossadegh, PM of Iran; 1950s (mid) – Claro M. Recto, Philippines opposition leader; 1955 – Jawaharlal Nehru, PM of India; 1957 – Gamal Abdul Nasser, President of Egypt; 1959, 1963, 1969 – Norodom Sihanouk, leader of Cambodia; 1960 – Brig. Gen. Abdul Karim Kassem, leader of Iraq;

1950s–70s – José Figueres, President of Costa Rica, two attempts on his life; 1961 – François 'Papa Doc' Duvalier, leader of Haiti; 1961 – Patrice Lumumba, PM of the Congo (Zaire); 1961 – Gen. Rafael Trujillo, leader of Dominican Republic; 1962 – Sukarno, President of Indonesia; 1963 – Ngo Dinh Diem, President of S Vietnam;1960s – Fidel Castro, President of Cuba, many attempts on his life; 1960s – Raúl Castro, high official in government of Cuba; 1965 – Francisco Caamaño, Dominican Republic opposition leader; 1965–66 – Charles de Gaulle, President of France; 1967 – Che Guevara, Cuban leader; 1970 – Salvador Allende, President of Chile; 1970 – Gen. Rene Schneider, Commander-in-Chief of Army, Chile; 1970s, 1981 – General Omar Torrijos, leader of Panama; 1972 – General Manuel Noriega, when Chief of Panama Intelligence; 1975 – Mobutu Sese Seko, President of Zaire; 1976 – Michael Manley, Prime Minister of Jamaica; 1980–86 – Muammar Gaddafi, leader of Libya, several plots and attempts upon his life, not including those attempted by Britain's SIS of course; 1982 – Ayatollah Khomeini, leader of Iran; 1983 – Gen. Ahmed Dlimi, Moroccan Army commander; 1983 – Miguel d'Escoto, Foreign Minister of Nicaragua; 1984 – the nine comandantes of the Sandinista National Directorate; 1985 – Sheikh Mohammed Hussein Fadlallah, Lebanese Shiite leader (80 people killed in the attempt); 1991 – Saddam Hussein, leader of Iraq.

See also WEAPONS.

ASSESSMENT   Analysis of the reliability or validity of information, intelligence or a statement resulting from this process.

ASSET   Any resource human, technical or otherwise available to an intelligence or security service for operational use.

ATOMAL   Classification used by NATO to identify Restricted Data provided by the USA to NATO.

ATOMIC SPY RING   In the late 1940s and early 50s, an extensive ring of Soviet informers uncovered US atomic secrets. Perhaps the most famous were Julius and Ethel Rosenberg, whose controversial trial garnered attention even years after their execution. Julius Rosenberg secretly organised military engineers to obtain secrets. Other members of this ring included David Greenglass (Ethel Rosenberg's brother) and Klaus Fuchs, who worked at Los Alamos military lab. Because of this spying, the Soviets were able to develop an atomic bomb more quickly than otherwise would have been possible.

ATTACHÉ Military and naval attachés are officers assigned to foreign capitals as liaison with those nations armed forces. Their duties include the overt collection of information and, if appropriate, intelligence gathering. These officers may be intelligence specialists or general service officers; however, typically all Soviet-Russian attachés are GRU or military intelligence officers.

AUDIO SURVEILLANCE Clandestine eavesdropping procedure usually with electronic devices.

AUSTRALIA *AIB Allied Intelligence Bureau* was established in 1942. It was created by the US and Australian military intelligence services to collect intelligence on Japan. The AIB operated under the auspices of Col. Charles Willoughby, General Douglas MacArthur's chief Intelligence Officer, and Col. C.G. Roberts, of Australian Military Intelligence.

The AIB operated a group called the Coast Watchers, whose mission it was to gather important intelligence on Japanese naval activities in particular, in New Guinea, Solomon Islands and the Philippines. Other Australian special operations personnel would also drop behind enemy lines to collect intelligence, and sabotage Japanese activities. The AIB was disbanded soon after the end of WWII. By 1946, however, Sir Charles Spry, head of Australian Military Intelligence, and several other senior security officials in the Australian Government felt there was a need for an Australian postwar intelligence service. Taking men and resources from the now defunct AIB, they began to create the new organisation.

ASIO (Australian Security and Intelligence Organisation) was finally established on 16 March 1949 with considerable help from senior British officers including Roger Hollis, later Director-General of the Security Service (MI5). The organisation is responsible for internal security and counter- intelligence. The first director of the ASIO was to be Col. C.G. Roberts the head of the AIB during WWII. The threat facing his new service was to be very different, Australia had to concern itself with Soviet and E European agents often disguised as innocent immigrants. These agents, once established as Australian citizens, concentrated on gathering intelligence on Australia's uranium mining operations, an essential element in the massive postwar atomic bomb programme.

ASIS Australian Secret Intelligence Service (also known as MO9) was established on 13 May 1952 as Australia's prime foreign intelligence service, though it was not officially acknowledged until October 1977.

Created very much in the image of SIS (MI6) the relations between the two services have remained extremely close and indeed as with ASIO a senior British intelligence officer Col. C.H. 'Dick' Ellis played an influential role in its early years and strangely both Ellis and Roger Hollis who worked with ASIO were either accused of or in the case of Ellis confirmed as being a traitor.

In April 1954, Vladimir Petrov, a Soviet legal, and KGB intelligence officer was recalled to the Soviet Union for 'Consultations'. Petrov assumed that he was to be purged in the post-Stalin upheavals and decided to defect. KGB officers at the Soviet Embassy quickly seized Mrs Petrov and attempted to return her to Moscow. When the aircraft carrying the Soviet Intelligence officers and their 'hostage' landed at Darwin airport to refuel, the ASIS ordered the passengers off and into an airport building where in front of the media Mrs Petrov was handed a phone with her husband on the other end who then told her to ask for political asylum. 'I do not want to return to Moscow,' she announced. The guards, who had been ordered to return with her, realising what was happening, seized Mrs Petrov. The ASIS field officers intervened and ordered the KGB intelligence officers out of the country, without Mrs Petrov, and with cameras rolling the entire time.

Petrov subsequently named two officials in the Australian Department of External Affairs as Soviet moles. He further divulged an extensive spy network that was interested in Australia's Uranium Production. The Petrovs were eventually given new identities while the Soviet Union broke off diplomatic relations with Australia temporarily, leaving the care of their embassy to Switzerland.

In 1959, the ASIS took part in OPERATION MOLE with MI5. The Soviets were talking about returning to Canberra. So with the help of MI5, the Australians bugged the future Soviet Embassy. The ASIS then waited a year to activate the listening devices in case the Soviets were monitoring the Embassy for microwaves in the first few months of their reoccupation. The operation was an abysmal failure. Every sound was recorded; there was only one hitch. The person being monitored never said a word.

In 1983 Valery Ivanov, a well-liked Third Secretary at the Soviet Embassy, who had tired of using low-level government contacts, attempted to develop 'agents of influence' in Australia. To that end he cultivated a friendship with David Combe, a leading lobbyist, former Labour Party official and, most importantly, a personal friend of Prime Minister Bob Hawke. Ivanov who had learned of the 'bugging operation at the Embassy, presumably from his Australian contacts, was finally exposed as a spy by ASIO the counter-espionage service and expelled. Hawke, under tremendous pressure from opposition leaders, also announced that Combe was banned from having any contact with Australian government officials. The Hope Commission was then established to examine the affair minutely and their investigators discovered that special minister Mick Young had leaked information to a friend that Ivanov was about to be expelled. Young not unsurprisingly, was forced to resign.

Towards the end of 1983, John Ryan the Director of ASIS authorised an intelligence exercise that caused great criticism of the service. The exercise simulated the rescue of a hostage held in a hotel room. Without informing local police or hotel management, the ASIS officers raced thorough the lobby of the Melbourne Sheraton Hotel. The agents wore carnival masks and carried sub-machine guns, brushing aside and even knocking down guests as they stormed their way to a hotel room where they battered down the door. When the hotel manager came running to investigate the disturbance, he was manhandled and shoved aside as the agents 'rescued' the mock hostage. Police were summoned and five ASIS agents were arrested as they left the hotel. Arresting officers stated that the agents were 'under the influence of alcohol'. The result was ridicule from the press, police and politicians alike, labelling the ASIS officers 'a bunch of stumblebums', and following severe political criticism Ryan resigned.

In 1990, it was learned that the ASIS, along with the help of 30 NSA technicians, had bugged the Chinese embassy. The story had originally been picked up by an Australian paper, but the ASIS had persuaded them not to publish. Finally the story was leaked to the US *Time* magazine, where it was promptly published, compromising the entire operation and doing little for Australian–Chinese relations.

DSD Defence Signals Directorate: the origins of DSD are in the Australian involvement in the Signals Intelligence (SIGINT) organisations formed during WWII to support US and Australian forces in the Pacific theatre. The Central Bureau, the Fleet Radio Unit Melbourne (FRUMEL), the RAAF Wireless Units, and the Army's Australian Special Wireless Group. Both Australian and US personnel were integrated in Central Bureau, which was established in Melbourne early in 1942. Late in 1942 Central Bureau moved to Brisbane with General MacArthur's HQ, and elements of the Bureau deployed with him to the Philippines later in the war. The operations of the Australian Sigint units were gradually wound down after the war. The growth of Cold War tensions however were quickly to see a SIGINT capability rebuilt and approval for the formation of a new peacetime organisation was given by the Australian Government on 23 July 1946. The Signals Intelligence Centre, to be located at Albert Park Barracks in Melbourne under the name of the Defence Signals Bureau (DSB), the forerunner of DSD, began to take shape in late March 1947. Final Australian Government endorsement occurred on 12 November 1947. DSB's role was both SIGINT and COMSEC, Communications Security for both the Australian Government and Defence communities. The organisation was retitled Defence Signals Branch in October 1949, a title it retained until January 1964 when it was renamed Defence Signals Division. DSD's intelligence role was formally acknowledged in 1977 in the Prime Minister's statement to the House of Representatives on the Royal Commission into Intelligence and Security. Part of the outcome of the review was that the organisation was restyled the Defence Signals Directorate and made directly responsible to the Secretary of the Department of Defence. The new Directorate was approved by Cabinet on 13 July 1978, and in 1979 relocated from its long-term HQ in Albert Park to a new purpose-built facility in Melbourne's historic Victoria Barracks.

In June 1988 the Government decided that DSD should be relocated to Canberra to new facilities at the northern end of the Russell Defence complex in 1993. The DSD operates a number of highly sensitive joint facilities with the NSA including Bamaga, Nurunggar, Pearce, Pine Gap (and the CIA), Shoal Bay and Watsonia. These are in addition to the ECHELON site at Geraldton and other SIGINT bases at Harman and Riverina.

AUSTRALIA, SPECIAL FORCES   The threat of a terrorist outrage during the run-up to the 2000 Sydney Summer Olympics was taken very seriously indeed by the Australian authorities. Every possible action that could be taken by the Special Air Service in co-operation with the counter-terrorist branch of the ASIO Internal Security Service was rehearsed and refined in the weeks leading up to the Games. The Tactical Assault Group (TAG) of the Australian Special Air Service Regiment and its Helicopter support unit had been training in the city area to familiarise themselves with local operating conditions from road traffic flow, to mapping the sewers. This level of training is now more important than ever as the threat of international terrorism has grown. While the Special Forces have long been a prime source of covert intelligence gathering and recruits for both the ASIS and ASIO, its role as the executive arm of the intelligence community in 2002 has been confirmed.

The Tactical Assault Group has been Australia's primary Counter-Terrorist Force since 1996 when some $45 million was spent on upgrading the units weapon, communications and command systems to enhance its overall capabilities considerably. The Australian Special Air Service, to whom the Tactical Assault Group belongs, was formed in July 1957 as a squadron or company sized unit. By the time of Australia's involvement in the Borneo Campaign and Vietnam War both in the mid-1960s, two further squadrons had been raised and along with Signal and HQ units formed the new 1st SAS Regiment. The SAS had earned a high reputation by the time it ceased operations in Vietnam, racking up an amazing record and firmly established itself as a major player in the Special Operations Field. The SAS had a confirmed kill rate of 500-to-1 and had won the highest possible honours for gallantry with four Victoria Crosses (equivalent of the Congressional Medal of Honour) to confirm its reputation.

The present organisation of the 1st Special Air Service regiment includes the 1st, 2nd and 3rd Squadrons, 152nd Signal Squadron and HQ Squadron Group. Recent years have seen greater attention being paid to the task of countering terrorism and the creation of the Tactical Assault Group in 1978 saw the first dedicated such unit assigned for this task. Later an Offshore Installations Group, with combat swimmers trained to parachute into the sea among their many skills, was added. This extra responsibility has placed some considerable strain on the limited manpower available to the Australian Special Air Service. The SAS training, skills and requirements follow closely those of the leading Special Force units including being HALO (High Altitude-Low Opening) and HAHO (High Altitude-High Opening) qualified; proficiency at Heliborne insertion and familiarity with a wide range of weapons including M16A2 and locally produced F88 (Steyr) 5.56mm Assault Rifles and Heckler & Koch MP5K Sub-Machine Guns.

AUSTRIA Despite being at the centre of international intelligence operations for much of the early Cold War period, Austria maintains a relatively small counter-intelligence capability based on the *Heeres-Nachrichtenamt* of the Ministry of Defence. Probably the most important elements of Austrian Intelligence are, however, the two major SIGINT sites at Kongswarte and Neulengbach. It is reported that both stations have provided the German BND with additional coverage, particularly during the Balkan conflicts.

AZERBAIJAN   Ministry of National Security, effectively a revamped local version of the old Soviet KGB. It still maintains close links with Russia's SVR.

AZORIAN   Overall codename for the CIA operation to use the specialist heavy lift vessel the *Hughes Glomar Explorer* to lift a sunken Soviet ballistic missile submarine off of the Pacific ocean floor (JENNIFER PROJECT).

B

BABYSITTER   Intelligence slang for a bodyguard.

BACKSTOPPING   Verification and support of COVER arrangement for an AGENT in anticipation of enquiries or other actions to test the credibility of that cover.

BANG AND BURN   Demolition and sabotage operations.

BARNETT, David (1933–)   The first CIA officer to be charged with espionage against the USA. Barnett worked in the Far East during 1958–63 and was involved in covert actions in Korea. There followed two years at the Langley HQ and a posting to Indonesia. He resigned in 1970, but after a business failure in 1976 offered his services to the Soviet KGB. He was asked by his Soviet controllers to rejoin the CIA, but was unable to do so. However, Barnett gave the KGB the names of some thirty undercover CIA agents, enough information to identify a number of CIA collaborators in foreign countries and details of highly secret CIA operations to obtain information on modern Soviet missile systems. In 1979, the CIA offered to rehire him as a contract employee; urged on by his KGB controller, he accepted. The CIA had probably been warned of his treachery and decided to 'bring him in' so that he could incriminate himself fully. The FBI detected his 'communications' with his KGB controller Vladimir Popov and Barnett was arrested. Indicted in October 1980 he was convicted of spying for the KGB and sentenced to 18 years' imprisonment on 8 January 1981. Whether he was detected by accident, good counter-intelligence or 'blown' to protect another more important Soviet source remains open to question.

BASIC INTELLIGENCE   Fundamental, factual and largely permanently accepted information obtained from OSINT sources about a nations main characteristics such as its physical, social, economic, political and cultural properties.

BAY OF PIGS   (CIA-backed invasion of Cuba) Following Fidel Castro's 1959 revolution and overthrow of the Batista regime in Cuba, relations with the USA deteriorated rapidly until in 1961 diplomatic relations were severed by Washington. Tens of thousands of Cuban refugees fled to exile in the USA and these included many members of Batista's hated secret police and Mafia crime syndicates as well as some of the country's political leaders, intellectuals and businessmen. Appealing to President Eisenhower, the Cuban exiles found a sympathetic ear. The US President conferred with Allan Dulles, the CIA Director, who was given the go-ahead to create plans for terrorist attacks, invasion and eventual counter-revolution in Cuba. When Kennedy became President in 1961, he embraced these plans wholeheartedly and, following approval from the Joint Chiefs of Staff, ordered the clandestine operation to proceed. The CIA and Cuban exiles established an HQ and secret network of bases in Florida where some 1,200 anti-Castro exiles were trained in 'black operations' including assassination and paramilitary activities. The Cuban Brigade invaded Cuba in April 1961. The operation proved to be a disaster. Richard Bissell, the CIA's deputy director of plans, conferred with Attorney General, Robert Kennedy a few days before the invasion. 'He told me at that time', Kennedy wrote in a memorandum dated 1 June 1961, 'that the chances of success were about two out of three and that failure was almost impossible. Even if the force was not successful in its initial objective of establishing a beachhead, the men could become guerrillas and, therefore, couldn't be wiped out and would become a major force and a thorn in the side of Castro.'

The administration had counted on the Cuban people rising up against Castro's regime but the poorly equipped, badly trained invasion force did not establish a strong position beyond the beach. Moreover, no uprisings took place. Worse, the ammunition ships promised by the CIA did not appear when the rebels quickly ran out of ammunition. According to Robert Kennedy, the President, closely watching the situation, urged the CIA to bring the ammunition ships close inshore to resupply the invaders. This would have directly involved US vessels that could later identify the invasion as being directly sponsored by the US. President Kennedy was in favour of direct support, if needs be; Robert Kennedy later claimed, 'he'd rather be called an aggressor than a bum'. However, communication between the CIA controllers and the Cuban right-wing invaders was poor and it was soon learned that Castro's heavily mechanised forces had responded far more quickly than had been expected. The invaders called for air support. Again, according to Robert Kennedy, 'Jack was in favour of giving it.' Dean Rusk cautiously advised the President to deny air cover and added that the US had openly stated that no American forces would be employed in the operation and that to do so would be to make a liar out of the

President. With no air cover provided, the Cuban army quickly destroyed the rebel Brigade. US warships later picked up about 30 exhausted invaders. Others managed to escape back to the US but the Brigade was effectively destroyed. Most of its members were either killed or captured. The fiasco was later placed squarely at the door of the CIA; a failure based on its inability to produce workable military tactics, an effective strategy or sound methods of support and supply. Though President Kennedy publicly took full responsibility for the fiasco, he pointedly blamed CIA Director Allen Dulles in private for not properly informing him in advance of the real chances of the invasion's success.

So devastating was the failure of this CIA operation that it caused Dulles to resign. Reflecting upon the disaster, Dulles later refuted the contention of various presidential advisers that the 1,200 men who invaded Cuba expected to be supported by a general uprising against Castro. Other CIA officers have privately claimed that the administration was fully informed of the risks of failure and that Kennedy had simply lost his nerve in a crisis and abandoned US allies to their fate. The Bay of Pigs disaster enabled Castro to convince the Soviet Prime Minister Nikita Khrushchev to openly support Cuba with military aid, which lead directly to the Cuban missile crisis of 1962. The embittered Cuban exiles and Mafia crime bosses, denied the return of their highly lucrative drugs, gambling and prostitution rackets in Havana and fuelled by the burning contempt for the President of many disenchanted CIA officers, are believed by many conspiracy theorists and impartial analysts to have been directly responsible for the assassination of John F. Kennedy in 1963.

DCRA Bureau Centrale de Renseignements et d'Action, the covert action and sabotage organisation established as part of the free French forces in London during WWII by Gen. Charles de Gaulle. It worked closely with Resistance groups through co-operation with the British SOE (Special Operation Executive).

B-DIENST Beobachtungdienst, the German Navy's CRYPTANALYSIS service that proved highly effective in decoding allied radio traffic to guide U-boats to convoy positions for much of WWII.

BELARUS Committee on State Security – Komitet Gosudarstvennoi Bezopasnosti (KGB), effectively still an offshoot of the KGB's successors the SVR and FSB in Moscow.

BELGIUM   Sûreté de l'Etat (SE) or Staats Veiligheid (SV) Belgium Security Service or BSS. This is the internal security service controlled by the Ministry of Justice. Like the SDRA or Service de Documentation de Recherche et d'Action, the military security service, it appears to have a wide range of political interests, opening computerised files on such diverse subjects as free radio stations, Oxfam shops, radical and left-wing parties, the peace movement, student activists and homosexuals. Indeed their activities go further: trade union officials have been harassed and Belgian Labour Party meetings and even (in 1987) a gathering of the Rainbow Group of the European Parliament were bugged. In 1990, the then Director of the SE was forced to resign after revelations surfaced of collusion between his organisation and the extreme right wing in Belgium; this followed earlier accusations that the SE had deliberately sabotaged the police investigations of a murder in which the neo-Nazi Westland New Post militia were believed to have been involved. A political oversight committee was established to reduce abuse of the system, but it is believed that the CIA intervened in the reform process by demanding guarantees of the confidentiality of their information sources and operations in Belgium.

BERIA, Levrente Pavlovitch (1899–1953)   A fanatical Bolshevik from an early age, Beria was Stalin's personal assassin as well as head of the NKVD and MVD. Cruel and ruthless, he later relished the role as head of the Soviet Union's dreaded secret police. Joining the Bolshevik party first Beria later joined the Cheka, the secret police established by Lenin to protect the revolution. Beria rose through the ranks of its successors, the GPU, OGPU and the NKVD by a combination of treachery and talent. He compromised countless party functionaries to obtain their jobs. Those he could not compromise, he murdered, some by his own hands. Stalin became increasingly indebted to his fellow Georgian who had carried out a large number of murders on his behalf. Following Lenin's death in 1924, Beria had supported Stalin's bid for power and in 1934 Stalin named Beria a member of the Central Committee of the Communist Party in gratitude.

Stalin was supported by a succession of mass murderers, Vyachesiav Menzhinsky who headed the OGPU in the 1920s, having poisoned his predecessor Felix Dzerzhinsky. Menzhinsky was purged by Stalin in 1934 and replaced by the mass murderer Genrikh Yagoda. Nicolai Yezhov, a bloodthirsty fanatic who became the first chief of the NKVD, deposed Yagoda in 1936. Stalin soon realised that he had placed a maniac at the head of the secret police, a man who potentially wielded more actual power than he did himself. Stalin turned yet again to Beria in December 1938 and Yezhov soon disappeared for ever, control passing to Beria for the best part of the next 16 years. One report had it that Beria personally strangled Yezhov, known as 'the bloody red dwarf' as he sat at his desk in NKVD HQ.

When the Germans invaded Russia in 1941, Beria was named deputy Prime Minister, in charge of all security behind the Russian lines. Beria's execution squads summarily executed any soldier who malingered or appeared disgruntled. They shot tens of thousands of old-style Bolsheviks at the same time since, in the chaos of war, Stalin thought it the perfect time to eliminate the last of his political enemies. Those whom Beria did not execute he sent to labour camps but these became an embarrassment as the Germans threatened to overrun these camps as they pushed deep into Russia. As the German Army approached Minsk, Beria ordered the political detention camp in that city to be eliminated. The NKVD machine gunned to death more than 10,000 prisoners then blew up the camp with explosive charges. What was left of the camp and its inmates was then burned. Stalin had no intention of allowing political prisoners to escape and possibly mount opposition to his dictatorial regime either from Germany or the West and similar atrocities were carried out in other areas as the Germans advanced. Even at the height of the war with Germany, Beria, a man of perverted habits would tour the darkened streets of Moscow in his official car to kidnap young girls who would then be raped brutally and often murdered or handed over to his favourite henchmen to be tortured for his amusement. A serial rapist and murderer, Beria was probably ultimately responsible directly or indirectly for the deaths of over 10 million Soviet citizens. Beria was to be deeply involved in the takeover of postwar E Europe and the creation of what Churchill was to call 'an Iron Curtain'. It was Beria who directed the imposition of a Communist regime on Czechoslovakia and who planned the murder of the Czech Foreign Minister, Jan Masaryk who was proving such stubborn opposition to the Soviet Union's ambitions. In 1948 Masaryk's body was found sprawled in the courtyard of the Czernin Palace in Prague in a crude Soviet attempt to make it appear to have been a suicide, jumping to his death from a balcony several floors above.

After the war ended Beria made several ill thought out attempts to streamline the Soviet intelligence and security services, but only succeeded in creating confusion and fear within the newly created MVD and its many offshoots. Indeed the constant purges and changes of direction led to an increasing number of defections by Soviet intelligence officers to the West. Beria continued to increase the power of his secret police within the Soviet Union and, with its enormous strength of over 250,000 and a vast budget, Stalin became increasingly suspicious of Beria, believing that he was actually plotting to replace him. Although Stalin died before he could effectively deal with Beria, his successors had no intention of allowing Beria to take over. He had little support within the Communist Party and the Army never forgave him for the vicious murder of tens of thousands of their colleagues before the war. He was arrested, tried in secret and condemned as a traitor. On 23 December 1953, Beria was placed before a wall in the Lubyanka HQ of the new KGB and shot by a firing squad.

BERLIN TUNNEL The Anglo-American intelligence project that involved digging a tunnel from the then West Berlin into East Berlin to access underground cables and tap Soviet–East German communications. The idea was inspired by a little known tunnel, but with similar concept, dug in postwar Vienna, a city very much in the image of that in the film *The Third Man*, while it was under joint Allied–Soviet control. The Berlin Tunnel was planned by the British Secret Intelligence Service (MI6), and the US Central Intelligence Agency (CIA). It was CIA financed and staffed, but with SIS expertise. Exact details of the project are still classified and confirmable information scarce. The then Director of the CIA, Allen W. Dulles authorised the project in early 1954 and promptly ordered that paperwork be kept to a bare minimum to ensure maximum security.

The Berlin project was codenamed OPERATION GOLD; the Vienna tunnel had been OPERATION SILVER. It was German agents, operating on behalf of the Gehlen Bureau, the forerunner of W Germany's BND (Bundes-Nachrichten-Dienst, Foreign Intelligence Service) and run by former Nazi Gen. Reinhard Gehlen, who had first alerted the SIS. They disclosed the location of the crucial telephone junction where at a depth of only 2 metres three major trunk cables joined together close to the edge of the American sector.

CIA and SIS intelligence officers met at the MI6 HQ at Broadway Buildings to plan the tunnel operation. However, among those present from the earliest meetings was SIS officer, George Blake, a deep penetration GRU (Soviet Military Intelligence) agent. Blake alerted his controlling officer immediately, the KGB being quickly informed by their military counterparts. This first breach of security resulted in the capture of two of Gehlen's agents while trying to lay a long-distance wiretap across the border.

The KGB, working on Blake's information, decided to let OPERATION GOLD continue, giving them an unprecedented opportunity to run a major disinformation game. In December 1953 the former FBI official, William K. Harvey, was transferred to the CIA to direct operations. Using a US Army supply depot as the western terminal of the tunnel, US Army engineers spent more than a year secretly digging the tunnel and carefully removing large amounts of earth and stones. The tunnel, some 300 metres long and at least 5 metres deep, still allowed a working headroom of 2 metres. At the eastern end under Communist Berlin was the electronic housing for the wiretapping equipment and the German and CIA monitoring staff. Their task was to record the flow of conversations from Soviet Military HQ in Zossen, near Berlin, to Moscow, the Soviet Embassy in E Germany and to Soviet military units throughout the Eastern Bloc. Back in Washington, DC, teams of CIA translators and intelligence analysts worked round the clock on the vast amount of intercepts collected. Ranging from high-level conversations to barrack room gossip, this flow of information dazzled the CIA and blinded them to some very obvious anomalies in the traffic patterns.

On 21 April 1956, about a year after the wiretapping operation had begun, Soviet and East German forces broke into the eastern end of the tunnel. The KGB made an immense propaganda coup out of discovery of the tunnel, calling it a 'breach of the norms of international law' and a 'Western gangster act'. There had been major problems of security during the project, including the fact that during the first snowfalls of the winter of 1954–55 the snow above the line of the tunnel melted because of the heat rising from below. While it is true that any sharp-eyed East German police officer could hardly fail to notice this, it was indeed George Blake who actually gave the game away.

It was not until after Blake's arrest, trial and conviction in 1961 that Senior CIA and SIS Intelligence Officials were finally forced to admit that the operation had been compromised from the very beginning and that they had been the victims of a massive and very successful KGB disinformation scam. CIA analysts have secretly argued over the results of the tunnel fiasco ever since. But it has been suggested that the Soviets in fact used the tapping operation to allow the West to discover that they had no aggressive intentions towards West Berlin and thereby reduced tensions during the heights of the Cold War.

BERTRAND, General Gustave Leading French cryptologist of the 1930s and 40s who played a major part in breaking the German ENIGMA ciphers. He commanded PC Bruno, the French Cryptanalysis centre at the Chateau de Vignobles in Gretz.

BERZIN, Yan Karlovich (1889–1939)   Chief of GRU, soviet military intelligence (1924–39) and commander of Soviet forces (1936–39), supporting the Republicans in the Spanish Civil War. Upon returning to the Soviet Union, Berzin continued to head the GRU until his arrest on 13 May 1939. He was shot on Stalin's orders in the basement of the Metropole Hotel in Moscow on 29 July 1939.

BETTANY, Michael (1950–)   Bettany was recruited by the Security Service (MI5) in 1982 at a time when the service was coming under increasing pressure to recruit more staff from the 'working classes'. His unsuitability quickly became apparent when on one occasion, after he had been working for MI5' for only a brief period, police stopped Bettany after he had staggered onto a train, heavily under the influence of alcohol, offering no ticket and attempting to evade the guard who had to chase him down the aisle of a coach. He shouted: 'You can't arrest me. I'm a spy!' to police officers. Irrespective of this incident and many others like it, MI5 kept him on its payroll. He was then promoted to the Russian desk, even though he had little or no background or knowledge qualifying him for that appointment. In his new position, Bettany had access to information that identified all known KGB agents in England. Bettany made copies of secret documents and then attempted to make contact with the KGB. Ironically, it was the KGB itself that informed MI5 of Bettany's treachery, believing that they were being 'set-up' by the Security Service. The Soviet intelligence service lost a potentially priceless contact within MI5 who could have identified which of their agents and operations were compromised. For Bettany had top secret clearance and the information to which he had access was so sensitive that even the Attorney General Sir Michael Havers, who was to prosecute Bettany in court, was apparently prevented from fully reviewing the information.

Bettany, tried 'in camera', claimed innocence but was convicted of ten charges dealing with violations of the Official Secrets Act. Lord Chief Justice Lord Lane, in sentencing Bettany said, 'You have made treachery your course of action. It is quite plain to me that in many ways you are puerile. It is also clear to me that you are both opinionated and dangerous. You would not have hesitated to disclose names to the Russians, which almost certainly would have led to death for more than one person.' Bettany was sentenced to 23 years in prison. The case, along with other recent breaches of British intelligence, including that of Geoffrey

Prime who had worked at GCHQ at Cheltenham, so alarmed the CIA that it demanded that MI5 take immediate steps to improve its chronic lack of internal security precautions.

While on remand in Wandsworth prison in late 1984, Bettany befriended Pat Magee, the Brighton bomber who had been arrested and charged with bombing the Tory Party conference. Subsequently, the IRA man knew that there was a British spy close to Martin McGuinness in Londonderry, who had been recruited by MI5 in 1974 while a soldier in the Queen's Royal Irish Hussars, and who had spent 11 years undetected by the IRA. His main role had been to report on McGuinness's political development and encourage him and others to abandon their military campaigns for a political solution. Republicans quickly relayed the information to McGuinness, who ordered an investigation into him. Other informants inside the Provisional IRA told the spy's handlers that his cover had been blown and the man's covert career came to an abrupt end. On 3 March 1985, the Army spirited him and his family to England.

The key IRA informer, in hiding for 16 years, risked his life in 2001 to give evidence to the Saville inquiry investigating the killing of unarmed Catholics in Londonderry on 'Bloody Sunday' in January 1972. He was to affirm that the former IRA commander Martin McGuinness did not fire any shots on the day of the fateful civil rights march that ended in the deaths of 14 civilians.

BIOGRAPHIC LEVERAGE – BLACKMAIL Use of secret background information to induce or blackmail a person to work for an intelligence service or a particular covert operation.

BIOTERRORISM In comparison to the real and enormous threat of emerging, re-emerging and transported naturally occurring infectious diseases, the problem of deliberately caused disease appears to be almost insignificant. However, the truth is somewhat different. The old Soviet Union expended vast amounts of money and energy on its highly advanced Chemical & Biological Warfare (CBW) programme and Russia has continued this programme on a reduced scale. Appalling new and deadly diseases have been hybridised in facilities that are now considered less than secure. The chance that rogue Russian scientists have helped expand the Iraqi, Iranian, Libyan and North Korean CBW capabilities is very high and while Western governments have officially abandoned CBW research, some development has probably continued. Indeed Western commercial companies have supplied much of the infrastructure of Middle Eastern programmes.

The fear that really haunts the West is the acquisition by dedicated terrorists of these silent killers, so just what weapons might the terrorists have and how are they likely to use them? *Anthrax* is easy to produce, cheap and probably the most obvious terrorist weapon. It is a bacterium that attacks the lungs and bronchial passages in its most lethal form, inhalation or pulmonary anthrax *(Bacillus anthracis)* and causes toxaemia, septicaemia and death, often within 48 hours if not promptly treated with high doses of antibiotics. Inhalation Anthrax, though deadly, needs a higher exposure level to develop and would certainly require a spray or aerosol dispenser to be truly effective and that of course led to the threat of stolen crop-dusting aircraft being taken so seriously in the USA. Tularemia is found in rodents and its causative agent *(Francisella Tularensis)* can infect people through contaminated water, it is extremely contagious, easily produced and persists in the environment for a long time. The pneumonia-like symptoms appear after two or three days and mortality varies, but can be as high as 40 per cent. There is a 'devils box' of such biological weapons, but there are many others, such as one of man's oldest natural enemies. Plague or *Yersina Pestisis* is spread by blood-sucking fleas. A cultivated variant of the Mosquito-borne Venezuelan *Equine Encephalitis* has been known to be fatal in humans and its white powder-like base could be spread from the air or in aerosol form and *Cholera*, a microscopic water-borne bacterium, have too low a death rate to be likely choices for a terrorist attack, however there is one more in particular, that strikes mortal fear into government health authorities everywhere. *Ebola*. Simply put, *Ebola Hemorrhagic Fever* or the closely related *Crimean-Congo HF* is a nightmare, causing horrific symptoms, highly contagious with no known cure or vaccine and could be dispensed in aerosol form directly into the air-conditioning system of a high rise office block to be carried quickly to every corner of the building. While few scientists would be prepared to accept that a terrorist organisation would have the expertise or resources to create large quantities, only one or two outbreaks would be sufficient to cause worldwide panic.

Smallpox The Soviet Union and later Russia, conducted research on the nuclear *polyhedrosis* virus, an insect virus that secretes a protective protein crystalline coat that renders the organism resistant to ambient effects of heat, cold and sunlight and also vastly increases its overall viability. During the 1980s and 1990s they experimented with the insertion of smallpox genes into the *polyhedrosis* virus and are believed to have succeeded in producing an even more hardy and deadly killer virus. Even in its original form, smallpox is often considered the ideal killer virus because it is readily cultured, highly contagious and relatively resistant to environmental changes. However in its new forms, Smallpox would probably be responsible for more deaths in London or New York than the detonation of a crude nuclear bomb by terrorists. Dispensed by aircraft using aerosol suspension it will invariably survive long enough in a 'mist' to be carried on the wind to reach and eventually kill a high percentage of those infected. The airborne droplets are small (1–5 microns) and remain suspended long enough to spread over a 50-mile-wide area, even if released at an altitude of under one thousand feet.

Chemical agents have been mass-produced in a number of Middle Eastern countries, including Iraq, Iran and Libya and there is little doubt that Osama bin Laden has been more than a little interested in the possible catastrophic effects of these weapons for some time and the psychological barrier against their use was finally crossed on 20 March 1995 when the Japanese sect, Aum Shinrikyo, unleashed a primitive chemical attack against commuters on the Tokyo subway. Using home-made *Sarin*, a nerve agent, in polyethylene pouches placed in five subway cars, the terrorists simply punctured them with sharpened umbrella tips and ran like hell! *Sarin* is sufficiently volatile that no special dissemination technique was required, poisonous fumes quickly filled the carriages and despite the crude delivery system, twelve commuters died and a staggering five thousand were taken ill. In a foretaste of what may one day happen on the London underground, this fanatic Japanese terrorist group had already planned a far more terrible outrage, again aimed at the subway system. Japanese Police, in September 1996, discovered a bottle containing just one ounce of VX, a more advanced nerve agent and sufficient to kill more than fifteen thousand if dispensed properly. Who could now doubt, following the 11 September destruction of the World Trade Center, that Al-Qa'ida is both merciless enough and quite capable of organising just such an attack on a major American or European city. A simple fire-extinguisher, suitably modified and placed in the central lobby of a major shopping mall, railway station, airport, school or hospital would be able to dispense enough VX chemical agent or the Smallpox virus in aerosol form to kill many tens or even hundreds of thousands, while a light aircraft could dump just two hundred kilograms of Anthrax spores over the capital which would be enough, in theory, to kill 6 million Londoners.

Even as the international terrorist threat grows, scientific developments are making it far easier than ever before to produce both biological and chemical weapons, it is perfectly possible for a bright sixth-former to produce some form of a chemical weapon in the local comprehensive school lab. So what can be done to protect against this terrible menace? In essence, the answer is very little, except maintaining good intelligence of terrorist intentions and the eternal vigilance of the security forces.

BISSELL, Richard M. (1910–94)   A protégé of Allen Dulles, Bissell had no espionage background before joining the CIA. A former Professor of Economics, working in postwar Germany, Bissell also held a position with the Ford Foundation in Washington DC. His initial speciality at the CIA was to be in photographic reconnaissance and in 1954 Bissell supervised the U-2 spy plane project approved by the Eisenhower administration with the aircraft becoming operational the following year. With the coming of the space age however, Bissell foresaw the use of spy satellites and began ordering unique camera equipment to operate in special CIA satellite projects. Bissell also became involved in many covert operations, including a coup d'état that overthrew the Guatemalan government of President Jacobo Arbenz after that country nationalised the assets of the United Fruit Company, a lucrative monopoly which controlled all the banana plantations. Bissell's position at the CIA was gravely weakened after the disastrous Bay of Pigs operation, which Bissell had played a large part in planning, failed in its aim of overthrowing the Cuban regime. A desperate Bissel had tried to persuade the President to support the flagging invasion with a massive intervention of US forces, but Kennedy refused and the invasion became a fiasco that would eventually cost Bissell and his boss, Dulles, their jobs and, according to some, the President his life.

Part of Bissell's plans had involved assassinating Castro and he had considered many bizarre murder schemes put forward by his chief adviser, the decidedly odd Dr Sidney Gottleib. Assassinations of Third World leaders believed to take an anti-American stance were also reportedly planned by Bissell and Gottleib. It has been suggested that these were aimed at General Kassem of Iraq, the Dominican Republic's Dictator Rafael Trujillo and Patrice Lumumba of the Congo. This latter operation was eventually believed to have been carried out by Belgian intelligence officers with British assistance. These operations were eventually revealed in reports from the Church Commission, which studied alleged assassination plots of foreign political chiefs. Following the Cuban invasion fiasco, Kennedy in

November 1961 forced the venerable Dulles to leave the CIA. His protégé Bissell resigned three months later and returned to private business.

BLACK In espionage terms, 'black' usually means 'black-bag job', slang for the surreptitious entry into an office or home to obtain files or materials illegally. Such activities have commonly been used by the major intelligence services, often to install electronic and other surveillance devices.

BLACK CHAMBER   The Cryptographic bureau or Section 8 of US Military Intelligence set up by Master Cryptographer Herbert O. Yardley in 1912. Later shut down by Secretary of State, Henry L. Stimson in 1929, reputedly saying 'Gentlemen do not read each other's mail'.

BLACKLIST   Counter-intelligence listing of hostile collaborators, suspects, sympathisers or politicians viewed as threatening the security of a nation or its allies.

BLACK OPS   Clandestine or covert operations not attributable to the organisation carrying them out.

BLACK PROPAGANDA   Propaganda that purports to emanate from a source other than the true one and designed to undermine morale or to create tensions that can seriously destabilise an enemy nation.

BLACK TRAINEES   Nickname given to foreigners recruited for CIA undercover training at 'The Farm'. At one time these trainees were allegedly not supposed to know they were on US territory.

BLAKE, George (1922–)   Born 'Georg Behar' in Rotterdam, Holland, Blake had all the advantages his wealthy family could provide: good schooling, a comfortable home and a bright future. After the German invasion of the Netherlands he served in the Dutch underground before escaping to Britain. Once in England he changed his name to Blake and joined the Royal Navy. Because of his language skills, he was accepted by SOE, which sent espionage agents to Nazi-occupied countries in Europe to work with underground fighters against the Germans. After the war he was accepted into the Foreign Office and eventually posted to the British Embassy in Seoul. During the Korean War he was captured by the advancing N Koreans in 1950. Blake was held for three years while the Communists painstakingly and successfully conducted brainwashing techniques on the prisoner. This was the turning point in Blake's life. Upon his release, he requested that the FO transfer him permanently to SIS (MI6) so he could fulfil his deepest ambition, to become a British Intelligence Officer. His excellent WWII service with SOE suggested high qualification for the job and SIS accepted Blake. This was quite unusual in that British Intelligence had a strict rule that all officers of SIS had to have complete British parentage.

Security checking also either ignored or failed to discover that in his teens Blake had been very close to his cousin Henri Curiel, who later helped establish the Egyptian Communist Party in 1943. Curiel was to be shot dead in his Paris home in May 1978 by members of the extreme right-wing 'Delta' group, thought to have links to SDECE, the French Intelligence Service. An hour later a news agency received a call saying 'The KGB agent, Henri Curiel, a traitor to France, which adopted him, finally ceased activity today.' This was one of a number of odd aspects of Blake's background that remained unexplained and that were to come back later to haunt those responsible for clearing him for top-secret work.

Blake became an SIS field officer in 1953. From this time until he was exposed by a German double agent, he would serve the KGB with stubborn loyalty, identifying more than 40 Western agents to the Soviets, resulting in the death of most or all of them. Posted to West Berlin in 1955, Blake exposed the existence of OPERATION GOLD (the Berlin Tunnel) in 1956. As soon as the KGB received Blake's report they began feeding false information through the system until eventually breaking into the tunnel and closing down the Western intelligence operation. Blake was to move back to London to work at SIS HQ. He would regularly meet his Soviet controller, Rodin (alias Korovin) in the Netherlands, using the excuse that he was visiting his Dutch relatives. Eventually he was transferred to the Arabic Language School at Shemlan just outside Beirut in the Lebanon. This establishment was known throughout the intelligence world as a 'training school for British spies'.

Blake would be finally compromised by German double agent Horst Eitner. SIS brought Blake back to London with the offer of a high-paying desk job at their HQ. Blake flew back to have what he thought would be a routine interview, but was arrested at Heathrow airport. After many long hours of interrogation, he admitted that he had been a triple agent and had fed the KGB everything he knew. Moreover, he admitted that he had embraced Communism as early as 1953 and had planned to spy for the Soviet Union from then on. Blake's trial was held in secret and few details of its records are available to this day. He was found guilty and was given the maximum sentence of 14 years for each of three main charges, 42 years in all. He would serve less than six of those years. Sent to Wormwood Scrubs Prison he appeared to be a model prisoner. However on 22 October 1967, Blake escaped to Moscow, where he was eventually given a post with the KGB.

BLETCHLEY PARK   Until 1938 it had been the residence of Sir Herbert Leon. Purchased by the SIS, 'The Mansion' became the HQ of GC&CS (1939–46). Located 50 miles N of London in Buckinghamshire, it was the centre for ULTRA and therefore home of one of the most important events of WWII; the cracking of the German ENIGMA ciphers. With just 200 staff in 1939 it grew to some 7,000 by 1944.

BLIND DATE   A meeting by an intelligence officer with an agent at the time and place of the agent's choosing. These are potentially dangerous, as the officer could be set up for capture or an attempt be made to 'turn' him.

BLOCH, Felix   A former Foreign Service officer in the State Department that the FBI investigated for spying in 1989. Robert HANSSEN is suspected by the FBI of tipping off the Soviets to the FBI's investigation of Bloch, who was videotaped passing a briefcase to a Soviet official in Paris but was never charged with spying. Bloch was fired and stripped of his pension in 1990 on grounds that he lied to FBI investigators.

BLOWBACK   A disinformation or deception programme carried out by an intelligence service in a foreign country deliberately to mislead with the intention of the deception being picked up in the country of origin. Here it would further mislead; usually aimed at newspapers and broadcasters, but sometimes even at the Government itself

Former Director of the Central Intelligence Agency, William Colby in testimony given to the Church Committee on Intelligence in 1977, admitted the involvement of the CIA in planting information that later 'blew' back to the US news media as the 'truth'.

BLOWN   Exposure of personnel, facility or other elements of a covert activity. The phrase is also used to describe a network of agents which has been infiltrated.

BLUNT, Anthony Frederick (SIR) (1907–83)   Pampered with an upper-class education and a comfortable lifestyle, Anthony Blunt embraced espionage as easily as he would later accept the honours of the country he later betrayed. At the outbreak of WWII, Blunt applied for and received a commission in the British Army. Following the fall of France Blunt joined the Security Service (MI5). Already a Communist agent from his days at Cambridge, he was now in a position to obtain and pass on secrets to the Soviet Union. From 1940 to 1945, Blunt was a dedicated NKVD double agent, passing secrets regularly to Soviet contacts in London. Blunt served in F Branch and was in charge of 'The Watchers' by the end of 1940. He later became Guy Liddell's personal assistant, then to B1(b) where he was responsible for checking the diplomatic pouches of neutral countries till 1944. He also represented MI5 at meetings of the JIC.

At the end of the war, Blunt was discharged from MI5 and immediately began to pursue his passion for the History of Art. Within three decades he had become one of the foremost authorities in the field. The honours early heaped upon him paved the way to his becoming the pre-eminent art historian in Europe.

Blunt had come under suspicion following the defection to Moscow of his close friend Guy Burgess, but had persuaded his interrogators of his non-involvement. However, the search continued for the 'Third Man' who had warned Burgess and Maclean. When 'Kim' Philby was identified as being responsible, rumours began to circulate about a 'Fourth Man' who had actually passed the warning to Philby and perhaps had even co-ordinated the escape of Burgess and Maclean with KGB agents. The intelligence community never gave up its search for the evidence that Blunt was the 'Fourth Man', and finally in 1963 this was provided by Michael Whitney Straight, a wealthy American who had known Blunt at Cambridge in the early 1930s.

When Blunt was shown the testimony of his American friend, he promptly confessed. Blunt stated that he was the man they were looking for, the 'Fourth Man', openly admitting that he had warned his friends, Philby, Burgess and Maclean. Blunt then struck a bargain with MI5. He would tell them everything in exchange for not being exposed and prosecuted. Though Blunt thought himself safe, he was dogged by journalists and authors writing about the 'Fourth Man'. Finally, Andrew Boyle's book *The Climate of Treason* identified the 'Fourth Man' as Blunt even though it was under the alias of 'Maurice'. Blunt's treachery was later confirmed by the Prime Minister, Margaret Thatcher in 1979. Stripped of his knighthood Blunt retreated from public life and died in disgrace in 1983.

BND BUNDESNACHRICHTENDIENST West German foreign intelligence service, established 1956.

BODYGUARD Codename for the overall DECEPTION plan for the Allied invasion of Europe in WWII and developed to obscure the real date, time and place of D-Day, the Normandy landings on 6 June 1944.

BOMBE   High-speed calculating machine used originally by the British GC&CS at Bletchley Park and later by the American crytanalysts in Washington, DC. It owed much to the Bomba developed by Polish military intelligence in the late 1930s and the great skill and bravery of the Polish mathematicians and cryptanalysts led by Marian Rajewski.

BONA FIDES   Establishing an operative's true identity, affiliation or intentions.

BOOT   British codename for AJAX, a joint SIS (MI6)-CIA operation.

BOSSARD, Frank Clifton (1912–)   British spy believed to have been 'blown' by a controversial Soviet defector known as TOP HAT in 1965. Though not as well known in England as George Blake, Kim Philby, Guy Burgess and David Maclean, Frank Bossard proved almost as devastating to British intelligence. Bossard's espionage activities were important because the secrets he sold were of a highly technical nature and of great value to the Soviet Union. Money was the only real motive for Bossard's treason

In 1940–46 Bossard served in the Royal Air Force where he specialised in radar. He later lectured on this subject at the College of Air Services at Hamble, Hampshire and eventually became assistant signals officer at the Ministry of Civil Aviation. SIS recruited him in 1956, moving him as an attaché to the British Embassy in Bonn, Germany. Bossard's technical background called for him to interview any scientist, engineer or technician who had escaped from behind the Iron Curtain.

When reassigned to London Bossard, always a heavy drinker, ran up debts and was so short of money that, in addition to his duties at SIS, he ran a small business for Coin Collectors as a sideline. In 1961, he was recruited by a Soviet agent codenamed 'Gordon'. For some four years Bossard provided the Soviets with the latest information on military radar and guided missile systems. Bossard always lived in high style but he now lavished too much cash on women and drink and this finally brought him to the attention of MI5 who began a surveillance operation on Bossard. After obtaining enough evidence, he was arrested on 12 March 1965. Bossard was tried at the Old Bailey on 10 May 1965. Upon conviction he was sentenced to 21 years in prison.

BOXSHALL, Lt. Colonel Edward G. (1897–1984)   Boxshall was probably the longest serving officer in British intelligence history. In Military Intelligence in WWI, he joined SIS in 1919; he had an ability to make influential friends and so developed a wide circle of important contacts. Among these was the immensely rich arms magnate, Sir Basil Zaharoff. Through Sir Basil's good offices Boxshall was to acquire the cover of being the representative of the Vickers Armament Company in the Romanian Capital of Bucharest for some twenty years as SIS Head of Station. Boxshall married the daughter of the Romanian Interior Minister, Prince Barbo Dimitrie Stirbey, whose real name was Bibescu. Boxshall's station obtained much intelligence on the Balkans and the Soviet Union from agents, defectors and refugees, and following his return to Britain, Boxshall was to spend much of his time in the E European sections of SIS. Indeed he became such an invaluable asset that he was still being regularly consulted until his death at the age of 87 in 1984.

BRAVO, Raphael (1972–)   The Cold War may be over, but a willingness to spy for Russia continues. Bravo, a guard working for Crusader Security at British Aerospace offices at Stanmore in North London, offered an MI5 officer posing as a Russian intelligence agent top secret documents on advanced radar, electronic warfare and other defence systems in return for, in his own words, 'Money, as much as I can get'. He was detained by the Special Branch as he left the meeting at the White House Hotel in Central London. Bravo was convicted and sentenced to eleven years on 1 February 2002.

BRAZIL   *SNI The National Information Service*: created in June 1964, just after the military coup that ousted the populist government of João Goulart. The SNI was linked to the National Security Council and would be responsible to direct intelligence and counter-intelligence activities in the country. It was made up of a Central Agency, divided into sections on Strategic Information, Special Operations and Internal Security. The rules that created the SNI exempted the agency from the need to inform Congress about its organisation and operations. Without the need for accountability to anyone, with the exception of the Presidency it served, the SNI grew rapidly in the 1960s. Since its organisation and functions were not established in law, it was possible for the agency to adapt itself to the circumstances that the new authoritarian regime faced. This 'elasticity' also allowed the SNI systematically to penetrate all levels of government.

During the presidential elections of 1989, the SNI monitored the movement of left-wing candidates in the country and infiltrated agents in the Sixth National Meeting of the Workers' Party (PT). In other words, the SNI still concentrated most of its resources on the internal surveillance of groups and actors capable of affecting Brazilian politics in a direction contrary to the preferences and interests of the Federal government. However, with the inauguration of President Fernando Collor in 1990, the SNI was dissolved, beginning a very confused period of transition in the Brazilian intelligence community but it is certain that the end of the SNI was not the end of traditional security and intelligence practices of the Brazilian armed forces or of the police. There have been changes, but the ideological base remains very much the same.

SAE (Secretaria de Assuntos Estratégicos or Secretariat of Strategic Affairs): a transitional agency, which was created to oversee security matters in the absence of a national intelligence authority. Almost immediately however, an Intelligence Department (DI) was established inside the new Secretariat of Strategic Affairs with many of the structures and something of the 'modus operandi' of the former discredited service were preserved. Far from the promised intelligence reforms, the ID simply became the heir to the personnel, operations, abuses and targets of the SNI.

ABIN (Brazilian Intelligence Agency): established by Presidential degree in 1995 and operational by 2000, the ABIN has taken over the operations and personnel of the SAE, effectively a holding organisation until an acceptable replacement for the SNI could be organised. ABIN will be responsible through a number of directorates for External Intelligence, Internal Security, Counter Terrorism, the Amazon Regional, the New Development Areas and Organized Crime. It will also have a certain amount of operational control (OPCON) over the rest of the Brazilian intelligence community and will be responsible for implementing the new Brazilian Intelligence System (SISBIN). This will give the ABIN a massive electronic information surveillance capability and has raised considerable disquiet about its potential use by an authoritarian government.

Brazilian Military Intelligence Services: the reorganisation of intelligence activities of the Brazilian armed forces during the first half of the 1990s was slow and did not seriously change public perception of the authoritarian character of such activities. It is a view well justified by the widespread abuse of civil rights and the repressive use of force by all the military information services throughout the period of military dictatorship (1964–85). The changes were mainly cosmetic and involved their official titles. Thus the Air Force Security Information Center (CISA) became the Air Force Intelligence Secretariat (SECINT) in 1991, the Navy's CENIMAR, created as long ago as 1955, became the Naval Intelligence Centre (CIM) also in 1991, while the huge Army Information Centre (CIE) simply exchanged 'Information' for 'Intelligence'.

BRAZIL, SPECIAL FORCES Brazil's involvement with Counter-Terrorist operations dates back to 1953 when a special intervention squad was formed by the Ministry of Aviation. The first truly dedicated unit was established only in 1983 as the Counter-Terrorist (CT) Detachment of Brazil's 1st Special Forces Battalion, which is in turn part of the Army's Airborne Brigade based at the HQ in Villa Mittor (Rio de Janeiro).

The Counter-Terrorist Detachment is similar in organisation, training and tactics to the US Delta Force and is closely linked to the ABIN, the main Brazilian Intelligence Service. In 2002 a new intelligence and counter-terrorist policy is likely to merge the interests of these organisations into a joint overall command structure. Only those with Parachute or Special Forces background and an exemplary record are allowed to volunteer; even so many fail to get past the initial training period. According to reports the attrition rate during the 14-day selection phase is as high as 90 per cent. Those lucky enough to survive go on to a 13-week training programme at facilities near Rio de Janeiro. Skills developed include marksmanship, combat shooting, parachuting and heliborne insertion. However, because of Brazil's varied terrain, special emphasis is placed on long-range patrol groups and intelligence gathering in the dense jungles and rivers of the Amazon.

Further emphasis is placed on intelligence gathering; security surveillance of the long borders with Venezuela, Colombia, Ecuador, Peru and Bolivia; ability to track the 'narco-gangs' smuggling drugs across national borders; and clandestine insertion of Special Forces into hostile areas. Brazilian Intelligence can call upon the assistance of the 1st Special Forces Battalion, a Commando Company, two Special Forces Companies and a Counter-Terrorist Detachment. The Detachment personnel must become proficient with a wide range of explosive demolitions, machete, dagger, Heckler & Koch MP-5 sub-machine guns, Colt M1911 automatic pistol, M870 Remington Combat shotguns and the much favoured PSG-1 sniper rifles.

BRIDGE AGENT An agent who acts as courier or go-between from a case officer to an agent in a denied area.

BRIEF ENCOUNTER   Any brief physical contact between a case officer and an agent under threat of surveillance.

BRITISH DISEASE, THE   The fascination with espionage and the willingness of generations of, in particular, the so-called upper classes, to become traitors. The obvious ones make a long list including Philby, Blunt, Burgess, Maclean, Capt. John King, Harry Houghton, Ethel Gee, David Bingham, John Vassall, Blake, Alaistair Watson, Driberg, Ernest Oldham, Fuchs, Tudor-Hart, Goronwy Rees, Percy Glading, Leo Long, Michel Bettaney, Geoffrey Prime, Denis Proctor and many others. But what is somewhat disconcerting is the sheer range of other spies largely unknown to the general public and an even bigger list of those suspected of treachery.

The revelation that little-known ex-MP Raymond Fletcher was a KGB agent shocked many who knew him well. Mr Fletcher, who sat for Ilkeston, Derbyshire, was codenamed PETER and died in 1991. He was always thought to be a moderate in the Labour Party, but had a maverick streak which led him to abstain on a key vote on entry into Europe. As a result he was sacked by Harold Wilson from his only government job, as parliamentary private secretary to Roy Mason after only three months. He was a part-time journalist with the left-wing *Tribune* newspaper but apparently moved to the right over the years. He quit politics and the Labour Party in 1983 and moved to the south of France.

So many others have been named that this list will be less than complete, but includes Michael Smith, John Symonds, Melita Norwood, Victor Allen and so on. In fact it appears that the Soviets had as many as 200 spies operational in the UK and US alone during WWII and many more in the late 1940s and 50s. Most have never been identified, not even turned or offered non-prosecution deals in return for 'co-operation'. The number of known Soviet codenames for undiscovered British spies includes BOT in the League of Nations; BUNNY, a member of the Oxford network; JOHN, KORONA PFEIL, VALET and VITYAZ, unidentified spies in London; PAUL, unidentified spy at Bletchley Park (not to be confused with Burgess who also used the same codename at times); and SCOTT, leader of an Oxford network.

BRIXMISS   For forty dangerous years from 1948 onwards BRIXMISS, the British Military Mission, in common with similar missions belonging to France, the USA and the Soviet Union, were allowed under the four power agreement in Occupied Germany to observe the Armed Forces on both sides of the Iron Curtain. This provided the

Allies with a unique opportunity to travel legally around parts of Eastern Germany and gather, covertly of course, intelligence on the vast Soviet armed forces facing NATO. The BRIXMISS officers were drawn from Military Intelligence, the SAS and SIS (MI6). Fluent linguists, they were able to penetrate secret training areas and even mix with ordinary Soviet troops. Occasionally when the Soviets weren't looking they smuggled out unexploded bombs and small missiles. They snatched photographs of troop trains, new tanks and missile systems, radars and communications gear. They even managed to break into hangars and steal new pieces of equipment from armoured vehicles. Sometimes when the Soviets noticed, their efforts were met with violence. BRIXMISS provided more information and valuable knowledge, not to mention actual equipment than many of the major intelligence agencies. The skills and experience gained was to be put to great use by SIS and the special SAS teams at their disposal, often called 'The Increment' who, at great risk, entered Afghanistan during the Soviet occupation. They were to reach and strip downed Soviet helicopters of secret items and to recover captured modern Soviet weaponry from the Mujhadeen.

BROADWAY HQ of British Secret Intelligence Service (MI6) (1924–66). Broadway Buildings, 54 The Broadway were in the West End of London and situated opposite St James's Park. The Broadway HQ backed on to 21 Queen Anne's Gate, the official residence of 'C', the chief of SIS.

BRUCE Lockhart, John (1914–95)   In a sphere that is sometimes regarded as suspect, Bruce Lockhart was motivated by deep patriotism. He was often irritated by the writings of past members of SIS and their frequent inaccuracies and distortions. The nephew of Sir Robert Bruce Lockhart, a famous WWI SIS officer and author of *The Memoirs of a British Agent*, he was involved in military intelligence in the Italian Campaign in 1943–44. His subsequent career in SIS saw him in charge of operations in France, Germany, the Middle East, Africa and importantly the USA where he did much to restore trust after the Burgess and Maclean defection. Bruce Lockhart would effectively become Sir Dick White's deputy at SIS until his retirement in 1965. Despite his renowned charm and a confident and cavalier manner, Bruce Lockhart was a modest and shy man. A generous and delightful companion he would dispense wisdom over a glass of wine. However, Bruce Lockhart was also one of the last of the 'robber barons' in SIS, patriotic, determined, freewheeling and willing to use covert action and dirty trick operations to ensure success. He was one of the true 'intelligencers' and unreplaceable. As one close colleague remarked 'when they made John, they broke the mould afterwards'.

BRUSA   British–US Agreement signed 17 May 1943 as a formal pact for the exchange of Communications Intelligence (COMINT) information between the two countries.

BRUSH CONTACT/PASS   A brief public but discreet encounter between an agent and their case officer or handler where information, documents or funds are exchanged.

BSC   British Security Coordination. Cover organisation set up in New York City by SIS (MI6) in May 1940. The office, established for intelligence and propaganda operations, was headed by the Canadian William Stephenson. It was openly known as the British Passport Control Office (PCO) and operated out of the Rockefeller Centre. It played a leading part in ensuring a reasonably smooth working relationship between the SIS, MI5, SOE and the FBI throughout WWII.

BUCKLEY, William (1928–85)   CIA Chief of Station in Beirut and the CIA's top counter terrorism expert. He was kidnapped in Beirut by the Islamic Jihad on 16 March 1984. Buckley was interrogated and tortured for more than a year before being finally murdered in June 1985, ostensibly in revenge for an Israeli attack on PLO facilities in Beirut.

BUGGING   A popular term referring to all manner of eavesdropping from telephone tapping to electronic surveillance devices.

BURGESS, Guy Francis De Moncy (1911–64)   In many ways Burgess was the most improbable spy, frequently drunk, a compulsive homosexual, his social behaviour and habits were outrageous and yet he charmed his way through Eton and Cambridge, becoming a member of the secretive and elitist Apostles society. Recruited at university as a Soviet agent, he joined various pro-Fascist or pro-German organisations as a cover. When WWII began, Burgess was working for the BBC. However, his involvement with members of the intelligence community grew, partly at Soviet insistence, but more because Burgess with friends like Blunt naturally moved in the right social circles. Also like Blunt, Burgess used homosexual blackmail to win over and then retain agents. In 1941, to ensure a wavering Donald Maclean's allegiance, he got his old friend drunk and photographed him nude and in a sexual embrace with a young man. In 1944 he joined the Foreign Office, being appointed personal assistant to the Minister of State, Hector McNeil. Burgess spent a short time billeted upon Philby at the Washington embassy in 1950, much to Philby's embarrassment, the horror of the embassy and the puzzlement of his American hosts. Warned either before or after his return to London that Maclean was under suspicion, Burgess decided to flee Britain with Maclean, thus creating the first serious doubts about his friend Philby in the minds of the security services. Burgess spent his last unhappy years with a succession of pretty boys in Moscow, thoroughly disapproved of by his Soviet colleagues both for his outlandish habits and for wrecking an important espionage network, and died of a heart attack in 1964. However, there has been increasing interest in the idea that Burgess was a far more important Soviet asset than his biography would suggest. He may indeed have been the link with a number of other important spies who, after his defection, simply went to ground and who have never been positively identified.

BURN   Slang for the deliberate sacrifice of an agent in order to protect a more important intelligence asset. Quite often an agent will be *burned* (*burnt*) when there are indications that he has been compromised and often in such a manner as to reinforce the credibility of a MOLE.

BURTON, Sir Richard (1821–90) Burton was an adventurer in the purest sense of the word and in the course of his many travels in Africa, Asia and the Middle East became a 'gentleman' spy. Certainly when the British army captured the Indian province of Sind his abilities were greatly appreciated by Sir Charles Napier, the Commander in Chief of the invading forces. As a young officer, Burton had disguised himself as a native of the area and, speaking the local language, opened three shops in Karachi. Burton sold cloth, trinkets and tobacco for a few rupees and gathered a mass of useful intelligence. Burton had his own peculiar habits which he indulged with much restraint: staining himself with henna and calling himself Mirza Abdullah of Bushire, he would spend night after night in the male brothels of Karachi. He was so skilful at becoming an Indian at will that he could walk past his commanding officer sure of not being rescued. One of the great Victorian eccentrics and an amateur spy.

C

C   Head of the British SIS (MI1c/MI6) – more correctly CSS or Chief of the Secret Service.

CABINET NOIR   French BLACK CHAMBER, a secret office set up under King Henry IV as the Poste aux Lettres in 1590 to intercept important mail. It was further developed by Cardinal Richelieu when he was made minister to Louis XIII in 1624. It would eventually be known as the Haute Police, which was the service concerned with foiling plots and conspiracies against the crown. The fear of political plots was considerable and a network of spies was established throughout Paris. It was the secret police attitude, that under the Ancien Regime their purpose was the suppression of 'private disorder' and to prevent scandals from undermining the Royal Court and the aristocratic families of France, that was to influence Fouché's idea of secret police work and it also spawned the development of cryptographic systems for the encrypting and decrypting of letters throughout Europe.

CAIRNCROSS, John   (1913–1995)   Born in Scotland, John Cairncross came from a long line of civil servants. He entered Cambridge in the early 1930s to study modern languages and was almost immediately converted to Communism by Anthony Blunt and Guy Burgess who turned him over to their NKVD controller, Samuel Cahan. Given a short course in espionage, Cairncross had joined the Foreign Office by 1936. During WWII, he worked at the Government Code and Cipher School, then part of SIS, at Bletchley Park. A large number of important codes and ciphers used by GC&CS and the Allies were copied by Cairncross and passed to the Soviet Union. He later admitted that he had decoded German messages and driven straight to the Soviet Embassy to make the delivery. The Soviets had even provided the car. Later in the war, Cairncross moved into the Broadway HQ of SIS. From the mid-1930s to 1952, Cairncross had been a dedicated Soviet mole. He provided secret information on the German military to the Soviet Union during and after the war. Cairncross also passed considerable amounts of secret material to other members of the Cambridge spy ring and indeed to other Soviet contacts.

Cairncross first came under suspicion in 1951, when Blunt, in the haste of clearing out incriminating material from Burgess's flat in London following his friend's defection, missed notes on British Economic Policy written by Cairncross. Interviewed later by MI5, Cairncross admitted passing only low-grade official material to the Soviets and, to avoid yet another security scandal, he was allowed to resign without being prosecuted.

MI5 finally caught up with Cairncross in 1964. After he was confronted with insurmountable evidence of his involvement with the Soviet intelligence services provided by Blunt, he confessed in return for again not being prosecuted. Cairncross was undoubtedly one of the Soviet Union's most important intellience coups and his immunity was granted as much to hide his importance than in return for for his co-operation. The British Government and Security Services were determined to avoid yet another highly damaging public spy scandal. Cairncross was then given a 'safe' job at the United Nations Food and Agricultural Organisation in Rome and on his retirement settled permanently in Italy.

CALL OUT SIGNAL   A method for triggering contact between the intelligence officer and the agent.

CAMBRIDGE SPIES   A group of Marxist Cambridge University graduates who, despite their upper class origins, became Soviet spies while working for the British intelligence during WWII. These included Burgess, Maclean, Blunt, Philby and Cairncross.

CAMP PEARY (THE FARM)   CIA Special Operations training school near Williamsburg, Virginia. The 10,000-acre site is known to generations of CIA officers from the Clandestine Service as 'The Farm'.

CAMP SWAMPY   A euphemism for the CIA's secret domestic training base at Camp Peary.

CANADA   *Canadian Security Intelligence Service or Service Canadien du Renseignement de Sécurité*: the Canadian Security Intelligence Service or CSIS is a domestic security intelligence service. The Service uses a variety of collection methods to monitor individuals or groups whose activities are suspected of constituting a threat to national security and it took over responsibility for these duties from the Security Service of the Royal Canadian Mounted Police (RCMP) only in 1984. In its early years, much of the CSIS resources were devoted to countering the espionage activities of foreign governments. In response to the rise of terrorism worldwide and the ending of the Cold War, the CSIS devotes a high proportion of its resources to counter-terrorism. CSIS has also assigned more of its counter-intelligence resources to investigate the activities of foreign governments that conduct active economic espionage or who attempt to acquire technology in Canada that can be used for the development of weapons of mass destruction. The CSIS is organised into Operational Branches with the Counter-Intelligence (CI) Branch which monitors espionage threats to national security from other national governments' intelligence operations, the Counter Terrorism (CT) Branch which provides the Government with advice about emerging threats of serious violence that could affect the national security of Canada and finally the Analysis and Production Branch which acts as the Service's main research department. It underwent a major reorganisation in 1996–97 with a new structure of three divisions: one responsible for counter-intelligence and foreign-intelligence matters, a counter-terrorism division and an administration division.

The Communications Security Establishment (CSE) is Canada's national Signals Intelligence (SIGINT) organisation. The actual collection of the SIGINT, however, is conducted by the Canadian Forces Supplementary Radio System (SRS), a component of the Canadian Armed Forces that operates under the direction of CSE. CSE and the SRS in turn work in close co-operation with the National Security Agency (NSA) and Government Communications HQ (GCHQ), Australia's Defence Signals Directorate (DSD), New Zealand's Government Communications Security Bureau (GCSB), and a number of other SIGINT agencies in a global intelligence alliance known informally as the UKUSA community. CSE maintains permanent liaison officers at NSA HQ at Fort Meade, Maryland (CANSLO/W) and GCHQ in Cheltenham, UK (CANSLO/L). There are also NSA and GCHQ liaison officers at CSE HQ (SUSLO/O and BRLO, respectively).

CSE was originally established as the Communications Branch of the National Research Council (CBNRC) on 1 September 1946 and was the direct descendent of Canada's wartime military and civilian SIGINT operations. In 1947, CBNRC took on the additional responsibility of serving as the Canadian Government's communications-electronic security (COMSEC) agency. Prior to 1947, the Government's encryption systems and keys had been provided by the British GC&CS. Between the CBNRC and the military SRS, a large number of monitoring bases have been operated by Canada and these are known to include the following: Aklavik, Northwest Territories (NWT), Alert, NWT, Augsburg, Germany (SRS detachment), Bermuda, Churchill-Manitoba,

Coverdale-New Brunswick, Fort Chimo (now Kuujjuaq)-Quebec, Frobisher Bay (now Iqaluit)-NWT, Gander-Newfoundland, Gloucester-Ontario, Grande Prairie-Kingston, Ontario, Ladner-British Columbia (BC), Leitrim-Ontario, Masset-BC, Ottawa-Ontario, Victoria-BC and Whitehorse-Yukon. However, probably only the main complex at Leitrim and the remote-stations at Alert and Masset remain as major operational sites in 2002. On 1 April 1975, the CBNRC was transferred from the National Research Council to the Department of National Defence and its name changed to the Communications Security Establishment.

CANADA, SPECIAL FORCES Canada's Joint Task Force-2 is the Armed Forces elite Counter-Terrorist and Special Operations unit and works in conjunction with the CSIS at all times. Activated in April 1993 taking over such duties from the Royal Canadian Mounted Police (RCMP). It has three Counter-Terrorist Operational Squadrons, a Command Group and several Specialist Intelligence Detachments. Commanded by a Lt. Colonel with some 250 highly trained and motivated soldiers, organised into specialist two or four man teams, they come under the operational control of a 25–30-man squadron. The Joint Task Force is very secretive and keeps much information about its size, weapons, exact roles and missions confidential. Although this unit is supposedly trained only as a Counter-Terrorist force, it is in fact a Special Operations Intelligence unit tasked to perform the same range of missions as the Special Air Service, Delta Force, French GIGN or German GSG-9. They do in fact operate closely with those units with cross-training and shared intelligence.

Based at the Dwyer Hill Training Centre in Ontario, the counter-terrorist facilities there include a DC 10 Airliner, a range of other vehicles including a bus and multi-storey building for hostage rescue training. Close Quarter Battle (CQB) building, state-of-the-art shooting range, gymnasium and Olympic sized pool. Training includes hostage rescue, marksmanship, combat shooting, combat swimming, explosives ordnance disposal, intelligence gathering, communications, unarmed combat, strength and stamina, heliborne insertion, mountaineering, arctic warfare, HAHO (High Altitude-High Opening), and HALO (High Altitude-Low Opening) Parachuting. It uses a range of weapons including SIG Sauer P226/229 and browning HP automatic pistols, Canadian C7 assault rifles, C8 carbines, Canadian C3A1, SIG Sauer-3000 and Heckler & Koch PSG-1 sniper rifles, with Heckler & Koch MP5 and Canadian C9A1 sub-machine guns.

CANARIS, Wilhelm Franz (1887–1945)   The great enigma, Admiral Wilhelm Canaris was the Director of the Abwehr (1935–44). Canaris undoubtedly worked secretly against the Nazis while trying to preserve and protect his country. He failed on both accounts but his efforts were heroic and admirable. Canaris was one of the few Germans who held power and rank in the Third Reich who plotted against its leaders from the beginning and almost certainly quietly co-operated with the British SIS and perhaps the OSS where and when it was possible to do so without becoming a traitor to his country.

On 19 February 1944, Hitler fired Canaris and replaced him with Walter Schellenburg. Made chief of the Dept of Economic Warfare in Potsdam, Canaris continued to be one of the key figures in the conspiracy of the Black Orchestra (underground) to overthrow Hitler in 1944. Before the military plotters attempted to assassinate Hitler on 29 July 1944, Canaris learned that Himmler suspected certain officers who were actually part of the plot. Canaris warned these men who nevertheless went ahead with the attempt that failed to kill Hitler. Thousands were rounded up and imprisoned as suspects in the abortive assassination including Canaris. The Admiral survived for some time in the Flossenberg concentration camp; however in March 1945 Hitler signed the death sentence. Canaris was horribly executed, dragged from his cell naked on 9 April 1945, paraded before jeering SS guards and then hanged, his corpse left to rot – an ignoble end to one of the great spymasters of the century.

CANNON   Name given to a professional thief employed by an intelligence agency whose sole purpose is to steal back an 'inducement' given to an enemy agent or target in exchange for information.

CARNIVORE   An FBI system to monitor email and other traffic through Internet service providers.

CASE   An intelligence operation in its entirety or the record kept of a past operation.

CASE OFFICER   An intelligence officer who acts as a controller or handler.

CASEY, William (1913–87)   Served in the Office of Strategic Services (OSS) during WWII and was appointed as Director of Central Intelligence (DCI) (1981–87). When Casey became the DCI he was given the task of rebuilding the agency after the effects of President Carter's 'reorganisation'. His aim was to give intelligence officers unrestricted authority to carry out operations throughout the world in the USA's best interests. Casey also wanted the CIA to be able to operate legally in the USA and in the interests of combating terrorism, have the right to break into private property, carry out physical surveillance and to infiltrate US domestic organisations. The CIA counter-intelligence staff was seen as seriously weakened following the dismissal of Anleton and several hundred experienced officers. Casey, however, as a non-career DCI was widely and probably rightly criticised for his lack of experience and, despite a good analytical brain, was often inarticulate. In the end, although he raised moral at Langley, increased the budget and staffing levels and had some success at lifting some of the restrictions previously imposed, he failed to rebuild the CIA that both he and the Reagan administration had wanted. He failed miserably at persuading his political opponents and as one CIA colleague commented, 'He has taken mumbling and turned it into an art form.' While serving as DCI, he was heavily involved in one of the major scandals of President Ronald Reagan's administration. The Iran-Contra affair involving the trading of arms to Iran for the attempted release of Americans held hostage in the Lebanon, the illegal transfer of arms to anti-Communist forces in Nicaragua and the deep involvement of the CIA in drug-related crime. Casey resigned in February 1987 after undergoing brain surgery for a malignant tumour. He died in May 1987.

CAT   Civil Air Transport, later the CIA's private air service. Founded in 1946 in mainland China and from 1949 based in Taiwan from where it supported clandestine air operations in Korea, Vietnam and elsewhere in Asia.

CAVENDISH-BENTINCK, Victor 'Bill' F. William (later the 9th Duke of Portland, 1897–1990)   Appointed to the Joint Intelligence Committee in 1939, he was soon to turn this singularly unimpressive organisation into one of the most important elements of wartime Britain's intelligence effort. The JIC contained representatives of the three Service Intelligence departments, the Foreign Office, SIS and MI5. Cavendish-Bentinck successfully by-passed inter-service rivalries to create a highly effective committee. Virtually everyone in the inner circle of intelligence came to trust him and his judgement. He was rightly called the 'Intelligence Chief Extraordinary' and the fact that the JIC was right in its assessments more often than not is a great tribute to him.

CC&D   Camouflage, concealment and deception.

CELL   The lowest and most expendable group in an espionage network.

CENTRE – MOSCOW   KGB HQ in the Lubyanka, Moscow.

CENTURY HOUSE   HQ of the SIS (MI6) at 100 Westminster Bridge Road from 1966 till its move to Vauxhall Cross in 1994.

CHAOS   An ill-advised FBI domestic surveillance operation which involved the infiltration of US radical and anti-war groups during the Vietnam War to discover whether there was a serious Communist element.

CHEKA   (Chrezuvychainaya Komissiya po Borbe s Kontrrevolutisnei I Sabottazhem: The Extraordinary Commission for the Struggle Against Counter-Revolution and Sabotage) Formed following the Russian Revolution of 1917 by the Polish Communist Feliks Dzerzhinsky, a forerunner of the KGB.

CHI   The Cipher Office of the German armed forces during WWII. The agency was responsible for interception, cryptanalysis and the developing and distribution of ciphers to the German forces.

CHICKEN FEED   Information knowingly provided to an enemy intelligence service through an agent or double agent. It must be of sufficient quality to convince the recipients of its authenticity and the value of its source.

CHILE   DIDN (Directorate of National Defence Intelligence or Dirección de Inteligencia de la Defensa Nacional). The notorious DINA Security Service was responsible for a reign of terror following General Pinochet's overthrow of the Allende Government in 1971; thousands were illegally imprisoned, tortured, assassinated or simply disappeared. When DINA's reputation became a major embarrassment to the Military Dictatorship it was simply replaced in 1977 by a new organisation known as the National Information Centre (Centro Nacional de Información – CNI). The functions of the CNI combined those of an external intelligence and an internal security service. Although human rights abuses decreased significantly after the abolition of DINA, its successor, CNI continued to draw worldwide criticism and was disbanded upon the election of a civilian government in 1990. Most of its 1,800 staff were largely absorbed by a new co-ordinating body for military intelligence, operating under the aegis of the National Defence

Staff and known as the Directorate of National Defence Intelligence (Dirección de Inteligencia de la Defensa Nacional – DIDN). The DIDN now concerns itself primarily with defence rather than with internal intelligence. The Chilean security services and their communications monitoring sites played an important role on behalf of Britain during the Falklands War of 1981 and the CNI and its successor the DIDN continue to maintain a close relationship with Britain's SIS and GCHQ.

CHINA, PEOPLE'S REPUBLIC OF   The main Chinese Communist intelligence organisation prior to 1949 was the *Central Department of Social Affairs*, which subsequently became the *Central Investigation Department* and finally the *Ministry of State Security* in 1983.

After the Party consolidated state power in China, the intelligence system played an increasingly important role. Li Kenong, head of the Central Investigation Department, was also deputy chief of General Staff, and vice minister of foreign affairs. During the 1950s every Chinese embassy had an Investigation and Research Office for intelligence collection by staff from the Central Investigation Department. Analytical tasks were the responsibility of the Central Investigation Department Eighth Bureau, publicly known since 1978 as the 'Institute of Contemporary International Relations'. Shortly before the Cultural Revolution, Li Kenong died and Kang Sheng assumed responsibility for the work of the Central Investigation Department.

During the Cultural Revolution the Central Investigation Department was abolished and most of its leadership sent for 're-education'. The PLA General Staff Second Department temporarily took over its responsibilities. The Central Group for the Examination of Cases, composed of Central Investigation Department cadres acting on orders of Kang Sheng, was instrumental in the removal from power of major figures such as Deng Xiaoping. This extreme group was also responsible for the killings of hundreds of thousands of loyal party members, liberals, artists and others who did not fit comfortably within the Party's tight new guidelines.

With the death of Lin Biao in the early 1970s the Department was re-established. When Hua Guofeng and Wang Dongxing assumed power in 1977 they sought to enlarge the Central Investigation Department and expand the CPC's intelligence work as part of their more general efforts to consolidate their leadership positions. This initiative was resisted by Deng Xiaoping, who had returned to power. Deng Xiaoping argued that the intelligence system should not use Chinese embassies to provide cover, and that intelligence personnel should be sent abroad under the cover of reporters and businessmen. Consequently, the Central Investigation Department withdrew its men from Chinese embassies abroad, apart from a small number of secret intelligence agents.

Zhou Shaozheng, a veteran of the Central Investigation system, became head of the General Office of the Central Investigation Department in 1976. In June 1983, a Ministry of State Security was finally established that would merge the whole Central Investigation Department with the counter-intelligence elements of the Public Security Ministry. Lin Yun, deputy minister of Public Security, was appointed the first minister of the Ministry of State Security Ministry, but was removed in 1985 and replaced by Jia Chunwang following the defection of a senior intelligence officer to the USA.

The Ministry of State Security (MSS) aggressively target the USA, placing particular emphasis on the high-tech sector heavily concentrated in Southern California, and in the Silicon Valley and indeed similar targets in W Europe. However this concentration on economic and technical intelligence has led to serious mistakes elsewhere. In 1987 the Chinese overestimated the Khmer Rouge and believed that the invading Vietnamese Army would prove incapable of capturing Phnom Penh and therefore continued to support the Pol Pot regime much to the indignation of Hanoi and much damage was done to long-term relations between Vietnam and China. On the eve of the collapse of Romania's Communist dictatorship, the MSS assessment was that the situation in Romania was fairly good. As it turned out, Ceausescu was executed shortly afterwards.

The Chinese Government's contributions to US political campaigns had been discovered by the FBI as early as 1991. There is evidence that China sought favourable American treatment on trade policy by contributing millions of dollars to the re-election of Bill Clinton and members of Congress. The US National Security Agency intercepted communications indicating that China was targeting 30 Congressional candidates (mostly Democrats) for influence buying campaign contributions. Newt Gingrich, Republican Speaker of the House, was one of those candidates and the CIA believe, based on FBI counter-intelligence surveillance, that Beijing's diplomatic community and espionage network helped Democratic fundraiser John Huang and other political operatives get millions of dollars in campaign donations for the 1996 election. The public disclosures were a severe setback to China's long-term plans to gain lasting influence in the USA.

The MSS is organised into the First or Domestic Bureau which resembles the *First General Bureau* of the old KGB and mainly operates within China. The Second or Foreign Bureau is responsible for operations abroad. The *Second Bureau* provides tasking for collection priorities and analysis. The *Third* or *Taiwan Bureau* is responsible for operations against Taiwan. The *Fourth* or *Technology Bureau* researches and develops intelligence gathering and counter-intelligence techniques. These include tracking, wiretapping, photography, recording, communications and intelligence transmission. The *Fifth* or *Local Intelligence Bureau* is responsible for directing and co-ordinating the work of local departments and bureaus of the Ministry of State Security at the provincial and municipal levels. The *Sixth* or *Counter-Intelligence Bureau*'s primary task is counter-intelligence activity against overseas Chinese pro-democracy organisations. The *Seventh* or *Circulation Bureau* is required to check, verify, prepare and write intelligence reports and special classified reports on the basis of first-hand intelligence obtained from open or secret sources. The *Eighth Bureau* or *Institute of Contemporary International Relations* is now one of the largest institutes for research on international relations, with a staff that at one time numbered over 500 research fellows. The Bureau is divided into some 10 research offices, specialising in general international relations, global economy, the USA, Russia, E Europe, W Europe, the Middle East, Japan, Asia, Africa and Latin America. One of its main objectives is to collect open source information. The *Ninth* or *Anti-Defection and Counter-Surveillance Bureau* is responsible for countering efforts by foreign intelligence services to recruit personnel of the Ministry of State Security and among cadres of Chinese institutions abroad. It also counters surveillance, wiretapping and infiltration by foreign intelligence services against Chinese embassies and consulates. This has required the import in recent years of sophisticated state-of-the-art surveillance equipment. The *Tenth* or *Scientific and Technological Information Bureau* is focused on collecting economic, scientific and technological intelligence, following the example of Russian agencies in stepping up the work of collecting scientific and technological information from the West. The *Eleventh* or *Electronic Computers Bureau* is responsible for analysing intelligence gathered with electronic computers, and operating the computer network of the Ministry of State Security and indeed also attempts to acquire state-of-the-art computer technology from foreign countries. The *Foreign Affairs Bureau* co-ordinates and develops co-operation with foreign intelligence services. In particular the ISI from Pakistan and despite its open support for Arab nations, with Mossad, the Israeli intelligence services. The main HQ of the Ministry of State Security remains at Xiyuan (Western Garden), situated next to the Summer Palace. The Xiyuan HQ includes the living quarters for dependants in the compound of the Ministry of State Security and is closely guarded by armed police.

Military Intelligence Department: the MID of the PLA General Staff HQ is responsible for basic order-of-battle intelligence, studies of foreign weapons systems, and analyses of the capabilities of foreign military organisations. It obtains information through military attachés, review of open source literature, clandestine HUMINT operations, and joint business ventures. The MID is believed to play an integral role in obtaining advanced military technologies to bolster China's military capabilities and improve weapons systems vital to China's export arms business. The MID has also played a significant role in the development of clandestine relationships with Israel and other nations to gain expertise in the development of advanced weapons systems. Together with the Commission on Science, Technology and Industry for National Defence (COSTIND), the MID works to obtain military technologies for application to the Chinese military. Much of this technology is obtained through technological diversion and reverse engineering of products purchased from the West.

The *Second Department* of the PLA General Staff is traditionally responsible for collecting military information through the activities of military attachés in Chinese embassies, clandestine operations and the analysis of OSINT or Open Source Intelligence; it now increasingly concentrates on military scientific and technological intelligence.

The Technical Department, or Third Department of the PLA General Staff, is the national agency responsible for managing China's Strategic SIGINT programme. The Department was established in 1953 with considerable Soviet assistance to provide the Chinese General Staff with a limited SIGINT capability and strategic communications support, a lack of which had seriously affected China's military ability in the Korean War. China now probably maintains the most extensive SIGINT capability of any nation outside the USA, UK and Russia. The Technical Department provides the Chinese Government and its armed forces with a wide range of SIGINT capabilities operating as many as 30 SIGINT ground interception stations deployed throughout both China and increasingly overseas. Their major monitor programmes appear to concentrate on Russia, Taiwan, Japan, S Korea, India and the USA.

Widespread coverage is given to monitoring the signal traffic of US military units located in the Pacific region; several large SIGINT facilities on Hainan Island are principally concerned with monitoring US naval activities in the South China Sea. The Chinese have successfully developed a limited space-platform ELINT system which is mounted on their most recent photo-reconnaissance and communications satellites. While there is no clear indication that this capability presents a significant threat to US forces in the region it is clear that China intends to achieve a significant ability to monitor effectively US communications in the very near future. Commercial Communications are monitored by a range of ground stations stretching from Hainan to Beijing and are considered to be of great importance to China's future economic development. The Chinese have developed a series of SIGINT collection vessels that constantly monitor US military operations and exercises in the Pacific region and are now believed to have a significant Submarine EW capability, while the Air Force has converted a number of large four-engined commercial aircraft for long-range EW and maritime surveillance duties.

The massive network of Signals Interception (SIGINT) facilities constructed throughout China in recent years have now been extended to a number of overseas locations. It is significant that at a time when the Russians are withdrawing such facilities from Lourdes in Cuba in early 2002, the Chinese are believed to have opened two new stations at nearby locations on the Caribbean Island. The main monitoring sites are believed to include the following:

- *Beijing, Zhangye* in Gansu Province – tracks foreign surveillance satellites.
- *Chengdu, Dingyuanchen* – in early January 2000 US reconnaissance satellites photographed the addition of several new large parabolic dish antennas to the already extensive antenna field at the Dingyuanchen SIGINT facility near the Russian border. This base was used to monitor US communications during the Afghan campaign in late 2001. China has an abiding interest in this area, since former Soviet Central Asian states such as Uzbekistan and Tajikistan are suspected of giving clandestine support to Muslim Uighur separatists in Xingjiang province in Western China. However it is also possible that intelligence gained from this facility and passed to the Pakistan ISI, known to have close connections to both the Taliban and Al-Qa'ida organisations, may have been 'leaked' to Osama bin Laden's intelligence officers and that this enabled many more of the terrorists to evade the US bombing attacks and possibly to escape from Afghanistan.

- *Erlian*, *Hami* and *Jilemutu* – near the Sino-Russian and Sino-Mongolian border.
- *Guangzhou* – monitors SE Asia and the South China Sea.
- *Hainan Island* – the large SIGINT complex on Hainan had been vastly expanded by 1995 and is presently undergoing a further enhancement in early 2002.
- *Lanzhou* – responsible for monitoring Russian signal traffic and at one time provided strategic early warning of a Soviet missile attack.
- *Nanjing* – this large site monitors Taiwan's communications.
- *Shanghai* – there are three SIGINT sites in and around Shanghai, two of which are dedicated to economic and commercial espionage.
- *Shenyang* – responsible for covering signals from Russia, Japan, and Korea.
- *Rocky Island (Shi-tao)* – in the Paracel Islands. One of the first major projects reflecting growing Chinese interest in activities in the South China Sea was the major expansion of its SIGINT capability with a new station on Rocky Island (Shi-tao) near Woody Island (Lin-tao) in the Paracel Islands which entered operational service in the summer of 1995. Located on one of the highest points in the region, the new station significantly improved coverage of the entire Spratly Islands area, the Philippines and the Strait of Malacca. This site concentrates on monitoring commercial and naval vessels.
- The *Coco Islands* – leased from Myanmar since 1994. The electronic intelligence station, on Great Coco Island in the Bay of Bengal some 180 miles south of the coast, is the most important Chinese SIGINT installation in Myanmar. The Chinese Army have also constructed a base on the *Small Coco* Island in the Alexandra Channel between the Indian Ocean and the Andaman Sea N of India's Andaman Islands. But of strategically the greatest importance are the Chinese Naval maritime reconnaissance and surveillance facilities on the Coco Islands. Their location is ideal for monitoring Indian naval and missile launch facilities in the Indian controlled Andaman and Nicobar Islands to the south and the movements of the Indian and other navies at a crucial point on the sea lanes between the Bay of Bengal and the Strait of Malacca.
- *Sittwe* – Myanmar has also granted China access to other islands, including Sittwe in Western Arakan State, for the construction of intelligence collection facilities. In addition during 1994 Chinese technicians also built a series of small SIGINT stations along the Myanmar coast of Bay of Bengal, providing overlapping coverage of the Bay of Bengal and Strait of Malacca.

- *Zedetkyi Kyun* – or St Matthew's island off the Tenasserim coast in the southeast is especially sensitive because it is located off the coast of Myanmar's southernmost tip at Kawthaung or Victoria Point. Close to the northern entrance to the Straits of Malaccait enables China to monitor the approaches to the Strait of Malacca.
- *Sop Hau in Laos* – this SIGINT site, in use since the early 1960s, has been significantly upgraded and expanded since 1995; it will give China almost complete SIGINT coverage of the entire Strait's area from the South China Sea to the Indian Ocean.

CHINA, SPECIAL FORCES The Chinese Counter-Terrorist units are known as Immediate Action Units (IAU) and are effectively an operational department of the MSS Intelligence Service. The personnel are mainly from Special Operations units and the training, weapons and support are all provided by the Army. Significant terrorist activity is dealt with by a regional Immediate Action Unit and supported by the Army when required. These units are not comparable with Western Special Forces as they concentrate largely on martial arts and the 'elimination' of the threat, i.e. the intention is to kill, not to capture. Little emphasis is placed on clandestine operations, capturing terrorists, preventing incidents or indeed hostage rescue.

By 2003 China will have a number of the new, much more intensely trained long-range Operations Groups for Airborne, Reconnaissance and Amphibious warfare. Its personnel were drawn from the 6th Special Warfare Group, 8th Special Warfare Group and the 12th Special Warfare Group's own Special Forces Detachment, based in the Guangzhou Military Region (southern China), nicknamed 'Sword of Southern China' and equipped with advanced intelligence equipment, command, control, GPS (global position system) and a wide range of weapons including some specially purchased in W Europe. The Officers are all Staff College trained and it is believed that some 60 per cent of serving members have university degrees. This new generation of Chinese Special Forces specialise in electronic warfare and intelligence gathering but with its multi-role capability it can be used as a mobile counter-insurgency or counter-terrorism fire-brigade. The vast cities of China and the hinterland are now beset by growing ethnic and tribal conflict, but in particular the large-scale Muslim insurgency in western China on the borders with Afghanistan provides the requirement for more such intelligence based units.

CIA Central Intelligence Agency. Established by President Truman in 1947 to co-ordinate all US intelligence activities. The Agency has

CLASSIFIED

become a global intelligence service and covert action (paramilitary) force for extending and maintaining US influence. The head of the CIA, the DCI or Director of Central Intelligence is in theory in overall charge of all US intelligence gathering agencies.

See also DIRTY TRICKS; UNITED STATES OF AMERICA.

CIAink Classified computer intranet at CIA HQ.

CICERO (1905–70) German codename for the Albanian Elyeza Bazna who spied on Sir Hugh Knatchbull-Hugessen, the British Ambassador in Ankara while working as his valet from October 1943 to April 1944. Although compromised by a German defector, Bazna escaped with the £300,000 he had received from the Germans, mostly in forged £5 notes as it turned out.

CIG Central Intelligence Group. Created in 1946, it effectively acted as a 'bridging' organisation between the disbanding of the wartime OSS in 1945 and the creation in 1947 of the Central Intelligence Organisation (CIA).

CIPHER *see* CODES.

CLANDESTINE (SERVICES) Covert, unknown to an enemy or the operational arm of the CIA responsible for classic espionage operations usually with human assets. Also known as the Directorate of Operations (DO), formerly the Directorate of Plans (DP).

CLANSIG Clandestine Signals Intelligence.

CLASSIFIED Classified information is defined as materials owned by, and produced by or for or under the control of, the US Government that fall within one or more of the following categories: intelligence sources or methods, cryptology, military plans, and vulnerabilities or capabilities of systems, installations, projects or plans relating to national security.

The classification is made by a special authority that determines that its unauthorised disclosure could reasonably be expected to result in damage to national security. Normal levels of classification include: *Top Secret*: information whose unauthorised disclosure could reasonably result in 'exceptionally grave' damage (there are a number of higher levels of Top Secret, such as 'Cosmic', 'Ultra' and so on); *Secret*: information whose unauthorised disclosure could reasonably result in 'serious' damage; *Confidential*: information whose unauthorised disclosure could cause damage to national security. Access to classified information at any level may also be restricted by caveats like material that is not releasable to foreign nationals or not releasable to contractors or contractors/consultants.

CLEAN   An agent or intelligence material or facility that has never actually been used for an operation and therefore probably remains unknown to an opposing intelligence agency.

CLOAK   A sensitive disguise and deception illusionary technique first deployed by the CIA in Moscow during the mid 1970s.

CNA-WATCHCON   US intelligence assessment of cyberwar threat.

COBBLER   Usual Russian name for a forger.

CODES AND CIPHERS   A system used to obscure a message by use of a cipher or by using a mark, symbol, sound or any innocuous verse or piece of music. As important today as in the Middle Ages, they are an integral part of any secret communication, whether military or commercial. Antoine Rossignol, Louis XIV's personal adviser on security matters, declared, 'an unbreakable code was probably an impossibility, but a reliable code should take so long to crack that the hidden message would be useless to an enemy by the time this was achieved'. Today's computer generated codes, of course, can have so many possible combinations as to make them effectively unbreakable. Indeed, the NSA devotes considerable effort to ensuring that as many as possible of the commercial codes have a 'back door' for government cryptographers to be able to read a wide range of commercial and private electronic communications quickly and easily.

Other commercial coding companies around the world have been bought up by compliant US computer software giants like Microsoft, or persuaded to see the light or just 'closed down'. The USA and other members of the UKUSA network, have too much invested in the future and too many threats from terrorists and organised crime to let advances in commercial coding companies 'blind' the intelligence services with unbreakable codes.

COLBY, William (1920–96)   Colby saw his first espionage service as a member of the OSS during WWII. He operated behind German lines in France and was part of many dangerous missions, including the blowing up of a German communications centre in Norway, which was achieved after Colby and a team of OSS men parachuted to the site. Returning to Princeton to study law after the war, Colby then went to work for the CIA. Station chief in Saigon (1959–62), he later ran the

Phoenix Program which involved resettlement and pacification of Vietnamese villagers. The programme was seriously abused by the USA and its S Vietnamese allies, which resulted in over 20,000 civilians being killed, and thousands more illegally imprisoned as suspected Viet Cong supporters. The nightmare of this slaughter haunted Colby throughout his intelligence career. In 1973 Colby was appointed Deputy Director of Operations, a post he assumed after returning from Vietnam. In September 1973, Colby was named Director of the CIA, a post he held until January 1976. During this period, Colby, under pressure to admit CIA 'bad secrets' admitted that the agency had interfered in the internal affairs of such countries as Angola in 1975. Colby further turned over top-secret information to the Church Commission which compromised the public statements of his predecessor, Richard Helms, who was later indicted for perjury. Another victim of Colby's uncertain handling was James Angleton, long-time head of the CIA's counter-intelligence department. The dislike and distrust between the two senior CIA officers was such that Angleton left the agency. This and other arbitrary behaviour earned Colby considerable criticism and undermined the overall effectiveness of the CIA.

More scrutiny was directed on the CIA during Colby's tenure than at any other time. President Gerald Ford prohibited the CIA from involving itself in the assassination of any foreign leader and went on to establish the Rockefeller Commission to investigate the agency further. The commission eventually gave the CIA its tacit approval but confirmed that it was guilty of numerous unlawful acts. Frank Church, who headed the congressional committee also investigating the CIA in 1975, described the agency as 'a rogue elephant running amok'. Colby retired soon after, to be replaced first by George H. W. Bush and then by Admiral Stansfield Turner. In late April 1996 Colby, while canoeing down a Maryland river, apparently drowned. His widow later identified his body on 6 May 1996.

COLD APPROACH An often-risky attempt to recruit a foreign national as an agent or informer without any prior indication that the person might be receptive to such an offer. Usually made after evidence that the target is in desperate need of money, or is simply greedy or perhaps unhappy in his work or lifestyle.

COMMERCIAL ESPIONAGE *see* ECONOMIC INTELLIGENCE.

COMINT A sub-category of SIGINT that involves messages or voice information derived from the interception of foreign communications;

it does not include the monitoring of foreign public media or the intercept of communications obtained during the course of counter-intelligence investigations within the USA.

COMPANY, THE   In-house name for the CIA.

COMPROMISE(D)   When an operation, asset or agent is uncovered and cannot remain secret.

COMSEC   Communications Security (methods used to block or avoid hostile SIGINT).

CONCEALMENT DEVICE   Any one of a variety of devices secretly used to store and transport materials relating to an operation.

CONFUSION AGENT   An individual dispatched to confuse the intelligence or counter-intelligence services of another country rather than to collect information.

CONSIGLIO DEI DIECE   The Council of Tens played a very significant role during the early Renaissance period as the state security and intelligence service of the Venetian Republic. The Consiglio or Council was formed in 1310 when a political conspiracy lead by the Doge, Marino Falieri, was exposed only by one of the conspirators. The Council, originally only a temporary response to a crisis, quickly became a permanent body within the Republic. A remarkably efficient combination of secret police work and political, military and commercial espionage ensured near unlimited power as a security, judicial and intelligence organisation within the Venetian Republic till around 1454.

Members of the council covered their faces with masks at official meetings and when asked to identify themselves would open their cloaks to show the linings were specially embroidered with the insignia CDX. Most of the agents and spies employed by the Council against the Venetian Republic's enemies, in particular the City State of Genoa, were either priests or Jewish tradesmen. Both, by the very nature of their professions, were allowed entry to all manner of places in societies that were largely governed by the needs of religion and commerce.

CONTROLLER   Often used interchangeably with Handler. Refers to an agent's controller, a reasonably senior officer working under diplomatic cover at the local embassy or as an illegal, operating under deep cover as, perhaps a businessman, who controls the activities of agents or double agents in the target country.

COOKING THE BOOKS   Politicising or slanting intelligence analysis to support a particular political view or objective.

CO-OPTED AGENT   National of a country who assists willingly a foreign intelligence service.

COUNTER-ESPIONAGE   Activities taken to protect secrets from foreign intelligence operations, usually in the former of surveillance and other measures taken within your own country against an external threat.

COUNTER-INTELLIGENCE   Activities conducted to disrupt foreign intelligence operations, usually in the form of active measures taken against the service or the country posing the threat.

COUNTER-SURVEILLANCE   Actions taken to thwart hostile surveillance operations.

COUNTER-TERRORISM   Positive action taken to prevent terrorist operations from occurring.

COURIER   A reliable officer or agent detailed to transport and deliver secret documents, money or other sensitive material. They are also the links between the agents and their intelligence service controllers or handlers. They sometimes serve as 'cut-outs' or intermediaries who enable a network or system to work without the necessity of direct contact between the spy and those for whom they are spying. A courier's task is often dangerous and their fate is of less importance than that of the spy or the controller; it is therefore not unknown for them to be eliminated to avoid the compromise of the controller's cover or the exposure of the spy network.

COVCOM   Covert communications.

COVER   Protective guise assumed by an individual or activity to conceal its true identity and affiliation.

COVERT ACTION OPERATION   Activities carried out in a concealed or clandestine manner in order to make it difficult, if not impossible, to trace those activities back to the sponsoring intelligence service or nation.

Afghanistan in 2001–02 provides a perfect example of Western Intelligence agencies running covert action operations. The CIA had a clandestine paramilitary unit of about 150 strong from its Special Operations Group (SOG) conducting a hidden war in Afghanistan from before 20 September 2001. It was composed mainly of former US military personnel and it had entered Afghanistan well before any other US forces, paving the way for the arrival of the Army's Special Forces. It had been engaged in actual combat with the Taliban and Al-Qa'ida forces quite early in the campaign.

The SOG is part of the CIA's Directorate of Operations, whose primary mission is to conduct clandestine intelligence gathering. This includes traditional case officers, who work out of US embassies or under business or journalistic cover. The Special Activities Division, which directly controls the CIA's 'secret soldiers', has been provided with specialised CIA case officers from the agency's Near East Division who spoke the local languages and have had previous covert relationships with the Northern Alliance and other anti-Taliban groups since 1994.

The role of the CIA's paramilitary units has been particularly important in Afghanistan because much of the war has turned on intelligence and targeting information. Indeed the CIA-operated Predator UAVs provided intelligence resulting in three days of strikes that killed key Al-Qa'ida leaders and this capability may have also played a role in the successful attack on Mohammed Atef, the senior operations adviser to Osama bin Laden whose death was later confirmed by the Taliban.

The highly secret CIA capability provided by the Special Activities Division consists of teams of about half a dozen men who do not normally wear military uniforms. The Division can call upon the services of about 250 covert action specialists, pilots and communications experts and probably still has access to a number of professional assassins. Most are hardened veterans who have 'retired' early from the Special Forces The division's arsenal includes stealth helicopters, clandestine air assets and the unmanned aerial Predator drones equipped with high-resolution cameras and even Hellfire antitank missiles. The CIA's Special Operations Group co-operates closely with the British SIS, SAS and the US SEAL-6 and Delta Force.

The SOG or 'snake eaters' are virtually an independent 'secret army' with their own dedicated annual budget of over $4 billion. Depending on the particular unit, they are subjected to a gruelling training regime at 'The Farm' (Camp Peary) and other covert facilities in preparation for a wide variety of missions ranging from hostage rescue to deep-penetration reconnaissance behind enemy lines to small-scale strikes, sabotage, assassination and urban warfare.

Their use of offensive action has in the past required a presidential 'finding', such as the wide-ranging 'clear and present danger' declaration signed by President Bush authorising the CIA to make war on Al-Qa'ida following the 11 September attacks. Such findings lay out what activities are permitted and senior congressional leaders should be informed of the covert action as well; however, in the light of recent statements restraint may no longer be uppermost in the mindset either at Langley or for that matter the White House. This carries the inherent risk of a return to the CIA's unbridled used of covert action to destabilise foreign regimes. It was not unknown for the CIA to stage coups and carry out sabotage operations, and it was this behaviour that so nearly brought about the destruction of the Agency by President Carter and Admiral Stansfield Turner in the late 1970s.

Much less attention is paid, however, to the role of the 'field officers' provided by the British Intelligence Service, the SIS (MI6). These officers have a reputation for great skill and local knowledge and have already proved invaluable to the CIA in Afghanistan. The SIS operations group is made up largely of combat veterans from the SAS and SBS with years of experience in Oman, Yemen, Afghanistan and much of the Middle East. Expert in local traditions, habits, languages and the complicated political, ethnic and religious situation of the region, the SIS have much to offer the US intelligence community.

It will probably be asked to play an increasingly important role as the War on Terrorism spreads to other nations in the Middle East and Asia and in early 2002 SIS was recruiting up to 100 additional former Special Forces soldiers as they expand their covert action capability.

COVERT AGENT   An officer or agent who carries out covert action duties.

CRABB, Lionel Phillip 'Buster' (1909–56)   Royal Naval diver of considerable skill and bravery who served in Gibraltar 1942, Leghorn and Venice in Italy, clearing mines and unexploded bombs from the harbours in 1943–44. Used by SIS (MI6) for covert missions while still in the Navy, retired finally in 1955. Against the express orders of the Government SIS employed Crabb to conduct a covert underwater examination of the Soviet Cruiser Ordzhonikidze while on a courtesy visit to Portsmouth, UK in 1956. His disappearance, either due to an accident or to a hostile Soviet response, led to a 'botched' cover-up, which included his SIS handler Teddy Davies (alias Mr Smith) removing pages from the register at the 'Sally Port' Hotel in Portsmouth where he and Crabb had been staying for the duration of the operation. Both SIS and the Admiralty did everything possible, including trying to involve MI5, to prevent a scandal and Government backlash. Though they managed to prevent public knowledge of the incident for some time, it seems certain that the Soviets were aware that something had been occurring. The response of the Government left little doubt of their displeasure. They dismissed the Chief of SIS, Major-General Sir John Sinclair, and replaced him with Sir Dick White, head of their rivals, the internal security service MI5.

One of the more likely explanations surfaced in 1996 when an Israeli journalist interviewed Joseph Zverkin, the former senior officer in Soviet Naval Intelligence who had also spent some years as a Soviet undercover agent in Britain. Zverkin claimed, 'Crabb was discovered when swimming on the water next to the ship by a watchman, who was at a height of 20 metres. An order was given to inspect the water and two people were equipped with sniper guns, small calibre. One of them was an ordinary seaman the other an officer, the equivalent of a lieutenant, who was in charge of an artillery unit on the boat, and an exceptional shot ... Crabb dived next to the boat and came up and swam, perhaps because of air poisoning. The lieutenant shot him in the head and killed him. He sank. All the stories about him being caught by us or that he was a Russian spy are not true.'

In other words, a Soviet Marine officer killed Crabb with a single shot from a small calibre, probably silenced rifle using modified ammunition that blew most of Crabb's head apart. Time and sea life did the rest, until Crabb's headless body was recovered from off Pilsey Island near Chichester Harbour on 9 June 1957, 14 months later and 10 miles (16 kms) away.

When KGB defector Anatoli Golitsin was interrogated in 1963 he admitted that Soviet Naval Intelligence knew in advance that an attempt by a diver would be made to examine the Ordzhonikidze in Portsmouth harbour. None of those later known to have been Soviet spies at the relevant time, such as Vassall, would have been aware of the operation and it is believed that MI5 only learned about the incident when the Admiralty asked them to help cover it up. SIS were certainly not then in the habit of discussing their operations with what they then still considered a junior service.

CRACKING Illegally gaining entry to a computer or computer network in order to do harm.

CRITICAL (CRITICAL INTELLIGENCE) Highest urgency message flashed to the top of the US Government to warn of imminent hostilities or other critical threats to US national security.

CROATIA The Croatian intelligence community remains split between a group of small agencies, each competing for a share of a restricted budget; however, this has also often been used as the excuse to take extreme and often brutal action, particularly during the Balkan conflicts of the 1990s. The Croatian security services were guilty of considerable human abuse, torture and murder of civilians of both Serbian and Bosnian ethnic origin. The main agencies are largely civilian run and appear to come under the operational control of the SZUP or Constitutional Order Protection Service; *Security Information Service (OBS)*, *National Security Office (UNS)*, *Security Information Service (SIS)* and the *Croatian Army's Intelligence Service (OSH)*.

The NSA has used SIGINT facilities at Braco Island and at Zagreb-Lucko Airport. During November–December 2001 the Croatian *NSEI* or *National Electronic Surveillance Service* received the advanced Watson system and surveillance equipment from the USA for use in the fight against terrorism and illegal migration. The equipment and installations have now been fitted in all major Croatian towns. Importantly from a NSA view the new surveillance equipment effectively covers the territories of neighbouring countries: most forms of telephonic communication, digital and analogue communication equipment, especially mobile phones, email and fax messages can now be monitored in Montenegro, Bosnia and of course, Serbia. The equipping of Croatia with hi-tech espionage installations confirms its role as the region's foremost partner in the US anti-terrorist coalition. This is also recognition of Croatia's long years of co-operation in the exchange of intelligence data with the US intelligence service. This is especially true in the case of exchanging intelligence on the presence of terrorist groups and individuals in Bosnia-Herzegovina and Kosovo over the past few years. With the arrival of the new equipment and technology, Croatia has become the biggest source of intelligence in SE Europe for the needs of the anti-terrorist coalition. The Croatian intelligence service, in co-operation with the NSA, US forces and NATO's SFOR Command in Bosnia-Herzegovina, has been instrumental in keeping under surveillance and arresting collaborators of bin Laden's network in Bosnia-Herzegovina. Apart from listening in on digital communication and mobile phones, the US intelligence-gathering system in Croatia also traces the movements of a person under surveillance if the battery is in the mobile phone. It has greatly reduced the transfer of foreign nationals across the Croatian border and indeed even the indicted war criminals Ratko Mladic and Radovan Karadzic were being kept under successful surveillance from Croatia by early 2002.

The USA has maintained successful co-operation in the intelligence area with the Croatian intelligence community since the early 1990s, both in the planning of military operations in the Balkans, and in the struggle against terrorism. The Croatian intelligence community can now monitor all kinds of digital and mobile communication, whose surveillance has so far been hampered and limited. Previously Croatian intelligence operatives had at their disposal technology that could successfully monitor only the 099 analogue network, while with two German-made vans and NSEI surveillance equipment it monitored digital mobile phones. This kind of monitoring was exhausting for the operatives, so that their concentration would flag, while expenses far outstripped the hoped-for results. The equipment for monitoring digital mobile communication is very expensive and unavailable on the free market. It is no secret that the EU members have similar systems, which they use for discovering terrorist and criminal activities in the Union member states. However, they are all countries with long democratic traditions, political stability, and precisely defined mechanisms for the control and supervision of secret surveillance and tapping. Unlike Croatia where the new capability will undoubtedly eventually be used for internal political purposes of oppression.

CRYPTANALYSIS   The process of converting encrypted or encoded messages into plain text without initial knowledge of the appropriate KEY.

CRYPTOGRAPHY   The science of secret writing employed in intelligence and espionage activities to send messages in such a way as to conceal the real meaning from everyone but the sender and the intended recipient.

CSI   CIA Centre for the Study of Intelligence. Can also mean the Consortium for the Study of Intelligence, the Georgetown intelligence think tank and working group.

CTC   CIA Counter-Terrorism Centre. Increasingly important with the growth of international terrorism.

CUBA   *DGI* or *Directorate General of Intelligence*, is the principal foreign intelligence service and has been closely modelled on and associated with the Soviet and Russian intelligence services. The DGI was established under the Ministry of the Interior (MININT) in late

1961. The new agency included three Liberation Committees – for the Caribbean, Central America, and S America – collectively known as the Liberation Directorate (DL). In the early 1960s, the DL was also responsible for supporting liberation movements in Africa, including those who overthrew the government of Zanzibar in 1963. However Soviet economic pressure on Cuba in 1967–68 forced Castro to develop a more selective revolutionary strategy and subordinate the DGI to the KGB. The KGB compelled Castro to replace its chief, Manuel Piñeiro, with José Méndez Cominches in 1969. The DGI thereafter focused its efforts on collecting military, political and economic intelligence, with responsibility for supporting national liberation movements shifting to the new National Liberation Directorate (DLN), which was independent of the MININT. The DLN was subsequently reorganised into the America Department (DA).

The DGI now has six divisions divided into two categories of roughly equal size: the three operational divisions include the *Political/Economic Intelligence Division*, consisting of four sections: E Europe, N America, W Europe and Africa-Asia-Latin America. The *External Counter-Intelligence Division* is responsible for penetrating foreign intelligence services and the surveillance of exiles, and *the Military Intelligence Division* remains focused on collecting information on the US Armed Forces and co-operation with friendly intelligence services.

The three support divisions include the *Technical Support Division*, which is responsible for production of false documents, communications systems supporting clandestine operations, and development of clandestine message capabilities; the *Information Division* and the *Preparation Division* which are responsible for intelligence analysis functions.

Despite the overall economic failure of the Cuban regime, the DGI remains a viable threat to the USA. The Cuban mission to the United Nations has the third largest delegation and probably 40 per cent of its the personnel are assigned to the mission by DGI. The Cuban Intelligence service actively recruits from within the émigré community and has used refugees to cover the insertion of agents into the USA. The DGI collects political, economic and military information within the USA and has in recent years concentrated on operations to obtain technology that could prove useful in improving the regime's ailing economy. Cuba is still considered by the USA to be a sponsor of international terrorism and has worked closely with Puerto Rican separatist and Latin American terrorist groups. However, many Cubans would argue that their nation has been on the receiving end of US-sponsored terrorist-style attacks by right-wing Cuban exiles, assassinations, full-scale invasion and some forty years of economic sanctions and diplomatic isolation for being stubborn and independent.

Like the CIA, the DGI has become involved with drug-related crime throughout the Americas and in November 1982 four close aides of Fidel Castro were convicted on charges of smuggling drugs into the USA. The four included René Rodríguez-Cruz, a senior official of the DGI (Cuban Intelligence Service). On 7 February 1983, a former member of the DGI testified in the District Court for the Southern District of Florida, that Cuban involvement in international drug operations part of a widespread campaign aimed at undermining the USA. The 1988 testimony given by José Blandón Castillo, a former intelligence aid to Panamanian leader Manuel Noriega appeared to provide further evidence concerning Cuba's role in the drug flow of the USA. *The Military Counter-Intelligence Department* of the Ministry of Revolutionary Armed Forces is responsible for conducting counter-intelligence, SIGINT, and electronic warfare activities against the USA.

CUMMING, Sir Mansfield Smith (1859–1923)   First Chief of the Secret Intelligence Service (SIS) (1909–23). The title 'C' has been used by the Chief of SIS ever since, although the correct title is CSS or Chief of the Secret Service. Born into a middle-class family, Cumming attended the Royal Naval College at Dartmouth and, upon graduation, was commissioned a sub-lieutenant. He was posted to HMS *Bellerophon* in 1878 and for the next seven years saw sea duty in the East Indies. However in 1895 he was placed on the inactive list as unfit for service through chronic seasickness. He was recalled to duty in late 1898–99 and undertook many espionage missions on behalf of the Admiralty. He proved an adept intelligence officer and his reports were sufficiently impressive to gain his appointment as chief of the foreign section of the Secret Service Bureau established in 1909. In 1911, Cumming was asked to head a modern espionage agency which would serve all the military branches and high level political departments. This became the SIS and was later given the cover designation MI-IC in the military restructuring that took place in 1916, and again renamed MI6 in 1920–21 when overall control passed to the Foreign Office. Cumming preferred officers who were from the upper class and looked upon espionage as a 'game for gentlemen'. Sir Paul Dukes, who was to become one of the most effective SIS operatives during and after the Russian Revolution, wrote of Cumming that 'At first

encounter he appeared very severe. His manner of speech was abrupt ...
Yet the stern countenance could melt into the kindliest of smiles, and
the softened eyes and lips revealed a heart that was big and generous.
Awe-inspired as I was by my first encounter, I soon learned to regard
"the Chief" with feelings of the deepest personal admiration and
affection.'

By early 1914, Cumming had built up SIS networks in Brussels,
Rotterdam and St Petersburg. These networks continued to operate
throughout WWI, providing Cumming with valuable information on
German troop movements. The service that Cumming created was to
stay largely unchanged for many years and he undoubtedly played a
major part in the development of the modern intelligence community.
Often treated as an eccentric, with the much repeated stories of a 1914
car crash in France, a resulting wooden leg and scaring the female staff
by speeding around the corridors of SIS on a child's scooter, the fact is
that he so effectively guarded the anonymity of SIS that many of his
greatest successes were never to be recorded. Cumming signed all of his
documents and messages with the letter 'C' and usually in green ink. In
honour of Cumming who died in 1923, subsequent directors of MI6
have since signed their correspondence with the same letter and for
many years in green ink as well.

CURWEN, Christopher Keith (1929–)   During the past decade or
so there seems to have been an unfortunate tendency to appoint elderly
heads of MI6 who retire within a few years, and thus have hardly any
chance of making their mark. The appointment of Christopher Curwen
in the mid-1980s, however, was favourably greeted within MI6 as he
was a professional officer, recruited into MI6 in 1952 and who had
survived dangerous espionage field missions in the Far East. Curwen
was educated at Sherborne and Cambridge, served in the 4th Queen's
Own Hussars (1948–49), joined SIS and was stationed in both
Bangkok and Vientiane. He was a Counsellor in the Foreign Office in
1980.

CUT-OUTS   A mechanism or person used to create a compartment
between the members of an operation but to allow them to pass
material or messages securely.

CYBERWAR   A synonym for information warfare and an area of huge
importance to the future of intelligence gathering.

D

DAGGER   A sophisticated disguise first used in the Soviet Union in the 1970s.

DANSEY, Sir Claude (1876–1947)   One of the most extraordinary appointees ever to achieve a senior intelligence position. Devious and conspiratorial, Dansey engendered loyalty, loathing, respect and hatred in equal portions and was described by one senior SIS Officer as an 'absolute shit'.

He had been stationed in Switzerland before the war and took a personal interest in intelligence from this territory. One worthwhile criticism he made was that most opposing intelligence services knew that the British Passport Control office was in fact a cover for the local SIS Station. He successfully urged the creation of the 'Z' network. This parallel and highly secret section was to supplement the usual SIS activities run from the British Embassy. The idea was good in that it was intended to act as a safeguard if the main SIS network was broken, but it depended upon having highly efficient agents, and Dansey's choices were not particularly good.

There were therefore two British intelligence networks in Holland, one headed by Major Stevens and the other belonging to the 'Z' network headed by Captain Payne Best. When WWII broke out it was decreed, very foolishly as it turned out, that the two continental networks should merge. As a result, Best and Stevens were detected by German intelligence, fed with disinformation and lured to Venlo on the Dutch–German border where they were kidnapped. Thus two of Britain's key intelligence officers in Europe were made prisoners by the Nazi secret police. Too late did they learn that their German contact, whom they knew as Schaemmel, was none other than Schellenberg of the Nazi Central Security Agency. As a result SIS networks all over Europe were decisively broken in a single day.

Dansey may have been unfairly blamed for the failure of what was basically a good idea, but his choice of officers left much to be desired. At times he seemed almost paranoiacally jealous of the OSS and was highly displeased when, later in the war, copies of documents a German defector brought with him from Berlin reached the SIS via the OSS in Washington. Foolishly Dansey insisted that the documents were fakes and had been planted on the US service. The documents proved to be genuine and the OSS employed the German agent, obtaining valuable intelligence from him. However, President Truman was to award Sir Claude the Legion of Merit, Degree of Officer in 1945. The citation read, 'Dansey ... was indefatigable in his efforts to ensure the success of Anglo-American cooperation ...', and the French, with whom Dansey had often been at loggerheads, added the Legion d'Honneur. By 1945 both Dansey's career and his health were in sharp decline and he was soon to retire. Dansey died in the Lansdowne Grove Nursing Home in Bath on 11 June 1947. The Duke of Portland, who as Victor Cavendish-Bentinck was head of the wartime Joint Intelligence Committee commented 'Claude Dansey? He was the best of them.' Claude Dansey was to remain an enigma to the end.

DEAD DROP/DEAD LETTER DROP   A prearranged hidden location used for secret exchanges of packages, messages and payments. A dead drop prevents the intelligence officer and the agent from being present at the same time or a physical location where communications, documents or equipment is covertly placed for another person to collect without direct contact between the parties. Also known as dead-letter box. These were often in such places as a hole in a wall, a piece of hollow railing or even a niche in a fallen tree trunk.

DEAD TELEPHONE   A signal or code passed via the telephone without speaking.

DEARLOVE, Richard Billing (1945–)   Dearlove, previously the Assistant Chief, became the new Head of SIS (MI6) in 1999. He joined SIS in 1966 as a 21-year-old graduate. In 1968 he received his first overseas posting to the Kenyan capital, Nairobi. Several postings later, he became head of SIS Washington station in 1991. He returned to the UK in 1993 as director of personnel and administration. The following year he became director of operations and in 1998 he was additionally made assistant chief. His appointment will be seen as a shift of emphasis by the service after Sir David Spedding, who was an Arabist from SIS elite Middle East specialists, dubbed the 'camel corps'. It reflects a new commitment in the post Cold War era to combating international organised crime as well as the services' more traditional espionage activities.

DEE, John (1527–1608)   Considered by many of his contemporaries as a charlatan and black magician, Dee actually carried out many secret missions on behalf of Elizabeth I's spymasters Sir William Cecil (Lord Burghley) and Sir Francis Walsingham. One of his most valuable reports to Walsingham was a warning that the Spaniards knew England was committed to building new and even bigger warships and that the Spaniards intended to defeat this plan by attacking and destroying England's timber supplies. The methods were to include a small party of Frenchmen, acting as Spanish agents, to burn down the entire Forest of Dean. The warning proved accurate and the local Verderers were able to catch the agents who, having claimed squatters' rights in the area, were planning a series of simultaneous fires at key points around the Forest.

DEEP COVER AGENT Permanent well-prepared and well-constructed cover.

DEFECTOR An intelligence officer or diplomat who, usually voluntarily, abandons their original agency or government service and betrays it by giving information to a foreign intelligence agency or government. The 'walk-in' defector arrives unannounced, hopefully bringing valuable intelligence with them while the 'defector-in-place' plays the part of remaining loyal to their service, but effectively becomes a MOLE supplying information to a foreign state.

DENMARK *PET (Politiets Efterretningstjeneste or Internal Intelligence Service)*: the Internal Security organisation. This is Department G of the National Commissioners Office and therefore part of the Police. One of the most important and perhaps surprising elements of PET's operations is the close relationship it has had for more than 30 years with Israel's Mossad. It has maintained surveillance on Palestinian groups in Denmark and on occasions 'recruited' suitable Palestinians for the Israeli intelligence service. These 'agents' have then been returned to the occupied areas of Palestine, perhaps even 'deported' to improve their cover. PET also controls a small network of 'intelligence groups' run by Conservative or right-wing political parties, including the Danish Social Democratic Party who have maintained their own intelligence section since the 1930s.

FET (Forsvarets Efterretningstjeneste or Defence Intelligence Service): FET played a major role within NATO during the Cold War, monitoring Warsaw Pact ship movements in and out of the Baltic Sea. Its other main task was SIGINT aimed at both Poland and E Germany. It developed close co-operation with both the German BND and the NSA. It maintained major secret listening facilities at Aflandshage,

Gedser, Hjorring and Logumkloster. In addition the two bases at Almindingen and Dueodde are situated on the strategically placed Island of Bornholm and from here all Soviet communications in the Baltic States, Leningrad area and of course the Baltic Fleet could be intercepted.

DENNING, Admiral Sir Norman (1904–79)   Founder of the Royal Navy's Operational Intelligence Centre (OIC) in WWII which made highly effective use of ULTRA and other intelligence sources to plot the destruction of the German Navy and in particular its Submarine fleet. An outstanding intelligence officer who later served as the penultimate Director of Naval Intelligence (1959–64).

DENNISTON, Commander Alistair (Alexander) (1881–1961) Assigned to the Admiralty's Room 40 codebreaking centre, he joined its successor GC&CS in 1919. In 1921 he was appointed the Head of GC&CS in the reorganisation that saw its parent organisation SIS moved to Foreign Office control. With few resources and a small staff he managed to build the service which was to use ULTRA to such good effect in WWII. Never a 'political' officer he was pushed sideways in 1942 to Head the Diplomatic and Commercial codebreakers at 7–9 Berkeley Street in Mayfair, London, giving way to his deputy at Bletchley Park, Commander Edward Travis. Denniston retired mainly due to exhaustion in 1944 being replaced by Travis as head of the entire GC&CS, soon to be known officially as GCHQ. Denniston was an outstanding Director of GC&CS through very difficult times and he deserved far more recognition than he received from the British Government.

DEUXIÈME BUREAU   The Second Bureau of the General Staff. Main Intelligence organisation of the French Army for much of the 20th century.

DGER   Direction Générale des Études et Recherches (General Directorate of Studies and Research). The French Foreign Intelligence Service that succeeded DGSS in 1944.

DGSE   Direction Générale de la Sécurité Extérieure (General Directorate for External Security). Succeeded the discredited SDECE after it was abolished by President François Mitterand in 1981.

DGI   Cuban foreign intelligence service.

DGSS   Direction Générale des Services Speciaux (General Directorate of Special Services). Resulted from a forced merger of General de Gaulle's Free French BCRA and General Giraud's rival SR in 1942.

DIA

DIA Defence Intelligence Agency.

DIN Defence Intelligence Network (DIA's 'Classified CNN').

DIRTY TRICKS A whole range of intelligence operations carried out covertly, to confuse, disrupt or damage an opposing intelligence service. However, the use of dirty tricks does spill over to include the media, political parties and individuals among them. It can range from spreading false rumours about a person's sex life or financial situation to the 'elimination' of a supposedly dangerous foreign leader.

The CIA's interest in and involvement with dirty tricks is set to return in a big way. The new policies and framework of the CIA, post 9/11, would be familiar to those old Cold War warriors, Frank Wisner and Richard Bissell and it is of interest to view a few comments from the period. In a letter written to his decidedly odd colleague, Dr Sidney Gottlieb, often considered the prototype for 'Dr Strangelove', Captain George Hunter White wrote of his CIA service, 'I toiled wholeheartedly in the vineyards because it was fun, fun, fun.' Adding, 'Where else could a red-blooded American boy lie, kill, cheat, steal, rape and pillage with the sanction and blessing of the all-highest?'

A CIA case officer with twenty years' experience commented, 'I never gave a thought to legality or morality. Frankly, I did what worked.'

The CIA has been involved in many operations of doubtful legality or morality over the last fifty years. Much can be forgiven if the Agency is ultimately proved to protect the national interests of the USA successfully, work for genuine justice and uphold democratic virtue and not infringe the sovereign integrity and human rights of other nations. Unfortunately this does not really apply to the overall performance of the CIA. A review of the dark side of covert action and dirty tricks would include, for example, OPERATION MIDNIGHT CLIMAX. This involved CIA-run brothels in San Francisco and New York. The operation paid prostitutes $100 a day to lure men into the net. The prostitutes spiked the client's drinks with LSD. The CIA, plentifully supplied with martinis, recorded the action from behind closed doors and one-way mirrors. Not only was this operation illegal as were many others, but the men who were 'experimented' upon had no idea that they were the objects of experimentation. The prostitutes were guaranteed their safety should they get caught plying their trade while engaged in this 'special operation'. A secret laboratory was established and funded by CIA director, Allen Dulles in Montreal, Canada at McGill University in the Allen Memorial Institute headed by psychiatrist Dr Ewen Cameron. What is ironic about Dr Cameron is that he served as a member of the Nuremberg tribunal who heard the cases against the Nazi doctors.

At the height of the drug experiment period, super-secret OPERATION MK-ULTRA was initiated. This was the brainchild of Richard Helms, later the DCI. It was designed to defeat the 'enemy' particularly communist China and N Korea, in brainwashing techniques. MK-ULTRA had another arm involved in Chemical and Biological Warfare (CBW) known as MK-DELTA. The 'doctors' who participated in these experiments used some of the same techniques as the Nazi 'doctors'. Those doctors who were not indicted in the Nuremberg trials were imported from Germany under the programme called OPERATION PAPERCLIP. The Nazi doctors were a valuable source of information to the CIA since many of the US techniques mimicked what had already been done by the Nazis. German doctors were prosecuted at the Nuremberg trials for similar acts to those now being carried out in the name of the US Intelligence service.

Just as Nazi Germany had its 'expendables' the CIA soon discovered theirs. Among the expendables the CIA had were prisoners of war, prostitutes, sexual psychopaths, prison inmates, certain war objectors, mentally retarded people, the elderly, terminally ill patients, schizophrenics, drug addicts, unwitting foreign nationals and occasionally even their own staff. Some of the CIA techniques involved sensory deprivation, bodily function deprivation and sleep deprivation in rooms with no windows and both continuous light and white noise. Other forms of mind control involved drug-induced comas, a wide variety of hallucinogenic drugs, brain surgery (pre-frontal lobotomy), massive Page-Russell electric shocks, and electro-convulsive treatments combined with endless interrogations that were tape recorded. These interrogations were calculated to induce certain required answers from the 'patient'. These tape-recorded sessions were then played back to the patient by means of a helmet outfitted with headphones. The helmet was worn for days at a time with the tape playing endlessly. It was not unknown for a combination of these techniques to result in the death of the 'patient' and it is believed that large numbers of the dysfunctional, seriously ill and those with no traceable relatives who were used during these experiments may have indeed died. To suggest that it would have been a living nightmare for many of those involved would not be an overstatment.

These 'special operations' were funded by the CIA through various intermediaries. Some had large financial interests in drug experiments. One such company was believed to be the Eli Lilly Company who told the CIA at its height of LSD manufacture that it could supply tons of the drug. George Bush (Sr), who was a CIA director and head of the President's US Drug Task Force, was also a director of the Eli Lilly Company from 1977–79. These programmes were additional to the CIA's involvement in organised crime, vice, drug dealing, torture, extortion, political interference in foreign countries, assassination plots, murder implications, presidential assassination conspiracies, money laundering, propaganda and covert operations domestic and abroad. While the agency says it has 'cleaned up its act' and has released to public scrutiny some of its past operations under the Freedom of Information Act (FOIA), can the CIA or any be trusted or even expected to tell the truth? Richard Helms as acting CIA director was asked about secret CIA operations. He attempted to justifiy CIA activities in an address to the National Press Club when he said: 'You've just got to trust us. We are honourable men.'

A democratic USA would not ordinarily be suspected of bribing foreign politicians; invading other countries with secret armies; spreading disinformation and outright lies; conducting medical experiments; building stocks of poison; training subversives to assassinate their leaders; or plotting to overthrow foreign leaders who had displeased Washington. The CIA has been accused of these actions, and much more, over a long span of years. The allegation that these actions were carried out on the orders of respected presidents – Eisenhower and Kennedy went after two enemies in particular in the years between 1959 and 1963, Lumumba in the Congo and Castro in Cuba – is astounding. An example of the CIA and dirty tricks would be its involvement with Cuba.

The Bay of Pigs clearly marked the beginning, not the end, of John F. Kennedy's determination to get rid of Castro; the moment when Fidel Castro ceased to be merely an enemy inherited from Eisenhower. Kennedy's mandate to General Maxwell Taylor in April 1961 was not to fix the blame for the failure of the invasion, but to find out why it hadn't worked, so the next plan would. Knowing of Kennedy's growing obsession with unconventional warfare, Taylor proposed a broad, government-wide effort to combat insurgencies from Vietnam to Latin America. The result, after Taylor joined the White House full time as the military representative of the President on 4 July 1961, was the establishment of the Counter-Insurgency (CI) Group. This began to meet on a regular basis with Taylor as chairman in October 1961. The first order of business for the CI Group was Cuba. The CIA was heavily involved in both Laos and Vietnam at the same time, but the covert operations launched against N Vietnam, beginning in autumn 1961 under the then Saigon station chief, William Colby, were still in the early stages. Cuba was where the Kennedys wanted immediate results. A second committee, the Special Group Augmented (SGA), was established to oversee OPERATION MONGOOSE, run by Colonel Edward G. Lansdale, a counterinsurgency specialist with experience in both the Philippines and Vietnam, where he had helped Ngo Dinh Diem to consolidate his control over the country.

No Kennedy programme received less publicity than MONGOOSE, or more personal attention from the Kennedys, and in particular from Robert. The importance of the undertaking did not take long to establish. In the early stages of MONGOOSE, a CIA officer working on the operation, Sam Halpern, asked Lawrence Houston, the CIA's general counsel, if the operation was even legal. He pointed out that the Bay of Pigs landing had been organised outside the USA, at least partly in order to avoid violating the Neutrality Acts, which prohibited the launching of attacks on foreign targets from American soil. Even though MONGOOSE was being run from Miami, Houston still argued that it did not break the law. The answer, it appeared, was that if the President says it's okay, and if the attorney general says it's okay, then it's okay.

After the first few months of covert operations, MONGOOSE gradually shifted its emphasis from resistance-building to sabotage, paramilitary raids, efforts to disrupt the Cuban economy by contaminating sugar exports, circulating counterfeit money and ration books, and the like. 'We want boom and bang on the island,' Lansdale said. Robert Kennedy took a particular interest in efforts to sabotage the Matahambre copper mines in western Cuba, on one occasion even calling repeatedly to learn if the agents had left yet. Had they landed? Had they reached the mines? Had they destroyed them successfully? He is reported to have demanded. Kennedy, like Lansdale, wanted boom and bang, and a number of CIA officers at the operational level grew to know his voice as he called to find out how they were coming along and to press them forward. The Matahambre copper mines were never destroyed, despite the launching of three separate full-scale raids, but other attacks on sugar refineries, oil storage facilities, and other economic targets were more successful. Still, they fell far short of wrecking the Cuban economy, even in its weakened state following the dislocations of revolution, and the paramilitary programme held little promise of Castro's eventual overthrow. There is a certain opaque quality to all of the CIA's plans to eliminate Castro. The invasion force that landed at the Bay of Pigs was too big to hide and too small to defeat Castro's huge army and militia. MONGOOSE in 1962 never got much beyond an intelligence-gathering effort, and while it succeeded in raising the level of 'boom and bang on the island' in 1963, it was hardly enough to do the job. Lansdale's scenario for a triumphal march into Havana was illusory. Desmond FitzGerald took over in 1963, but a lot of people who worked for FitzGerald never quite grasped how his plans were supposed to work either. FitzGerald was adamant. 'You don't know what you're talking about,' he told one of his doubting officers. The CIA was still going to get Castro!

However, John F. Kennedy was assassinated in Dallas on 22 November 1963 and the impetus behind the Cuban operation began to wither away. The last exile groups, boats and maintenance facilities in Florida were not abandoned until 1965, but Lyndon Johnson never gave his full attention to the Cuban 'problem'. In March 1964, Desmond FitzGerald, by then the new Western Hemisphere division chief, visited the CIA station in Buenos Aires. There he told some of his officers, 'If Jack Kennedy had lived, I can assure you we would have gotten rid of Castro by last Christmas. Unfortunately, the new President isn't as gung-ho on fighting Castro as Kennedy was.'

DISCARD   An agent betrayed by his own intelligence service to protect a more valuable source of information.

DISINFORMATION   The creation and disinformation of misleading or false information to damage the image of the targeted nation. Developed by the KGB, such operations frequently involved forged documents designed to undermine the credibility of the USA and its allies.

D NOTICE   Formal British censorship request issued to the news media by the D-Notice Committee (Services, Press & Broadcasting Committee). It is circulated confidentially to editors requesting restraint in publishing certain intelligence or defence material.

DOCTOR   Russian intelligence name for the police.

DOIHARA, Major-General Kenji (1883–1946)   One of the most brilliant of Japan's Senior intelligence officers between the two world wars. He spent many years in China, but it was after the Japanese withdrew from Siberia in 1922 that he came into his own. He was reputed to speak nine European languages and four Chinese dialects. He organised a network of renegade Chinese to work for him and used brothels as listening posts in Mukden and Harben. Thus by diligent intelligent work he paved the way for the takeover of Manchuria by Japan.

At the age of 49 he was promoted to rank of general and created what became known as the puppet state of Manchukuo, at the same time forming Tokumu Kikau or Special Service Organisation in Mukden. This was an organisation which, effectively controlled and collated all intelligence operations in the territory. So thorough was he in his gathering of intelligence that he set up a Refugee's Bureau, exercising authority not only over all White Russian refugees, but their banks, factories and restaurants and this proved to be a vital instrument of espionage. Doihara was in Shanghai (1938–39), operating his Tokumu Kikau in China and having spies right in the heart of Chiang Kai-shek's entourage. Later in the war with China Doihara was given command of a division in the field.

However, he had a complete disdain for human life, and the Chinese in particular. His treatment of prisoners of any age or sex was appalling and it is not surprising that Doihara was one of six senior Japanese officers to be hanged as a war criminal at the end of WWII.

DONOVAN, Major General William 'Bill' (1883–1959) Forceful and effective Director of the Office of Strategic Services (OSS) during WWII, Donovan created a highly capable US clandestine intelligence and special operations organisation following its establishment in 1941. OSS was limited by the fact that it was unable to operate either with the USA or Latin America because of Hoover's political influence and in fact Hoover was constantly trying to undermine both Donovan and the work of OSS for much of the war. Donovan also believed that both the US and British were giving far too much intelligence material and help to the Soviet Union. Fearing that the Soviets would quickly become an enemy again once Nazi Germany had been defeated, he pressed the President to retain OSS as a permanent postwar organisation. Hoover, however, had far more influence in the White House and Congress than Donovan and in concert with the US Military, who disliked the paramilitary role of the OSS, persuaded Truman otherwise. Although President Truman precipitately abolished the OSS on 20 September 1945, the experience gained laid the groundwork for the creation of the CIA in 1947. Donovan's far-sighted views would be vindicated with the onset of the Cold War and the future development of US Intelligence.

DOUBLE AGENT These are agents who are turned against the intelligence service that originally recruited them and work for a foreign agency, while at the same time making the original service believe that their loyalty has not altered. There are obvious reasons (see MICE) for this behaviour, but it may indeed be simply to save the officer's life after falling into an enemy agency's hands, particularly if their own service remains unaware of the incident. These operations can prove to be a two-edged sword, however. For if the original service is informed by the officer of the offer to spy for a foreign agency or if the original service discover this without the officer's knowledge, then they may be used to supply false or misleading information to the foreign agency. There is a reasonable expectation that any information supplied under these circumstances will be fully accepted by the foreign agency as true.

DOUBLE-CROSS SYSTEM   (XX Committee or Twenty Committee) Controlled by John Masterman, later Sir John, under the control of 'TAR' Robertson head of section B1A of MI5 (1941–45), the Double-Cross System involved the complete compromise of captured German agents in Britain. Some of the Abwehr agents were allowed to continue operating as German spies, but all the false information they transmitted was tightly controlled by their MI5 controller. Those agents who were caught and controlled inside the UK totalled 39 in all, most of them with intriguing codenames. There was a MUTT and JEFF, a LIPSTICK and a PEPPERMINT, but what was most remarkable was how their codenames rang true to character. There was CARELESS whose 'personal conduct and the impossibility of controlling him except in prison spoiled a promising case', and WEASEL who had to be dropped because he was 'believed to have contrived to warn the Germans'. The absolute gem of them all was Hans Schmidt, codenamed TATE, who operated successfully for more than four and a half years after being captured when parachuting into England. The Germans lapped up his (faked) radio messages so eagerly that they awarded him the Iron Cross. GARBO was another great success, awarded the Iron Cross by the Germans and the MBE by the British. Sometimes, however, the authorities failed to get the best value from double-agents, an example being TRICYCLE. False information fed back to Germany by captured agents included details about where the Allies were likely to land in France, armaments production and the disposition of troops. Some of the manipulated German agents were able to convince their masters in Berlin that more funds should be dispatched to them. TATE was particularly successful in this respect; he was instructed by the Germans to wait at the terminus of the number 11 bus route at Victoria Station. Here he was to get on a bus with a Japanese who would be carrying a copy of *The Times* newspaper and a book in his left hand. TATE was to wear a red tie and also carry a newspaper and a book. Having established his identity in this way, TATE was handed £200.

The most effective results of the Double-Cross System were seen in OPERATION BODYGUARD, a masterstroke by the MI5 misinformation department. One of MI5's best double agents, Luis Calvo, a Spaniard using the codename GARBO, convinced the Abwehr that the invasion of Europe would be launched from SE England and directly at Pas de Calais. Supporting this notion was a complete dummy US Army commanded by General George Patton who travelled about the area inspecting endless rows of tanks, troops and planes which looked real from the air. However, upon closer inspection they proved to be of wood, cardboard and rubber. So convinced was Adolf Hitler that the invasion would, indeed, come at the Pas de Calais, that he concentrated his forces at this point and refused the German Army General Staff's increasingly urgent requests for reinforcements long after the Allies had actually landed in Normandy, 6 June 1944.

Although the system's use is best known in W Europe, it was actually more skilfully applied in the Middle East, where it deceived the Germans about allied intentions in both N Africa and the Eastern Mediterranean. Virtually an MI5 shadow organisation, Security Intelligence Middle East (SIME) achieved even more surprising coups through the double-cross system. Linked with 'A' Force, under Brigadier Dudley Clarke, it proved to be highly effective in its use of the system. It was through this that the Germans lost the battle of El Alamein and were deluded as to the British plans for the invasion of Sicily and Normandy. Not only did SIME agents win over German agents, but they also created fictional agents to provide misleading intelligence.

One of the oddest of these operations involved a prostitute named GALA, who was actually in jail in Palestine. For the purposes of misleading the Germans, she was portrayed as a '*poule de luxe*' in Beirut with a whole string of lovers, including Allied Officers and an Air Force technician who was supposed to be preparing Turkish airfields for Allied occupation. The two double-agents who were kept in jail were codenamed QUICKSILVER and PESSIMIST. It was essential that while they were sending out their messages it should appear that QUICKSILVER was transmitting from Beirut to Athens, while PESSIMIST was radioing from Damascus to Sofia. The Gemans were apparently totally fooled for the entire length of the operation.

See ROBERTSON, LT COL THOMAS ARGYLL 'TAR'.

DRIBERG, Tom (Lord Bradwell) (1905–76) It will come as no surprise to contemporaries of the flamboyant former MP Tom Driberg that he was a KGB spy, codenamed LEPAGE. The notoriously homosexual MP for Barking, who had a predilection for public lavatories and young 'rough trade' was a close friend of Guy Burgess and visited Moscow with him. He was a supporter of Stalin and throughout his time in the House of Commons and later the Lords, there were persistent rumours that he was a Soviet agent. It is claimed it was during one visit to Moscow that the KGB used his habit of 'cottaging' to entrap him when he allegedly attempted to seduce RAVEN (a homosexual, in this case, used for *sexpionage* purposes) in the urinals behind the Metropole Hotel. But it was probably unnecessary, as he did nothing to hide his political sympathies, which were well known in Westminster and more widely in the media. He rose to prominence as a journalist working for Lord Beaverbrook's *Daily Express* where he used his contacts to start the hugely successful 'William Hickey' gossip column. He gave up his parliamentary seat in 1955, soon after the Burgess and Maclean defection, and the suspicions that Blunt, Cairncross and Philby were also Soviet agents.

Driberg's social circle included a huge variety of celebrities from politics, the media, show business, sport and the criminal underworld, ranging from Guy Burgess to the Kray twins. A supporter of the 'Youth Culture', pop festivals and legalising cannabis, his interest did not end there. Fascinated with Rolling Stones singer Mick Jagger and his original approach to life in the 1960s, he tried to persuade him to take up a career in politics. Once eyeing Jagger's tight jeans he remarked loudly, 'What a big basket you have, Mick!' apparently causing the rock star to blush profusely. Driberg was made a peer by Harold Wilson in 1975 and when he died a year later, his coffin was draped in a red flag.

What many were wondering in Westminster was exactly how much use LEPAGE would have been to the Soviets. He would not have been party to any great state secrets and he had a reputation for unreliability but, at the height of the Cold War, both sides were eager to recruit anyone near the centre of power, which he certainly was. And if gossip and information that might be used to blackmail someone of importance was required, then Driberg would have been the ideal source.

DROP The action of placing material in a clandestine location to be picked up by a specific individual.

DRY CLEAN Actions taken to determine if one is under surveillance by a hostile security service.

DST   French security and counter-intelligence service.

DUFF, Sir (Arthur) Antony (1920–2000)   The epitome of the wise and reliable civil servant, Duff was also the submariner awarded a DSC for his part as Commander of HMS *Stubborn* during an attack on the giant German Battleship *Tirpitz. Stubborn* was badly damaged and hit the sea floor on four occasions before the 23-year-old Duff succeeded in bringing her home without a single casualty among his crew. He went on to become a career diplomat. Serving in Cairo, Paris, Bonn, Kuala Lumpur and as Ambassador to Nepal, he was High Commissioner to Kenya at the time of the Rhodesia crisis and was brought back to London to head the Foreign Office's Africa Department. Thatcher appointed him to the position of Deputy Governor of Rhodesia and he was credited as playing a major part in the transition of that country into an independent Zimbabwe. He was to be appointed to head JIC to co-ordinate the activities of MI5, SIS and GCHQ in the Cabinet Office. However, his lasting influence on British intelligence will be that, at the age of 65, he took on the task of revitalising and modernising MI5. He steered the Security Service into more relevant targeting, including Irish terrorism and brought a new generation of younger officers into positions of responsibility. Having had more than enough of Whitehall and after a long and successful career, Duff finally retired, actually for the third time, in 1987. As simple Tony Duff he was to spend the next five years making tea for the 'down and outs' as a member of the board of London's Homeless Network. A great human spirit still burned with the suave shell of the traditional pinstriped civil servant.

DUKES, Paul (1889–1967)   Dukes, following his graduation from Charterhouse in 1909, went to St Petersburg to study music at the conservatory and was attached to the famous Marinsky Theatre. In 1915 he was appointed to a position with the Anglo-Russian Commission and carried the passport of a King's Messenger, effectively a diplomatic courier. His job was to study and report on the Russian press. Dukes was appointed to the British Foreign office with an unusual 'roving commission' in 1917, the year of the Russian Revolution. At one point in 1917, Dukes was in Samara ostensibly working for the American YMCA but his duties, other than 'training Boy Scouts', were never explained.

Dukes formally became a member of SIS in 1918 as Agent ST-25 much to his delight as one who thought of espionage as 'high adventure' and loved intrigue. He was first summoned to London where he met the SIS Chief Commander Cumming who later stated that Dukes was his 'top mate' or agent in Russia. After brief training in invisible inks and codes, Dukes returned to Russia. There he travelled throughout the country making great use of his linguistic skills, becoming a master of many disguises and aliases and an expert in the use of forged identification papers. Dukes observed the chaos the revolution had brought and encouraged Britain to side with the White Russian forces attempting to overthrow the fragile Red or Bolsheviks government. Dukes was eventually placed in overall control of all SIS networks inside Russia. He established contact with the National Centre, the organisation that represented the interests of the White Russian monarchists who maintained armies in the field against the Bolsheviks. Using money provided by Cumming, often in the form of gold coins, Dukes helped finance widespread espionage, sabotage and insurrection against the Reds.

Much of Dukes's activities were directed towards rescuing prominent White Russians from prison and smuggling them out of the country through Finland. Working with SIS Dukes was able to save hundreds of lives. He also worked with Lt Augustus Agar, a RN lieutenant stationed in Finland who operated a squadron of specially modified fast motor torpedo boats stationed at a base near Helsinki. Dukes supplied information on Russian warships to Agar, which allowed him to lead a highly successful attack which resulted in the sinking of several major Russian warships. Meanwhile, using yet more disguises, he managed to join both the Communist Party and the Red Army, while in 1919 Dukes actually obtained an internal passport which showed him as an officer of the Cheka secret police – extraordinary feats in themselves. Dukes was able to obtain important political as well as military information. Double agents operating for the Cheka, however, were eventually able to identify the top leaders of the National Centre in 1919 and they arrested its chief, N.N. Shchepkin, on the night of 28–9 August 1919. Dozens of other White Russian spies and a courier from Admiral Alexander Kolchak, head of the White Russian armies, were also seized. In the following months more than a thousand members of the National Centre were arrested. Shchepkin and 67 others were later executed.

The Cheka had managed to identify Dukes but its officers could not find the elusive spy. He fled to the Finnish border where he attempted to contact Lt Agar, but failed. To avoid detection from spies at the Kronstadt forts, Dukes crossed nearly impossible terrain to reach Lake Luban and then escaped by foot into Latvia.

When he reached Reval, Dukes was compromised when he injudiciously confided in White Russian friends. The Latvian press obtained some of his comments and these were promptly quoted in Finnish and Swedish newspapers, effectively ending his undercover career in the new Soviet Union. Cumming was so elated with Dukes and Agar that he arranged for both men to meet King George V. Agar was awarded the VC, while Dukes's award came in 1920 when he was knighted, becoming the only British agent to receive a knighthood as a direct reward for espionage. In 1939, just before the onset of WWII, Dukes was to have another spectacular involvement with British intelligence. He was sent to Germany by the head of SIS, Admiral 'Quex' Sinclair, acting on behalf of a group of London industrialists. His actual mission was to discover the truth about the disappearance of a wealthy Czech businessman, Alfred Obry, on his way from Prague to Switzerland. It was known that the Germans wanted him to sign over to the Nazi state the huge commercial enterprises he controlled and may have discovered his plans to escape using a false passport. Dukes, ever meticulous and resourceful, searched local newspapers and noticed a report on the mysterious death of Friedrich Schweiger, a tailor from Prague whose mutilated body was found on a railway line. Suspecting the worst, Dukes tricked the local German authorities into exhuming the body, which did indeed turn out to be that of Alfred Obry.

Dukes's exact role during WWII has not been properly recorded, but that he remained in contact with his old service and had, at the very least, an advisory role seems certain.

DULLES, Alan Welsh (1893–1969)   Allen Dulles entered Princeton in 1910 and received his bachelor's degree in 1914. He was awarded his master's degree in 1916 and immediately entered the diplomatic service, spending much of the intervening years in Europe and Switzerland in particular. Dulles joined COI, forerunner of OSS in October 1941. One of his first major tasks were to establish the agency's HQ on the 25th floor of 30 Rockefeller Plaza in New York City. By mid 1942 Dulles was already deeply involved in running covert operations against both Germany and Japan. In late 1942, Dulles was relocated to Bern, Switzerland to run operations against Germany. Dulles moved to Berlin in 1945 where he became the OSS chief in the American Zone of occupied Germany. He worked closely with the former Nazi intelligence officers in the Gehlen organisation identifying Soviet spies, as well as helping to find German scientists and engineers to join the new US electronic, nuclear, chemical warfare and ballistic missile projects.

President Truman disbanded the OSS in 1945. However the need for an intelligence service soon became apparent even to Truman and the CIG was established in 1946, becoming the CIA or Central Intelligence Agency in 1947. Dulles joined the agency and became the deputy director in 1951. By 1953 he was appointed as DCI and ushered in the most sweeping US intelligence operations in history. Dulles, backed by his brother, John Foster Dulles, who was then Secretary of State, achieved virtual autonomy for the agency. Dulles planned and set in motion spectacular espionage operations, including covert interference in the affairs of many Third World countries, assassinations of political enemies of the US and the introduction of the first strategic U-2 spy planes. In 1961 he strongly advised President Kennedy that the CIA-backed Bay of Pigs invasion of Cuba would prove successful and bring about the destruction of Cuban regime. When the invasion turned into a disaster, an onslaught of criticism destroyed Dulles, who then 'resigned' as Director of the CIA. Allen Dulles died eight years later, respected throughout the world as the most talented and celebrated US Director of Intelligence in history.

DUNLAP, Jack (1928–63) A combat veteran, awarded a Bronze Star for coolness under fire in the Korean War. Dunlap was a US Army Sergeant assigned to the NSA where he was the driver for Major General Garrison B. Cloverdale, NSA Assistant Director and Chief of Staff. More importantly, the trusted Dunlap was also a courier for highly classified documents between different sections of the NSA and vitally for his role later as a Soviet spy, as driver to the NSA Chief of Staff he had the rare privilege of a car that would not be searched. In fact at least six other NSA employees used Dunlap's vehicle to smuggle out office equipment that they had stolen from the HQ building, further increasing Dunlap's ability to obtain favours and information.

Sometime in 1960, Dunlap, a womaniser, married with a large number of children and deeply in debt, walked into the Soviet Embassy in Washington and offered to spy for money. His GRU controller was to receive a simply amazing quantity of top-secret and highly classified intelligence material ranging from instruction books and repair instructions for cipher machines, codebooks and manuals and even CIA appreciation of Soviet and East German force structures and much more. The Soviets were to pay highly for this prized material and Dunlap lived the high life on the proceeds of his treachery.

His sudden wealth, a mistress, a Jaguar, two Cadillacs and even a 30-foot boat failed to arouse the suspicion of NSA security officials. However the strain of his double life began to tell and after failing a routine polygraph test in May, he admitted to 'petty thievery' and 'immoral conduct' and was transferred to a lesser position within the NSA. Several months later he drove to an isolated spot, ran a hose from the car exhaust in through the partly open side window and died from carbonmonoxide poisoning. Dunlap was buried with full military honours at Arlington cemetery on 25 July 1963, still apparently unsuspected. A month later however his widow handed over to the FBI a box she had discovered, containing a large quantity of top-secret documents. The measure of damage done to US intelligence was believed to be immense, but some doubt must be cast over the last few months of Dunlap's life. It is likely that the polygraph test was a blind to remove Dunlap from access to secret material. He was probably unmasked by information from an important CIA double agent, Major General Dimitri Polyakov who spied for the USA for nearly twenty years. Polyakov was later one of the US agents betrayed in turn by Aldrich Ames, the Soviet 'mole' within the CIA.

DZERSHINSKY, Felix Edmundovich (1877–1926) A Polish aristocrat and dedicated Communist, Lenin entrusted the establishment of the CHEKA intelligence service and secret police to Dzershinsky in December 1917. Dzershinsky would famously declare that 'We stand for organised terror ... terror is an absolute necessity during times of revolution.' When the new Communist Government moved to Moscow, the Cheka transferred its HQ to Lubyanka Street, while its chief office in St Petersburg moved to Gorochovaya Street under the bloodthirsty fanatic Uritsky. The men Dzershinsky chose to lead Cheka were often brutal and semi-educated peasants, but usually loyal to him personally. He divided the new secret service into two main divisions, a *Counter-Espionage Section* and a *Secret Operations Section*, and imposed total discipline on his officers; those that made too many mistakes, were disloyal or simply unsuitable were simply killed out of hand. Those citizens that fell into the hands of the Cheka fared no better and indeed were often tortured before execution, usually without bothering with the inconvenience of a trial first.

In December 1921, the Soviet Government ordered a reorganisation of the secret service with the Cheka to be replaced by the GPU, and the replacement of summary murder with a trial, still followed by execution in most cases however. During this time Dzershinsky created the apparently anti-Communist organisation known as the Trust, to lure enemies of the state to their deaths. Victims included Boris Savinkov and former British SIS agent Sidney Reilly. Dzershinsky died in 1926, apparently without the help of his colleagues, unlike many of his successors.

DZERSHINSKY SQUARE   The site in Moscow of the Lubyanka, long-time HQ of Soviet Security organisations from the Cheka, through the KGB, to today's FSB.

E

EARS ONLY   Material that is so highly classified that it cannot be committed to print but only discussed orally in special facilities.

ECHELON   A multinational surveillance network, the overall control for which comes from the National Security Agency (NSA) at Fort Meade in Maryland, intercepting all forms of electronic communications. Based on the UKUSA network which includes both the NSA and GCHQ, although the sites within the British network have been known as Composite Signals Organisation Stations (CSOS) since 1964, along with the SIGINT agencies of Australia (DSD), Canada (CSE) and New Zealand (GCSB). Each station in the ECHELON network has computers that automatically search through the millions of intercepted messages for ones containing pre-programmed keywords or fax, telex and email addresses. For the frequencies and channels selected at a station, every word of every message is automatically searched (they do not need your specific telephone number or Internet address on the list).

All computers within the main UKUSA network are known as ECHELON dictionaries and have been designed to interconnect and allow the stations to function as components of an integrated whole. It replaced a system where, although UKUSA allies carried out intelligence collection operations for each other, each agency then usually processed and analysed the intercept from its own stations with the finished reports, rather than raw intercepts, being exchanged. The UKUSA system also neatly gets round the ticklish problem of getting warrants to intercept your own nationals' international calls. The NSA intercept British calls at the American sites and relay them back to GCHQ and Britain returns the compliment. You scratch my back and I'll …! However since the building of Menwith Hill and the routing of most telephone calls through Hunters Stone, many internal British phone calls could be legally intercepted by the NSA here in Britain.

Each station's dictionary computer contains not only its parent agency's chosen keywords, but also a list for each of the other agencies. Thus allowing each station to collect all the telephone calls, faxes, telexes, Internet messages and other electronic communications that its computers have been pre-programmed to select for all the allies and automatically sends this intelligence to them.

The international communications-monitoring network has grown spectacularly over the last twenty years, as throughout most of the 1970s only two stations were required to monitor all the Intelsat communications in the world. A joint GCHQ-NSA station at Morwenstow in Cornwall had two dishes, one each for the Atlantic and Indian Ocean Intelsats, and an NSA station in the western USA had a single dish covering the Pacific Intelsat. By 2002 the ECHELON network largely targeted at private or commercial communications and tasked more for gathering economic and industrial intelligence is still growing as countries outside the original UKUSA alliance are building their own major interception facitilies, in most cases to co-operate, but occasionally in competition.

The supposedly secret global network is now believed to include *CSOS-NSA Morwenstow*. Opened in 1972–73, this is located only some 65 miles from the British Telecom satellite station at Goonhilly in southern Cornwall. Throughout the 1980s and 90s seven additional dishes were installed to keep up with the expansion of the Intelsat network. Two were inclined towards the main Indian Ocean Intelsats, three towards Atlantic Ocean Intelsats, three towards positions above Europe or the Middle East and one dish was covered by a radome and was used for US surveillance satellite downlinks.

NSA Yakima, Washington State in the NW USA: established in the early 1970s, the Yakima Research Station initially consisted of a single large dish pointing west, out above the Pacific to the third of the three Intelsat positions. Two additional west-facing dishes are now targeted on the main Pacific Intelsat satellites. Two new east-facing dishes target the Atlantic Intelsats, intercepting communications relayed towards N and S America. The fifth dish at the station is smaller than the rest and faces to the west. Given its size and orientation, it appears to be the UKUSA site for monitoring the Inmarsat-2 satellite that provides mobile satellite communications in the Pacific Ocean area. If so, this is the station that would, for example, have been monitoring Greenpeace communications during the nuclear testing protests in the waters around Moruroa Atoll in 1995.

A new generation of Intelsat 4A and 5 series satellites launched from the late 1970s onward differed from earlier models in that they now also had 'east and west hemispheric' beams that transmitted separately. These changes required at least two new stations with enhanced facilities to maintain the global coverage provided by NSA and GCHQ.

NSA Sugar Grove, a new satellite interception station fully operational by 1980 on the east coast of the USA, covered Atlantic Intelsat traffic, beamed down towards N and S America. Sugar Grove is also only 60 miles from the Etam international satellite communications earth station.

CSOS Stanley Bay, the other new station, was established in Hong Kong in 1978–79. The station had one dish pointing east towards the Pacific Intelsats, another towards the Indian Ocean Intelsats and a third, for the station's own communications, pointing to a US Defence Satellite Communications System satellite above the Pacific. Because Hong Kong was to be handed back to Chinese control in 1997, work began to dismantle the site in 1994 and to move the main facilities to DSD Geraldton and DSD Shoal Bay in Australia.

By the late 1980s coverage of the southern hemisphere was vastly expanded with the introduction of three ground stations available to monitor the new Intelsat 7 satellites introduced in 1994, at *GCSB Waihopai* in New Zealand, *DSD Geraldton* in West Australia and *CSOS Two Boats* on Ascension Island. The British intelligence facility on Ascension Island had played an important role monitoring Argentinian communications during the Falklands War in 1981.

In addition to the UKUSA stations monitoring Intelsat satellites, there are another group of stations targeting other nations' communications satellites and are also part of the overall ECHELON dictionary system. US surveillance or 'spy' satellites, designed to intercept both military and commercial communications are also likely to be connected into the ECHELON system. These satellites either move in orbits that criss-cross the Earth or, like the Intelsats, sit above the Equator in geostationary orbit. They have antennae that can scoop up very large quantities of radio communications from the areas below.

The main ground stations concerned are *CIA Pine Gap*, near Alice Springs in central Australia, and *NSA Menwith Hill* in N Britain with its 22 satellite terminals; this is undoubtedly the largest station in the UKUSA network. It taps directly into the British Telecom microwave network, purposefully designed with most major microwave routes converging on the Hunters Stone junction-tower, which is connected by underground cables to the station. Menwith Hill also intercepts satellite and radio communications and is a ground station for US electronic surveillance satellites. Each of Menwith Hill's powerful interception and processing systems has its own dictionary computers connected into the ECHELON system. As an example of the station's global reach, it was awarded the NSA's Station of the Year prize for

1991 for the part it played in the Gulf War. The activities at Menwith Hill are undoubtedly capable of infringing directly on the civil liberties of people throughout the world. The final station is *NSA Bad Aibling* in Germany. This site was slated for closure by 2001, its main operations moving to Menwith Hill, but closure is believed to have been considerably delayed due to the 'War on Terrorism' declared in the aftermath of 11 September.

The interception of communications relayed by Intelsat and Inmarsat is only one component of the global spying network co-ordinated by the ECHELON system. Other elements include: radio listening posts, interception stations targeted on other types of communications satellites; overhead signals intelligence collectors (spy satellites) like those controlled from the *CIA Pine Gap* facility in Australia; and secret facilities that tap directly into land-based telecommunications networks. These satellites can intercept microwave trunk lines and short-range communications such as military radios and walkie-talkies. Both of these transmit only line of sight and so, unlike HF radio, cannot be intercepted from faraway ground stations.

The ECHELON system also covers a largely undocumented and still highly sensitive area of communications interception. A combination of under-ocean cables and huge networks microwave towers carry a vast amount of traffic and its monitoring therefore provides UKUSA with near total worldwide coverage. Microwave communications are intercepted in two ways: by ground stations, located near to the microwave routes and by satellites. Because the facilities required to intercept radio and satellite communications are difficult to hide for long, that network is reasonably well documented. Because all that is required to intercept land-based communication networks is a discreet facility situated along the microwave route or an underground connection cable running from the legitimate network far less is known about the huge network of ECHELON sites involved.

An example is provided by CSOS-NSA Morwenstow in Cornwall, for not only does this highly sensitive facility have a large number of dish aerials for both commercial and intelligence spy satellites, it also sits on a 'dog-leg' in the National Microwave network leading to Goonhilly SATCOM Ground Station. Morwenstow also began operations just before GCHQ closed its CSOS Goonhavern base, which had monitored the major transatlantic communications cables from a site in southern Cornwall for many years. The traffic from these under-sea cables can now be monitored once it enters the terrestrial microwave network.

Secret 'Embassy collection' operations involve sophisticated interception receivers and processors placed in the embassies of UKUSA nations to intercept communications in foreign capitals. Since most countries' microwave networks converge on the capital city, embassy buildings, protected by diplomatic privilege, are an ideal site for microwave interception.

The ECHELON system has created an awesome spying capacity for the USA, allowing it to monitor continuously most of the world's communications targeting civilian as well as military traffic. It is an important component in the growing power and influence of the USA since the collapse of Communism brought about the end of a Cold War. However there is now a highly unstable 'Warm War' of major regional conflicts, US military intervention, multinational crime and the worldwide threat of terrorism to contend with.

The NSA has lobbied hard for the creation of the ECHELON system and has achieved a position of overall control. The NSA has subsidised its allies in UKUSA by providing the sophisticated computer programmes used in the system and provides for the largest number of interception operations. In return, the NSA gets to set the agenda, choose the targets and has, theoretically at least, access to all the intelligence material gained by its allies around the world.

ECONOMIC INTELLIGENCE Economic intelligence, commercial intelligence or industrial intelligence, corporate espionage or the good old private 'spook' are all slices from the same intelligence pie. Economic espionage is as old as greed itself. But with huge sums to be made stealing designs for computer chips and patents for hormones, the threat is growing. Rapid changes in technology are tempting many countries to try to acquire intellectual properties in underhanded ways, thus bypassing the enormous costs of research and development. New global phones, faxes, voice transmissions and data on the Internet make this type of spying easier than ever. Industry analysts estimate slightly more than 85 per cent of the world's companies with a market capitalisation of more than US$1 billion have a formal intelligence programme either to gather information on competitors or protect their own information. Corporate espionage can all too often mean the DGSE against IBM, or even Japanese Motor Corporation against a giant US automobile manufacturer. Economic and industrial espionage is being carried out around the world and US companies are prime and often sitting targets.

The FBI has taken the lead role in what is a relatively new campaign to stop economic espionage. The bureau is currently investigating allegations of economic espionage activities against the US by individuals and organisations from 23 different countries. In recent years, FBI agents have recorded more than a 100 per cent increase in economic spying and now have more than 800 cases under investigation – espionage attempts from the super sophisticated to the downright crude.

France, Israel, Russia and China have made economic espionage a top priority of their foreign intelligence services, while the CIA and NSA provide economic intelligence to policy-makers and leading commercial companies. However, the idea of using the US intelligence community to give companies an edge is an explosive subject that has divided the CIA and provoked bitter debate in Congress. It also raises doubts about whether a free society can accept the kind of help that an intelligence service can provide when the question is not one of national security but simply of commercial advantage. The giant US corporations will, no doubt, continue to be the recipients of 'stolen goods' provided by the CIA and its expert 'black-bag' operatives. According to sources in the intelligence community, the CIA has long run a major clandestine effort to help, among others, the US automobile industry. Since the end of the Cold War, Washington has regularly been abuzz with talk about the use made of economic espionage provided by the CIA. Stripped of euphemism, this simply means that US intelligence officers target major commercial concerns in both friendly as well as hostile nations and then covertly pass stolen trade secrets and technology to their US-based corporate competitors. In a form of 'intellectual asset stripping' the NSA, CIA and the Pentagon have for years shared industrial or technological intelligence with US industry and in particular defence contractors or those involved in advanced electronic research. Economic intelligence is certain to be a major growth industry throughout the intelligence world, whether national or corporate in the 21st century.

ELECTRONIC WARFARE   Overall term for efforts to detect, locate, exploit, reduce or prevent an enemy's use of the electromagnetic spectrum. It applies in differing forms to:

● *Electro-Optical Intelligence (Electro-OPINT)* – intelligence gathered from the optical monitoring of the electromagnetic spectrum from the ultraviolet (0.01 micrometres) through to the far infrared (1000 micrometres);

- *Electronic Intelligence (ELINT)* – electronic intelligence (emissions other than communications, such as radar, but not including atomic detonation or radioactive sources); and
- *Electronic Counter Measures (ECCM)* – covers any actions taken to retain the effectiveness of one's own use of the electromagnetic spectrum against hostile Electronic Warfare activities.

ELICITATION The acquisition of intelligence from a person or group when the collector does not disclose the intent of the interview or conversation.

ELLIS, Charles 'Dick' (1895–1975) An Australian who joined SIS (MI6) in the 1920s. Admitted to handing low-grade service secrets to the Germans for money in the 1930s, he came under suspicion as a Soviet agent in later years. A senior SIS officer and later a consultant to the Australian ASIS, Ellis continued to deny working for the KGB and no hard evidence against him has been produced so far.

EMISSION CONTROL (EMCON) AND SECURITY The avoidance or reduction of the use of radio or radar to prevent hostile forces from detecting or intercepting the emissions from sensitive equipment or buildings, and the measures taken to deny intelligence to enemy activities from the interceptions and analysis of electronic emissions.

ENIGMA Electrical cipher machine used by German armed forces and Government during WWII. A brilliant Allied campaign to read the ciphers produced by ENIGMA resulted in the intelligence usually known as ULTRA and which probably helped shorten the war by several years.

ENTERTAINERS AND SPIES Cary Grant, the quintessential English hero, worked for British Intelligence monitoring suspected Nazi sympathisers in Tinseltown such as Errol Flynn and Gary Cooper. After the war and under his real name of Archie Leach, Grant was awarded the King's Medal. Grant is but one of many internationally known movie and theatre stars who have acted as spies. Leslie Howard worked for SIS, Sir Anthony Quayle and Bill Travers for SOE. Sir Noël Coward was certainly an SIS asset. Even Greta Garbo was suspected of dabbling in intelligence. Sir Alexander Korda (1893–1956), who produced so many famous movies such as *The Private Lives of Henry VIII* with Charles Lawton and *Things to Come*, *The Scarlet Pimpernel* and *The Third Man*, worked for Col Claude Dansey. Korda's own company, London Films, had been set up with money provided by the intelligence service. It operated as an SIS (MI6) front for many years throughout prewar Europe and provided vital cover for SIS officers as movie cameramen wanting to film sensitive locations. The Nazi party were only too pleased for a British film company to want to film the beautiful fatherland and extended considerable help on a number of occasions.

ESCAPE AND EVASION Techniques taught both to both intelligence officers and special operations personnel on how best to escape capture in a hostile country. A branch of British Intelligence MI9 operated the escape routes for aircrew shot down over enemy territory in WWII. Today the 23rd SAS (TA) fulfil this role within the British armed forces.

ESPIONAGE Clandestine intelligence collection. Espionage is spying. To historians, it's the world's second oldest profession. To criminologists, it's a crime against national government. To practitioners, it's the exercise of simple tradecraft.

The *history of espionage* goes back at least to 500 BC–AD 1900. The importance of espionage in war has been recognised since the beginning of recorded history. The Egyptians had a well-developed secret service and spying and subversion are mentioned in the Iliad and in the Bible. The ancient Chinese treatise *The Art of War*, by an original master of espionage Sun Tzu in c. 500 BC devotes much attention to deception and intelligence gathering. Spying is often quoted as being the second oldest business in the world. It has been around as long as civilisation itself. Clearly any ruler or leader needs to know the strengths and weaknesses of his or her neighbours as they are the most likely to become the enemy at some point in time. Hence the need for reliable intelligence. The Bible makes over 100 references to spies and intelligence gathering. That gives some indication of how old the art of spying actually is. The word eavesdropping derived from the Middle Ages when spies for the king or queen of the time would listen at the eaves of the houses of prominent people to see if they could get news of any plot to overthrow the ruling party before it happened.

In the Middle Ages, political espionage became important. Joan of Arc was betrayed by Bishop Pierre Cauchon of Beauvais, a spy in the pay of the English and Sir Francis Walsingham developed an efficient political spy system for Elizabeth I. The Renaissance period of the 15th and 16th centuries in Europe saw the foundations of modern espionage established. Many of the tools of the trade in use then such as spy networks and polyalphabetic ciphers are still in use today, albeit in a far more complex form. During the American Revolutionary War

(1775–83), General George Washington and patriots such as Benjamin Franklin and John Jay directed a broad range of clandestine operations that helped the colonies win independence. They ran networks of agents and double agents, employed deceptions against the British army, launched sabotage operations and paramilitary raids, used codes and ciphers, and disseminated propaganda and disinformation to influence foreign governments.

The US founders all agreed with General Washington that 'the necessity of procuring good intelligence is apparent and need not be further urged'. Nathan Hale, of course, was America's most famous spy, and everyone knows his famous quote in 1776 when he was about to be hanged: 'I only regret that I have but one life to lose for my country.' With the growth of the modern national state, organised espionage became a fundamental part of government in most countries. Joseph Fouché is credited with developing the first modern political espionage system and Frederick II of Prussia is regarded as the founder of modern military espionage.

The American Civil War (1861–65) between the Northern or Union and Southern or Confederate States saw new technologies slowly starting to be used for information gathering. The major new development of the time was the advent of photography. It was so new that many commanders did not even see it as a threat; hence both sides were allowed to take pictures of military installations. Eventually this led to the miniaturisation of pictures in order to hide them and then led to an early form of microdots. Telegraphy was quickly taken up for fast communications and gave rise to the use of ciphers for sending and receiving.

The USA's first formal, permanent intelligence organisations were formed in the 1880s: the Office of Naval Intelligence established in 1882 and the Army Military Intelligence Division. They posted attachés to several major European cities principally for open-source collection. When the Spanish-American War broke out in 1898, the attachés switched to espionage. They created informant rings and ran reconnaissance operations to learn about Spanish military intentions and capabilities – most importantly, the location of the Spanish Navy. One US military officer used well-placed sources he had recruited in the Western Union telegraph office in Havana to intercept communications between Madrid and Spanish commanders in Cuba. The US Secret Service, which was placed in charge of domestic counter-intelligence during the war, broke up a Spanish spy ring based in Montreal that had planned to infiltrate the US Army.

1900–90 By WWI, all the great powers except the USA had elaborate civilian espionage systems and all national military establishments had intelligence units. The British established an interlocking structure of Intelligence and Counter-Intelligence services in 1909 with the establishment of the Secret Service Bureau. The Home section later became the Security Service and in 1916 gained its military cover-title of MI5, while the Foreign Section became the Secret Intelligence Service, with the military cover title of MI-1C in 1916 being changed to MI6 in 1921 when responsibility for foreign intelligence passed to the Foreign Office. WWI saw the establishment by the British Admiralty of Room 40 which achieved outstanding success in the field of codebreaking and was to be merged with other military and civilian sections to form a full-time codebreaking and making service in 1919. It was given the rather odd cover-name of the Government Code & Cipher School and was placed under the operational control of SIS by the Foreign Office in 1921.

The GC&CS were responsible with the outstanding help of the brilliant Polish and French cipher services for breaking the German ENIGMA code and producing the ULTRA intelligence that helped first save Britain from defeat and then shorten the war; today its successor, GCHQ, is second only to the giant NSA in skill and worldwide capability.

To protect the country against foreign agents, the US Congress passed the Espionage Statute of 1917 and this proved the first tentative step towards the creation of the huge US intelligence community of today. It is also important to mention the Russian Revolution 1917 since some of the intelligence-gathering techniques developed then led to modern-day practices. The Russians failed to use a cipher when giving troop movements in WWI. Consequently the Germans were able to read their plain Morse code and gained a crucial advantage and these led directly to the disasters that befell the Russian Imperial Armies on the battlefields of 1914–15. Okhrana, the Tsarist secret service, were therefore painfully aware of the possibilities of signals intelligence and it later employed spies to assist in codebreaking activities. They also set up a highly effective network of informers and agents in Europe to penetrate the revolutionary groups and the information gathered was of such quality that the Okhrana files are now a major source of historical information on the Bolsheviks. The Bolsheviks were in turn to quickly set up their own secret police called the Cheka who, through the clever use of these files and surveillance techniques, inherited from the Okhrana in 1917, soon became an effective secret service.

At the start of the war in Europe in 1939, Germany, Japan, the Soviet Union and Britain had well-established foreign intelligence networks; however, the most effective intelligence operations were perhaps those of the Allied codebreakers. British cryptographers broke the ciphers of the German ENIGMA and its derivatives, while the USA broke the Japanese Purple cipher. The information gathered did not guarantee victory, but had far-reaching effects on their conduct of the war. The war also demanded new organisations and Britain was to create the Special Operations Executive (SOE). This was the first service that combined intelligence gathering with clandestine warfare and direct support for resistance groups. The USA soon followed with the Office of Strategic Services (OSS) which was to play a similar role, but with a greater emphasis on information gathering as the USA did not have a dedicated intelligence service such as Britain's SIS. Together the SOE, OSS and the many national resistance groups caused chaos behind the enemy's lines both in Europe and in Asia.

Since the end of WWII, intelligence and counter-intelligence activity has grown enormously, initially through the Cold War between the Western Allies and the former USSR. Russia and the Soviet Union have had a long tradition of espionage, ranging from the Czar's Okhrana to the Committee for State Security (the KGB). In the USA the 1947 National Security Act created the Central Intelligence Agency (CIA) to co-ordinate intelligence and later, in 1952, the National Security Agency for research into codes and electronic communication. In addition to these, the USA has seven other intelligence-gathering agencies. A major element of the Cold War was the arms race and in particular the ballistic missile and weapons of mass destruction programmes. During this period existing Western techniques for intelligence gathering proved inadequate for assessing the nuclear strength of the Soviet Union. This led to the development of the U-2 high-altitude photographic reconnaissance aircraft and besides flying over the Soviet Union, the U-2 was used in 1962 to monitor developments on the island of Cuba, revealing the presence of Soviet SS-4 Sandal medium-range nuclear missiles. This precipitated the Cuban Missile Crisis, the most dangerous event of the Cold War, resolved eventually by a public climbdown by the Soviets and a private agreement by the USA to remove similar missiles from W Europe. By 1961 satellites were being used for photographic reconnaissance, although early technology necessitated jettisoning the film for recovery and development back on Earth. In 1976 the US began using digital technology which enabled satellites to beam high-definition images back to Earth as soon as they were taken. Such developments in technology have become a prime target for espionage. The KGB found that the lure of money was the easiest way to recruit agents. The two most important KGB agents to be exposed in the USA in recent times, John Walker and Aldrich Ames, both offered their services for money. Ames operated as a mole inside the CIA, while Walker sold secrets from within the US Navy.

Espionage since 1945 has been constantly highlighted by a large number of incidents, defections and spies. However, a shortlist might include the capture by Communist China of two CIA agents in 1952 and in 1960 Francis Gary Powers, flying a U-2 on a CIA reconnaissance mission over the Soviet Union was shot down and eventually given a show trial. Many Soviet intelligence officials were to spy for or defect to the West, including Gen. Walter Krivitsky, Victor Kravchenko, Vladimir Petrov, Peter Deriabin, Oleg Penkovsky and Oleg Gordievsky.

Among Western officials who defected to the Soviet Union are Britain's Guy F. Burgess and Donald D. Maclean in 1951, Otto John of W Germany in 1954, US cryptographers William H. Martin and Bernon F. Mitchell in 1960 and of course the 'third man' Harold (Kim) Philby in 1962.

China has developed a very cost-effective intelligence programme that is especially effective in monitoring Asian countries and a major programme to acquire hi-tech intelligence from the USA. Smaller countries can also mount effective and focused espionage efforts, both the Viet Minh and later N Vietnam had consistently superior intelligence during much of the Vietnam War. Israel probably has one of the best espionage establishments in the world while India, France and Germany all having highly effective intelligence services.

1990 The end of the Cold War and the collapse of Communism has not brought the expected slow-down in the growth of espionage activity; far from it. For instead of one major enemy the Western allies are now confronted with an ever-changing pattern of alliances and threats. The Gulf War, the Balkan Wars, Afghanistan, the War on Terrorism, global crime and huge advances in technology will ensure that espionage and the attempts to defeat it, will remain a major influence on the world indefinitely.

ESTABLISHED SOURCE A standard or accepted source of intelligence requiring little further checking.

EWING, Sir Alfred (1855–1935) A scientist who played a considerable part in establishing modern British codebreaking activities. Served as Head of Room 40 (1914–17).

EXECUTIVE ACTION   Intelligence term for assassination sanction directly by an intelligence agency.

EXFILTRATE (OPERATION)   A clandestine rescue operation designed to bring a defector, refugee or an operative and his or her family out of a hostile environment to a place of safety.

EXPLOITATION   Determined attempt to obtain the most information possible from any source.

EYES ONLY   Security restriction applied to documents indicating that they may only be read and should not be discussed orally except in certain restricted facilities.

F

FALSE FLAG   Approach usually by hostile intelligence officers who misrepresent themselves as members of a friendly intelligence service.

FAMILY JEWELS   The list of secret but 'Questionable Activities' that came to light during the Senate investigations of the CIA.

FBI   Federal Bureau of Investigation (US internal security and national anti-crime organisation).
   See also UNITED STATES OF AMERICA.

FEDORA   US codename for a Soviet Intelligence Officer who provided information to the SIS (MI6), CIA and the FBI. CIA Counter-Intelligence Chief James Jesus Angleton firmly believed that Fedora was in fact part of a major Soviet disinformation operation designed to undermine the Western Intelligence community.

FENCE   Russian term for the border or frontier with another country.

FERRET   Electronic intelligence collection platform, usually an aircraft or a satellite.

FIELD   British term for foreign territory, hence 'in the field' for an overseas operation.

FIGURES, Sir Colin Frederick (1925–)   Succeeded Sir Arthur Franks as head of MI6 in 1982, Sir Colin originally worked with the Control Commission in Germany (1953), then went to Amman as first a Third, then a Second, secretary and served for a few years in Warsaw. In 1966 was appointed First Secretary and Head of the Visa Section in Vienna. He was given the rank of Counsellor in the Foreign Office in 1975. Not without a sense of humour, when asked what his recreations were, he replied, 'Watching sport, gardening and beachcombing.' He retired a few years later.

FINCEN   Financial Crimes Enforcement Network (US Treasury Dept, intelligence clearing house on money laundering).

FINESSE   Sensitive disguises developed by the CIA using movie consultants and special-effects contractors. The CIA established close contacts with a number of Hollywood's leading make-up artists, designers, special-effects experts and even screenwriters to make the best possible use of their unusual skills and perhaps provide an alternative view on problems faced by the Agency.

FIRM, THE   Term occasionally used for the CIA among its own personnel, alternative to 'The Company'.

FISH   Advanced German WWII online Cipher Machine (Geheimschreiber) and a significant improvement over the more widely used ENIGMA.

FIX   CIA term meaning to compromise, blackmail or simply to 'con' or fool.

FLAPS AND SEALS   The tradecraft involved when making surreptitious openings and closings of envelopes and seals on packaging.

FLASH   The highest precedence for CIA cable communications.

FLOATER   A freelance agent used for a one-off or occasional intelligence operation. Usually a low-level operative such as a taxi-driver, waiter or similar.

FLOWERS, Thomas Harold 'Tommy' (1905–98)   The father of the modern electronic computer. At the request of GC&CS, Flowers then working as a Post Officer engineer at Dollis Hill in London, designed and constructed one of the world's first electronic digital computers, the Colossus. It was urgently needed to speed up the deciphering of the vast amounts of ENIGMA intercepts pouring into Bletchley Park. Its development notably helped shorten the war. In all some 11 Colossus computers were built, the last being destroyed by GCHQ only in 1958. T.H. Flowers was indeed, as one newspaper commented in its obituary column, 'The Colossus of Codes'.

FLUENCY COMMITTEE   Established in October 1964 under the chairmanship of MI5 officer Peter Wright and included Anthony Motion and Arthur Martin from MI5 and Stephen de Mowbray from SIS. A joint MI5 'D' Branch (Internal Security) and MI6 (CI Directorate) tasked to determine whether British intelligence had been deeply penetrated by the Soviet Union. Two Directors of the Security Service (MI5) came under suspicion in an overheated atmosphere reminiscent of the worst excesses of Angleton's last days at the CIA. Michael Hanley was quickly cleared and no evidence of note was ever produced to Sir Roger Hollis's detriment. The Fluency Committee could hardly have undermined British Intelligence more if it had been a Soviet disinformation operation. Closed down in 1970, the Fluency Committee had achieved little beyond a useful re-examination of past material.

FOOTS   Members of a surveillance team who are working on foot and riding as passengers in a car.

FORGERS BRIDGE   Technique for bracing the forger's writing hand with the fingers of his other hand as an aid to making fluid handwritten entries.

FOREIGN ARMIES EAST   (Fremde Heer Ost) 12th Branch of the German General Staff, concerned with military intelligence on the Soviet (Eastern) Front during WWII.

FOREIGN ARMIES WEST   (Fremde Heere West) Dealt with military intelligence on the Western Front in WWII.

FORT MEADE   Built in 1957, Fort Meade near Laurel in Maryland is the HQ of the National Security Agency (NSA).

FORTY COMMITTEE   The National Security Council (NSC) group assigned the task of approving Covert Action operations conducted by the CIA.

FOUCHÉ, Joseph   (Duc D'Otrante) (1754–1820) He joined the religious Oratorian order in 1779; however he abandoned his clerical career and was elected to the National Convention. He became a leading radical and soon gained a position of great power as the Minister of Police and spymaster to Napoleon. In 1802 he was dismissed on the grounds that he had become far too powerful and threatened Napoleon's own position.

Fouché was a Jacobin who had used the Revolution to create a fortune for himself and had become one of the richest men in France. Napoleon reinstated him in 1804 realising that the security of the state needed Fouché's particular brand of patriotism. Napoleon was considered a hero by many in Ireland and Fouché recruited many of the 'Wild Geese' to his organisation: they were to prove of great value, in particular in the war with England. However his major mistake came when he began to believe that there was little left to gain from continuing the war with England and sent secret intermediaries to a number of countries to open negotiations. Napoleon was furious and, regarding Fouché virtually as an English agent, dismissed him from office. Fouché cleverly removed a vast number of incriminating documents and names from his secret office, more than sufficient to ensure his survival from the revenge of his enemies. As a result Napoleon only banished him from France. Fouché died in exile in Trieste in 1820.

FRANCE *Direction Générale de la Sécurité Extérieure – General Directorate for External Security (DGSE)* Subordinate to the Ministry of the Defence, it is responsible for military intelligence as well as for strategic information, electronic intelligence and for counter-espionage outside the borders of the national territory. Based for many years at the Caserne des Tourelles, 128 Boulevard Mortier, 75020 Paris, in the 20th arrondissement, this is now being supplemented by the new HQ complex at the Fort of Noisy-Le-Sec. Situated in the communes of Noisy-le-Sec and Romainville, the project began in 1992 and is generally referred to as 'Fort-2000'.

The DGSE has its origins in the integration of the diverse agencies of French intelligence from WWII. The Free French forces in 1942 created the Central Bureau of Information and Action (BCRA), which in November 1943 relocated to Algiers as the General Directorate of Special Services (DGSS). On 6 November 1944 the intelligence networks of the French Resistance were integrated to the DGSS, which was redesignated the Directorate of Studies and Research (DGER).

In 1946 the service was renamed the External Documentation and Counter-Espionage Service (SDECE). After abolition of the French Indochina opium monopoly in 1950, SDECE imposed highly illegal and covert controls over the illicit drug traffic that linked the Hmong poppy fields of Laos with the opium dens operating in Saigon. The French intelligence services generated huge profits from the drug trade and these funded clandestine operations throughout the rest of the war in Indo-China. The French defeat at Dien Bien Phu in 1954 barely interfered with the SDECE control of the trade routes and this continued until the CIA took over the local drug trade in the early 1960s.

By 1960, the SDECE was being used increasingly as a strategic intelligence service and was particularly efficient in the struggle against the rebellion in Algeria, where it established a reputation for the ruthless and permanent elimination of its enemies. In 1962 General De Gaulle decided to subordinate the SDECE to the Minister of the Defence, and the institution adapted to the military environment.

And this was followed by a Presidential order for SDECE to

undertake covert operations in Canada using nationalist and separatist movements in Quebec. Undercover of 'Assistance et Cupertino Technique' or OPERATION ASCOT, SDECE dispatched officers to Quebec in a failed attempt to promote the growth of separatist movements. In 1968 SDECE tried to gain control of the Nigerian oil from Britain and the US by arming and supplying rebel forces in the oil-rich Biafra region. The resulting war cost some 500,000 lives before the attempt at secession was crushed.

On 4 April 1982 the SDECE became the Directorate of the External Security (DGSE). It is presently organised into a *Strategic Directorate*, which provides analysis of economic and political intelligence, and an *Intelligence Directorate* which is responsible for the collection of information, mainly from human sources (HUMINT), including the employment of illegal agents. It is responsible both for collecting and disseminating intelligence and works closely with the Operations Directorate.

The ID is deeply involved in industrial espionage, particularly against the USA. In early 1993 the CIA obtained a long list of the most important DGSE targets in the USA, which included Boeing, among other companies. The DGSE agents were mainly interested in the navigation system of Boeing's new jumbo-jet to pass on to French companies, particularly Airbus Industries.

The *Technical Division* was constituted from the former Groupement des Contrôles Radioélectriques (GCR – Radioelectronic Communications Group). This is responsible for strategic electronic intelligence and maintains a number of collection stations throughout the world, including the newly enhanced Djibouti facilities in NE Africa. At a listening station west of Paris, the DGSE can intercept international telephone and fax traffic and this is part of France's version of ECHELON

The *Operations Division* is responsible for planning and implementing clandestine operations. The 1995 OPERATION SATANIC had the objective of neutralising the *Rainbow Warrior* ship that was part of the Greenpeace campaign against French nuclear tests in the Pacific. On 10 July 1985 DGSE agents detonated a bomb on the ship while it was in port of Auckland, New Zealand, killing the photographer Fernando Peira.

The DGSE also has its own Covert Action section: the 'Division Action' has training camps in Cercottes (Loiret), Roscanvel and Perpignan (Pyrenees Orientals) (formerly situated in Margival, in the Aisne). In 1992, during the DGSE reforms and the creation of the

special force HQ, it was decided to leave the 11th RPC to the DGSE, given the particular missions of the Division Action in peacetime. On 30 June 1995 11th Shock was dissolved and its functions were replaced by three 'stations', the CPES in Cercottes, the CIPS in Perpignan and the CPEOM in Roscanvel. These sections combine the operations of the CIA's SOG and the SAS teams dedicated to SIS, and have a distinct and well-earned reputation for being quite ruthless in their dealings with terrorists.

Direction du Renseignement Militaire – Directorate of Military Intelligence (DRM): its HQ and activities devoted to administration and current intelligence are located in Paris, while technical and processing sub-directorates are located in Creil (Oise). This new organisation was formed in the light of lessons learned during the Gulf War in 1991 and it amalgamated the main Intelligence Directorates of the French Army and Air Force on 16 June 1992. The DRM is responsible for planning, co-ordinating and leading investigations, and for the overall control of military intelligence. The DRM concentrates on gathering information from open sources rather than from clandestine operations; however, it has begun to step on the toes of the DGSE as it moves into both political and economic intelligence gathering. Its present organisation includes:

- *The Research Sub-Directorate* – responsible for human and electronic operational and works closely with the Intelligence and Electronic Warfare Brigade (BRGE);
- *The Exploitation Sub-Directorate* Imagery Interpretation Centre – responsible for production and dissemination of intelligence;
- *The Proliferation and Armament Sub-Directorate* – responsible for study and analysis of threats from nuclear technology proliferation, chemical weapons, and other armaments;
- *The Technical Sub-Directorate* – responsible for providing technical support to the other elements of the Directorate;
- *BRGE Brigade de Renseignement et de Guerre Electronique – Intelligence and Electronic Warfare Brigade* – created 1 September 1993 and providing the Defence Ministry and military commands with Signals Intelligence (SIGINT) support. It is also responsible for communications security (COMSEC) within the armed forces and for the development of new electronic equipment.

DST Direction de la Surveillance du Territoire – Directorate of Territorial Security – established in 1944 this is the prime French internal security service. Following the collapse of Communism in 1991 the DST redeployed many of its officers previously working on the Soviet threat and assigned them to deal with new threats in Britain, Israel and the USA in particular when DST counter-espionage officers noted that the CIA were regularly 'approaching' senior civil servants and military personnel holding sensitive positions.

The DST with HQ situated at 1 rue Nélaton in Paris, since July 1985, is organised into five sub-directorates (for counter-espionage, internal security, international terrorism, technical administration and general administration) and a special office of national and international relationships which includes countering the illegal drug trade, organised crime, money laundering and arms proliferation. The DST also has a provincial structure with seven regional directorates and overseas territories departments with several 'brigades' and four stations installed in former French colonies.

The DST also has an *Economic Security and Protection of National Assets* department established in the mid 1970s with units in the 22 regions to protect French technology, not only in the defence industry, but pharmaceuticals, telecoms, the automobile industry, manufacturing and service sectors, from foreign intelligence activities.

FRANCE, SPECIAL FORCES The French have a very wide range of Special Forces units available from both the Armed Forces and the National Police and all of which are tasked for intelligence and counter-terrorist operations under the direction of the DGSE and DST Intelligence and Security services.

The 1st Parachute Infantry & Marine Regiment is the French army's primary Special Operations unit. The Black Berets are very similar to the Special Air Service and indeed owe many of their traditions to the Free French Special Air Service units that served with such distinction during WWII. The Ist Paras are an extremely effective and well-equipped force, with their main missions being intelligence gathering, direct action, special operations, and counter-terrorism. Training includes marksmanship, combat shooting, unarmed combat, combat swimming, desert, mountain and amphibious warfare, heliborne-insertion, para-gliding, HAHO (High Altitude High Opening), HALO (High Altitude Low Opening) and a wide range of clandestine and intelligence-gathering techniques. They are trained to use most weapons and have a stock of standard service, commercially bought and captured terrorist weapons that run into hundreds of makes of rifles, sub-machine guns, automatic pistols, machine guns, grenades and explosives. The 1st Paras are supported by *ALAT (Special Operations*

Aviation Unit) with two Special Operations Helicopter Squadrons, the first with Puma and Cougar Transports and the second with Gazelle Gunships. It is now part of the Special Operations Command formed in the aftermath of the Gulf War in 1991 and designed to ensure full co-operation between the various Special Force units and their parent services.

The Special Scout Team of the 2nd REP (Legion Para regiment) is a particularly well-proven and effective Intelligence and Counter-terrorist unit with a speciality in 'hard skirmishes', sabotage of hard value targets, long-range reconnaissance and patrol, POW (prisoner of war) rescue, psychological warfare, deep clandestine penetration behind enemy lines and the elimination of terrorist targets.

GIGN (Intervention Group of the National Gendarmerie) was formed in 1974 and has never had more than 100 personnel. GIGN has always been inventive and effective, from soon after its establishment it quickly developed a reputation for being one of the world's busiest and finest counter-terrorist units. They have taken part in over 1,200 operations worldwide and because of this they are trained to act effectively in a myriad of situations. Their training includes every technique from HALO (High Altitude-Low Opening) to parachuting into the sea in full scuba gear. Even to be considered for GIGN you must have five years of experience with an exemplary record; the training then takes ten months and as many as 90 per cent of volunteers fail to make the grade.

FRANKS, Sir Arthur Temple (1920–) Educated at Rugby and Queen's College, Oxford, Sir Arthur entered the SIS largely on the strength of his wartime service in the SOE. Joining the Foreign Office in 1949, he went to Tehran as second Secretary the following year at the time of the Iranian coup, and after another spell in London was appointed MI6 Chief of Station in Bonn in 1962. He succeeded Sir Maurice Oldfield as head of MI6 in 1978, and retired in 1981.

FRASER-SMITH, Charles (1904–92) Brilliant inventor of espionage devices for SIS (MI6) and SOE during WWII, who was the inspiration for Ian Fleming's 'Q' in the James Bond stories. His task was to supply the clandestine services with 'Q' gadgets, named after WWI 'Q' ships, which had been effectively warships disguised as ordinary merchant vessels. Many of his 'Q' gadgets were concealed as everyday objects, for instance a pack of playing cards which, when the top layer of these cards was soaked off, would reveal numbered map sections. Once reassembled the sections formed a master from which escape maps were then copied. Other items included a hairbrush, pen and a pipe, all with hidden maps, compasses or knife blades.

FRENCH OPENING   Technique for the surreptitious opening of an envelope by slitting one end and then restoring this cut.

FRIEDMAN, William Frederick (1891–1969)   After codebreaking work during WWI, Friedman was made chief of the Signal Intelligence Services (SIS). By the late 1930s, US intelligence realised that war with Japan was inevitable and stepped up its intelligence preparations and codebreaking activities. By 1941 US intelligence experts, Friedman at their core, were able to translate the Japanese orders to break off negotiations on 7 December which had clearly indicated Japan's intent to go to war, although the messages did not pinpoint Pearl Harbor as the site of the first sneak attack. Friedman visited the British codebreaking operations at the Government Code and Cipher School (GC&CS) at Bletchley in 1941 to establish close co-operation. Not only did the wartime partners produce a codebreaking capability that probably shortened WWII by several years, saving countless millions of live, but laid the groundwork for the global intelligence-gathering network that still exists today. Following the end of the war, Friedman remained an intelligence officer, becoming in 1952 the chief cryptologist for National Security Agency (NSA). He died in 1969, exhausted by decades of brilliant but mind-numbing codebreaking, one of the great unsung American heroes and one the leading cryptologists of his era.

FRIENDS   Term used for the British Secret Intelligence Service (MI6) within the British establishment.

FRONT   A legitimate-appearing business created by an intelligence agency or security service to provide cover for spies and their operations.

FSB   Russian counter-intelligence and internal security (formerly part of Soviet KGB).

FUMIGATING   Checking premises for listening and other surveillance devices and ensuring either their removal or to neutralise them.

FUCHS, Klaus (1911–88)   Of all the atomic spies working for the Soviets, probably the most important and dangerous was the naturalised British scientist Klaus Fuchs. He did not become a spy for any of the usual reasons, money, revenge or blackmail. His motive was purely ideological.

Fuchs was a dedicated Communist and moved to England in 1933. When Fuchs's file was reviewed in 1940 his pronounced anti-Nazi sentiments convinced British officials that he was not a risk as an enemy alien. Moreover, Fuchs, a brilliant physicist, was soon recruited to work on various projects and moved to Glasgow. A short time later, Fuchs was sent to Birmingham University to work with Professor Rudolf Peierls who was also a German refugee and who was a friend of Fuchs. It is likely that Peierls personally requested that Fuchs join him in his research for the 'Tube Alloy Project' (cover name for the atom bomb research programme). Rudolf Peierls, many years later, had accusations made against him of being a Soviet spy, in part because of his close connection with Klaus Fuchs. Fuchs required and received a security clearance after being vetted by MI5 officers. He was also required to become a British citizen, which he did, again without protest, early in 1942.

In December 1943 Fuchs was sent to America, to continue his atomic research at Columbia University in New York. However, in 1949 the FBI conducted sweeping investigations in the US and uncovered a network of Soviet agents. One of the Soviet spies admitted to FBI that he had been passed secret material by a British physicist working at Los Alamos. Fuchs was the immediate suspect but neither the FBI nor MI5 could obtain sufficient hard evidence to arrest him.

However by a strange twist of fate, Fuchs asked to see the security officer at Harwell in 1949 to discover whether his father's recent appointment to a teaching position at Leipzig University in E Germany would compromise his security clearance. MI5, informed of this request, promptly sent one its best investigating officers, William Skardon, a former detective, to visit Fuchs. Having quietly established a friendly and sympathetic relationship with the suspected spy, Skardon persuaded Fuchs to confess. Following his conviction, Fuchs received 14 years in prison, the maximum sentence. Fuchs was sent to Wormwood Scrubs Prison where he soon became the librarian. After nine years, Fuchs was released and immediately left for E Germany where he was appointed by the Soviets to head the Nuclear Research Institute at Dresden. Fuchs died of natural causes in 1988.

FUSION The process of examining all sources of intelligence and information to derive a complete assessment of potential foreign activities, intentions and most importantly, capabilities.

G

GAMBIT   A disguise technique first deployed by the CIA in SE Asia in the early 1970s with the help of a Hollywood consultant. It made a quick ethnic change possible.

GAMEKEEPER   British term for an agent controller or HANDLER.

GARBO   Codename for Juan Pujol Garcia. Originally a German agent he was captured and 'turned' by the British XX Committee (Double Cross Committee) to become one of the most effective double agents in history.

GARDENING   British term for an operation that forces an enemy to send a message in cipher or code, thereby giving codebreakers a crib to help in their cryptographic efforts.

GC&CS   Government Code and Cipher School cover name for codebreaking centre from its establishment in 1919 to its 'official' change of title to GCHQ in 1946. It probably took its new title on its move to Bletchley Park but as much for reasons of convenience as security the title GC&CS continued to be used for some time.

GCHQ   Government Communications Headquarters (British counterpart to the NSA and part of Foreign Office).

GEHLEN, Reinhard   *see* GEHLEN ORGANISATION.

GEHLEN ORGANISATION   Major General Reinhard Gehlen headed the *Foreign Armies East* which was responsible for collecting intelligence on the armed forces of the Soviet Union. Gehlen had begun planning his surrender to the USA at least as early as autumn 1944. In early March 1945 a group of Gehlen's senior officers microfilmed their intelligence archives on the Soviet Union and packed the film in steel drums which were then buried throughout the Austrian Alps to be recovered later with the help of US Intelligence Officers. On 22 May 1945 Gehlen and his top aides surrendered to an US Army Counter-Intelligence Corps team. After the war, the USA recognised that it did not have an intelligence capability directed against its wartime ally, the Soviet Union. Gehlen negotiated an agreement with the USA which allowed his operation to continue in existence despite postwar denazification programmes. Quickly reconstituted as a functioning espionage network under direct US control, it played a hugely important role in the early years of the Cold War. The many hundreds of German army and SS officers who were released from internment camps to join Gehlen's HQ in the Spessart Mountains in central Germany certainly saw this as a chance to pursue their anti-Communist crusade and indeed influence the CIA and US foreign policy in Europe.

As the size of the organisation grew, Gehlen with funding from the CIA moved it to a 25-acre compound near Pullach, south of Munich, operating under the innocent name of the South German Industrial Development Organisation. In the early 1950s it was estimated that the organisation, made up mainly of former Army, SS, Abwehr and even Gestapo officers, operated networks of spies, saboteurs and black-propaganda agents throughout Soviet-controlled E Europe.

Under OPERATION SUNRISE, some 5,000 anti-Communist E European and Russian personnel were trained for operational missions at a camp at Oberammergau in 1946, under the command of General Sikes and SS General Burckhardt. This and related operations supported anti-Communist rebels throughout E Europe and these were not entirely suppressed by Soviet Security until 1956.

In April 1956 control of the Gehlen Organisation passed to the newly created West German Federal Republic as the BND Bundesnach-richtendienst, or 'Federal Intelligence Service'. Gehlen was to remain Director of W Germany's Intelligence service until he retired in 1968.

GERMANY *Bundesnachrichtendienst – The Federal Intelligence Service (BND)*: established in 1956 with its HQ in Munich-Pullach and which since 2000 has had a Federal Government liaison Office in Berlin. The Pullach site also includes the Situation and Information Centre (LIZ) which is responsible for the analysis of all information collected from around the world from OSINT, HUMINT and SIGINT sources. The reports are analysed, compiled and integrated with political evaluations for dissemination to government and military departments. The BND operates a number of secret SIGINT interception stations including Hoefen on the border with Belgium and Husom in Schleswig-Holstein in addition to receiving information from the US controlled Echelon network.

The BND is a global intelligence service with officers, usually under diplomatic cover in the local embassy, or agents in more than 100 countries. Administratively the BND is part of the Federal Chancellor's Office and is structured to include Department 1 for Operational

Procurement, Department 2 for Technical Surveillance; Department 2A, based in the high security building No 109 in Pullach, is responsible for Counter-Narcotics and Countering Money-Laundering Activities and Department 3 for Intelligence Analysis and Interpretation. The highly sensitive Department 4 is for Administration, but also maintains the BND Central File for Persons (PEZD) which contains files on every person with contacts with the intelligence services; Department 5 is for Internal Security and Defence and finally Department 6 for Central Tasks. The BND now devotes a large amount of its efforts to Middle Eastern terrorism and has succeeded in a limited penetration of Islamic, Turkish and Kurdish groups in various German cities and has intensified its activities in Central Europe and the Balkans in particular.

The BND has been deeply involved in a co-ordinated European effort to stop arms deals and smuggling and even has an agreement with the Russian SVR and FSB covering the threat of nuclear proliferation. In August 1994 three members of a criminal gang smuggled some 363 grams of plutonium from Moscow to Munich on a Lufthansa airliner. Detectives from the Bavarian Office of Criminal Investigations arrested them at Munich Airport, but later it was revealed that two BND agents, Karsten Uwe Schnell (ROBERTO) and Rafael Ferreras Fernandez (RAFA) had earlier encouraged the plutonium deal, codenamed OPERATION HADES, in a meeting with the criminals in Madrid. The BND were privately unrepentant about the 'sting' and though there has been an enormous amount of controversy and not a little disinformation surrounding the Munich incident, the BND has continued to use such techniques to good effect against arms smugglers, terrorists and organised crime.

MAD Militaerischer Abschirmdienst – Military Security Service: MAD is the Security Service of the German armed forces. Established in 1956 it was known as the Office for Security of the German Armed Forces (Amt für Sicherheit der Bundeswehr – ASBw) until 1984. MAD maintains close contacts through its S-Group with the military intelligence departments of all NATO countries and has established working relationships with a surprising number of overseas countries including Israel and China.

ANBw Amt für Nachrichtenwesen der Bundeswehr-Office of Intelligence of the Federal Armed Forces: this is the primary office of military intelligence for evaluation and analysis of foreign armed forces weapons and ORBAT.

Bfv Bundesamtes für Verfassungsschutz – Federal Office for the

Protection of the Constitution: its duties are those of an internal security service, though the Bfv has no executive police powers. It can not arrest, interrogate or conduct house searches. It gathers and evaluates information and passes this on to the appropriate agencies of the Federal and State governments. The information from the BfV serves in legal proceedings as important evidence.

GERMANY, SPECIAL FORCES GSG-9 (Grenzschutzgruppe-9) formed as a direct result of the humiliating failure of the German anti-terrorist groups at the 1972 Munich Olympics. The inept police response to the Black September Terrorists led to the death of innocent Israeli athletes and officials. A decision was quickly made to ensure that Germany would have an effective counter-terrorist organisation because the German Army had again proved unwilling to create elite units, the paramilitary Border Guards were chosen in 1973 to host the new unit. In the aftermath of the 11 September terrorist attacks in the USA, GSG-9 has increased its operational strength and now comes under the control of the Counter-Terrorist Division of the Federal Intelligence Service, the BND. GSG-9's highly skilled personnel can conduct long-term clandestine operations and infiltrate terrorist groups, carry out intelligence surveillance and counter-terrorist operations in any environment.

GSG-9 recruits only volunteers from within the Border Guards and ex-Army personnel. The training is extremely thorough and GSG-9 has a higher proportion of graduates than most similar organisations due to the greater demands made on the personnel's intellectual abilities by the combination of Intelligence, Special Forces and Detective work. Rigorous screening still ensures that there is an 80 per cent dropout rate, however. Cross-training is conducted with other NATO elite units and some graduates attend the international LRRP (Long Range Reconnaissance Patrol) School at Weingarten. Training includes HALO (High Altitude-Low Opening) and LALO (Low Altitude-Low Opening), SCUBA diving, combat swimming, demolition and explosives disposal, mountain warfare, skiing and heliborne insertion.

Based at a state-of-the-art centre at Saint Augustin Centre near Bonn, the GSG-9 (Grenzschutzgruppe-9) is organised into GSG-9/1 Counter-Terrorist Group, GSG-9/2 Maritime Counter-Terrorism and GSG-9/3 Airborne Special Operations. It usually operates in five-man teams and uses a wide variety of weapons including Austrian Steyr AUG assault rifles, PSG-1 sniper rifles and MP5/SD3 silenced sub-machine guns.

GESTAPO (Geheimes Staatspolizeiamt) The GESTAPO (Amt IV of the RSHA) was the political police force of the Reich and was originally founded in April 1933 by Hermann Goering. The GESTAPO, through its great powers of arrest and confinement to concentration camps without recourse to law, was the principal means for eliminating enemies of the Nazi regime.

The GESTAPO was eventually organised into: Section A, dealing with opponents, sabotage and protective service; Section B, dealing with political churches, sects and Jews, and subdivided into four offices, including B4, responsible for Jewish affairs, matters of evacuation, means of suppressing enemies of the people and State, dispossession of rights of German citizenship with Eichmann as its chief; Section C, dealing with card files, protective custody, the press and the Nazi Party; Section D, dealing with the regions under greater German influence; Section E, dealing with security; and Section F, dealing with passport matters and foreign police forces.

Subordinate offices of the GESTAPO were established throughout the Reich and designated as Staats Polizeileitstellen or Staats Polizeistellen, depending upon the size of the office. These offices reported directly to the RSHA in Berlin but were subject to the supervision of Inspekteurs of the Security Police in the various provinces. In the occupied territories the regional offices of the GESTAPO were co-ordinated with the Criminal Police and the SD under Kommandeurs.

The GESTAPO was one of the main agencies for eliminating the Jewish population of Europe and indeed Obersturmbannfuehrer Eichmann estimated in his report to Himmler on the matter that 2 million Jews had been killed by shootings, mainly by the Einsatz Groups of the SIPO and SD during the campaigns in E Europe and the invasion of the Soviet Union. This did not include the estimated 4 million sent by the GESTAPO for extermination in annihilation camps. The 'Einsatz Groups' controlled by the GESTAPO carried out mass murders of hundreds of thousands, if not millions of civilians in the occupied countries as a part of the Nazi programme to exterminate political and racial undesirables, those killed including liberals, socialists, Communists, conservative opponents of the Nazis, ethnic minorities, gypsies, homosexuals or in fact anyone who didn't match the mythical 'Aryian' ideal. The most casual remark of any German citizen or resident of an occupied country could bring them to the attention of the GESTAPO, where their fate was decided without recourse to law. In Nazi Germany the rule of law was replaced by the oppressive and tyrannical rule of fear; the GESTAPO was the primary instrument of that oppression.

GLOBAL ORGANISED CRIME   Global organised crime along with international terrorism has been recognised as the key threat to national security. It has been described as a continuing criminal conspiracy having a firm organisational structure, a conspiracy fed by fear and corruption. The internationalisation of crime includes drug trafficking, extortion, money laundering, arms smuggling, bribery and fraud schemes.

In recent years these criminal groups have dramatically increased the scope of their activities by taking advantage of the many changes that have occurred since the end of the Cold War, the creation of the new Europe which has resulted in the lowering of economic and political barriers. An added important factor is the huge advances made in technology, global communications and transport.

Certain distinctions can be made between global organised crime and terrorism, for while many terrorist groups motivated by specific political, ethnic or religious causes, most organised crime groups are only interested in political power for the security it would provide their organisation and their primary motivation remains financial.

Co-operation between global organised crime groups has markedly increased but has not yet been adequately match by a global law enforcement response, despite Interpol, Europol and the many bilateral agreements between the FBI and foreign police forces. When police activity in Florida reduced the amount of Colombian cocaine being smuggled into the US through the Caribbean islands, the Colombian drug cartel leaders simply began working with their Mexican counterparts instead of their Caribbean partners. Multinational economic crime groups are a distinct threat to international financial markets, as the world economy becomes increasingly interdependent. Laundering billions of dollars in organised crime money worsens national debt problems because the large sums of money are then lost as tax revenue to that country's government. The Russian Mafia are actively involved in banking simply because public financial institutions are vulnerable and lucrative targets, while the Russian Interior Ministry has estimated that organised crime 'controls' one way or another, most of Russia's 200 or so banks.

The global networks of criminals, terrorists and corrupt government officials and their complex methods of smuggling goods have been widely used in international drug trafficking which poses an immense threat to the social fabric of all countries. The increase in the scale of these operations has led to an increase in drug use, addiction and general crime level. The common US–Mexico border alone is responsible for some 70 per cent of the Colombian cocaine on the streets of America's major cities. Other European organised crime groups use this border to transport heroin, marijuana and meth-amphetamine. It has become increasingly difficult to track the flow of narcotics into the USA as the drug cartel methods become more technically sophisticated, even to the extent of redesigning the interiors of Boeing airliners to hold enormous amounts of illegal drugs, transferring drug profits electronically to dozens of banks around the world in less than 24 hours and using falsified export documents and invoices for goods in order to disguise drug trafficking transactions. The involvement of intelligence services, including the French SDECE and the CIA with its use of 'proprietary' or front companies has often seen the misuse of drugs and the vast revenue they generate for illegal and controversial clandestine activities. These same techniques used by the drug traffickers could also be used for the smuggling of nuclear materials on a massive scale. As global organised crime groups become more powerful and as nuclear materials become more vulnerable through poor management, underpaid workers in nuclear facilities and widespread government corruption, the threat becomes more serious.

There are many criminal organisations now operating within Europe and the USA, the Italian Mafia, the French Union Corse, Chinese Triads, Japanese and SE Asian gangs, Jamaican Yardies, E European Mafia-style groups and even front-organisations for terrorists, including the Real IRA and ETA. But perhaps the biggest threat comes from over 200 of Russia's estimated 6,000 organised crime groups which operate with their American counterparts in 18 or more cities spread out across at least 14 states. Global crime can now be rated as a primary threat to the stability and economic well-being of the world in the 21st century.

GOLD   Codename for Berlin Tunnel operation.

GOLITSYN, Anatoli (1923–) In December 1961 Golitsyn approached the CIA Head of Station in Helsinki, Finland and announced that he was a major in the First Directorate of the KGB. His offer to defect included the promise that he could identify hundreds of Soviet agents working in the West. Golitsyn was able to tell CIA officials exactly where NATO information had been leaking and provided a list of KGB agents in Helsinki. Upon his arrival in the USA, Angleton, then head of the CIA's counter-intelligence supervised his interrogations. Though Angleton eventual became a Golitsyn supporter, others at the CIA believed the Russian was an 'agent provocateur' who had been planted to spread disinformation. Much of the distrust was caused by Golitsyn's arrogant, quarrelsome and temperamental behaviour. Angleton was to demand that he should provide proof of his claims. Golitsyn identified three Soviet agents in the US who, he said, would begin to spread disinformation about him in an effort to discredit his information and it is believed that CIA investigations may have identified the individuals concerned. British Intelligence officers later visited CIA HQ to meet with Golitsyn and the information he provided succeeded in the identification and arrest of three top Soviet agents working in England. Moreover, Golitsyn was able to provide new information on the British SIS Officer Kim Philby. The Soviet defector visited England to work more closely with MI5 and SIS (MI6) but his cover was blown in an article published by the *Daily Telegraph* and, fearing assassination by KGB agents, he immediately returned to the US.

GORDIEVSKY, Oleg (1938–) His defection was announced by the British Foreign Office on 12 September 1985. Gordievsky, one of the more believable and level-headed defectors, proved to be of immense value to Western Intelligence and provided a vital insight into the final years and internal collapse of the Soviet Union. Gordievsky's defection was a huge blow to KGB prestige and both the information he was able to provide Western counter-intelligence services and the ensuing major reorganisation it forced on his old service played a crucial role in undermining Soviet espionage operations in the remaining years of the Cold War.

GOTTLIEB, Dr Sidney (1918–99) Sidney Gottlieb was everything you could dream of as a mad scientist in a spy novel, except that he was very real. His most notable feat was to introduce the world to the joys of LSD or lysergic acid diethylamide. He discovered by accident that the drug developed by Dr Albert Hoffman in 1953, could be used in a Cold War super-secret mind control programme, codenamed MK-ULTRA. The real 'Manchurian Candidate' operation in fact. Gottlieb, in something reminiscent of the illegal actions of Nazi doctors in German wartime concentration camps, proceeded in 1958 to initiate a secret series of tests. At least 149 experiments, some 25 involving large doses of LSD, were carried out. At first on CIA officers, sometimes unknowingly in drinks, but later deliberately using prisoners, mental patients and prostitutes as human guinea pigs. One of his colleagues,

Maj. General William Creasey of the US Army's Chemical corps, believed that LSD placed in huge quantities in an enemy city's water supply offered a 'humane' alternative to the bomb. He argued that it was 'absurd' when denied the opportunity to test his theory by spraying a cloud of LSD over a US city.

Gottlieb's colleague, Dr Frank Olson, suffering from acute depression and paranoia resulting from a 'bad trip', was to jump to his death from an upper floor of New York's Statler Hilton after taking LSD for the first time at the CIA's special facility at Camp Peary. Gottlieb was to stay in charge of MK-ULTRA for twenty years; however he was also involved in an array of other extraordinary schemes: a poisoned handkerchief for an Iraqi agent, a poisoned dart to kill the Congolese leader Lumumba and a whole arsenal of devices to kill Castro. He retired in 1973. The infamous movie character Dr Strangelove is reportedly based on Sidney Gottlieb.

GOUZENKO, Igor (1919–82) Gouzenko was one of the first important Soviet intelligence officers to defect after WWII and effectively it was one of the first signs of the impending Cold War. In 1943 Gouzenko, a lieutenant in the GRU, worked as a cipher clerk in the Soviet Embassy in Ottawa, Canada. By 5 September 1945, Gouzenko had had enough of the GRU and apparently the Soviet Union. After making contact with the RCMP Security Service, he stole a large number of files and documents from Room 12 (cipher and secrets room) of the Soviet Embassy which would prove the existence of a large Soviet spy ring operating throughout Canada. Roger Hollis from MI5 and Peter Dwyer from SIS visited Gouzenko in Canada and prepared reports on his accusations of Soviet penetration of Western security. At least 18 Soviet agents were exposed and eleven were prosecuted in Canada alone.

Gouzenko and his family were given sanctuary in Canada and put under protective custody, while sweeping arrests were made in Canada, especially of those who were in the Canadian Communist Party and were serving as Soviet agents. Gouzenko's information eventually exposed the British nuclear scientist Dr Alan Nunn May. Nunn May's and the later unrelated arrest of Klaus Fuchs led to the exposure of a number of American Communists who were then accused of providing the Soviet Union with atom bomb secrets, including Gold, Greenglass and the Rosenbergs. Gouzenko later condemned British intelligence for not acting sooner on his information in the case of Klaus Fuchs, pointing out that when he first provided his information, Fuchs's name was prominent in the documents yet MI5 waited almost five years before finally organising his arrest. He also claimed that the NKVD had infiltrated MI5 as early as 1942. The erroneous belief that (Sir) Roger Hollis, later Director General of MI5, was the Soviet agent referred to caused enormous distress and turmoil within Western counter-intelligence for many years and was based on a misreading of information that could just as easily have pointed at a genuine traitor, Kim Philby.

GREAT GAME   The term first used in Rudyard Kipling's novel *Kim* in 1901 to describe the massive British intelligence activity in India and Afghanistan during the 19th century often aimed at thwarting Imperial Russia's designs on the region.

GREECE   *National Intelligence Service (EYP)*: the EYP replaced the KYP in the late 1980s and has undergone a major reorganisation in recent years. This was largely forced upon it by the end of the Cold War, the increase in international terrorism, the ever present threat of wars in the Balkans, in a divided Cyprus and with its fellow NATO neighbour, Turkey. The Greek Intelligence Service, in its various incarnations from its creation towards the end of WWII, has developed a tough reputation and an unenviable record of human rights abuse, kidnapping, torture and murder particularly during the Military Dictatorship which overthrew the monarchy in 1967. However recent presidential decrees have gone some way to making EYP more accountable for its actions and require a greater concentration on intelligence gathering. It is organised into an *Intelligence Study Centre* created for the purpose of collaborating with scientific organisations, universities and specialised research institutes. It will undertake the drafting of security studies and analyses of strategic issues. The EYP has seven directorates covering National Security, Military Security, Political and Economic Intelligence, International Terrorism and Organised Crime, Counter Espionage, Analysis and Distribution and Administration.

It is also responsible for the overall control of EKAM; a battalion-sized Special Anti-Terrorist unit, which after a number of bungled operations in the early 1990s was partly taken out of service for thorough retraining. Further development of this unit has involved the close co-operation of US anti-terrorist officials.

GREECE, SPECIAL FORCES   The primary Greek Special Forces unit is known as ETA (Ediko Tmima Alexiptotiston) or Special

Airborne Unit. Formed in 1959 as an LRRP (Long-Range Reconnaissance Patrol) and tasked for conducting operations similar to the British Special Air Service or the US Delta Force, it specialises in, among other techniques, intelligence gathering, counter-terrorism, and direct action raids, sabotage missions and strategic reconnaissance. This is a highly secretive unit, but it is known that they regularly carry out clandestine intelligence operations inside FYR Macedonia and other former Yugoslav Republics. ETA's main intelligence mission however and its prime areas of operation are the borders with Turkey, Cyprus and the disputed islands of the eastern Aegean Sea.

ETA is organised into 1st Commando Special Operations Regiment, created in 1946 for specialist anti-Communist operations and now a primary Counter-Insurgency unit with B Commando and D Commando in Macedonia, A Commando and E Commando in Thrace, while C Commando (Amphibious Warfare) and 13th Commando Counter-Terrorist Regiment are based in Athens. Training for ETA as with most elite units is rigorous and concentrates on physical strength and stamina, with an extra emphasis, because of Greek terrain, on rock climbing and the rigours of mountain warfare. This is complemented by further courses on intelligence, surveillance, parachuting, unconventional warfare, combat swimming on the Greek Navy's MYK (underwater warfare) course and at NATO's LRRP School in Germany. ETA uses a wide variety of NATO and commercial weapons, including M16 assault rifles, M203 40mm grenade launchers and Belgian MINIMI 5.56mm light machine guns.

GREY MAIL   Threat by a defendant in a trial to expose intelligence activities or other sensitive information if prosecuted.

GRU   (Glavnoye Razvedyvatelnoye Upravlenie or Chief Intelligence Directorate of the General Staff) The military intelligence agency for both the former Soviet Union and now the Russian Federation.

GUBBINS, Major General Colin (1896–1976) Director of the British WWII Sabotage and Covert Action Service, the Special Operations Executive (SOE) (1942–46), Gubbins lobbied hard with the Labour Government of Clement Atlee to retain SOE in some form and though he failed, Gubbins succeeded in ensuring that many of the special abilities developed during the war and many of SOE's leading personnel were absorbed into SIS (MI6) in 1947. In fact, large parts of the SIS Clandestine services were run for much of the Cold War by former SOE officers or their protégés and Gubbins also maintained close contacts with SIS for a number of years after his official retirement. While the value of SOE's contribution to the overall outcome of WWII remains a matter of some controversy, there is little doubt that in Colin Gubbins it had a leader of genius and with a remarkable aptitude for the exceptional wartime activities he directed.

H

HALL, Admiral William Reginald (Blinker) (1870–1943)   Entering the Royal Navy, Hall saw considerable service at sea, rising to the rank of captain and the command of the battle cruiser HMS *Queen Mary* at the outbreak of WWI. Ill health forced him to give up his command when the war was only three months old. Hall, however, was promptly named Director of Naval Intelligence (DNI). Hall was able to reap the awards of the deciphering system set up by his predecessor, Captain, later Admiral, Sir Henry Oliver. Hall's first move was to organise tightly and consolidate the Navy's cryptography section, moving it into Room 40 of the old Admiralty Building in London. With a largely civilian staff of brilliant cryptographers such as Nigel de Grey, Thomas Inskip, later Lord Chancellor and Sir Philip Wilbraham, a Fellow of All Souls, it was to become famous for its ability to monitor German diplomatic and military codes and break their ciphers. Hall had more than a little good luck as well: the Magdeburg codebook, which detailed the operating, ciphers and codes of the German Navy, had been captured early in the war and Hall's cryptographers used it against all intercepted transmissions of the German fleet. Every German squadron, for instance, was required to radio its position regularly. These communications were intercepted by Room 40 and decoded so that the British knew the position of every German ship, from battle cruiser to submarine almost throughout the entire war.

It was Hall's policy to share Naval information with the rest of British intelligence community. To that end, he established valuable lines of co-operation with MI5, SIS and the Special Branch of Scotland Yard. Though Hall supervised a host of naval intelligence operations, it was Room 40 that proved to be his prize operation, including the interception of German Navy battle orders in December 1914 which called for raids along the British coast and led the British fleet to intercept the German warships. The greatest coup, however, involved the notorious 'Zimmerman Telegram', a coded message intercepted by Room 40 on 17 January 1917 from German Foreign Minister Arthur Zimmerman to the President of Mexico. The decoded message bluntly proposed that Mexico and Japan join Germany in a war on then neutral USA. Zimmerman boldly proposed that, if Mexico attacked the

US, it could regain its lost territories. Germany, then, would be free of any interference from America in crushing the forces of England and France. Three months later, on 6 April 1917, the US declared war on Germany. It was Admiral 'Blinker' Hall, far more than any other senior British intelligence officer that struck fear into the hearts of the Germans and thoroughly alarmed intelligence services elsewhere. He was certainly one of the most formidable, devious and ruthless heads of a major intelligence service there has ever been.

Following WWI, Hall entered politics and was elected as Conservative Member of Parliament for West Derby in Liverpool in 1919. When WWII broke out, he was too old for the intelligence service but he nevertheless became an active member of the Home Guard until his death in 1943.

HANDLER   Usually a case officer who is directly responsible for the operational activities of agents.

See also CONTROLLER.

HANSSEN, Robert Phillip (1945–)   Hanssen was arrested 18 February 2001 and accused of spying for the former Soviet Union and Russia since 1985. US security officials say Hanssen, a 25-year FBI veteran who never underwent a polygraph test, provided information that betrayed US agents and other US intelligence operations, including a tunnel built underneath the Soviet Embassy in Washington for eavesdropping purposes. Unlike the NSA and CIA, the FBI didn't have a policy requiring all employees to undergo polygraph tests after they are hired. Since Hanssen's arrest, the FBI has changed its policy and is starting to make all employees undergo random polygraph tests.

HELMS, Richard McGarrah (1913–)   Richard Helms was part of the CIA during the agency's most controversial period. Through CIA associates such as Richard Bissell and Sidney Gottlieb he became involved in bizarre schemes to assassinate Third World leaders and in plans to interfere with the national interests of many foreign governments. In August 1943 Helms was accepted into the ranks of the Office of Strategic Services (OSS), where he served in both England and France and, unlike many other OSS agents, Helms stayed on after VE day. Although the OSS was dismantled by President Harry Trueman in 1946, Helms remained at his post in Germany, as station chief first for the Central Intelligence Group and then the CIA.

Helms worked with Reinhard Gehlen's West German espionage operations and advised Washington in the early stages of the Cold War that the Russians had established a worldwide espionage network and were intent on using any and all means of covert operations to accomplish world domination of Communism. Returning to Washington, Helms served in CIA middle-management until, following the Bay of Pigs fiasco in 1962, Helms was made Director for Plans at the CIA and served in this capacity until 1966 when he was named Director. It was Helms's bad luck that he became DCI at a time when President Lyndon B. Johnson was obsessed with Vietnam. The controversy still rages over whether or not Helms advised Johnson to stay out of Vietnam.

Helms was also compromised by Watergate, which involved the CIA's aid to an ex-CIA man, E. Howard Hunt. When it appeared that the CIA would be directly drawn into the Watergate affair, Helms did his utmost to protect the agency, a posture that President Richard Millhouse Nixon interpreted as treacherous, and one that caused Helms to be fired by Nixon on 2 February 1973. The firing of Helms was not unexpected; Helms was considered by some to be a poor leader and a failure as director, more of a caretaker in fact. More trouble was in store when Helms appeared before the Foreign Relations Committee, prior to his assuming the ambassadorship to Iran. He swore at the time that the CIA had no part in attempting to overthrow the government of Chile under President Salvador Allende. Evidence supplied by CIA officials succeeding Helms proved him to be a liar. Helms was found guilty of perjury in 1977. He was fined $2,000 and given a two-year prison sentence, which was suspended. President Ronald Reagan, however, attempted to rehabilitate Helms's much-tarnished reputation in 1983 by awarding him the National Security Medal. Helms, by then a consultant on Middle East investments, remarked: 'I have no feelings about remorse or exoneration.'

HF DF   ('Huff-Duff') High Frequency-Direction Finding: a means of determining the direction and through the use of multiple receivers,the location of the source of radio transmissions.

HOLLIS, Sir Roger (1905–73)   Hollis first attempted to join SIS in 1938 but was rejected on grounds of ill health; however, he was accepted by MI5 in 1939. For the next six years he worked on the Russian desk. A born bureaucrat, Hollis was promoted to deputy director in 1953 and director three years later. After being knighted by the Queen, Hollis retired in 1965.

In 1945 Gouzenko, a GRU Officer at the Soviet Embassy in Ottawa defected, exposing a vast Soviet spy network. Hollis was the man chosen to go to Canada to debrief the defector. Kim Philby, the Soviet double agent working inside MI6, was supposed to perform this chore but was busy hushing up another defector. In Hollis's debriefing of Gouzenko he was told there was an important Soviet mole deep inside British Intelligence Section Five, which was taken by the anti-Hollis brigade as meaning MI5, but could indeed refer to R5 of MI6 which could then refer to Philby. Hollis faithfully reported Gouzenko's statements in full to his superiors in London. Still later, it was said that Hollis was the man who, in 1963, warned Kim Philby that he was about to be interrogated by MI5, information that caused Philby to leave Beirut and escape to the Soviet Union. In that same year Hollis is accused of failing to warn Harold Macmillan that the Soviet GRU spy Yevgeny Ivanov was at the centre of a scandal involving War Minister John Profumo and a number of call girls supposedly run by society osteopath, Stephen Ward. Hollis was also accused of being too supportive of the traitor and Soviet agent Sir Anthony Blunt when he was given immunity in exchange for his confession in 1964. Hollis was under such a cloud of suspicion that he was later asked to return to MI5 offices where he volunteered to be grilled by his accusers.

Hollis repeatedly denied having anything to do with Soviet espionage and Sir Martin Furnivall Jones, his replacement as Director-General, rightly allowed the matter to drop. A decade later, Margaret Thatcher admitted that Hollis had been interviewed but stated that he had been cleared of any wrongdoing.

There is little doubt that, in the absence of new and highly damning evidence to the contrary, Hollis must be considered one of the most 'wronged' officers in British security history. His innocence has been supported by many impartial intelligence sources and such leading figures as Sir Dick White, the only officer to head both MI5 and SIS (MI6). Even following the collapse of Communism and the access allowed to former Soviet intelligence archives; not one single shred of believable evidence has been discovered to prove that Hollis was ever a spy for the NKVD, KGB or the GRU.

HONEY TRAP   Intelligence term for a sexual entrapment operation.

HOOVER, J. (John) Edgar (1895–1972)   No other American law enforcement official in the 20th century wielded as much power as did Hoover. His influence on eight presidents and the US Congress was enormous. His name became synonymous with the FBI, which he headed for five decades. Hoover established the best forensic laboratory in the world and the identification systems he established within the

FBI have become the benchmark for other investigative services worldwide.

However, Hoover abused the power he gained, often putting himself above the law, ignoring the civil rights of citizens it was his legal duty to protect. He was determined to maintain his power base and would tolerate no criticism of the FBI or of himself. He assembled illegal files on individuals whom he then subtly blackmailed. The OC, or Official and Confidential, files were kept in his private office and these contained potentially embarrassing sexual, financial and political information about government officials and various public figures whom he might at some time need to 'persuade' in order to ensure his own position. Sometimes when his agents found a particularly sensitive snippet of information, Hoover would pass it on to the White House for the amusement of the President and members of the Cabinet. However the OC files were also said to contain information about the extramarital affairs of Franklin D. Roosevelt and his wife Eleanor, as well as numerous indiscretions from the lives of, among many others, Richard M. Nixon and both John F. Kennedy and his brother Robert.

Hoover had become the head of the Bureau of Investigation on 10 May 1934 and developed a fearsome reputation as a gangbuster; however, with the start of 1940 the FBI was required to become a counter-espionage service. Hoover began to work closely with the SIS (MI6) which had its BSC or British Security Co-ordination HQ in Rockefeller Plaza in New York, run by William Stephenson. At first, the FBI chief, under the watchful eye of Roosevelt and Churchill, extended enormous help to the BSC which grew to a force of some 2,000 officers. Hoover's insistence on ultimate control began to dominate his relationship with the British who believed that Hoover, well intentioned or not, could not set aside the police mentality or his heavy-handed methods which constantly proved more of a hindrance than a help.

The British, for instance, provided information to Hoover through one of their double agents, Dusko Popov. From his German connections, Popov had learned that the Japanese intended to attack Pearl Harbor. Hoover thought little of the information, chiefly because he regarded Popov as a playboy. He dismissed Popov's warnings because of the spy's supposed sexual prowess. According to Hoover Popov 'had a liking for bedding two girls at a time'. Hoover's obsession with the sexual activities of others would, throughout his long career, prejudice his evaluations of usable information.

Hoover deeply resented and indeed opposed the creation of OSS and, in particular, its energetic director 'Wild Bill' Donovan and he was forever objecting to the existence of OSS agents operating in any area outside of its HQ. However, Hoover's counter-intelligence operations during WWII were generally effective. It was the FBI laboratory which had discovered the Abwehr's development of the microdot, known as the *mipu* or *mikropunkt*. A Professor Zapp at the Dresden Institute had developed a process of reducing a sheet of paper to the size of a postage stamp. Then by photographing the reduced image through a reversed microscope, reducing the document once more to the minuscule size of a dot on a typewriter's 'i'.

Throughout the Cold War the FBI's counter-intelligence activities were successful in eventually breaking many Soviet Spy-networks in the USA, but had failed either to notice or prevent their activities in some cases for many years before doing so. The FBI Cointelpro programs were expanded in 1961 to include those citizens demonstrating against the Vietnam War. Hoover considered such anti-war demonstrators as a threat to national security as he did any vocal black leader and this became one of his most obvious personal vendettas. The FBI began tapping King's phone in 1957; eventually in 1964 Hoover got his 'proof' that King had been indulging in extramarital activities. Hoover made the information available to President Johnson, Congress, members of the press and even the Pope just prior to a visit paid by Dr King in August 1964. When King was about to collect his Nobel Peace Prize, Hoover launched a vicious assault on his character, branding him 'the most notorious liar in the country'. The FBI Director also sent a copy of the now infamous 'hotel tapes' which apparently proved King's infidelity, to King's wife along with an unsigned note which further revealed Hoover's personal feelings by calling King 'filthy, abnormal and fraudulent'.

Cointelpro was to come under severe criticism throughout the 1960s with critics claiming that Hoover was violating constitutional and civil rights by spying on US citizens. With political pressure mounting, Hoover was finally forced to disband Cointelpro in 1971. By that time, Hoover had also been exposed as a neurotic who felt that Moscow was behind every protest in America, a racial and sexual bigot who refused to accept minorities and women into the FBI and a scheming conspirator who kept secret files with intentions of using their contents to blackmail those who opposed him. On the night of 1 May 1972, Hoover had dined at the home of Clyde Tolson, his lifelong friend and Associate Director of the FBI, before returning home. The next morning his housekeeper found Hoover on the floor of his bedroom, the victim of a heart attack. The most powerful and devious man in America for almost fifty years was given a state funeral. However, the man the USA buried had used the instruments of power to abuse the State and the civil rights of countless people and to hide his own bigoted closet homosexuality. A final and fitting epitaph for the nation's most powerful law officer came in an interview given not long before he died when Director of the FBI, J. Edgar Hoover commented that 'law and order is first, justice is incidental'.

HOSPITAL   Russian security term for prison.

HOSTILE   Service or surveillance posing an immediate threat; term used to describe the organisations and activities of the 'opposition' services.

HOUGHTON, Harry (1906–)   Houghton served in the Royal Navy (1922–45). Houghton then joined the Navy's Underwater Weapons Establishment at Portland in Dorset, where he met Ethel 'Bunty' Gee with whom he formed a close relationship, despite the fact that he was married.

Houghton and Gee were contacted by a Canadian businessman, Gordon Lonsdale, who was later identified as the Soviet Intelligence Officer Konan Molody. The Soviet agent asked for information on British submarine detection. At the time British and NATO expertise in underwater technology was far in advance of the Russians. Both Houghton and Gee passed the information on to Lonsdale in return for several hundred pounds. Lonsdale gave the information to Peter and Helen Kroger (Morris and Leona Cohen), an 'American' couple who had a bungalow in West London where they transmitted information to Moscow via shortwave radio. Houghton was anything but discreet when it came to spending the money he earned through espionage. A naval security officer witnessed some of Houghton's sprees and found it strange that the ex-chief petty officer could have so much money on a meagre salary and navy pension. He called this to the attention of Special Branch, which put Houghton and Gee under surveillance.

In early 1962, officers from MI5 and the Special Branch arrested three members of what soon became known as the Portland Spy Ring as they were meeting near London's Old Vic Theatre. At that moment Gee was turning over a shopping basket to Lonsdale that contained a tin filled with microfilm and four large Admiralty files. The developed film produced several hundred photographs of British warships, including specifications for the nuclear submarine HMS *Dreadnought*.

The Krogers were also arrested and all five were placed on trial and sent to prison. After serving eight years Houghton and Gee were released. Lonsdale and the Krogers were later exchanged for British subjects who had been held on spying charges in the Soviet Union.

HOWARD, Edward Lee (1952–)   Aldrich Ames was not the first CIA agent to sell secrets to the Russians. That dubious honour arguably went to Edward Lee Howard, a drug-taking, heavy-drinking adventurer who, despite his suspicious background, was accepted by the CIA and trained to occupy an important position in Moscow, even though Howard had admitted to a CIA colleague that he had contemplated selling US secrets to the Soviets.

Howard joined the CIA in 1981 and in his application had admitted that he was a 'moderate' drinker and had confided that he had occasionally used drugs, such as marijuana, cocaine, Quaaludes and even LSD. None of this disquieting information caused his rejection by the agency, which concluded that his education, overseas experience and expertise with firearms made him a good candidate. He was eventually trained for special duty with the CIA's Soviet/E European (SE) division which ran all of the agency's espionage operations in the Soviet Union and the Eastern block. Howard was about to be assigned to a position in Moscow, one of the most sensitive assignments the CIA could make. He was thoroughly briefed on most of the important agent contacts the CIA had in Moscow, as well as important espionage operations the CIA was then conducting elsewhere behind the Iron Curtain. A short time before Howard was to be sent to Moscow, CIA officials became more concerned with his drinking problems. He was ordered to take a polygraph test that revealed Howard was still using drugs; following this he resigned. A Soviet defector, Yurchenko, some time later claimed that a CIA agent who bore the KGB codename ROBERT had met with Soviet officials in Austria in late 1984 and had turned over secrets in return for large sums of cash. Yurchenko did not know ROBERT personally, but he did know that this agent had been specially trained for a post in Moscow but had been suddenly 'removed' before being sent to Russia.

The CIA quickly realised that ROBERT could be none other than Edward Lee Howard. Yurchenko's information dovetailed with recent CIA setbacks in Moscow. The chief of station there had been sending in disturbing reports that many of the agency's operations had been 'blown'. In one recent incident, CIA officer Paul M. Stombaugh Jr, who had diplomatic cover, had been expelled from the Soviet Union for conducting espionage. Six weeks later, one of Stombaugh's agents, Adolf G. Tolkachey, a defence researcher, was arrested and later executed for treason. Other CIA agents fell victim to the KGB, all exposed by the traitorous Howard. The CIA's reaction was one of silence. Although Howard still lived in Santa Fe, working as an economic analyst for the New Mexico State Hospital, the CIA decided not to inform the FBI. On 7 August 1985, however, CIA officials finally decided to come clean and informed the FBI that it had identified ROBERT as Edward Lee Howard.

Howard may have been warned by the KGB as by then he was on a flight to Denmark. He later travelled about Europe, went to Helsinki, then back to Canada, S America, then again to Europe. Six months after he had fled the USA, he walked into the Soviet Embassy in Budapest, Hungary to be greeted warmly by his KGB caseworkers. He was flown on to Moscow where he was to be given an apartment, a country retreat, work as a consultant and a comfortable salary.

HUGGER-MUGGER Originally a British public school expression meaning close, secretive or stealthy. Often used to mean a confused or disorderly intelligence operation.

HUMINT Human source intelligence – intelligence collected by means of agents or informers.

I

ILLEGAL   An intelligence officer or agent who operates in a foreign country in the guise of a private person, often under a false identity. A KGB or SVR operative infiltrated into a target country and operating without the protection of diplomatic immunity.

IMINT   Imagery intelligence; electronically generated images. Has replaced PHOTINT or Photographic Intelligence in common usage.

IMMEDIATE   The second highest precedence for CIA cable communications.

IMPERSONAL COMMUNICATIONS   Secret communication techniques used between a case officer and an agent when no physical contact is possible or desired.

INDIA   *JIC Joint Intelligence Committe* The JIC is responsible for the analysis of intelligence data provided by the Intelligence Bureau and the RAW, the Directorate of Military Intelligence, the Directorate of Naval Intelligence and the Directorate of Air Intelligence. The Joint Intelligence Committee has its own secretariat, which works under the overall control of the Cabinet Secretariat. It would also be called upon to advise the CCS or Cabinet Committee on Security along with the JCOS or Joint Chiefs of Staff of the Indian Armed Forces in the event of a crisis that might lead to a war. Ultimate control of the intelligence services should rest with the National Security Council (NSC) established on 24 August 1990, and which includes the Prime Minister as Chairman, and the Home Minister, External Affairs Minister, Defence Minister and Finance Minister as members. *RAW Research and Analysis Wing* established in 1968, The Cabinet Secretariat Research and Analysis Wing is India's most powerful and the main external intelligence agency. RAW has become an effective instrument of India's national power and has assumed a significant role in formulating India's domestic and foreign policies. Working directly under the Prime Minister, the structure of the Research & Analysis Wing is largely kept secret from Parliament.

The RAW has so far had only limited success in dealing with separatist movements in Manipur and Tripura in the northeast, Tamil

Nadu in the south, and Punjab and Kashmir in the northwestern part of the country. However, RAW was specifically targeted on Pakistan from the beginning and its formation was based on the belief that Pakistan was supplying weapons to Sikh terrorists, and providing shelter and training to the guerrillas in Pakistan. Pakistan has accused the Research and Analysis Wing of sponsoring sabotage in Punjab, where RAW is alleged to have supported the Seraiki movement, providing financial support to promote its activities in Pakistan and organising an International Seraiki Conference in Delhi in November–December 1993. RAW has an extensive network of agents and anti-government elements within Pakistan, including dissident elements from various sectarian and ethnic groups of Sindh and Punjab. A disproportionate amount of its operations are directed to defeating the widescale Muslim insurgency in Kashmir which had already cost some 35,000 lives by early 2002.

RAW also has a long history of activity in Bangladesh, supporting both secular forces and the area's Hindu minority. The involvement of RAW in East Pakistan is believed to date back to 1969 when it promoted dissatisfaction against the largely West Pakistan Government in East Pakistan, including funding Mujibur Rahmanh's general election victory in 1970 and providing both training and weapons for the separatist Mukti Bahini.

The RAW and the Ministry of External Affairs are provided with a considerable budget each year for use as 'discretionary grants' for foreign influence operations. These funds have supported organisations fighting Sikh and Kashmiri separatists in the UK, Canada and the US. An extensive network of Indian operatives is controlled by the Indian Embassy in Washington DC while the embassy's covert activities are reported to include limited COMINT activities. In 1996 an Indian diplomat was implicated in a scandal over illegal funding of political candidates in the US. Lalit H. Gadhia, a naturalised US citizen of Indian origin, was sentenced to three months imprisonment by The US District Court in Baltimore for funnelling campaign contributions to influence US lawmakers. Over $46,000 provided by Devendra Singh, a RAW intelligence officer working out of the Washington embassy in 1995 reached some twenty Democratic Congressional candidates including Senators Charles S. Robb, Paul S. Sarbanes and Representatives Benjamin L. Cardin and Steny H. Hoyer.

The origin of the Indian Intelligence Services is in the Colonial Period when the British were not only interested in preventing internal unrest but defending their Empire against the threats from Central

Asia posed by Imperial Russia. The first real organised intelligence organisation was established in British India during 1892–93 with the appointment of Major General Charles McGregor to the leadership of the nascent *Department of Intelligence*. Russia had strong imperial ambitions and a special interest in South Asia and the intelligence office in St. Petersburg collected information about the Indian government. Russian officers on the borders disguised themselves as the workers of the East India Company to collect information on the British Indian administrative, political and military structures.

Before General McGregor's appointment, an organisation called the Survey of India, located in Dehra Dun, had performed the basic intelligence functions. It gathered topographical information, made maps based on the information provided by its agents on the borders and also assessed the fighting order of the Russian military, troop disposition and composition.

The Department of Intelligence structure had its roots firmly in the state institutions of British colonial India and its military organisation. The Department of Intelligence predated the formation in Britain during 1909 of what would later become the Secret Intelligence Service (MI6). Its creation was partly the result of the activities of Russian interests and its well-placed intelligence machinery, and partially due to the domestic needs of consolidation within the British Raj in India. Both SIS of what would become the Secret Intelligence Service (M16). To some extent the DoI outperformed the SIS in collection of the most sensitive information within Southern Asia and both SIS and MI5 were to recruit many of their intelligence officers from the Indian services over the years to the extent that MI5 was at one time accused of being staffed by retired Indian colonial 'policemen'.

IB Intelligence Bureau The Intelligence Bureau is the Indian government's domestic intelligence agency, and reputedly the world's oldest intelligence agency. It is rather difficult to ascertain what the IB does, since its operations are carefully shrouded in secrecy. In addition to domestic intelligence responsibilities, the IB is particularly tasked, since 1951, with intelligence collection in border areas. This was a task entrusted to military intelligence organisations prior to independence in 1947. The IB is also responsible for 'black bag' operations such as the interception of mail, phone tapping and has an active disinformation department.

Joint Cipher Bureau The inter-services Joint Cipher Bureau has primary responsibility for Cryptology, SIGINT and COMSEC providing co-ordination and direction to the other military service organisations with similar mission. It controls the activities of a number of listening sites including the major SIGINT facility at Charbatia. These are often maintained by the military and are mainly sited along the Pakistani, Kashmiri, Chinese, Nepalese and Myanmar borders and on the coast opposite Sri Lanka. It also maintains SIGINT and Maritime Surveillance sites on a number of the Islands groups in the Bay of Bengal. A number of Indian Air Force aircraft have been modified for Electronic Warfare (EW) and ELINT (Electronic Intelligence), while some Indian warships and merchant vessels have also been fitted out for surveillance operations. *CBI Central Bureau of Investigation* The Central Bureau of Investigation is India's premier investigating agency and responsible for a wide variety of criminal and national security matters and was established on 1 April 1963. It evolved from the Special Police Establishment established in 1941. The CBI was responsible for the inquiry into the Bofors Case when associates of the late prime minister Rajiv Gandhi were linked to alleged pay-offs made in the mid-1980s by the Swedish arms firm AB Bofors. It is reported that some US$40 million in illegal payments were moved from Britain and Panama to secret Swiss banks for assistance given during the US$1,300 million arms purchase of 410 howitzer field guns.

Defence Intelligence Agency Created in March 2002 in response to the growth of advenced technology, external threats and international terrorism to co-ordinate all the activities of the army, navy and air force intelligence services. It also finally breaks the civilian stranglehold on military intelligence maintained for decades by the RAW and IB, and unlike its predecessors including the Directorate General of Military Intelligence (DGMI), the DIA will have a major operational section dealing specifically with terrorism and perceptions of threats to internal security.

Special Protection Group The Special Protection Group provides protection for the President, Prime Minister and members of their immediate families, as well as VIPs and foreign dignitaries. They are trained like the US Secret Service and include recruits from the NSG commandos. The protection provided includes close bodyguards, during a journey by road, rail, aircraft or any other means of transport. It includes the venues for functions, engagements, residence or halts and comprises ring round teams, isolation cordons, the sterile zone around the rostrum and access control to the person or members of his immediate family. The SPG is divided broadly into the following main categories: *OPERATIONS* responsible for the actual protection duties with components like the Communications Wing, Technical Wing and

Transport Wing; *INTELLIGENCE* and *TOURS*: this last category looks after the threat assessment, internal intelligence vetting of personnel and organisation of tours.

INDIA, SPECIAL FORCES The Para-Commandos are now India's premier Special Forces, formed after the 1965 Indo-Pakistan war highlighted the need for an enhanced elite special operation capability. The first two Battalions, the 9th and 10th, first saw major conflict during the 1971 war, when they took part in the invasion of East Pakistan, now Bangladesh. Both units were also to play a part in the ill-fated peacekeeping operation in Sri Lanka in 1988 during the height of the civil war with the Tamil separatists. Further units have been added – the late 1970s saw the formation of the 1st Punjab and in 1990 the 21st Maratha Light Infantry which now form the 'Red Devils' Parachute (Special Forces).

Since 1978–79 the Para-Commandos have been trained in HALO (High Altitude-Low Opening) parachute techniques, with their trademark black jumpsuits, wrist altimeters, square canopy, leaf pattern parachutes, and armed with modern automatic weapons, grenades, and a jack knife. This unit provides the Indian Army with a powerful and adaptable special force capability, tasked for a wide range of counter-insurgency and anti-terrorist missions. Their tasks include clandestine operations, sabotage and intelligence gathering behind the enemy's front line. Their training is of the highest quality: marksmanship, combat shooting, heliborne-insertion, combat swimming, explosives ordnance disposal, mountain warfare techniques, prisoner of war rescue, surveillance, and HALO and HAHO (High Altitude-High Opening). They regularly cross-train with Special Forces from other armies and personnel are sent on specialist courses abroad. They can call on the whole range of standard issue Indian Army weapons for counter-insurgency operations. For clandestine operations they have access to specially bought in small arms, such as the 9mm Israeli UZI & 9mm German MP5A2/3 submachine guns, 5.56mm US M16A2 assault rifles, and a range of specialist sniper rifles including the 7.62 mm Mauser SP66, PSG-1/MSG-90 and the SSG-2000. They are equipped with a wide range of specialist communications and GPS.

However, the Counter-Terrorist units will increasingly be provided by the *National Security Group (NSG)*: this elite 12,000 strong force is known as the 'Black Cats' because of the distinctive black dungarees worn by its Commandos. In addition there is a small Special Protection

Group (SPG) formed in 1984 after the assassination of Mrs Ghandi to provide VIP bodyguards and protection for both National Government and visiting foreign officials.

INDICATION AND WARNING Intelligence activities directed to detect and report time-sensitive intelligence information relating to potential threats from hostile nations or terrorist groups against a country or its allies.

INDONESIA *Badan Koordinasi Intelijen Negara – State Intelligence Coordinating Agency (BAKIN)*: the central intelligence-gathering body, which provides analysis of both domestic and foreign intelligence gathered by its own personnel and from other civilian and military sources. It is under the direct control of the President and has its own secure communications network. A major reorganisation in 1992 strengthened the President's independent access to intelligence when BAKIN took over many of the security and intelligence functions formerly performed by BAKORSTANAS and its predecessor, the infamous KOPKAMTIB.

In the wake of Suharto's US-inspired military coup and the birth of the New Order regime in 1965, hundreds of thousands were detained in a vast number of prisons, hastily prepared detention centres, work camps and military units. Known by the acronym TAPOL (Tanahan Politik or political prisoner), even official estimates admit to up to 750,000 prisoners. The military quickly established the intelligence body, KOPKAMTIB, to administer the arrest, interrogation and trials of TAPOLs.

KOPKAMTIB later became the foremost intelligence agency, which focused primarily on mounting internal security operations and collecting intelligence data. However, its original function was to purge the government and armed forces of the PKI or Communist Party members and others suspected of complicity with the Communists. By the late 1960s, that task had been largely completed with over one million Indonesians having been killed or simply 'disappeared' in an orgy of violence. The lists used by the Indonesian intelligence and security services to arrest, torture and murder their victims had been largely compiled by the CIA and handed to the new Military Dictatorship in late 1965. Political offences and acts regarded as threats to national security were usually prosecuted under Presidential Decree No. 11 of 1963 concerning the eradication of subversive activities. Promulgated as a statute in 1969, it granted far-reaching authority in dealing with almost any act that did not conform to government policy and carried a maximum penalty of death. The special statutes also contained special procedures that differed in important respects from those in the Criminal Procedures Code. Thus, for example, while the code stated that a suspect could only be held a maximum of 120 days before being brought to trial, the subversion law allowed suspects to be held up to one year.

The most prominent use of the special procedures regarding political offences involved KOPKAMTIB's use of mass arrests and detention of hundreds of thousands of persons in connection with the 1965 coup attempt, most of whom were never charged or tried. These prisoners were classified as group A, B or C, according to the government's perception of how deeply they had been involved in the events of 1965 or in any of the banned organisations, including the PKI. Between 1969 and 1979 KOPKAMTIB ran a separate penal colony on Buru Island for Group B prisoners, who were convicted on charges of indirect involvement in the 1965 attempted coup. In late 1979, following the nationwide release of Group B prisoners, the penal colony on Buru Island was closed and the island was designated a transmigration site. The majority of KOPKAMTIB's many victims, however, simply ceased to exist with no documentation or record kept marking their elimination and disposal. As part of the 1985 armed forces reorganisation, KOPKAMTIB was disbanded.

BAKORSTANAS (Agency for Coordination of Assistance for the Consolidation of National Security): this agency inherited KOPKAMTIB's widespread powers; however, the changes reflected both a consolidation of the national security situation and a streamlined intelligence and security apparatus able to operate within the reorganised armed forces structure. The key organisations in the revised BAKORSTANAS system were the ten army KODAMs and the two intelligence agencies, the State Intelligence Coordinating Agency (BAKIN) and Armed Forces Strategic Intelligence Agency (BAIS), the ABRI (Armed Forces) agency for intelligence dealing with external defence and internal security, analysis and operational functions. After the elimination of KOPKAMTIB in 1985, BAIS received a major infusion of personnel, funds and power. The BAKORSTANAS operates outside the legal code and has wide discretion to detain and interrogate persons thought to threaten national security. It is probably this organisation that plays the leading role in organising and directing the brutal suppression of countless separatist groups in Indonesia by well-armed paramilitaries. The torture, murder and wide-scale intimidation of such groups was highlighted by the events in East Timor in 1990–99 when only the intervention of an Australian-led UN peacekeeping force prevented yet another bloodbath at the hands of the Indonesian nationalist militia.

INDONESIA, SPECIAL FORCES   The Indonesian Army's Special Operations Command (KOPASSUS) is a strike force whose main missions are intelligence operations, counter-insurgency and anti-subversive operations. KOPASSUS, often known as the Red Berets, has seen its areas of operation expanded recently to cover all the main areas of Indonesia vulnerable to foreign intervention, such as Borneo or Irian Jaya.

It conducts missions such as intelligence gathering, infiltration, reconnaissance and 'militia' training behind the lines in areas liberated by anti-government insurgents or in the case of a possible intervention by a foreign power. Its training, while of a high commando standard, falls well short of the multi-role capability expected of Western elite units. KOPASSUS receive the best of new weapons and have an interesting array available including French FNC SSIV-1, Russian AK47 & US M16 assault rifles, Belgian FN MINI light machine guns and Israeli UZI sub-machine guns.

Indonesia is full of separatist movements and while most are poorly armed and trained, KOPASSUS has still been called upon to support the local territorial garrisons on many occasions, often with brutal effectiveness. In the major reorganisation of June 1996, KOPASSUS was not only increased in size with the addition of two extra battalions, but also returned to the original 'formation' of its establishment in 1952. This was done to simplify its structure and to allow the better use of manpower to ensure that at least 25 per cent are on active duty at any one time. KOPASSUS has long been considered the elite corps of the Indonesian Army and it has traditionally emphasised its compact size and rapid strike potential. KOPASSUS operates throughout Indonesia and in clandestine intelligence operations in neighbouring countries, particularly with Group-4 CIS based in Jakarta. It also has gained the unfortunate reputation of being very closely associated with human rights abuses and 'disappearances', as well as with being responsible for the arming and training of militias guilty of the mass slaughter of civilians in East Timor and elsewhere.

It now has five groups and a Presidential Guard Group with around a total of 6,000 personnel. Its HQ is at Cijantung, Jakarta, Java; Group-1 Strike-Para Commando (three Battalions) are based in Western Java; Group-2 Strike-Para Commando (three Battalions) are based in Central Java; Group-3 Training Command are based in

Western Java; Group-4 Combat Intelligence Squadron-sized are based in S Jakarta, Java; and Group-5 Counter-Terrorism Battalion-sized are based in S Jakarta and are trained in a wide range of hostage rescue and anti-hijack techniques; Group-Presidential Guards (PASPAMRES) battalion-sized are based in S Jakarta, providing close protection for the President and senior government ministers.

INDUSTRIAL ESPIONAGE   *see* ECONOMIC INTELLIGENCE.

INFILTRATION   Secretly or covertly moving an operative into a target area with the idea that their presence will go undetected for the appropriate amount of time.

INMAN, Admiral Bobby Ray (1931–)   A US intelligence officer of considerable importance and intellect, Inman was successively the Director of Naval Intelligence (1974), Vice Director NSA (1975), Director of NSA (1977) and Deputy Director of Central Intelligence (DDCI) (1981). Apparently disillusioned with the Intelligence community and struggling with a personality conflict with the DCI William Casey, he resigned in mid 1982.

INSCOM   US Army Intelligence and Security Command since 1977. HQ at Fort Belvoir, Virginia.

INTELLIGENCE   The product of collection, processing, evaluation and analysis of information concerning foreign countries or areas.

INTELLIGENCE CYCLE   Planning and direction, collection, processing, production and analysis, and dissemination or distribution make up the several parts of the process by which an agency matches production with requirements.

INTELLIGENCE ESTIMATE   (UK: INTELLIGENCE APPRECIATION) The appraisal of all available intelligence relating to specific requirement relating to potential hostile actions or developments.

INTELLIGENCE OFFICER   A professional member of an intelligence service.

INTELLIGENCE OVERSIGHT   Political 'management' of intelligence activities. The CIA has been 'accountable' to the President of the USA through the National Security Council since 1947 and this oversight capability was in theory strengthened by the formation of the Presidents Foreign Intelligence Advisory Board (PFIAB) by President Eisenhower in 1956.

INTELLIGENCE PRODUCER Intelligence service or staff that participates in the production stage of the INTELLIGENCE CYCLE and INTELLIGENCE REQUIREMENT.

INTELLIGENCE REQUIREMENT A general or specific subject upon which intelligence is required.

INTERCEPTION OF ORAL COMMUNICATIONS Euphemism for bugging.

INTERDEPARTMENTAL INTELLIGENCE Synthesis of intelligence gathered by numerous agencies and departments that transcends their individual needs.

IRAN *Vezarat-e Ettela'at va Amniat-e Keshvar* (*Ministry of Intelligence and Security, VEVAK*): little is publicly known about the Ministry of Security (SAVAK)'s successor agency, SAVAMA, which was formed soon after the Islamic revolution that overthrew the Shah of Iran in 1978–79. The new revolutionary government's keen desire to gain an upper hand over leftist guerrilla organisations and the war with Iraq influenced leading IRP leaders to relax their previously unrelenting pursuit of military intelligence personnel which had resulted in the execution of countless innocent and sorely needed senior officers. The 1984 reorganisation of the security services created the VEVAK; the Ministry of Information and Security which then assumed the role formerly played by SAVAMA. Key religious leaders, including Majlis speaker Hashemi-Rafsanjani, insisted on recalling former intelligence officers to help the regime eliminate domestic opposition. Consequently, some intelligence officers and low-ranking SAVAK and army intelligence officials were asked to return to government service because of their specialised knowledge of the Iranian left. Others had acquired in-depth knowledge of Iraq's Baath Party and proved to be invaluable in helping decision-makers.

Indeed some of SAVAK's intelligence-gathering operations and networks were re-activated and turned, and then handed over to VEVAK. The Islamic Republic of Iran adopted Khomeini's philosophy of Velayat-e Faqih, or 'Islamic Rule', calling for the imposition of absolute authority over the populace and also extending this authority to all Muslims, i.e. 'exporting revolution'. This is used to justify Iran's support for international terrorism.

VEVAK personnel are either attached as diplomats in Iranian embassies and consulate offices or as Ministry of Guidance and Propaganda representatives. Non-official covers include Iran Air or students, businessmen or tradesmen as well as members of opposition groups. VEVAK has frequently relied on the foreign branches of Iranian state-controlled banks to place intelligence agents and to finance terrorist operations. In Germany, for instance, the most prominent is Bank Melli, which maintains branches in Hamburg, Frankfurt and Dusseldorf.

Iran is widely recognised as the world's leading supporter of international terrorism and, since the creation of the Islamic state in 1979, the country has used terrorism as an integral part of its foreign and military policies. Iranian leaders view terrorism as a valid tool to accomplish their political objectives. Despite a marked Western reluctance to deal with Iranian-sponsored terrorist outrages and accept its widespread use as a political tool, many impartial observers have concluded that Iran has either been directly responsible for or, at the very least, heavily involved in numerous major incidents. These quite probably included the destruction of Pan Am Flight 103 over Lockerbie in 1988 and the attacks on 11 September 2001 in Washington, DC and New York.

Terrorist operations are reviewed and approved at the highest levels of the Iranian government, and the President of Iran is involved in the approval process of all major terrorist operations. Iranian sponsored terrorism has had two major goals: punishing opponents of the Islamic regime and expanding the Islamic movement throughout the Persian Gulf region. VEVAK is also responsible for intelligence collection to support terrorist operations and for liaison activities with supported terrorist groups and Muslim fundamentalist movements such as Islamic Jihad and even Al-Qa'ida. The VEVAK Special Operations Department has also conducted terrorist operations in support of Iranian objectives and against Iranian dissidents. VEVAK-supported Mujahedin units have assisted in the training of selected Bosnian army elements since 1993 and along with Osama bin Laden's Al-Qa'ida organisation played a major role in supporting and arming the Muslim Albanian separatists of the KLA in the Yugoslav province of Kosovo in 1998–99. In a strange twist of fate, the KLA also received considerable help and weapons from Al-Qa'ida's bitterest enemy, the CIA.

The Joint Committee for Special Operations consists of Iran's president, its top religious authority, and other senior security officials, including representatives of the Pasdaran or Guardians of the Revolution, the Ministry of Foreign Affairs and the Ministry of Security and Intelligence. It is responsible for co-ordinating activities devoted to gathering intelligence and special weapons technology abroad, as well as activities within the Iranian exile community.

The headquarters of Iranian intelligence in Europe was for many years housed in the diplomatic mission in Bonn at Godesberger Allee 133–137. Here some twenty staff members worked for VEVAK, while representatives from other agencies also used the building's specially secured third floor, where six offices and a radio room were reserved for agents. Some 100,000 Iranians living in Germany today are still being monitored and opposition members harassed by VEVAK. Operations also continue to try to obtain commercially or by covert means, advanced nuclear, chemical and biological weapons technology from both Europe and the USA. Other operations bases include the consulate in Frankfurt and in Hamburg both the consulate and the 'Imam-Ali Mosque', one of the largest Muslim religious centres outside the Islamic world. Iranian intelligence agencies are also mounting extensive operations in Bosnia, Kosovo and Albania to gather information and counter Western influence. The JCSO is collaborating closely with a pro-Iranian faction in Bosnia's intelligence service, the Agency for Investigation and Documentation. But Iran's intelligence operations extend far beyond the training programme and are aimed at influencing a broad range of Bosnian institutions.

Qods (Jerusalem) Force Iranian Revolutionary Guard Corps (IRGC – Pasdaran-e Inqilab): while the Constitution of Iran entrusts the military with guarding Iran's territorial integrity and political independence, it gives the Revolutionary Guard, established under a decree issued by Khomeini on 5 May 1979, the ultimate responsibility of guarding the Revolution itself. The foreign operations include the activities of Hizbollah and Islamic Jihad is usually carried out through the *Committee on Foreign Intelligence Abroad* and the *Committee on Implementation of Actions Abroad*. As with agents of Ministry of Intelligence, Pasdaran personnel operate through front companies and non-governmental organisations, employees or officials of trading companies, banks, cultural centres or as representatives of the Foundation of the Oppressed and Dispossessed (Bonyade-e-Mostafazan), or the Martyrs Foundation. The Qods Force is also responsible for extraterritorial operations, including terrorist operations and training Islamic fundamentalist terrorist groups, and for gathering the intelligence required for targeting and attack planning. The Pasdaran has contacts with underground movements in the Gulf region, in particular Kuwait, Bahrain, Qatar and the United Arab Emirates and Pasdaran members are assigned to Iranian diplomatic missions, where, in the course of routine intelligence activities, they monitor dissidents.

The largest branch of Pasdaran foreign operations consists of approximately 12,000 Arabic speaking Iranians, Afghans, Iraqis, Lebanese Shiites and N Africans who trained in Iran or received training in Afghanistan during the Afghan war years. Presently these foreign operatives receive training in Iran, Sudan and Lebanon, and include the Hizbollah 'Party of Allah' intelligence, logistics and operational terrorist units in the Lebanon. Pasdaran foreign operations also involve training and arming Kurdish groups, Kashmiris, the Balouchis, Afghans, Bosnians and the Kosovan separatists. The Pasdaran has also supported the establishment of Hizbollah branches in the Lebanon, Iraqi Kurdistan, Jordan, Somalia, Sudan and Palestine and the Islamic Jihad terrorists in many other Muslim countries including Egypt, Turkey, Chechnya, Kosovo and in Caucasia. The obvious overlap of the areas of interest between the Iranian sponsored terrorist groups and those of Osama bin Laden's Islamic Jihad movement, which has at least 12 separate groups including Al-Qa'ida, is so considerable that close co-operation between the two is highly probable. Hizbollah has been implicated in the counterfeiting of US dollars and European currencies, both to finance its operations and to disrupt Western economies by impairing international trade and tourism.

SAVAK (Ministry of Security): Shah-an-Shah Mohammad Reza Pahlevi was restored to the Peacock Throne of Iran with the assistance of the Central Intelligence Agency and Britain's Secret Intelligence Service in 1953 in a coup organised against the left-leaning government of Dr Mohammad Mossadeq. The catalyst for this action was Mossadeq's imminent nationalisation of Western interests in Iran's oil industry. CIA subsequently provided organisational and training assistance for the establishment of an intelligence organisation for the Shah. Formed under the guidance of USA and Israeli intelligence officers in 1957, SAVAK developed into an effective secret agency. It increasingly came to symbolise the Shah's rule from 1963 to 1979, a period of corruption in the royal family, one-party rule, the torture and execution of tens of thousands of political prisoners, suppression of dissent, and alienation of the religious masses. The USA reinforced its position as the Shah's protector and supporter, sowing the seeds of the anti-Americanism that later came to a head during the Islamic revolution against the monarchy. SAVAK became a law unto itself, having legal authority to arrest and detain suspected persons indefinitely. SAVAK operated its own prisons in Tehran, including the infamous Komitch and Evin facilities. SAVAK's torture methods included electric shock, whipping, beating, inserting broken glass and pouring boiling water into the rectum, tying weights to the testicles and the extraction of teeth and nails. Many of these activities were carried out without any institutional checks and occasionally in front of the victim's family.

In 1978 the increasing opposition to the Shah erupted in widespread demonstrations and rioting. SAVAK and the military responded with brutal repression that resulted in the deaths of some 15,000 people and seriously injured at least another 50,000. Recognising that even this level of violence had failed to crush the rebellion, the Shah abdicated the Peacock Throne and fled Iran on 16 January 1979. Despite decades of oppressive surveillance by SAVAK and with the unstinted co-operation of the CIA, the massive anti-Government and anti-American demonstrations that so quickly swept the Shah from power came as a considerable surprise to the US intelligence community and the White House. However, it was no surprise that SAVAK was later singled out as a primary target for reprisals with its HQ destroyed and many prominent senior officers tried and executed by 'komiteh' representatives.

IRAN, SPECIAL FORCES While the Iranian Special Operations Command includes a full Special Forces Division with at least three Light Infantry Brigades, in addition the 23rd Commando Division has raised special force units trained in mountain warfare, particularly along the border with Afghanistan. The Iranian Special Forces, although tough, motivated, reliable and with a considerable ability to conduct clandestine operations, lack the true special operations skills necessary to be considered an elite fighting force and Iran simply does not have the infrastructure or finances to produce a true Special Force capability at the moment.

Within the Revolutionary Guards Corps (Pasdaran Inqilab) are a range of small covert action units whose tasks go well beyond the normal range of Special Operations. These include maintaining Islamic purity, assassination and the training, arming and control of Islamic Terrorist groups both within the Middle East, and increasingly throughout the world. Pasdaran-trained special force personnel are attached to the main Iranian Intelligence services and often operate within Europe and the USA on clandestine intelligence gathering and subversive missions.

IRAQ Virtually every aspect of internal security and intelligence gathering within Iraq appeared to have one particular aim and that was to protect the political power base of the repressive one-party apparatus that had been dominated by Saddam Hussein since July 1979. The overall control of the Intelligence community was through the National Security Council headquartered at the Presidential Palace in Baghdad and which met on a weekly basis, chaired by Saddam Hussein.

Special Security Service – *Al Amn al-Khas*: this highly secretive organisation, also known as the Presidential Affairs Department, or Special Security Organisation, was the least known but most feared of the Ba'athist security organisations. The Amn al Khas acted as an elite guard unit and was established at the end of the Iran–Iraq War in 1988. Iraq had developed an extensive arms and technology procurement network in the 1980s to acquire technology, hardware and personnel for its nuclear, chemical, biological weapons and missile programmes. Amn al Khas played a major role in the co-ordination and implementation of a covert network of front companies operating in the USA and Europe to acquire equipment, technologies, supplies and material. The organisation's primary task was to protect the Ba'ath leadership in Iraq and in consequence the Amn al Khas only accepted the most loyal troops serving in the Iraqi armed forces, and whose dedication to Ba'athism and to Saddam Hussein personally had been tested on numerous occasions. These elite personnel face considerable danger because of the frequent assassination attempts on Saddam Hussein and on his close associates, which usually lead to loss of life among the personal bodyguards. Survivors are, however, generously rewarded. Among its various responsibilities, the Special Security Organisation carried out surveillance of senior officers holding the most sensitive positions within Intelligence, Military Intelligence, Military Engineering, and the military security agencies. It was organised into *Office of the Director General* which is located in the Hai Al Tashriya district of Baghdad. *The Special Branch* was located in Hai Al Tashriya district next to the Director General's Office. It included the Security Office that monitored personnel to ensure their loyalty to the regime and included the Identification Department, which produced all credentials for this service, the special Hai Al Tashriya prison and the security department.

The Al Amn al-Khas HQ was in Palestine Street in Baghdad, while the main operational facilities were in a large multi-storey building near the Rashid Hotel, and the Communications security and intelligence office was housed in the Al Hayat Building. Considerable attempts were made both to harden and conceal a back up HQ, with in-built redundancy particularly for the command and communications facilities and to some considerable extent the buildings listed above had become symbols of the state, rather than actual operational facilities. This indeed applied to many of the high prestige buildings that would figure so prominently in the first few days of the US air attacks on Iraq in 2003. To lessen the chances of assassination either from his own officers, dissident elements, foreign special forces or by a selective mission flown by the USAF, Saddam Hussein used a vast network of 'safe-houses', disinformation about places, times and routes when travelling or holding meetings and a number of 'lookalikes', at least one of whom is believed to have died during an attempted assassination.

Iraq's own clandestine arms-purchasing agencies, set up in the 1970s and controlled during much of the 1980s by Hussein Kamil, used operatives of the Amn Al Khas or special security to run the operations outside Iraq. The acquisition network used front companies throughout Europe and the USA, and although many were identified in 1990–92, a large number survived and were used in sanction busting until 2003. Indeed UNSCOM's 8th report confirmed that these organisations were still very active as late as 1998. It is interesting to note that the Iraqis placed an agent, a Syrian translator, inside UNSCOM who is believed to have successfully kept the Iraqi Intelligence service informed of the United Nations investigations.

The Amn al-Khas controlled illegal payments, bribes etc. via its Audit office in Hai Al Tashriya, Baghdad. It was the effective paymaster for the Abu Nidal Organisation established in 1974, and although expelled from Iraq in 1982, was thereafter still controlled by the GID and played a part in smuggling weapons and technology into Iraq and also to Palestine. However, another major part of the smuggling operation concerned the Office of the Presidential Palace or OPP in Baghdad, and this organisation in turn controlled a spider's web of groups. A special department of the Military Intelligence Security Battalion of the OPP liaises with the Republican Guard Forces Command or Al Faris Command, which passed its requests for action and funds through the National Security Council and Joint Operations Room to the appropriate clandestine action department. These organisations provided the weapons and other items such as communications equipment via supply depots at Al Qaim in western Iraq and the Rumashid staging post near H3 on the Jordanian border for transport via Syria and Lebanon or through Jordan. The actual movement was the ultimate responsibility of the Amn al-Khas and its smuggling network in Syria and the Lebanon, i.e. the Syrian Army, Intelligence Service, Abu Nidal, Hezbollah and Hamas. Weapon training for Palestinian personnel on new equipment was carried out under cover of Syrian Army activities in the Bekaa Valley in eastern Lebanon.

Da'irat al Mukhabarat al Amah – Department of General Intelligence (GDI): the Mukhabarat was by far the most infamous and most important part of Iraq's state security system. It is very much a part of Saddam Hussein's own rise to power. Hussein had taken part in the unsuccessful attempt by the Ba'ath Party to assassinate Iraq's then ruler Abd al Karim Qasim in October 1959. He controlled the Jihaz al Khas or Special Apparatus department from 1964 to 1966, which concentrated on intelligence and security work. After the Ba'ath Party finally took power on 17 July 1968 Hussein expanded the Jihaz al-Khas and extended his control to the Amn or state internal security department. In 1973 the Jihaz was transformed into the Da'irat al Mukhabarat al Amah after an attempted coup by the Director of Internal Security. Saddam Hussein relied heavily upon his loyal Mukhabarat for vital support during his takeover of the presidency in 1979 and they continued to protect him very effectively thereafter. The main elements of the Mukharabat are believed to have been:

- *The Special Bureau or 1st Directorate* – conducted sensitive and highly confidential operations, including the interrogation and torture of suspects, internal security and assassination of 'enemies of the state';
- *3rd Directorate – Surveillance* – targets included suspects and possible recruits; situated in the National Security Institute in the Jihad district of Baghdad;
- *5th Directorate – Counter-Intelligence* – responsible for detecting and countering foreign agents; concentrated in particular on the US, British, Israeli, Iranian, Syrian and Turkish intelligence services; worked closely with the 3rd, 4th, 14th & 18th Directorates;
- *6th Directorate Mukhabarat Security* – located inside the main Mukhabarat complex, the Sixth Directorate is responsible for the conduct of officers and other ranks within the organisation; its members worked within all departments as this directorate is responsible for issuing security passes, passports, 'legends', i.e. the creation of false or misleading personal biographies, identification papers and a wide range of other material required for clandestine or 'black' operations;

- *7th Directorate – Al Haakimiya prison* – the Mukhabarat conducted interrogations in a variety of 'safe' houses and buildings, but still used the old main interrogation centre located on 52nd Street opposite the Passport Office as a holding centre; it was a large prison building with two or three floors underground;
- *9th Directorate – Secret Operations* – these were controlled from Khandai, 23km west of Baghdad;
- *19th Directorate – Personnel Supervision* – this directorate was responsible for surveillance of all Mukhabarat employees, including opening mail, bugging property, phone tapping and mobile surveillance;
- *22nd Directorate* – Protection – provided bodyguards and other personal protection for senior Mukhabarat officials and visiting VIPs;
- *14th Directorate – Office of Special Operations* – conducted the training of agents for clandestine and sensitive special operations outside the country. The main training facility was located in Salman Pak 12 miles southeast of Baghdad, and was one of the most important and largest in the Mukhabarat. This directorate undertook the most secret operations and was responsible for the attempted assassination of former President George Bush during a visit to Kuwait in April 1993 and the assassination of Talib Al Suheil. It conducted joint operations with the Mujahideen Khalq Organisation, and undertakes training of specially selected officers for this type of operation. Agents also attended a special school which provided language courses and orientation concerning the country to which they were to be assigned.

The Salman Pak complex was also the base for intensive training courses for terrorist groups where they were schooled in hijacking techniques, sabotage, assassination and other 'black' operations. This was confirmed in 2001 by two Iraqi military intelligence defectors who reported that there were mixed nationality units including Saudis, Egyptians and Chechens at Salman Pak. Usually about 40 strong, these terrorist units received up to five months of intensive training. However the terrorist units were actually under the control of Iraq's Al-Mukhabarat Intelligence Service and in particular a section called the Directorate of Special Operations. The foreign fighters were segregated from Iraqi military personnel, except during certain specific training sessions. The overall training programme included assassination, kidnapping, sabotage or hijacking of aircraft, buses, trains, sabotage of public utilities and most importantly of all, in the use of chemical, biological and possibly crude nuclear devices. However, the training also included how to prepare and carry out suicide attacks and involved how to get access to the flight cabin, getting weapons on board, security weakness, terrorising the passengers and crew. The Arabs are volunteers and arrive in small teams with the sole intention of eventually carrying out suicide operations directed towards US targets.

● *Brigade of Mukhabarat.* Acted as a rapid military intervention force responsible for the protection of buildings and senior personnel. It is this unit that is responsible for the removal of senior officers to safe locations in the event of a major external attack.

Al-Istikhbarat al-Askariyya – Military Intelligence Service: since the early 1980s until 2003, this organisation was under direct presidential control. Its main HQ complex is in the Aladhamia area of Baghdad and included a prison and interrogation centre in addition to a variety of support facilities. The Istikhbarat also had a facility at Al Rashid camp in Baghdad and regional HQ with special responsibilities for geographical areas of interest. Kirkuk – Iran and the Kurdish region of N Iraq; Mosul – Turkey and Syria; Basra – Gulf states and Iran and Baghdad, but separate from the main HQ – Jordan, Syria, Saudi Arabia, Iran and opposition groups.

Al Amn al-Askariyya – Military Security Service: the Askariyya was responsible for detecting and countering dissent within the armed forces. Initially constituted as part of the Special Bureau of the Estikhabarat, in 1992 it was established as an independent entity reporting directly to the Presidential Palace. It was headquartered in the Aladhamia district of Baghdad near the Military Intelligence Service HQ and was responsible for monitoring the political reliability of the armed forces.

Mudiriyat al-Amn al-Amma – General Security Service: effectively a Secret Police force which had been an element of the Ministry of the Interior until the late 1970s, when it was established as an independent agency reporting directly to the Presidential Palace. Between 1990 and 2003, the Amn had their HQ in the Al Baladiat area of the city, with the Bataween building becoming the agency's main prison. The Amn had a wide authority concerning political and economic activities defined as 'crimes', including smuggling and manifestations of disloyalty or opposition to Saddam's regime and it operates an extensive network of informers. With its pervasive local presence Amn remains an important local element in a national security environment.

However, following the defeat of Iraq in the war launched by the United States and Britain in March 2003, the entire intelligence structure had been dismantled. Certain internal security elements will probably be re-established with former Iraqi exiles and US officers of Iraqi origin. Trainined, equipped and directed by the CIA and FBI, this new service will work closely with the US Forces and the United Nations to counter any ongoing resistance by members of the former regime. It will probably be greatly expanded as soon as an Iraqi-controlled government is formed in due course.

IRAQ, SPECIAL FORCES   The Iraqi Special Forces, having gained a considerable reputation during the 1980–88 war with Iran, surprisingly gave a poor performance in the 1991 Gulf War. A major reorganisation took place during the late 1990s to address the perceived weaknesses and greater emphasis has been placed on intelligence, physical fitness, mental toughness and motivation with the help of a small number of Russian ex-Spetsnaz Special Force officers. The problems caused by UN sanctions have been partly overcome by the widespread 'black market' smuggling of new weapons, communications and other specialist surveillance equipment from mainly Russia and the Ukraine.

Under the control of the Office of the Presidential Palace, with its HQ in Baghdad, there were a number of ultra-reliable Special Forces with just one major mission, the protection of Saddam Hussein. These units included the 'Green Berets' or 33rd Special Forces Brigade, and the Special Republican Guard Motorised Infantry Brigade; both were Rapid Reaction units. There were also a number of specially trained detachments for dedicated Counter-Terrorist and Hostage Rescue operations.

Following the defeat of the Iraqi armed forces in March and April 2003 it is very likely that some form of counter-insurgency force will be quickly re-established with the help of the US Special Forces to provide an effective Iraqi-based counter to any possible outbreak of guerrilla warfare by members of the former regime in the Kurdish territories in the north or amongst the Iranian-backed Shia majority.

IRELAND, NORTHERN ('THE TROUBLES')   On 8 May 1992, the British Home Secretary, Kenneth Clarke, announced that the Security Service, MI5, was to be given the lead responsibility for intelligence work against the IRA in Britain, taking over from the police Special Branch. MI5 already had primary responsibility for intelligence work in relation to loyalist (e.g. Ulster Volunteer Force, Ulster Freedom Fighters) and international terrorism, as well as IRA activity in Europe and elsewhere. The new policy reflects a substantial shift in the priorities of British intelligence compared to the period of the Cold War. Nearly half of MI5's staff now works on the conflict over N Ireland, though this is likely to change following the events of 11 September 2001. In N Ireland the Royal Ulster Constabulary's Special Branch (RUC SB) plays the main role in gathering intelligence and, in theory, has overall responsibility for policing and intelligence work. It works alongside three other bodies: MI5, Military Intelligence (intelligence units of the British Army) and the Secret Intelligence Service (MI6). MI5 is thought to have an active staff of about 100 in Ireland, most of whom are based in the North. The British Army has a number of units mainly concerned with surveillance and intelligence analysis, but it also runs informers and has operational control over the elite Special Air Service (SAS) which has killed around 50 people, including 30 IRA volunteers, since 1969.

Since the early years of the current conflict in Ireland, there has been rivalry and conflict between MI5 and MI6, as well as between the British military and the RUC. The co-ordination of intelligence agencies has therefore been a long-standing issue. In the late 1970s, the first of three Tasking and Coordination Groups was established. Based at Castlereagh in Belfast, the TCGs proved so successful in 'tasking the SAS for executive action', i.e. for assassination, that two more were established soon afterwards for the RUC's other regions – one at Gough Barracks, Armagh, and the other in Derry. The TCGs combine the intelligence of RUC Special Branch, MI5 and the Army, allowing the linking together of informer-based intelligence and the surveillance and ambush activities of undercover units. The Army representative on TCGs is almost always a veteran of an SAS or 14th Intelligence Company tour. The bulk of intelligence available to the TCGs comes not from MI5, FRU or 14th Intelligence Co., but from RUC SB. A review of policies governing the use of informers and the sharing of intelligence, conducted by a retired MI5 officer, led to the setting up of the Provincial Executive Committee in 1992. This provides top level coordination between the intelligence agencies within the North and includes the Army's Commander of Land Forces, the head of RUC SB, a Deputy Chief Constable with special responsibility for police/Army liaison, and MI5's Director and Coordinator of Intelligence.

ISRAEL Following the 'mandate' over Palestine granted to Britain by the League of Nations in 1922 the Zionist underground resistance force, the Haganah, established an intelligence service known as Sherut Yedioth. Later known simply as the *SHAI* it began worldwide operations as early as 1929; its task was to collect political intelligence for the sake of Zionist propaganda and to infiltrate the anti-Zionist and extremist groups in Palestine as well as the neighbouring Arab countries. An additional agency was also created to help the flow of Jewish immigrants into Palestine as Britain tightly controlled the numbers who could legally enter the country for fear of a serious adverse reaction from the majority Arab population. Mossad le Aliyah Bet was established in Austria, Bulgaria, France, Rumania, Switzerland and Turkey to help increase the numbers of illegal immigrants. This it did by obtaining false passports and papers, arranging undercover routes out of Europe and providing ships willing to take the risks involved in being caught smuggling Jews into British controlled Palestine.

The Haganah created a military arm, Palmach and Rekhesh, which was responsible for covert operations and arms smuggling for the underground Jewish forces that had infiltrated the Arab townships. After becoming an independent state in 1948, the SHAI was disbanded in favour of Israeli Defence Forces or IDF. Its political department became responsible for foreign intelligence, while *Sherut Bitachon Klali* was formed as a general internal security and counter-espionage service, often known as *SHABAK or Shin Beth* in Hebrew. In 1951, the decision was taken to create the Central Institute for Intelligence and Special Duties or Mossad Letafkidim Meouychadim, more commonly known as *Mossad 'The Institute'*. Its initial function was military intelligence, but after the establishment of *AMAN* Agaf Modiin Aman, a dedicated military intelligence organisation in 1953, Mossad quickly became the prime foreign intelligence service. In 1960, *LEKEM* or the Bureau of Scientific Relations, was instituted to collect scientific and technical intelligence for technological development, especially in relation to nuclear weapons.

Mossad ha-Mossad le-Modiin ule-Tafkidim Meyuhadim or *The Institute for Intelligence and Special Tasks*: Mossad, with its HQ in Tel Aviv, has overall responsibility for HUMINT collection, covert action and counter-terrorism. Its focus is on Arab nations and organisations and those nations thought to be enemies of Israel. It is also responsible for the clandestine movement of Jewish refugees out of Syria, Iran and Ethiopia. Mossad has a total of eight departments, the six most important being:

- *The Collections Department* – the largest, with responsibility for espionage operations, with offices abroad under both diplomatic and unofficial cover; the department consists of a number of desks responsible for specific geographical regions, directing case officers based at 'stations' around the world, and the agents they control;
- *Political Action and Liaison Department* – conducts political activities and liaison with friendly foreign intelligence services and with nations with which Israel does not have normal diplomatic relations; in larger stations, such as Paris, Mossad customarily had under embassy cover two regional controllers: one to serve the Collections Department and the other the Political Action and Liaison Department;
- *Special Operations Division* or *Metsada* – conducts highly sensitive assassination, sabotage, paramilitary, and psychological warfare operations;
- *LAP* or *Lohamah Psichlogit Department* – responsible for psychological warfare, propaganda and deception operations;
- *Research Department* – responsible for intelligence production, including daily situation reports, weekly summaries and detailed monthly reports; the Department is organised into 15 geographically specialised sections or 'desks', including the USA, Canada and W Europe, Latin America, Former Soviet Union, China, Africa, the Maghreb (Morocco, Algeria, Tunisia), Libya, Iraq, Jordan, Syria, Saudi Arabia, the United Arab Emirates and Iran; a WMD intelligence desk is focused on special weapons related issues;
- *Technology Department* – responsible for development of advanced technologies for support of Mossad operations.

Mossad has been highly successful over the years in penetrating hostile Arab and Communist intelligence services and gaining a privileged position within the Western intelligence community. During the 1960s Mossad officer Eli Cohen infiltrated the top echelons of the Syrian government. Cohen radioed information to Israel for two years before he was discovered and publicly hanged in a Damascus square. Another Mossad agent, Wolfgang Lotz, established himself in Cairo, became acquainted with high-ranking Egyptian military and police officers, and obtained information on missile sites and on German scientists working on the Egyptian rocket programme. In 1962 and 1963 Mossad succeeded in a well-planned operation to intimidate several key German scientists working in that programme.

In 1960, Mossad carried out one of its most famous operations, the kidnapping of Nazi war criminal Adolph Eichmann from Argentina bringing him to Israel for trial and eventual execution.

The Israeli intelligence community has a justified reputation for resorting to assassination as a matter of state policy. During the 1970s, Mossad assassinated several Arabs connected with the Black September terrorist group. However, on occasions they missed their target rather publicly as in Lillehammer Norway on 7 January 1974 when Mossad agents mistakenly killed Ahmad Boushiki, an Algerian waiter carrying a Moroccan passport, whom they mistook for PLO security head Ali Ahmad Salameh. Following the killing the Mossad agents were arrested and tried before a Norwegian court. Five Israeli officers were convicted and served short jail sentences. Believed to have masterminded the 1972 massacre of Israeli athletes at the Munich Olympics, Salameh was eventually killed in 1979 by a Mossad-inspired car-bomb explosion in Lebanon.

Mossad was able to destabilise the PLO seriously in April 1988. An assassination team travelled by fast naval craft from Israel to invade the well-guarded residence in Tunis of Arafat's deputy, Abu Jihad, considered to be the principal PLO planner of military and terrorist operations against Israel. In a well-planned and executed lightning attack, the Israeli team successfully eliminated their target and escaped safely. In another operation the Canadian scientist, Gerald Bull, who had developed the long-range 'Super Gun' for Iraq was killed by a Mossad special operations team at his Brussels apartment in March 1990, effectively halting the development of the Supergun project. On 24 September 1997 Mossad operatives attempted to assassinate Khalid Meshaal, a top political leader of the Palestinian group Hamas. The assassins entered Jordan on fake Canadian passports and injected Meshaal with a poison. The Jordanian Government was able to wring a number of concessions out of Israel in the aftermath of the fiasco, including the release of the founder of Hamas, Shaykh Ahmad Yasin, from an Israeli jail. By 2002, however, Mossad in concert with the Special Forces of the IDF had carried out many hundreds of assassinations of leading Arabs, particularly within the Palestinian community, thus giving the distinct appearance of having decided that in the absence of a negotiated peace, the planned and wide-scale use of assassinating their Arab opponents was a viable, if temporary alternative to all-out war.

Sherut ha-Bitachon ha-Klali or *Shin Bet – General Security Service*: Shin Bet, the Israeli counter-intelligence and internal security service, is organised into three main operational departments and five support departments. Arab Affairs Department is responsible for anti-terrorist operations, political subversion and maintenance of an index on Arab terrorists. Shin Bet detachments, known as HENZA, worked with AMAN undercover detachments known as the *Mista'arvim* to counter the Arab insurgency such as the Intifada. This Department also has active service detachments to counter the paramilitary activities of Hamas, Hezbollah and other Arab organisations. *Non-Arab Affairs Department* formerly divided into Communist and non-Communist sections, concerned itself with all other countries, including penetrating foreign intelligence services and diplomatic missions in Israel and interrogating immigrants from the Former Soviet Union and E Europe. *Protective Security Department* is responsible for protecting Israeli government buildings and embassies, defence industries, scientific installations, industrial plants, and the El Al national airline.

With a reputation for being tough, determined and astute, Shin Beth had run agent networks within Arab countries for many years. But one of their major successes came when their network of agents and informers in the territories occupied during the 1967 war quickly destroyed the PLO's effectiveness there, forcing their withdrawal to bases in Jordan. Shin Bet's reputation as a highly proficient internal security agency has been tarnished severely on occasions. In April 1984, Israeli troops stormed a bus hijacked by four Palestinians in the Gaza Strip. Although two of the hijackers survived, they were later beaten to death by Shin Bet agents. The resulting attempted cover-up, scandal and resignations rocked the Israeli intelligence community; however, the president granted pardons to Shin Bet's senior officers who had joined in the cover-up and to the agents implicated in the killings.

Aman Agaf ha-Modi'in or *Military Intelligence*: Aman is an independent military intelligence service, co-equal with the army, navy and air force within the IDF. It is responsible for producing comprehensive national intelligence estimates for the Prime Minister and the Cabinet, daily intelligence reports, risk of war estimates, target studies on nearby Arab countries, and communications intercepts. Aman also conducts across-border agent operations. *Foreign Relations Department* is responsible for liaison with foreign intelligence services and the activities of Israeli military attachés abroad. Aman was held responsible for the failure to obtain early warning of the joint Egyptian-Syrian attack that launched the October 1973 War as many indications of the attack were received but faulty assessments at higher levels prevented adequate warning being given to the IDF Chiefs of Staff. During preparations for the invasion of Lebanon in 1982, however, Aman correctly assessed the weaknesses of the Christian Phalange militia on which Israel was depending and correctly predicted that a clash with the Syrian garrison in Lebanon was inevitable. The Israeli Air Force operate advanced reconnaissance drones and specially equipped aircraft for Electronic Warfare and Intelligence surveillance as well as for covert special operations, while the Israeli Navy can provide both submarines and fast patrol craft for AMAN operations.

In addition AMAN controls Unit-8200, the SIGINT organisation with its HQ at Herzliyya. There are a number of interception facilities operated by this organisation including those located on the Golan Heights, Har Avital which monitors Syria, Iraq and Iran, Mount Hermon which monitors both Lebanon and Syria and Mount Meiron. Another site is found at Mitzpah Ramon, while the joint NSA-AMAN SIGINT complex on Dahlak Island off the Eritrean coast has proved of great value to the USA during the War on Terrorism in 2001–02 by monitoring possible terrorist communications between Somalia, Yemen, Sudan and Afghanistan, Iran and Iraq. Indeed it was probably Dahlak that provided the information that allowed Israel to seize more than 50 tonnes of Iranian weapons destined for Palestine in January 2002.

Lekem – Leshkat Kesher Madao or *Bureau of Scientific Relations*: until officially disbanded in 1986 Lekem collected scientific and technical intelligence particularly on nuclear and other weapons of mass destruction (WMD). Lekem was abolished following the scandal in the USA caused by the arrest of Jonathan Pollard for espionage on behalf of Israel. Pollard, a US naval intelligence employee in Washington, was sentenced to life imprisonment after receiving considerable sums of money for delivering vast quantities of classified documents to the Lekem officers in the Israeli embassy.

ISRAEL, SPECIAL FORCES *The AMAN Miltary Intelligence* have a further range of dedicated units such as unit Yachmam for intelligence and target acquisition, unit T'zasam for special reconnaissance duties in Palestinian areas, while unit-504 handles human clandestine intelligence resources. In addition there is Sayeret Duvedevan, a secretive unit based on the Israeli–Egyptian border. It is a 'mistaravim', or 'becoming an Arab' force for deep-cover clandestine intelligence operations inside Egypt and is expert at merging successfully with the local population.

The Sayeret MATKAL General Staff Deep Reconnaissance Unit is Israel's primary counter-terrorism and intelligence-gathering entity formed in 1958 and absorbing the operational experience gained by the original Israeli special operations force, Unit-101 and indeed adopting its SAS-style structure. In 1974 Matkal and other special force units started to acquire genuine Counter-Terrorist training provided by the British SAS and the US SEAL and Delta units, and by 1980 had a high degree of both operational experience and capability. In 1985 the Israelis established a discreet Special Forces base at Mitkan Adam with a Special Training Installation (Maha-7208) and the Counter-Terrorism Warfare School (Unit-707).

This now included hostage-rescue, close-quarter battle, combat shooting and other specialist facilities. Training, which is remarkably tough even by normal special force standards, includes advanced intelligence and surveillance techniques, assassination, 'booby-traps and specialist explosives, combat swimming, sniping, specialist para-chuting (high altitude-low opening HALO etc.), cold weather and desert warfare techniques, heliborne insertion and sabotage. Weapons used include US M16AI automatic rifles and its CAR-15 carbine version, 9mm Mini-Uzi, 9mm P226 automatic pistol, Remington 870 combat shotgun; sniper rifles include Mauser SR82, US M24 7.62mm and the long-range .5 Barrett M82A1. In addition they have available for use a wide range of captured or specially bought in small arms for undercover and non-attributable opera-tions. This highly capable force, the Sayeret MATKAL, which is tasked for intelligence operations outside Israel and along with its civilian counterpart, the unit Yamam, a GSG9 style counter-terrorist unit tasked for domestic operations, are required to provide two action-ready units at all times for counter-terrorist operations anywhere in the world.

ITALY *SISDE Servizio Informazioni Generali e Sicurezza – Service for Information & Democratic Security*: responsible for internal security and under the overall control of the Ministry of the Interio, SISDE was only established in 1977. It concentrates its activities on international terrorism, organised crime and political subversion. However, although it was formed to give Italy a non-military security service free of its reputation for corruption and political intrigue, it soon became apparent that its senior personnel were still involved with organisations not in keeping with their duties. A parliamentary commission investigating the influence of the Masonic Lodge P2 in 1981 found that both the Directors of SISDE and the SISMI were affiliated members. Some observers have commented that it is this very close connection with hidden channels of influence and organised crime that has led many to consider the Italian Secret Services and SISDE in particular, to be past masters at the art of intrigue. The CIA has often called upon these skills, particularly in the Balkans, and the Italian services have a justified reputation for getting a job done, even if in an unorthodox manner. There was acute embarrassment in the 1960s when it emerged that the military intelligence service had bugged the president's residence, the Quirinale Palace, and Pope John XXIII's library in the Vatican – as a courtesy to CIA director William Colby. In the wake of the 11 September attacks on the USA the Italian secret services will be authorised by the government to break the law from March 2002 and intelligence officers will be guaranteed impunity if they were carrying out state security operations at the time.

SISMI Servizio perle Informazioni e la Sicurezza Militare – Military Information Service: the Italian military intelligence services have gone through a series of cosmetic name changes since WWII, usually following a scandal involving organised crime, political manipulation or sponsored right-wing terrorism. SIFAR Servizio Informazioni Forze Armate was established in 1949 and replaced in 1965 by SID Servizio Informazioni Difesa only to see its entire staff taken on by SISMI in 1977. This was despite being disbanded for malpractice when the former SID Deputy Director and several other senior officers were jailed for illegal arms trafficking, association with organised crime, embezzlement, corruption and subversive activities. However, in this case the real key players escaped prosecution and retained their political power. SISMI also has responsibility for the activities of the *SIOS Secondo Reparto* Military Service Intelligence Units. SISMI also controls the activities at the SIGINT bases at Sorico and with the NSA at San Vito.

ITALY, SPECIAL FORCES   These include the NOCS (special operations division of the anti-terrorism state police), known as the *teste di cuoio* or leatherheads because of their distinctive headgear; a paramilitary force of only 50 men which achieved lasting fame with the rescue of US General James Dozier from the terrorist Red Brigade in January 1982. NOCS trains at the Abbosanta Special Base in Sardinia, where they train intensively in many special forces techniques, but with a considerable concentration on night operations and the use of sophisticated electronic surveillance equipment.

The GIS has a strength of only 100 and operates with a 30-man operations section and a specialist sniper squad; it was formed in 1977 and is made up of soldiers from the Ist Carabinnieri Parachute Regiment. It trains regularly for anti-hijack and hostage rescue missions at several major Italian airports and has a reputation for outstanding fitness and technical ability in such areas as demolition, breaching, rappelling and other entry techniques. The GIS also has its own SAS-style 'killing house' for combat shooting and hostage rescue scenarios and now operates both within and outside Italy. The GIS has rightly acquired a fearsome reputation and is considered an elite among the world's elite.

However, the main Special Forces unit is provided by the Folgore Parachute Brigade at Livorno, near Pisa. The Folgore forms part of the Italian Army's Rapid Reaction force, and within this it includes the 1st Carabinnieri Parachute Regiment, but more importantly the 9th Para-Assault Regiment 'col. Moschin' (the name refers to a mountain peak, col. Moschin) – this unit was created for sabotage and intelligence operations during the Cold War, but proved to be so well organised and flexible that their responsibilities were extended to cover all aspects of special intelligence operations and counter-terrorism; it is structured into the 1st Battalion 'Incursori' (raiders) with two companies, the 110th and the 120th 'Incursori' and one company of 'Guastatori' (long-range reconnaissance and patrol or LRRP) and, unlike the 'Incursori', it is part of the NATO's ACE Rapid Reaction Corps or ARRC.

The 'col. Moschin' regiment has taken part in counter-terrorist and special operations missions in the Alto-Adige (1960s), the 'Achille Lauro' hijacking of an ocean liner (1985), secret missions to Kurdistan and Ethiopia (1991), Somalia (1992–95), Rwanda (1994) and the Yemen (1994). They were also deployed in Bosnia, Albania and Kosovo (1996–2000). This regiment provides the Italian Army with one of the best trained, most effective and most widely experienced special force units to be found anywhere in the world today.

The training program for this regiment includes an initial eight-month period at the Pisa parachute school and it is a further year before the surviving volunteers, virtually all NCOs or officers, are passed fit to join the 'col. Moschin'. The training is aimed at ensuring that each soldier has the ability to operate in any environment, they are taught survival, evasion and escape techniques, interrogation, counter-interrogation and free-fall parachuting (HALO and HAHO), heliborne insertion, mountain, desert and underwater warfare, combat shooting and sniping, unarmed combat, clandestine intelligence operations, hostage rescue, counter-terrorism, sabotage and long-range patrol.

It can call upon a specialist squadron of the Italian Air Force from the 15th wing in the form of HH3F helicopters or from the 46th Air Brigade with G222 (US C27 Spartan) fixed wing transports for special operations. The weapons available to this unit include 9mm Beretta-92 automatic pistols, 9mm MP5 sub-machine guns, 5.56mm SCP70/90 para automatic rifle, MSG90, SP86 and Barrett M82A1 sniper rifles, Beretta RS202 combat shotguns, 5.56mm Minimi machine guns and even Milan anti-tank missiles.

J

JACK IN THE BOX   A dummy placed in a car to deceive surveillance teams about the actual numbers of persons in a vehicle.

JAPAN   *Naicho – Naikaku Chosashitsu Betsushitsu – Cabinet Research Office – CRO*: Japan's joint intelligence agency is the Naicho, a small section of the Prime Minister's Office which provides analysis of information from abroad. It is supposed to act as a co-ordinating agency for other groups in the government, but has appeared rather ineffectual. However considerable efforts are being made by the new Government to give Japan fully fledged foreign intelligence services with the CRO being strengthened to provide a clearing-house for intelligence material.

Security Bureau of the National Police Agency: the Bureau formulates and supervises the execution of security policies. It is also responsible for security surveillance of foreigners and radical political groups, including investigation of violations of the Alien Registration Law and administration of the Entry and Exit Control Law. A secret unit of the Japanese National Police Agency was set up to deal with potential sabotage and subversive activities by N Korea. It has recruited and trained N Koreans to gather intelligence on Japan's behalf. According to some reports, high-ranking members of the Chosen Soren, the N Korean residents' organisation in Japan, have been recruited to work for the Security Bureau and that this has resulted in the exposure of a number of Communist agents.

The Second Department of Investigation of the PSIA: this organisation was originally formed as a domestic, Cold War security service and is now being progressively run down as other services gain control of both internal and external intelligence. However, the 2nd division has provided liaison with over 30 intelligence agencies in the world, including the CIA, FBI, SIS (MI6), MOSSAD, ASIS, DGSE and BND and this will undoubtedly survive in one form or another.

The Intelligence and Analysis Bureau is responsible for stategic intelligence and is divided into the General Management Division, the First Analysis Division and the Second Analysis Division. The Bureau plans and formulates a comprehensive policy on how the Ministry as a whole collects, provides analysis and information. The system has also been further improved to meet the increasingly complex and volatile international situation, the functions of regional and international analysis of security, military and terrorist threats are being strengthened.

Jouhou Honbu – Defence Intelligence Office – DIO: a research office in the DA's Bureau of Defense Policy was created in July 1998, responsible for making recommendations on security and defence policy. Within the Bureau of Defence Policy, the First Intelligence Division in charge of domestic intelligence became the Intelligence Division, and the Second Division in charge of foreign intelligence, the International Planning Division. It is part of the overall restructuring to enhance the capability of the Japanese intelligence services in the 21st century.

The Defence Intelligence HQ – DIH: equivalent of the US Defence Intelligence Agency (DIA) or Britain's Defence Services intelligence (DSI), it integrates the five intelligence elements from its three services, the Japan Defence Agency (JDA) and the Joint Staff Council. Based in the new JDA HQ in Tokyo's Ichigaya district it is organised into five directorates:

- *The Administration/General HQ Division* – carries out administrative functions and provides logistic support;
- *The Planning Division* – concerned with HUMINT collection and has officers assigned to more than 40 overseas diplomatic missions as defence attachés;
- *The Imagery Division* – created by consolidating the Satellite Image Analysis Divisions of the three SDFs;
- *The Signals Intelligence (SIGINT) Division* – has 10 sections and is the largest division at the intelligence HQ; it maintains a network of listening bases at Futenma and Hanza on Okinawa, Higashi, Miho, Rebunto, Shiraho and Wakkanai; it also has a liaison section at the giant NSA base of Misawa; the electronic intelligence unit at the GSDF facility in Ichigaya, has three separate sections for monitoring N Korean communications; in addition there are six other communications offices in Kobunato in Niigata Prefecture, Oi in Saitama Prefecture, Tachiarai in Fukushima Prefecture, and Kikaijima (in Kagoshima Prefecture);
- *The Analysis Division* – responsible for summarising and assessing information.

JAPAN, SPECIAL FORCES   The Japanese intelligence services have had to deal effectively with the growing threat of extremist behaviour, such as the eight deadly attacks by members of the Japanese Red Army on the Tokyo subway since 1972 or the Aum Shinri Kyo religious group that used Sarin nerve gas in an attack that killed 12 and injured 5,500 Tokyo subway passengers in 1995. It resulted in 26 stations and two complete lines being shut down with the consequence that the city largely ground to halt. The National Police, who had to commit around a third of their available manpower to the incident for several weeks, responded in April 1996 by forming the Special Assault Team. This paramilitary force is organised into ten platoons each of twenty personnel and are trained to the highest possible military standards by, in particular, the French GIGN Gendarmerie special operations unit.

They are considered very skilled and proficient in a wide range of techniques from heliborne insertion, combat shooting, hostage rescue, counter-terrorism, anti-hijacking, with a particular interest in buses and subways, and close-quarter battle situations. There is in addition a small and very discreet special hostage rescue unit for highly delicate operations, and these extremely fit and well-trained personnel are known as the 'modern ninja'.

JEDBURGHS OSS and SOE covert teams dropped into occupied Europe after D-Day to help resistance organisations behind the German front lines.

JENNIFER, PROJECT On 11 April 1968, a Soviet Golf-2 class submarine, the K-129 capable of carrying three nuclear-armed SSN-5 SLBM (Submarine Launched Ballistic Missiles) sank after a series of explosions, in the Pacific. In 1974 the CIA secretly commissioned billionaire Howard Hughes, of the Hughes Aircraft company and a number of other enterprises, to salvage the submarine. Hughes Summa Corporation built a special salvage ship; the *Glomar Explorer* equipped with a 'moon pool' into which a 209-foot derrick could lift salvaged material up to 800 tons in weight. Refrigeration facilities were installed to handle up to 100 bodies and the *Glomar Explorer* set sail for the submarine's presumed position with its commanding officer carrying booklets containing both American and Russian burial services.

The results of the CIA operation, codenamed PROJECT JENNIFER, were never fully detailed. It is reported that only the bow section of the submarine's hull was salvaged; it is believed to have contained the bodies of 70 Soviet sailors who were later buried at sea after full naval ceremonies. However it is possible that the real object of the search, the fin containing the missile launch tubes, was partially recovered along with at least one of the missiles remaining intact. If this was the case, then it was an intelligence prize worth all the effort and great financial outlay by the CIA.

JIC   Joint Intelligence Centre. Draws together information from many sources within an intelligence community and acts as a distribution centre for vital intelligence.

JOHN, Otto (1909–97)   John was an energetic anti-Nazi and, at the onset of WWII, exempted from military service because of his important job as legal adviser to the Lufthansa, enabling him to continue to travel widely and thus to act as a courier and contact man for the anti-Hitler groups. As such he worked with the British SOE, SIS (MI6) and the US OSS keeping these Allied intelligence services abreast of these group's activities when visiting neutral Lisbon and Madrid. It was in Lisbon in 1943 that John informed SIS that the head of the Abwehr, Admiral Canaris, wanted a high-level meeting with the British. There was no response as Britain had no wish to anger its Soviet allies by promoting internal German resistance to the Nazis and in addition all reports from Lisbon landed on Kim Philby's desk in SIS HQ. Philby instructed the Lisbon SIS Station to break off all contact with Otto John and his report about the plot to assassinate Hitler was suppressed by Philby on the grounds that it was 'unreliable'. After the failed bomb attempt on Hitler's aircraft on 20 July 1944, John escaped to Madrid and later to Lisbon and on to London where he spent the rest of the war working in the PWE or Political Warfare Executive. After the war he served as an interpreter at the Nuremberg war crimes trial.

In 1950 W Germany's President Theodor Heuss, one of John's old friends, appointed him director of the Federal Internal Security Office, which was later retitled the Bureau for the Protection of the Constitution or BfV. It was John's paramount duty to control Soviet espionage in W Germany. Since his experience in counter-intelligence was limited, the organisation was slow in developing into an effective agency. In 1954, however, John submitted a report that would have vastly improved the BfV.

In July 1954, on the tenth anniversary of the failed assassination attempt on Hitler, Otto John, president of the Bfv at the time, took part in the memorial service in West Berlin as one of the few surviving conspirators. That same night, he disappeared. Shortly afterwards, he reappeared in the East German media and criticised the rearmament of the Federal Republic of Germany as being an obstacle to the reunification of Germany. Soviet defector Piotr Deriabin would later claim that he had been blackmailed into defecting by the KGB over his wartime links to British intelligence.

In December 1955, he returned to the West and was arrested. A

West German court later opted not to believe Otto John's confused evidence or his explanations. It dealt with him severely, doubling the sentence demanded by the prosecution, giving John four years' imprisonment. Following his release, he fought tirelessly for the repeal of his conviction. His portrayal of events has been complemented by statements by, among others, Markus Wolf, the former head of the East German secret service and the Danish journalist Henrik Bonde-Henrikesen who made it possible for John to return to the Federal Republic. Otto John later moved to Austria and retired.

JOHNSON, Robert Lee (1920–72)   A US Army sergeant stationed in Berlin, Johnson contacted the KGB in Berlin in 1952. KGB officials patiently heard him out, then proposed to pay him for whatever small secrets he might be able to steal from US Army HQ in Berlin. They trained him secretly in West Berlin, providing Johnson with spy cameras and showing him how to take photos of documents. Johnson then introduced a fellow soldier, Sergeant James Allen Mintkenbaugh, to his KGB caseworkers. Mintkenbaugh also became a Soviet agent. Johnson eventually finished his tour of duty and returned to the US. Mintkenbaugh showed up in 1956 to reactivate Johnson for Soviet spy work, convincing him to re-enlist and attempt to get himself stationed to an important post in Europe. He did exactly that, asking that he be assigned to SHAPE. However, Johnson was given a post at the Armed Forces Station in Paris at Orly Airport instead. This had been one of the KGB's prime espionage targets.

Up to that time, the Orly Courier Station had proved to be impenetrable. Now, the Soviets would have a spy inside the very centre that dispatched all the important secrets between the Pentagon and US Army commands throughout Europe. On orders from his caseworker, Johnson volunteered for weekend guard duty, the most unpopular duty hours. He soon discovered that for several hours every Saturday night he was utterly alone at the Orly centre. It was at this time that he accessed the security vault, withdrew several packets of information from the vault and turned these over to KGB agents waiting in the parking lot outside. The information gained by the Soviets was invaluable, US contingency plans for international crises, cryptographic materials, codes, ciphers, military ORBAT, details of some US agents in Europe and up-to-date reports on North Atlantic Treaty Organisation (NATO) and Soviet military strengths and weaknesses. Johnson continued to raid the Orly security vault, making seven successful hauls before he was posted back to the US in April

1963. He was reassigned to the Pentagon where he continued to obtain information for the Soviets.

Though he had been paid well by the Russians, he began to drink even more heavily and finally in October 1964 staggered on to a bus heading for Las Vegas, mostly to escape the breakdown of his marriage. When Johnson failed to appear at his post, FBI agents investigated his disappearance. They interviewed his wife who broke down and, in a rambling statement, described what she knew of her husband's spying activities. Sober at last, Johnson turned himself over to the Las Vegas police and was later arrested and tried for treason, along with Mintkenbaugh. Both men were convicted and, in July 1965, were given 25-year prison sentences. In 1972, Johnson's son Robert, who had served in Vietnam, visited his father in prison and, for what he later described as 'personal reasons', suddenly produced a knife and stabbed his father to death.

JOINT INTELLIGENCE CENTRE (JIC)   Organisation that brings the intelligence capabilities of several individual agencies under the overall direction of a single body either permanently or for a specific operation.

JONES, Professor R.V. (Reginald Victor) (1911–97)   One of the most outstanding brains ever to be involved with Secret Intelligence work. 'RV' joined SIS (MI6) in 1939 as a Scientific Officer. His first major success came in identifying and helping to produce an effective counter to the German 'beams' used to guide their bombers on to targets in Britain. Henceforth Churchill hailed Jones as his 'boy wonder, the man who broke the bloody beams'. Jones became Assistant Director of Intelligence (Science) and SIS principal scientific adviser and his work on German secret weapons, including the V1 flying bombs and V2 ballistic missiles and on enemy radars throughout the rest of the war, was simply outstanding. Jones became the Director of Intelligence (Science) in 1946, but did not enjoy the political in-fighting it involved; he resigned and became Professor of Natural Philosophy at the University of Aberdeen. A brief period as Director of Scientific Intelligence at Churchill's direct insistence in 1952 convinced him of his preference for an academic life.

JORDAN   *General Intelligence Department – GID*: a small, but competent security service responsible for countering illegal organisations, sabotage, subversion and counter-espionage. Additional duties include combating corruption, the smuggling of arms and drugs, and counterfeiting operations. The focus of its efforts are intelligence gathering and analysis of terrorist activity, the Palestinians, Syria and Israel in particular. It works in close co-operation with the even smaller *Jihaz-al Radad – RASD* or *Directorate of General Intelligence*, the security and intelligence component of the Royal Jordanian Army General Staff.

JOURNALISTS AS INTELLIGENCE ASSETS   Intelligence services and, in particular, the CIA, KGB and SIS have long used journalism as a cover for officers serving abroad. More embarrassing to bone fide practitioners, are the number of journalists who become agents. Even a partial list covering Britain alone is interesting enough, Colin Coote of *The Times* and later editor of the *Daily Telegraph*; Frederick Voight of the *Manchester Guardian*; Geoffrey Cox of the *Daily Express*; David Walker of the *Daily Mirror*; Donald McCormick, later Foreign Manager of the *Sunday Times,* who had worked in Naval Intelligence and later wrote under the name Richard Deacon; Henry Brandon was an SIS asset; Cedric Salter formerly SOE; Anthony Terry doubled as both a journalist and an SIS officer in Vienna and Berlin. Journalists who mix spying with writing are at risk. David Holden, Chief Foreign Correspondent of the *Sunday Times*, was kidnapped and murdered in Cairo in 1977. Although the US has denied it, there is a widespread belief even among his many colleagues that he had been a long-term CIA agent. Others involved in the media with known intelligence links include Robert Maxwell and Tom Driberg.

J-STARS   Joint Surveillance and Target Acquisition Radar System. RC-135 airborne sensor and command platform designed to monitor and control the land battlefield and to provide near real time relay of the intelligence gathered.

JWICS   Joint Worldwide Intelligence Communications System (US DOD).

KAMARILLA, THE During the 18th and 19th centuries Austria established a national intelligence council called the Kamarilla with its own network of spies. The council was based on the ideas of Frederick II of Prussia brought to Vienna by the Habsburg Emperor Joseph II. There he created the new agency using espionage techniques practised in the Italian City States of Venice and Florence. Only high-level political and military officials of the Empire were appointed as members of the Kamarilla and they alone were allowed access to the secret reports prepared by the Supreme Chancellors of State or the Minister of Police, for the Emperor. The council developed a pervasive secret police network that was to become the first of its kind by involving agents of all classes and backgrounds in its networks.

The Kamarilla was primarily created to watch the armed forces and bureaucrats, but eventually would include sections on revolutionaries and subversives run by the political committee known as the Haute Police, particularly under the rule Chancellor Metternich in the first half of the 19th century. By the 1860s, Vienna had become the espionage capital of the world. Not only were there Austrian and Hungarian networks, but others run by France, Russia and Italy. The Kamarilla under pressure from these developments was disbanded but became the basis of the Austrian State and Military Intelligence services that served until the collapse of the Habsburg Empire in 1919.

K'ANG Sheng (1899–1975) The Director of Chinese Foreign Intelligence operations under Mao Zedong from 1949, K'ang was sent to Moscow in 1933 to study Soviet security and intelligence techniques, where he developed grave doubts about the Soviets' real commitment to the Chinese Communist cause and despite their obvious attempts to recruit him, remaining loyal to his beliefs. In 1934 K'ang largely took over responsibility for intelligence within the Party and made a determined effort to place agents within Chiang Kai-shek's Kuomintang intelligence services and the Chinese Nationalist armed forces. By the end of WWII and the upsurge of civil war, K'ang had achieved a paramount position within the Communist security and intelligence community. As early as 1951 he uncovered a hostile Soviet penetration of the Chinese Institute of Mathematics which had acquired a virtual Soviet control of the new computer techniques in engineering, aerodynamics and nuclear physics. It was to be the start of the serious breakdown of relations between the two Communist nations. K'ang's intelligence service compiled a dossier on Soviet hostile espionage operations, the falsification of historical documents including the clandestine redrawing of international borders in the Soviet Union's favour and much more. This sensitive document was presented to the leadership in Beijing, virtually ensuring the final split with Moscow. K'ang's greatest achievements were in the field of nuclear and scientific espionage where he was able to obtain vast amounts of information from Western sources, often quite legally. K'ang was also to plant a series of scientific 'moles', particularly within the US nuclear and hi-technology industries, most of whom have never been exposed by the security services. Kang, from his base in Beijing known as the 'Bamboo Garden', electronically monitored almost everything of importance that happened in China. This included surveillance of the Communist Party itself. He is known to have used a wide variety of eavesdropping devices to achieve this and is even believed to have bugged the personal office of Mao Zedong himself. K'ang, perhaps becoming too powerful, manipulative and tainted by the excesses of the Cultural Revolution, fell from favour in the mid 1960s and retired to die from cancer and largely in obscurity in 1975.

KELL, Sir Vernon (1873–1942)   Kell learned Polish and English as a small child. By the time he graduated from Sandhurst in 1892 and received his commission, Kell spoke many languages fluently and was immediately assigned as an interpreter to important missions abroad. He went to Moscow in 1898 where he quickly mastered the Russian language. In 1900 he was sent to China, serving with front line Western Powers troops in crushing the savage Boxer Rebellion which had threatened to annihilate the European legations in Peking.

In 1902, Kell returned to London where he was promoted to captain and assigned to the German desk at the War Office. Kell was by 1907 held in such high esteem that he was placed on the Committee of Imperial Defence. In 1909 Britain established the Secret Service Bureau, with a foreign section later to become the SIS and a Home or counter-intelligence section which would soon become known as the Security Service. Given the military cover name of MO5 or Military Operations 5 this would be changed to MI5 or Military Intelligence 5 upon the creation of a dedicated Military Intelligence Department in the reorganisation of the War Office in 1916. Vernon Kell was selected to be its first director in 1909 with two rooms, a tiny budget and a staff of three or four. Since Kell's service had no powers of arrest, he was given the services of a police detective as a temporary measure.

Kell and his tiny organisation put in a prodigious amount of work in the years preceding WWI and were in a position to delay rounding up many of the known German spies until just after England declared war on Germany in 1914. Kell waited until the last second so that his agents could arrest the entire network in one fell swoop. Among those caught in the net were: Karl Ernst, who operated a barbershop as a front for a mail drop centre; Dr Armgaard Graves; Heinrich Grosse; Frederick Gould; and George Parrott, a Royal Navy gunner working with the Germans. Throughout WWI Germany sent many more intelligence officers and agents to England but almost all of them were tracked down and imprisoned. Some of them were executed. It was Kell who directed the hunt for Germany's top spy in Great Britain, Karl Lody. This German agent used a fake US passport to enter Britain and successfully spied on several military installations in Scotland before he was tracked down in Ireland. Kell had a distinguished career throughout WWI and into the 1920s and 1930s. He rose to the rank of Major-General and was considered to be one of the world's top counter-intelligence chiefs. Under his direction MI5 gathered information on Soviet and German espionage activities throughout the 1920s and 1930s. However, by the start of WWII the Security Service was in dire need of a major reorganisation and an input of fresh blood and new ideas. Kell exhausted by more than thirty years of stress and overwork was simply not up to the task ahead.

Matters became still worse for Kell when on 14 October 1939, shortly after war between Germany and England had been declared, a German submarine under the command of Captain Gunther Prien picked its way around the Navy's anti-submarine defences in the Orkney Islands, penetrating the Royal Navy's anchorage at Scapa Flow. Prien sent a torpedo into the battleship HMS *Royal Oak,* which quickly sank, taking 834 men with her. Rumours had it that a German spy, undetected by MI5, had provided the German Navy with the information necessary to penetrate the Royal Navy's anti-submarine defences. Though this was later proved to be false, Churchill nevertheless blamed Kell for the disaster. As the new First Lord of the Admiralty, Churchill demanded action from MI5 and when he did not receive the detailed reports he expected, he again blamed Kell for dragging his feet. He also told confidantes that Kell's methods were old-fashioned and that he was not keeping pace with Willhelm Canaris' Abwehr. Then in January 1940 an explosion occurred at the Royal Gunpowder Factory, Waltham Abbey, right in Churchill's own constituency. It was attributed to German sabotage, which MI5 had again failed to prevent. Churchill blamed Kell once more, even though Scotland Yard's investigation of the explosion did not prove sabotage of any kind. Churchill apparently used the Scapa Flow sinking and the Waltham Abbey explosion as the reasons for demanding the dismissal of Kell on 25 May 1940. So embittered was Lady Kell, who managed a serviceman's canteen, that she called the staff together and snapped: 'Your precious Winston has sacked the General.' Kell retired to a small rented cottage in Buckinghamshire where he died on 27 March 1942.

KEMPEI TAI Following the 1936 army mutiny in Japan, one which was reportedly staged on orders from Emperor Hirohito to make it appear that he was merely a pawn in the hands of war-mongering militarists, the Emperor established the Kempei Tai. Hirohito, who was probably deeply involved in the military cabal ordered Lieutenant General Nakajima Kesago to head Kempei Tai, specifically stating that this secret police force was to keep order in Tokyo and throughout Japan and all lands conquered by Japan's invading armies. It was to be Kesago who presided over the terrifying 'Rape of Nanking' in 1937, delighting in the countless atrocities committed by his men, horrors which he himself detailed and directed: tens of thousands of brutal rapes; murders; the bayoneting of Chinese babies; the barbarous executions of tens of thousands of captured Chinese soldiers who were lined up, hands tied behind their backs, as they were slowly killed in bayonet practice.

Kempei Tai quickly expanded its operations, monitoring every move made by foreigners visiting Japan before WWII. Kempei Tai personnel were recruited from the Army and had to have at least six years of military service before they were accepted into the ranks of the counter-intelligence organisation. The ability to speak and learn new foreign languages, especially English, was much sought after as well as detailed knowledge of foreign countries, their people, habits, customs, political inclinations. Of the 70,000 agents – half this number being officers – working for Kempei Tai during WWII at least one-third of them spoke English and most of these had spent some time in the US. It also spent vast sums in propaganda among Japanese citizens, warning them to be alert to foreign spies, circulating millions of posters, flyers and pamphlets that urged distrust of all persons who were not Japanese. Anti-spy days were declared in which hundreds of thousands of people ranted and raved against foreign suspects, bringing to Kempei Tai officials any kind of evidence, no matter how trivial, that might implicate foreigners in espionage.

Hardly a shop or business in Japan did not display Kempei Tai posters that warned of spies in their windows. Kempei Tai monitored all radio programmes, newspapers, and periodicals, as well as all public speeches, propagandising against possible espionage agents. Through this relentless campaign, the Japanese people as a whole were whipped into fanatical distrust and hatred for all foreigners, a xenophobic passion that later led to mass genocide on the part of Japanese troops fighting on all fronts. The Kempei Tai ruled by fear, not co-operation. The Kempei Tai closely regulated the sale of all explosives, drugs, arms, electrical equipment, in fact anything that might be used by enemy agents, including those few Japanese citizens prepared to spy upon their own government. It had hundreds of thousands of informers who either volunteered information to protect themselves or were blackmailed into supplying information. Any citizen could be arrested without a stated reason and be charged with espionage, secretly imprisoned or even be executed.

As the most powerful organisation in Japan at the close of WWII, General Douglas MacArthur made it his personal business to dismantle Kempei Tai thoroughly. He exposed Kempei Tai leaders, who were held up in public disgrace as true oppressors of their own people, before sending them to prison or obscurity. However, the Kempei Tai didn't fade away, instead the tens of thousands of its surviving officers with considerable knowledge of the West and often fluent in the English language merely slipped away to offer their undoubted skills to the devastated Japanese business and industrial sectors. The former secret policemen, torturers and killers alike, played no small part in the vast resurgence of the postwar Japanese economy.

KGB (Komitet Gosudarstvenoy Bezopasnosti or Committee for State Security) The intelligence service of the former Soviet Union. The KGB's First Chief Directorate (FCD) was the branch responsible for intelligence, active measures and counter-intelligence outside of the Soviet Union. The Second Chief Directorate (SCD) was the KGB branch responsible counter-intelligence within the Soviet Union.

See also RUSSIA

KNIGHT, (Charles Henry) Maxwell (1900–68) Maxwell Knight became one of Britain's favourite radio and television naturalists as 'Uncle Max', and it is said that any visitor to his home at Camberley might find him nursing a bush-baby, feeding a giant toad, raising young cuckoos, or 'engaging in masculine repartee with a vastly experienced grey parrot'. He was also considered an excellent jazz musician who loved playing the clarinet, an avid cricketer and someone who had a keen interest in the occult. He is probably most famous for his career as an Agent Controller and anti-Soviet expert during WWII. Having joined SIS (MI6) in April 1925, Knight moved only after the political subversion section he worked for was transferred from SIS to MI5 in 1931. Knight would go on to be one of the most successful, but controversial officers in MI5, running his own department, B5(b), out of a set of rooms in Dolphin Square. Knight's close friend in NID was Ian Fleming, the author of the James Bond novels. In fact when Fleming was designing the character for Bond's boss whom he simply named 'M', he used his friend Maxwell Knight as the model.

Like Peter Wright much later in MI5 and Angleton in the CIA, Knight believed that the Soviets were a far greater threat than his superiors were prepared to accept. Eventually he would be forced to retire early on health grounds in 1956. His natural love of animals allowed him to create a full-time career as a TV naturalist in the late 1950s.

A genuine eccentric, Knight was already broadcasting on the BBC while still in MI5 and it was not unknown for a colleague in the service to be startled when a hamster suddenly poked its head out of Knight's pocket in the middle of discussing a Soviet spy network.

Aleister Crowley, 'the Great Beast', is believed to have met Knight through their mutual friend, Tom Driberg MP and Soviet spy. However, Knight had a strong interest in the occult and this attracted him to the writings of Crowley, whom he met several times around 1937. It is known that Crowley and Knight had another mutual and influential friend, Dennis Wheatley. Knight would later describe Crowley as 'a well-dressed middle-aged eccentric with the manner of an Oxford don'. It appears, according to one historian, that both Wheatley and Knight 'jointly applied to Crowley as novices and he accepted them as pupils'. Although Harry Smith, Maxwell Knight's nephew, has been quick to point out, 'My uncle stressed that his interest – and also Wheatley's – was purely academic.' According to Wheatley, he was merely studying magic for use in his novels. In fact, Crowley would later become a model for some of the characters in Wheatley's books. Unfortunately very little survives regarding the facts of Knight and Crowley's relationship.

Some writers have suggested there were more reasons why Knight wanted to meet Crowley than 'occult interest'. For example, some authors have hinted that Knight's first wife, Gladys Poole, apparently knew Aleister Crowley before marrying Knight. It is also rumoured that she had a bad personal experience with the Great Beast. What actually transpired between the two is not recorded. Some have gone so far as stating that this experience with Crowley might be directly responsible for her suicide on 17 November 1934, but there is absolutely no evidence which has ever surfaced to support this outlandish claim. It is still a mystery why Knight wished to meet the notorious Aleister Crowley. We can only speculate. Maybe Knight simply wanted to know the truth regarding his wife's suicide, and he felt that perhaps Crowley held some of the answers. However, most likely Crowley did not. His wife's suicide is fairly well documented and it is safe to say that it had little to do with Aleister Crowley. One of the more notorious if not famous incidents involving Crowley and Knight centred on the defection of a prominent Nazi, Rudolf Hess. This incident also involved the author Ian Fleming who, like Maxwell, also had a strong interest in Crowley.

On Wednesday, 27 January 1968 Maxwell Knight died peacefully of heart failure in a hospital at the age of 68.

KNUCKLE DRAGGERS Name given to the CIA's Special Operations Group case officers by the other members of the Directorate of Operations.

KOREA, NORTH *National Intelligence Committee of the Central Committee of the Korean Workers Party (NIC)*: all N Korea's intelligence organisations are under the supervision of the NIC and are directly responsible to the President. The majority of the N Korean intelligence agencies are actively controlled by the Cabinet General Intelligence Bureau of the Korean Worker's Party Central Committee.

- *The Liaison Department* – responsible for conducting intelligence operations in S Korea and Japan, its agents are used to undermine the S Korean Government by supporting internal subversion and to gather information on US forces in Korea;
- *The Research Department for External Intelligence (RDEI)* – the primary agency responsible for foreign intelligence collection, the RDEI is composed of four geographic subsections, one of which is N America;
- *Central Committee of the General Association of Korean Residents in Japan (Chosen Soren)* – supports intelligence operations in Japan, assists in the infiltration of agents into S Korea, collects open source information, and diverts advanced technology for use by N Korea;
- *Reconnaissance Bureau of the General Staff Department and the State Security Department* – responsible for collecting strategic,

operational and tactical intelligence for the Ministry of the People's Armed Forces; it is also responsible for infiltrating intelligence personnel into S Korea through tunnels under the demilitarised zone and seaborne insertion;

● *The State Security Department* – responsible for N Korea's counter-intelligence and offensive counter-intelligence programme.

N Korea primarily depends upon HUMINT for intelligence collection in S Korea and other parts of the world and has only a limited SIG1NT capability which is largely focused on S Korea, but with an increasing clandestine use of ELINT vessels, Japan has now become a major target.

8th Special Operations Corps: by any consideration N Korea has one of the world's largest special operations forces. With over 80,000 elite light infantry organised into 22 brigades and at least seven independent battalions, the special operations forces are believed to be the best trained and to have the highest morale of all N Korean ground forces. The *Ministry of the People's Armed Forces* controls the bulk of the special operations forces through one of two commands, *the Reconnaissance Bureau* and the *Light Infantry Training Guidance Bureau*. The Reconnaissance Bureau is the primary organisation within the Ministry of People's Armed Forces for the collection of strategic and tactical intelligence. It also exercises operational control over agents engaged in collecting military intelligence and in the training and dispatch of unconventional warfare teams. The Light Infantry Training Guidance Bureau is directly subordinate to the General Staff Department. The party directly controls approximately 1,500 agents. In the 1970s, in support of overland insertion, N Korea began clandestine tunnelling operations along the entire DMZ, with two tunnels per forward division. By 1990 four tunnels dug on historical invasion routes from the north had been discovered by S Korean and US tunnel neutralisation teams: three in the mid-1970s and the fourth in March 1990. The S Koreans suspect there will be as many as 28 tunnels by early 2003. However, the present level of ongoing tunnelling is unknown.

KOREA, SOUTH (ROK or REPUBLIC OF KOREA) *National Intelligence Service (NIS)*: in 1995, the ANSP was relocated to a new intelligence building equipped with up-to-date facilities in Naegok-dong, southern Seoul, from its 34-year-old site in Mt Nam in downtown Seoul and Imun-dong, eastern Seoul. With the inauguration of the People's Government, on 22 January 1999 the agency was renamed the National Intelligence Service (NIS). The NIS is also responsible for a large network of secret SIGINT sites including those on Kanghwa-Do and Pyong-Dong Islands. The main listening bases operate in conjunction with the NSA at Osan, Pyong'aek, Taegu, Tongduchon, Oijongbu and Yongsan.

ANSP or *Agency for National Security Planning*: established in 1981, its powers were redefined in presidential orders and legislation. The ANSP, like its predecessor, was a cabinet-level agency directly accountable to the president. The director of the ANSP continued to have direct presidential access and the agency was redesignated as the principal agency for collecting and processing all intelligence. There is a requirement for all other agencies with intelligence gathering and analysis functions in their charters to co-ordinate their activities with the ANSP. However, like its predecessors, its main task was to keep a very tight lid on political subversion and discontent whether instigated by N Korea or home-grown in the form of violent student demonstrations, strikes and riots. The security presence in city centres, near university campuses, government and party offices, and media centres continued to be heavy. Citizens, particularly students and young people, were subject to being stopped, questioned, and searched without due process. The typical response to demonstrations was disruption by large numbers of Combat Police, short-term mass detention of demonstrators, and selective prosecution of the organisers. Arrest warrants – required by law – were not always produced at the time of arrest in political cases.

The National Security Act was increasingly used after 1985 to suppress domestic dissent. Intended to restrict 'anti-state activities endangering the safety of the state and the lives and freedom of the citizenry', the Act was also used to control and punish non-violent domestic dissent. Its broad definition of offences allowed enforcement over the widest range, wider than that of any other politically relevant law in S Korea. Along with other politically relevant laws such as the Social Safety Act and the Act Concerning Crimes Against the State, it weakened or removed procedural protection available to defendants in non-political cases. Questioning by the security services often involved not only psychological or physical abuse, but also outright torture. The 1987 torture and death of Pak Chong-ch'ol, a student at Seoul National University being questioned as to the whereabouts of a classmate, played a decisive role in galvanising public opposition to the government's repressive tactics.

Discontent was kept under control until 1987 by the regime's extensive use of the security services, particularly the Agency for National Security Planning and the Defence Security Command (DSC). Both the civilian ANSP and the military DSC not only collected domestic intelligence but also continued 'intelligence politics'. The security services not only detained those accused of violating laws governing political dissent, but also put under various lesser forms of detention those people, including opposition politicians, who they thought intended to violate the laws. Aside from its controversial internal security mission, the ANSP was also known for its foreign intelligence gathering and analysis and for its investigation of offences involving external subversion and military secrets. The National Unification Board and the ANSP (and the KCIA before it) were the primary sources of government analysis and policy direction for S Korea's reunification strategy and contacts with N Korea. The intelligence service's reputation in pursuing counter-espionage cases was also excellent.

The KCIA (*Korean Central Intelligence Agency*): created in 1961 to supplant the Army Counter-Intelligence Corps (CIC), the KCIA came directly under the Supreme Council for National Reconstruction in the immediate aftermath of the 16 May 1961 military coup. Its duties were to 'supervise and co-ordinate both international and domestic intelligence activities and criminal investigation by all government intelligence agencies, including that of the military'. Its mission was akin to that of a combined US Central Intelligence Agency and Federal Bureau of Investigation. The KCIA maintained a complex set of interlocking institutional links with almost all of the government's key decision-making bodies and maintained a near monopoly over crucial information concerning national security under the charter of the Act Concerning the Protection of Military Secrets.

The KCIA's practically unlimited power to investigate and to detain any person accused of anti-state behaviour severely restricted the right to dissent or to criticise the regime. The frequent questioning, detention or even prosecution of dissidents, opposition figures and reporters seriously jeopardised basic freedoms and created an atmosphere of political repression. The lack of civil liberties continued to be justified by referring to the threat from N Korea. The S Korean Government often used martial law in response to political unrest. From 1961 to 1979, martial law or a variant was evoked eight times. The government grew even more authoritarian, governing by presidential emergency decrees in the immediate aftermath of the establishment of the Yusin constitution; nine emergency decrees were declared between January 1974 and May 1975.

Opposition to the government and its harsh measures increased as the economy worsened in 1979. Scattered labour unrest and the

Government's repressive reactions sparked widespread public dissent: mass resignation of the opposition membership in the National Assembly and student and labour riots in Pusan, Masan and Ch'angwon. The Government declared martial law in the cities. In this charged atmosphere, under circumstances that appeared related to dissatisfaction with Park's handling of the unrest, on 26 October 1979, KCIA chief Kim Chae-gyu killed Park and the chief of the Presidential Security Force, Ch'a Chi-ch'ol, and was then himself arrested. Emergency martial law was immediately declared to deal with the crisis, placing the head of the Defence Security Command, Major General Chun Doo Hwan, in a position of considerable military and political power. The continuing slow pace of reform led to growing popular unrest. In early May 1980, student demonstrators protested against a variety of political and social issues, including the Government's failure to lift emergency martial law imposed following Park's assassination. The student protests spilled into the streets, reaching their peak during 13–16 May, at which time the student leaders obtained a promise that the Government would attempt to speed up reform. In Kwangju, demonstrations to protest the extension of martial law and the arrest of Kim Dae Jung turned into rebellion as demonstrators reacted to the brutal tactics of the Special Forces sent to the city. The Government did not regain control of the city for nine days, after more than 200 deaths. The following year saw the final disbanding of a discredited, violent and oppressive KCIA; unfortunately the change was cosmetic as the new organisation, the ANSP, has continued to conduct its security operations in much the same way and with many of the same personnel.

KOREA, SPECIAL FORCES (SOUTH or ROK) The main Counter-Terrorist unit is the 707th Special Mission Battalion and part of the S Korean Army's Special Forces Command formed in April 1958. Some years after the tragic events of the Arab terrorist attack on Israeli athletes at the 1972 Munich Olympic Games, S Korea, in anticipation of hosting the 1988 Games, formed the 707th battalion in 1982. The unit, based in Songham, SE of Seoul, is organised into two companies each with four 14-man operations squads and supported by specialist women only, weapons, demolitions and intelligence teams. Counter-terrorism training, often provided by the German GSG9, is extremely tough, with some six months of developing advanced fitness, weapons and infantry skills. This is followed by a further six months of training in close-quarter combat skills, special warfare training, underwater warfare and parachute techniques. Mountaineering and cold weather warfare is also very important to a unit often called upon to operate in sub-zero conditions. The 707th uses a wide variety of foreign and domestically produced weapons, including the 9mm Daewoo automatic pistol, 9mm MP5 sub-machine guns, 5.56mm CAR15 carbines, Daewoo K1/2 assault rifles and PSG-1 and US M24 sniper rifles. The 707th has already seen considerable and successful action in operations mounted against N Korean infiltrators.

KRIVITSKY, Walter G. (1899–1941)   Krivitsky was the first high-ranking KGB officer to defect to the West, a decision that later cost him his life. Born Samuel Ginsberg, a Polish Jew in Galicia, Krivitsky became a dedicated Communist and took part in the 1917 Bolshevik revolution in Russia, earning a place in Cheka intelligence service. Following Lenin's death, Krivitsky displayed his loyalty to Stalin and rose even higher in military intelligence, being posted to the Netherlands in 1935 where he acted as the head of all GRU for western Europe with the rank of general. Using the alias of Dr Martin Lessner, he posed as an Austrian dealer of rare books and maintained offices in The Hague, which had been called 'The Spy Capital of the World', due to its neutrality during WWI. In late September 1937, he was ordered to return to Moscow. Krivitsky knew that in the midst of the purges under way in the Soviet Union he could be branded a traitor and summarily executed. Major General Krivitsky therefore went to French government officials and asked for asylum. This was granted and in return, Krivitsky turned over a great deal of information on Soviet intelligence and counter-intelligence operations

Fearing that SMERSH agents would find him in Paris, Krivitsky travelled to the USA where he provided the FBI with a complete description of Soviet espionage operations. British intelligence had been aware of Krivitsky since the mid-1930s and SIS (MI6) had kept his bookstore and art gallery in the fashionable Celebestraat in The Hague under surveillance. SIS agents had followed Krivitsky as he went to the French Ministry of the Interior to seek asylum and watched him later sail for America. In January 1940, Jane Sissmore (Archer), a lawyer and a leading MI5 officer, interviewed Krivitsky but apparently attached little importance to the defector's statements, even when he talked about how Soviet agents had recruited quite a number of Cambridge University students into the NKVD ranks and that a British journalist had been sent to Spain ostensibly to cover the Civil War but whose real NKVD job was to spy against France.

Krivitsky was to name 61 Soviet agents working in Britain and its Commonwealth, only six of whom were Soviet Intelligence officers working under diplomatic cover and a further 18 were operating under deep cover as illegals in Britain. Sixteen British subjects were full-time 'agents of the NKVD'. One was an 'independent' politician, three were Labour party members, four Trade union officials, three were in the Foreign Office (FO), three in SIS or MI5, with one definitely in the latter and two were well-known foreign correspondents of major British newspapers. This information was slightly complicated by the fact that one or more of those described as being in the FO and both the newspapermen could also have been SIS officers. All three of those described as being in SIS and MI5 may have been in the security service alone, but it is unlikely that we shall ever know for sure. However, Krivitsky described one of the agents in the FO as a 'Scotsman with Bohemian tastes'. This is not Donald Maclean, as first thought, but more likely an official of great importance, Sir Archibald Clark Kerr, later Lord Inverchapel.

MI5 did not pursue these unnamed British agents working for the Soviets. Had MI5 properly addressed Krivitsky's allegations and probed deeply, they would have had a good chance of breaking the Cambridge Spy Ring in 1940–41 long before serious damage had been done. Sissmore did manage to collect enough information from Krivitsky to have MI5 identify a British subject working as a cipher expert in the British FO who was regularly feeding the OGPU information. This was Captain John Herbert King who was to admit spying for the Soviets since 1935 when he had been stationed in Geneva as a member of the British delegation to the League of Nations. He was tried 'in camera' at the Old Bailey on 18 October 1939, found guilty and given a prison sentence of ten years. Krivitsky was found dead, shot in the head, in his room at the Bellevue Hotel, Washington DC on Sunday morning, 9 February 1941. His death was ruled as suicide but it is most likely that a member of SMERSH had finally assassinated Krivitsky.

KROGER, Peter (1910–95) and **Helen** (1913–*c*.1990) Born Morris Cohen in the Bronx in 1910 of Russian-Jewish parents he married Leona or Lona Petka of Adams, Massachusetts. Both became Communists at that time. Kroger fought for the Communist brigade against Franco in the Spanish Civil War, using the name of Israel Altman. Later he worked for the Russian-sponsored Amtorg Trading Co in New York until 1942, before serving in the US Army in WWII. The Cohens were part of the NKVD espionage networks in New York City which include those run by the Rosenbergs and Colonel Abel. Warned that the Rosenbergs were about to be arrested by the FBI in 1950, the Cohens fled first to Europe and then on to London where they reappeared as the Krogers in 1954. They had taken the name of a couple, Peter and Helen, who had died much earlier in New Zealand; a long-used identity-change tactic employed by the NKVD. It was not until November 1960 that MI5 picked up the trail of the Krogers in London, identifying them with the Soviet network operated by Gordon Lonsdale. Lonsdale delivered secret information he had obtained from the British traitors Houghton and Gee who worked at the Admiralty UWE in Portland, England.

MI5 agents kept the Krogers under surveillance until the other members of the Portland Spy Ring were arrested in early January 1961. Police officers then arrested the Krogers at their W London home. A search yielded a motherlode of espionage equipment, including cipher pads on quick-burning flash paper, ciphers, codebooks, sophisticated photo equipment, a device for reading microdots, a specially built Ronson lighter containing a coded message inside, and numerous other items. After a week the MI5 officers found a powerful transmitter capable of sending in rapid bursts. There could be no doubt that the Krogers' bungalow was the communications centre for sending information to Moscow and, some twenty years later, the new occupants of the Krogers' home dug up a second high-speed Soviet radio transmitter in the back garden. Fingerprints taken from the Krogers were sent to Washington where the FBI identified them as belonging to the Cohens who were still wanted in the Rosenberg case. Instead of returning the Krogers to the US the British authorities tried and convicted them of espionage. They were sent to prison for 20 years. The KGB went out of its way to secure the release of the couple by engineering the arrest of British lecturer Gerald Brooke who was visiting Moscow and who was accused of distributing subversive literature. The KGB offered to exchange Brooke for the Krogers. The US authorities stepped in, stating that the Krogers were US citizens and could not be bartered for a British subject and that, if they were to be released, they had to be extradited to the US for their part in the Rosenberg conspiracy. The Soviet Union claimed that the Krogers were in fact Polish citizens, not Americans, and the British, more eager to regain Brooke than to appease the USA, accepted the claim. The Krogers were exchanged for Brooke in October 1969. They vanished a few years later. Peter Kroger takes to the grave the name of the mole codenamed PERCY within the Manhattan Project who helped him pull off the century's espionage coup.

L

LCS (London Controlling Section) Consisting of a small but effective staff, the LCS established in 1941 was headed by Colonel John Bevan. It worked in co-operation with MI5, SIS, SOE and, to a lesser extent, with other Allied intelligence organisations. Its job was to spread disinformation, to hoodwink the Germans into believing armies, planes, tanks, paratroopers existed where none did. LCS spread disinformation on the Allied landings in Sicily and Italy in 1943 so that German intelligence was gulled into believing the invading forces would arrive where they did not. It was also very effective in planting false information that there would be an allied invasion of the Balkans so that many German divisions were diverted to that region and could not participate in repulsing the Allied invasion of Normandy in 1944. It was disbanded at the end of 1945.

LEBANON The security forces in the Lebanon have been riven with sectarianism and the effects of foreign invasions for the best part of 35 years. At times there has been a small central Government intelligence service, Christian Phalangist, Muslim and indeed Druze intelligence groups all competing with each other and with the presence of Syrian, Israeli, Iraqi and even Iranian intelligence networks. In addition the situation in the Lebanon, at times split between Government control, Israeli and Syrian areas of military occupation naturally retained the interest of the CIA, SIS and the French DGSE. The 2001 War on Terrorism is of particular importance as the Iranian-backed Hezbollah terrorist group has a complex of bases in the Beka'a Valley in the east of the country and though well protected by the Syrian armed forces, remains a major target for both the Israelis and the USA.

General Direction of State Security: the GDSS is responsible for internal security, monitoring foreign forces, terrorist movements and has a small overseas section.

Second Bureau (Army and Military Intelligence): provides a limited tactical intelligence capability; concentrates on liaison with the Syrian occupation force and monitoring Israel military activities.

LEGAL Intelligence agent who operates in a country using an official position such as a commercial attaché at the embassy as his cover.

British SIS officers for many years were rather too easily identified as the Embassy Passport Control Officers. Legals may now be 'declared' to the host country.

LEGEND (cover)   The complete cover story developed for an operative.

LIBERTY, uss   US Navy AGRT-Intelligence collection vessel deliberately attacked by Israeli air and naval forces off the Sinai coast on 8 June 1967 during the Six Days War between Israel and the Arab States. uss *Liberty* was attacked for 75 minutes in international waters by Israeli jet fighters and motor torpedo boats; 34 men died and 172 were wounded. The attack has been a matter of controversy ever since. Survivors and many key government officials including Secretary of State Dean Rusk and former JCS Chairman Admiral Thomas Moorer have admitted that the incident was not mistaken identity. The author, James Bamford, believes the attack was carried out because Israel feared that uss *Liberty* might have intercepted evidence of an Israeli massacre of Egyptian prisoners of war. Israel and its supporters insist it was a 'tragic case of misidentification', confusing the US Naval Intelligence vessel with an elderly Egyptian horse carrier, the *El Quseir*. Israel further charges that the survivors are either lying or too emotionally involved to see the truth.

However, the large US Naval vessel was cleared marked, in good clear weather, in international waters, far from any fighting and flew a bright, clean, new US flag. The commanding officer, Captain William Loren McGonagle, received the Congressional Medal of Honor for conspicuous gallantry at the risk of his life, above and beyond the call of duty during the attack. To avoid embarrassing the Israelis, Captain McGonagle's Medal of Honor was presented in a quiet ceremony in the Washington Navy Yard instead of in the White House by the President as is customary.

LIBYA   *Jamahiriya Security Organisation – Libyan Intelligence Service (JSO)*: Libya has only had a modern Intelligence service since the overthrow of the Monarchy in 1969 when the MUKHABARAT was formed. Modelled on the Soviet KGB and East German STASI, the Libyan Intelligence and Security Services concentrated on consolidating the power base of Colonel Gaddafi. However, it wasn't long before the MUKHABARAT and its successor the JSO began to promote revolution and terrorism throughout Africa and the Middle East in particular. Weapons, training and vast sums of money would be given to the Arafat's PLO, the Italian Red Brigades, the Provisional IRA, ETA, US Black Power groups, Muslim separatists in the Philippines and

Indonesia, terrorist groups in Venezuela and elsewhere. The Libyan and Syrian Intelligence services co-operated closely for many years and were guilty of assassinating each others' dissidents or defectors on several occasions, notably the killing by Libyan 'Green Brigade' assassins of Issam al-Attar, leader of the Syrian wing of the Muslim Brotherhood at his home in Aachen, W Germany. Libyan money also found its way to Western politicians and family or close friends in 'black operations', which often had disastrous results for those involved. The Libyan manipulation of a gullible Billy Carter proved highly damaging to his brother Jimmy Carter's chances of re-election in 1980. The JSO *Foreign Liaison Office* has overall responsibility for most overseas intelligence operations and a Sub-Directorate provides direct contact with international terrorist groups.

Two Libyan intelligence officers were accused of the bombing of PanAm Flight-103 over Lockerbie in 1988 and indeed one was surprisingly convicted. The Iranians have handsomely compensated Libya for this in the form of access to chemical and biological weapon technology and help in constructing an underground production complex. However, Libya has been guilty of involvement in many genuine acts of terrorism including the killing of political opponents in Britain and even the use of poisoned peanuts by a Libyan hit squad in one remarkable attempt in the early 1980s to assassinate a political opponent based in England. The hijacking of cruise liners and the provision of passports to members of the Abu Nidal Organisation, used to launch attacks in W Europe on Israel's national airline, El Al. Targeting Libyan students in the USA, while at various times from the mid-1980s onwards, Libya has backed plots to assassinate presidents in Egypt, Sudan, the former Zaire, Tunisia and Chad, according to the Israeli-based Institute for Counter-Terrorism. The second-in-command at the JSO, Abdallah al-Sanussi, is Gaddafi's brother-in-law, and one of six Libyan officers charged in 1991 with helping orchestrate the bombing of French UTA Flight 772 two years earlier, in September 1989.

Libyan intelligence is broadly made up of three distinct sections *Istikhbarat al Askariya – Military Intelligence,* the security battalions that enforce loyalty to Gaddafi across the country and which include the so-called *Green Brigades*; and the JSO. The latter is subdivided into separate units for domestic and external security, nuclear and chemical weapons procurement and terrorist liaison.

LIDDELL, Guy (1892–1958)   Liddell served in the field artillery during WWI, earning the Military Cross. In 1919 he went to work for Basil

Thompson, Head of Special Branch. His assignment was to identify political extremists living in England, chiefly Communists. Liddell worked closely with MI5 and the SIS which, since the Revolution of 1917, had been conducting widespread espionage operations in the Soviet Union. In 1927, after MI5 aggressively identified Soviet spies in the celebrated Arcos raid, Liddell joined MI5 in 1931 going to work in its 'B' Branch, which was responsible for counter-intelligence.

At the onset of WWII, Liddell's Counter-Intelligence Branch was successful in picking up virtually very agent the Germans had managed to plant in Britain. With the firing of Kell by Churchill in May 1941 Liddell became Director of MI5's B Branch. Liddell was ably assisted in his wartime duties by Maxwell Knight. The two organised a vast network of MI5 agents mounting surveillance operations on possible German agents or Nazi sympathisers. Following the war Liddell was expected to take over control of MI5 and it is often argued that the Labour Prime Minister Atlee was distrustful of the 'old school tie' background of MI5's senior officers and chose instead the police officer Sir Percy Sillitoe to head MI5. However, Herbert Morrison, the Home Secretary, had apparently been warned that Liddell may not be 'suitable' for political reasons and therefore he was passed over for that reason. Liddell was still made Deputy Director General in 1946. He continued his close friendship with Philby, Burgess, Blunt and the artist Tomas Harris, who was later to die in mysterious circumstances in 1964. By the time Burgess and Maclean defected in 1951, Liddell was already under investigation, but this was quickly hushed up. He was allowed to continue to serve in MI5 until 1953 when he accepted a post as the Atomic Energy Authority's Head of Security at Harwell. It was Blunt who warned Burgess in 1951 that Maclean was about to be arrested as a Soviet agent. Blunt had been passed the information probably by an informant inside MI5 or perhaps by Philby in the USA, as a result of seeing one of the VENONA transcripts mentioning HOMER, Maclean's Soviet espionage codename. Both Philby and Liddell were to be investigated, Liddell in particular. While Philby later confirmed his guilt by defecting, Liddell escaped probable exposure as a major Soviet spy by dying in 1958 of a heart attack.

LIMA SITES 'L' (landing) sites built by the CIA on mountaintops in Laos during the secret war. These were the bases of operations behind enemy lines.

LINK ENCRYPTION The application of online crypto-security to a communications link ensuring that all information using the system is totally encrypted.

LISTENING POST   Can be used to describe anything from a covert surveillance site in an embassy to a major monitoring site like Menwith Hill.

LITERARY SPIES   The lure of espionage over the centuries has attracted poets and dramatists from Chaucer, Marlow, Daniel Defoe to the novelist Graham Greene. Spies have to be liars, thieves and sometimes even murderers and for a variety of reasons many writers appear to wish or even believe that they could function more successfully in these roles. The list would include Erskine Childers, who was to write to great effect about the German spy menace before 1914; John Bucan, who was to be made a director of a military intelligence department in WWI; Somerset Maugham, who was to spy for SIS in both Switzerland and Russia; and Sir Compton Mackenzie, who operated for SIS in Athens. In WWII both Malcolm Muggeridge and Graham Greene joined SIS and were stationed in Africa while Dennis Wheatley worked within the super-secret London Controlling Section disinformation department, while several members of his family served in MI5. The journalist and Labour politician Tom Driberg, later to become Lord Bradwell, infiltrated the Communist party on behalf of MI5. Ian Fleming, creator of James Bond, worked in Naval Intelligence and John Bingham, the Lord Clanmorris, actually became a senior MI5 Counter-Espionage officer. In later years David Cornwall, better known as John Le Carré, served in both MI5 and SIS in the late 1950s and early 60s. Fay Weldon worked in the IRD, a propaganda unit attached to the SIS and Basil Bunting worked for SIS in Iran up to 1951; Charlotte Bingham, John Bingham's daughter, who famously once mislaid 29 files of classified documents, worked in intelligence, while Compton Mackenzie operated in Greece for SIS and Sir John Betjeman worked for military intelligence during WWII. The USA has had its fair share of literary intelligence agents, one of the best known of whom is Howard Hunt.

LONDON CAGE   Operated from 6–7 Kensington Palace Gardens in London where MI5 and SIS (MI6) interrogators handled important German prisoners during WWII. Rooms were bugged and 'false' POWs were often used to persuade German officers to talk and, indeed, it worked remarkably well. Britain was to gain a vast amount of useful information from unsuspecting senior German officers. Commanded by Lt. Colonel Alexander Paterson Scotland.

LONSDALE, Gordon (Konon Trofimovich Molody) (1922–70) Born in Russia, he was sent to live with an aunt in California at age seven in 1929. He lived there for nine years, English becoming his natural equal language. He returned to Russia in 1938 and immediately joined the KOMSOMOL. After fighting in WWII, he was accepted by the NKVD and was trained as a spy, and then sent to Canada in 1954 with a fake passport and the alias Gordon Lonsdale. A year later he arrived in London in the guise of a successful Canadian businessman. Lonsdale opened up substantial bank accounts and rented a luxury apartment in Regent's Park. He made friends easily and talked of opening up an importing firm to distribute amusement games in Europe. He was regularly seen at London's best nightclubs with an attractive woman on his arm.

Lonsdale (Molody) was by nature sexist, anti-Semitic and a philanderer, taking a large number of mistresses. Having established a believable front as a Canadian businessman, and with the Krogers acting as his communications and technical agents, he set about building an effective spy network at the top-secret underwater weapons research establishment at the Portland naval base in Dorset. Two of the other known members would be Harry Houghton and his mistress Ethel Gee. Eventually MI5 caught up with Houghton, Gee and Lonsdale at a meeting. The Krogers were also arrested and all five were placed on trial, now known as the Portland Spy Case. Convicted and sent to prison, Lonsdale was to receive a 25-year term. However, Lonsdale had in fact run more than one major espionage network in Britain and MI5 never discovered the full extent of the damage done to Western security. It is believed that the Soviets obtained considerable secret information on chemical and biological weapons from within the Microbiological Research Establishment at Porton Down from another of Lonsdale's networks. The Soviet defector Oleg Gordievsky certainly believes that Lonsdale's importance as a master spy has not been fully recognised in Britain.

The spymaster served less than four years in prison, released in 1964 when he was exchanged for Greville Wynne, an Englishman convicted by the Soviet Union in 1963 of being an SIS (M16) courier to the GRU traitor Penkovsky. Hailed as a hero upon his return to Moscow, Lonsdale received two medals, the Red Star and the Red Banner. He then wrote his memoirs, with the help of British defector Philby, publishing this fanciful tale under the title *Spy*, a specious, lying document that was made into a specious, lying film by the Soviets. In October 1970, Lonsdale collapsed in a small garden behind his Moscow apartment, dying of a heart attack as he was picking mushrooms, but brought on by a prolonged drinking bout.

L PILL   A 'lethal' cynanide capsule issued to intelligence operatives who would prefer to take their own life rather than be caught and tortured.

LUCY RING   Major Soviet WWII espionage network run from Switzerland by Rudolf Roessler (codename LUCY). It has been claimed that this spy network made all the difference between survival and defeat for the Soviet Union and indeed the Lucy Ring obtained a huge range of vital information on German plans, operations, units and weapons from a network of supposedly important German 'sources'. However, it is certain that Roessler was a witting or unwitting British double-agent and that the Lucy Ring was used by SIS and probably later the OSS to feed ULTRA material through to the Soviet Government in a form they would accept. Attempts to make selected ULTRA intercepts directly available to Moscow were rejected by a suspicious Soviet Government on the grounds that it was an attempt to mislead. The Soviet NKVD however, was fully aware of the existence of GC&CS and ULTRA through Philby, Cairncross and other Soviet agents. The NKVD probably went along with the ruse as it saved them a lot of problems convincing Stalin of the veracity of the information.

LYALIN, Oleg Adolfovich (1937–95)   A high-living womanising KGB officer, he defected in London in the early 1970s. Lyalin was an officer in the KGB's Department Five, which was responsible for sabotage. Lyalin blithely informed MI5 that he had been sent to England, attached to the Soviet trade mission at Highgate, with specific instructions to destroy the super radar station at Fylingdales on the Yorkshire moors which was operated under British and NATO direction and had cost £45 million to establish. The Soviet defector also began to identify scores of KGB Department Five operatives in the West. Moscow denied everything but, with the Lyalin defection and subsequent revelations that Moscow was preparing to go on a war footing by destroying key Western defence systems such as the radar complex at Fylingdales, they immediately called back to Moscow all of their Department Five agents who hastily left Mexico City, Athens, Bonn and Paris. Lyalin had not operated alone. He identified all of those in his sabotage ring, including two Cypriot tailors and a Malaysian. All were arrested. Following their confessions, they were convicted and sent to prison. In retaliation for the British actions, the Soviets expelled 18 British officials and diplomats from Moscow. But it was only window-dressing. The KGB had suffered a major setback from which they would not recover for some years.

M

McCONE, John (1902–91)   One of the most respected and capable Directors of Central Intelligence. Appointed as DCI in November 1961 he guided the CIA through the Cuban Missile Crisis, the aftermath of the Bay of Pigs and the assassination of President Kennedy. Relatively close to both the Kennedy brothers he worked tirelessly to rebuild the Agency's image and quietly to remove some of the wilder elements from the Directorate of Operations before he retired in 1965.

MACLEAN, Donald Duart (1913–83)   Possibly one of the least competent entrants to the diplomatic service, Maclean was largely accepted on his Cambridge background and the fact that his father was a Liberal Member of Parliament. Maclean was an alchoholic, a homosexual and frequently mixed drunkenness, sex and violent behaviour in, even for those rather libertarian circles, depraved orgies. In addition he was a committed Communist and a Soviet spy. Despite all of this – and quite a lot was known or suspected by his colleagues – Maclean was thought of as a future ambassador. Maclean was frequently discovered to be inadequate, irrational, violent, drunk, remarkably indiscreet and outspokenly anti-American, even at official functions during his various diplomatic postings including both Paris and Cairo. But to the surprise of many, Maclean was appointed First Secretary at the Washington Embassy. It was from this position that he was able to pass ever more vital intelligence to his Soviet controllers on nuclear research and much more. The CIA was suspicious of Maclean long before the penny dropped in Britain. Soon after his return to Britain, Maclean was warned by Burgess that he was about to be arrested and the two fled to Moscow. Maclean, by then a compulsive alcoholic, lived on unhappily in Moscow separated from his family. His wife had an affair with Philby before returning temporarily to Maclean who finally died in 1983.

MAFIA, THE   Under Mussolini every effort had been made to stamp out the Mafia secret society because it was feared that it might become a rival to his own Fascist party. The task of defeating the Mafia was given to the Duce's own Chief of Police, who arrested suspects by the thousand and shipped them off to penal islands, so that by 1927

Mussolini was able to announce to the Fascist Parliament that the war against the Mafia had ended. When the question of invading Sicily and Italy was being discussed during WWII the British SIS took the view that it would be extremely dangerous to revive the Mafia and allow it unbridled authority. However, it was agreed that some former Mafia members might be cautiously used as agents. The OSS had rather more robust ideas and in 1943 'Lucky' Luciano, born Salvatore Luciana in Sicily and head of the American Mafia, was approached in prison in the USA.

The OSS, aided by the US Navy, decided to make use of his services to contact the underground head of the Mafia in Sicily. In return for these services Luciano was officially given his freedom in 1945, though it is possible that he was secretly taken to Sicily and was seen in the vicinity of the US Seventh Army's HQ shortly after the invasion.

Extensive Mafia aid was given to the US troops in an area dominated by Don Calo, a local Mafia leader. Something like 15 per cent of the US troops were of Sicilian origin, deliberately selected for the operation on the suggestion of OSS. While it would be churlish to detract from the imaginative way in which the US exploited the Mafia in Sicily and so paved the way to a more or less bloodless invasion of the western area of the island, it cannot be denied that the co-operation went too far. Imprisoned Mafiosi were speedily released and, within weeks, most Sicilian towns had Mafia mayors. Meanwhile, in the area where the British operated, Scotland Yard was asked to send out men to round up the worst of the Mafia gangsters in stark contrast to the US policy.

The USA had made considerable use of the New York 'families' Sicilian connections and this was to become the start of a continuing relationship between US Intelligence and organised crime, whether in the form of the Mafia, SE Asia narcotics smugglers or Latin American drug cartels. Indeed, the CIA's long-term relationship with the Cuban and Florida Mafia both before and after the Bay of Pigs fiasco may have come back to haunt the USA in an appalling fashion on a November day in 1963 in Dallas. Some would argue that this was one of the most monumental 'own goals' in history.

MAGIC US WWII codeword for intelligence derived from deciphered Japanese signals.

MAIL COVER Intelligence agency request for the mail authorities to examine the exterior only of mail addressed to a particular target in search of helpful information such as return addresses, postmarks and the like.

MAIL DROP   *see* ACCOMMODATION ADDRESS.

MAJOR DOCS   The principal identity documents used to authenticate an alias identity.

MALY, Theodore (1884–1937)   A talented Soviet Intelligence officer famous for being the first to recognise Kim Philby's potential as a spy. Maly, a well-built, good-looking Hungarian had a colourful early career as an Army chaplain in the Austro-Hungarian army in WWII. Captured during the Carpathian campaign by the Russians, he abandoned Catholicism for Communism after several periods of re-education in POW camps. Known to have doubts about the extreme methods of interrogation used by his new employers, Maly nonetheless remained a loyal supporter of Communism throughout his career in OGPU, and later the NKVD, the state intelligence services. He was considered to be an officer of great potential with a gift for recruiting, inspiring and winning the loyalty of his agents. Late in 1932 Maly was posted as an Illegal (intelligence officer operating abroad and posing as a national of that country) to Germany and then later assigned to Vienna under the principal cover name of 'Mann'. Philby was working in Vienna at the time as a courier for the banned Communist party and their contacts in Prague and Paris. Maly spotted Philby's real worth and encouraged him to return to Britain in May 1934.

Maly and his wife arrived in Britain in April 1936 using false Austrian passports in the names of Paul and Lydia Hardt. As chief of the Illegal station in London, he controlled Captain J.H. King, the cipher clerk in the Foreign Office Communications department. However his main responsibilities, under the cover name of 'Theo', were to develop further and act as control for the Cambridge Ring of Five, Philby, Anthony Blunt, Guy Burgess, Donald Maclean and John Cairncross. Maly is known, however, to have recruited other British 'sleepers' or to use the modern alternative 'moles' (deep cover agents, activated only when they are in a position to have access to vital state secrets). Much effort has been expended by MI5, the British Security Service, over many years in a largely unsuccessful hunt for these traitors.

Recalled, along with most of his staff, to Moscow in July 1937. Maly may have thought that a commendation received from Stalin in 1936 would protect him from the fate that befell so many returning Soviet intelligence officers. It may also have been a conscious decision to accept the risk, as he remarked to a colleague that he returned to Moscow to give the lie to 'that priest may have been a real spy (for the anti-Bolsheviks) after all'. Maly was arrested and executed by a firing squad in the cellars of the NKVD HQ in Derzhinsky Square in late 1937.

MARLOWE, Christopher (1564–93)   English poet and dramatist who acted as a 'gentleman spy' on many occasions for Queen Elizabeth I's spymaster, Sir Francis Walsingham. He was recruited while still at Cambridge University (shades of the distant future). In 1587, posing as a Catholic student, he entered a seminary at Rheims in France. Here he learned of Jesuit plots against England. His death in a tavern brawl is believed to have been directly linked to his involvement with Elizabethan intelligence.

MARTIN, William H. (1931–) and **MITCHELL, Bernon F.** (1929–) The so-called 'NSA Spies' created probably the worst scandal in the history of that agency. Martin and Mitchell both joined the NSA in 1957, Martin after serving as a Naval cryptologist at the NSG intercept station in Kamiseya, Japan and Mitchell after completing his degree course in Mathematics at Stanford and his time at Kamiseya where he had originally met Martin. However they both soon became disillusioned, secretly accusing the NSA of being unscrupulous and of spying on friendly nations, but instead of just resigning they began planning first to spy for and then defect to the Soviet Union. They believed that the Communist superpower offered a more moral and honest home for their loyalty. Martin was actually awarded an NSA scholarship for a Master's degree in Mathematics at the University of Illinois, the first two-year scholarship ever awarded by the NSA. Martin, a mathematical genius, excelled, getting a straight A average, but he also took a course in Russian and began to associate with members of the Communist Party.

In December 1959 Martin and Mitchell flew to Cuba to meet with Soviet officials undetected by NSA security. They received a veritable shopping list of material the Soviets wanted them to steal from the NSA and apparently they more than fulfilled Soviet expectations. Indeed there is some suggestion that they had foreknowledge of the U-2 flight by CIA Pilot Gary Powers and that the information they supplied enabled the Soviet Union to spring the trap which successfully brought down his aircraft. In June 1960 they again took leave together first in Mexico City, then to Cuba where they boarded a Soviet cargo ship and defected. On 1 August the news was broken at last by a Pentagon news release. Both self-confessed traitors later took Soviet citizenship, Martin actually changing his name to Sokolovsky. In the security scandal that followed their defection, amazed observers were to discover that both men had severe personality defects and should never have been accepted for top-secret work. Martin has been described as an irresponsible and insufferable egotist, while Mitchell was employed by the NSA despite admitting to six years of sexual experimentations with both dogs and chickens until he was about 19 years old. During the selection procedure, their remarkable gifts as mathematicians were held to outweigh their personality defects and even their 'farmyard' experiences. It was revealed that they had been homosexual lovers and in the subsequent NSA purge, 26 employees were dismissed for 'indications of sexual deviation'.

MASINT Measurement and Signature Intelligence (techint; metric, angle, spatial wave length, time dependence modulation and hydromagnetic data; also, air and water samples).

MASTERMAN, Sir John (1891–1977)   Masterman, an MI5 officer, was the Chairman of the joint intelligence Twenty Committee which ran the highly successful XX Cross (Double Cross) System of turning captured German agents by offering them the choice of a trial and hanging or the opportunity to relay false or misleading information back to Germany. Some chose to die, the majority did not. The clever manipulation of information, mixing the verifiable with the deliberately misleading, was one of the outstanding intelligence triumphs of WWII.

MATINT   Materials Intelligence

MEASLES   'A case of the measles'. A murder or assassination carried out so efficiently by an intelligence service that death appears to have been from accidental or natural causes.

MEDICAL INTELLIGENCE   Intelligence on the health of leaders of potential or actual hostile nations such as the Soviet Union's President Breznev's heart problems, Russia's Boris Yeltsin's alcoholism, Iraq's Saddam Hussein's cancer or indeed the Al-Qa'ida terrorist leader's internal organs. The condition of Osama bin Laden's kidneys were of particular interest prior to the US operations against Afghanistan in 2001–02 and rumours, unsubstantiated, that he received treatment in an American hospital in a Gulf State a mere three months before the attack on the USA are intriguing, as are the equally unsubstantiated suggestions that he was visited by at least one official from a Western intelligence service in his hospital accommodation.

MENWITH HILL   The principal NATO theatre ground station for high altitude signals intelligence satellites. Although this facility is jointly operated with the UK's Government Communications HQ

(GCHQ), it is not privy to the intelligence down-linked to Menwith Hill. The tapes containing the data are returned via air to the USA for analysis. Menwith Hill Station was established in 1956 by the US Army Security Agency (ASA). Inside the closely guarded 560-acre base are two large operations blocks and a large number of satellite tracking dishes and domes. Initial operations focused on monitoring international cable and microwave communications passing through Britain. In the early 1960s Menwith Hill was one of the first sites in the world to receive sophisticated early IBM computers, with which NSA automated the labour-intensive watch-list scrutiny of intercepted but unenciphered telex messages. Since then, Menwith Hill has sifted the international messages, telegrams and telephone calls of citizens, corporations or governments to select information of political, military or economic value to the USA.

The official story is that the all-civilian base is a Department of Defence communications station. The British Ministry of Defence describes Menwith Hill as a 'communications relay centre'. Like all good cover stories, this has a strong element of truth to it. Until 1974, Menwith Hill's SIGINT speciality was evidently the interception of International Leased Carrier (LCC) signals, the communications links run by civil agencies, telecommunication ministries and corporations throughout the world. The National Security Agency took over Menwith Hill in 1966. Interception of satellite communications began at Menwith Hill as early as 1974, when the first of the large satellite communications dishes were installed.

MENZIES, Sir Stewart Graham (1890–1968) Born in London, 30 January 1890, into a wealthy family, but with the reputation of being an illegitimate son of the future King Edward VII, following Sandhurst military academy Menzies joined the Grenadier Guards. During WWI, he served in France and was injured in a gas attack in 1915. Unable to serve on the front lines, Menzies joined Field Marshall Haig's counter-intelligence section at Montreuil where he served with distinction. On the strength of this he entered SIS (MI6) in 1918. Later appointed head of the Military Liaison department, properly MI6, though this title came to used as a convenient cover name for the entire SIS, he later rose to be Sinclair's deputy.

In July 1939 obtaining one of his outstanding successes, Menzies was to personally travel to Warsaw to negotiate the final arrangements with the Polish Cryptographic Bureau for a copy of the German ENIGMA machine and much top secret information obtained by Polish Intelligence. This was to prove of incalculable value to British intelligence and it has to be said that the outstanding part played by Polish Intelligence, in particular their brilliant codebreaking section, has never been sufficiently and publicly acknowledged. Later in 1939 Menzies was named Chief of the SIS on the death of Admiral Sinclair. In addition to expanding the wartime intelligence and counter-intelligence departments of SIS, Menzies also supervised GC&CS at Bletchley and made astute use of its successes when at times there was little else to offer an ever-impatient Prime Minister. Menzies came to believe strongly that Britain and SIS in particular had made a serious mistake in the prewar period in not trying harder to make contact with anti-Nazi elements in Germany, and Admiral Canaris in particular. There can be little doubt that Menzies and Canaris were in communication on occasions, even after war broke out. Indeed, it was to be one of Menzies's great disappointments that he was unsuccessful in persuading other British intelligence organisations and the Government itself, to make a genuine alliance with Canaris against Hitler. Menzies was later credited with being one of the few intelligence chiefs who could maintain a working relationship with the demanding Churchill, the SOE, the Chiefs of Staff, the OSS and the French. Menzies would be honoured in full by Britain, the USA and many other nations once victory had been ensured. Following the war, Menzies oversaw the reorganisation of SIS to face a new enemy with the onset of the Cold War, the absorption of the best of SOE into its ranks and the difficult economic situation under an often hostile Labour Government.

To his great personal distress his position was to be undermined towards the end of tenure as C by internal conflict within SIS over the presumed treacherous activities of a number of officers, but particularly Philby. A clubman who married four times, Menzies lived a rather lonely life with few close friends. He resigned in 1953 to indulge his love of the countryside and field sports in rural Gloucestershire and was to die on 29 May 1968.

MI5 Military cover-name (still widely used by media) for the British Security Service; responsible for counter-intelligence and internal security (similar to FBI).

MI6 Military cover-name (still widely used by media) of British Secret Intelligence Service (SIS); responsible for foreign intelligence (similar to CIA).

MICE The four motivations for people to become spies are usually; *Money* Financial problems, such as being deeply in debt, having an extravagant lifestyle or a mistress or two, are fertile grounds for agent recruitment. This has proved successful in both the Communist and Western worlds. *Ideology* The belief in the ultimate superiority of a political, religious or social cause has produced a large number of agents whose spying activities often end with an unforced defection. *Compromise* The first step in the recruitment of many agents has been to identify an element in a person's lifestyle or a flaw in their personality that offers the chance of blackmail. Sexual, particularly homosexual, or criminal behaviour has traditionally offered the best levers. *Ego* Case officers are often trained specifically to appeal to a target's vulnerability to intellectual flattery in order to recruit them. The request to write articles for publication on the grounds of the candidate's 'expertise' and the importance of their views. By the time the target is requested for more sensitive material they are already trapped by the lifestyle provided by the earlier payments. The Case officer will have all the evidence he needs, the receipts signed for payment and perhaps even the information used in the commissioned articles suitably doctored to appear like a stolen intelligence document.

MICRODOT A photographic reduction of a secret message so small it can be hidden in plain sight or buried under the period at the end of this sentence.

MINARET Highly classified and compartmented programme of the NSA to intercept civilian communications from foreign nations to the USA.

MISSION The task, together with the purpose, that clearly indicates the action to be taken and reason therefore. In common usage, especially when applied to lower military units, a duty assigned to an individual or unit to task.

MK-ULTRA CIA drug and mind-control programme.
See also GOTTLIEB, DR SIDNEY

MOLE These are ostensibly loyal employees of one intelligence service who actively work on behalf of a foreign agency over a long period. They are potentially the most valuable source of high-grade intelligence for any hostile agency. The CIA has suffered at the hands of a least two important 'moles', Larry Wu Tai Chin who joined the agency in 1948 and secretly worked for Chinese intelligence until he committed suicide in 1985 and Aldrich Ames, arrested in 1994. In Britain, Philby, Blunt, Prime and Cairncross are but four of those who have spied for the Soviet Union over a period of many years. The West, of course, has had its successes as well, with Godievsky, Penkovsky and Lt. Gen. Dmitri Polyakov among others.

MONGOOSE   Secret operation ordered by President John F. Kennedy and Robert Kennedy to assassinate or overthrow the leader of a foreign nation, Cuba's Fidel Castro, following the disastrous Bay of Pigs invasion of Cuba in April 1961.

MORWENSTOW   A joint GCHQ–NSA Communications monitoring and intelligence satellite ground station. Operated by the Composite Signals Organisation at Cleave, 4 miles N of Bude. Work started on this 400ft-high Clifftop site at Coombe overlooking Lower Sharpenose point in February 1939 and was occupied by G & V Flights of No-1 AACU in May using a 2700ft (823m) runway. By 1942 Spitfires Whirlwinds and even a Mosquito had used Cleave. In May 1943 a USAAF B17 landed without difficulty. Cleave was finally taken over by Fighter Command and the large Army Camp built on the northern perimeter, now partially occupied by the US Army, saw numerous US Army Shows including one with Glenn Miller and Bob Hope on the same bill.

Reduced to Care & Maintenance on 16 May 1945, it was closed completely in November. It remained as Cleave Army camp for most of the 1950 and early 1960s. In 1967 a decision was taken to build a mirror site for the GPO Ground Station at Goonhilly Downs in order to access the new INTELSAT communications satellites and the old airfield and Army Camp proved an ideal site for this. It also became a replacement for CSOS Goonhavern at Perranporth which intercepted transatlantic undersea cable communications. Building began in 1969, with the first two dishes operational by 1971–72, with Goonhavern closing in 1971. The BT nationwide microwave tower chain was given a 'dog-leg' from Exeter via Morwenstow to allow the interception of all British and European communications transmitted by the Goonhilly Station and the undersea cables to both N and S America. For most of the 1970s NSA-GCHQ-DSD had just Morwenstow and Pine Gap in Australia operational, but with the next generation of INTELSAT-4 and 5 being launched more capability was quickly required and CSOS Morwenstow was greatly expanded. By the early 1990s there were at least nine major dishes operational and six other similar bases were to be built around the world operated as part of the ECHELON network by NSA, GCHQ, CSE, DSD and GCSB. This is undoubtedly one of the most important stations in the worldwide UKUSA network.

MOSCOW RULES   The ultimate tradecraft methods developed for use in the most hostile of the operational environments. During the Cold War, Moscow was considered to be the most difficult of the operating environments.

MOSSAD   Israel's foreign intelligence service.
   See also ISRAEL

MUSIC BOX Russian term for a clandestine radio set.

MUSICIAN Russian term for a radio operator.

N

NACIC   National Counter-Intelligence Centre (USA).

NAKED   Operating entirely alone and without the availability of immediate assistance.

NAVE, Captain Eric (1899–1993)   Leading Australian-British naval cryptographer. He was fluent in Japanese, and in 1925 the British Admiralty asked the RAN for the 'loan' of Nave as an interpreter in Hong Kong. He joined a Signals Interception Station and devoted his time to cracking Japanese diplomatic as well as naval codes. By 1927, Nave had unravelled the entire Japanese naval radio organisation. In 1928 Nave travelled to London to join GC&CS. His first success came when he discovered that the Japanese were paying a Labour MP, Cecil Malone, to pass on information about defence matters. Later in 1931 he returned to Hong Kong to build up the GC&CS station there. Returning to HQ in 1934 he was finally to break the Japanese naval attaché code and the first Machine cryptograph known as Type-91 or 'Red' which was used for diplomatic traffic as well. In June 1939, the Japanese introduced a new code, the D, known to the Allies as JN-25. It was in fact an old type of book code used by the US forces in the Spanish American War of 1898 and long since discarded as insecure. Nave successfully broke into JN-25 by November 1939. He returned to Australia on sick leave in 1940 and stayed, on loan to his own country, to create the Central Bureau, effectively a regional GC&CS. In 1947, he joined the newly established ASIO or internal security service, eventually becoming the Deputy Director before finally retiring in 1959 after 42 years of 'secret' service. It was Nave's ground-breaking work on Japanese naval codes that led some commentators to suggest that Britain had learned of the impending attack on Pearl Harbor and that either Churchill, or perhaps in concert with Roosevelt, withheld the information in order to draw an unwilling USA into the war.

NEED TO KNOW   A determination made by an intelligence agency to restrict the numbers of individuals entitled to hold or consult a particular classified document.

NEGATIVE INTELLIGENCE   Intelligence known to be compromised or to have been acquired by a hostile intelligence service.

NEIGHBOURS   Soviet GRU for the KGB. The present Russian GRU still use it to refer to the SVR, the successor to the old Ist Chief Directorate of the KGB.

NETHERLANDS   *Binnenlandse Veiligheidsdienst – National Intelligence and Security Agency (BVD)*: in 1945, the Bureau for National Security or BNV was established to track down wartime collaborators and to prevent left-wing sabotage and subversion. The BVD itself was established in 1949 with a responsibility to counter espionage by E European intelligence services and the activities of the Communists in the Netherlands. The BVD has a department for internal security and in 1994 assumed responsibility for foreign intelligence when the *IDB Espionage agency* was disbanded. Other departments deal with the illegal weapons trade, international terrorism established in the 1970s and international organised crime established in the 1990s. The BVD moved into its present HQ at Leidschendam, which is a suburb of the city of The Hague, in 1998–99. The BVD has some 'liaison officers' in various major cities such as Washington, Paris, Tokyo and London. The BVD is considered to be a reliable and efficient service, with a particularly close relationship to Britain's SIS (MI6).

Militaire Inlichtingendienst – Military Intelligence Agency (MID): the military intelligence service was originally known as the 'Section III of the General Staff', also called 'GSIII', shortly before WWI and was also the first Nertherlands intelligence service. The current MID was finally established in 1997. The MID collects information and, if necessary, takes active measures in the areas of military security, foreign intelligence and security agencies, terrorism, right-wing extremism, information security, industrial security and weapons proliferation.

The MID HQ (MIDCO) is in The Hague with only four small offices at various locations in the Netherlands, the Dutch Antilles and a larger liaison office at NATO HQ in Brussels. It is responsible for the *TIVC or Technical Intelligence Analysis Centre* which operates SIGINT sites at Emnes with the NSA and at Terschelling.

NETWORK   A group of undercover agents or illegals working in a foreign country or countries and who have a common HANDLER. Often broken down into individual and independent cells for added security.

NEWS   Usually taken to be 'Bad News'.

NEW ZEALAND   *Security Intelligence Service (NZSIS)*: the NZSIS was established on 28 November 1956 when it moved into its present HQ at 175–175a Taranaki Street in Wellington and it has since opened regional offices in both Auckland and Christchurch. The Service's principal role is the production of secret intelligence in support of government security, defence, foreign and economic policies. It meets these requirements for intelligence gathering and other tasks through a variety of sources, human and technical, and by liaison with a wide range of foreign intelligence and security services, but in particular the ASIS, ASIO, SIS and MI5.

Government Communications and Security Bureau – GCSB: established in 1977, collection is made from electronic communication transmitted through satellite, radio waves or other open means. GCSB does not intercept private or other communication transmitted by telephone landlines, though it operates a satellite monitoring station at Waihopai near Blenheim and a radio receiving station at Tangimoana near Foxton. These are both capable of receiving and collecting commercial as well as military and intelligence communications. Through the UKUSA agreements, GCSB has links with the US National Security Agency, the Communications Security Establishment Canada, Defence Signals Directorate Australia and the Government Communications HQ UK.

NICHOLSON, Harold James (1950–) CIA officer Harold James Nicholson was arrested in 1996 for giving the Russians top-secret material. He was the highest ranking CIA officer to be detected spying for another nation, according to the government. In 1997, he pled guilty and received 23.5 years in prison. 'Nicholson said that he sold defence secrets to Russia to make up to his children for the worry and disappointment he caused them due to a failed marriage and numerous overseas assignments,' according to the National Counter-Intelligence Centre.

NID 1. *National Intelligence Daily* (CIA's current intelligence newsletter; discontinued in 1999 and replaced with more restricted SEIB, the Senior Executives Intelligence Brief). 2. Naval Intelligence Department.

NIE National Intelligence Estimate (USA).

NIGERIA Until the mid-1970s, when the military regime deprived the nation of its civil rights through the widespread use of detention without trial, physical assault, torture, harassment and intimidation, the issue of human rights had not been a major concern for most people in Nigeria. However as the Government of Major General Gowon declined in popularity following his failure to return power to a civilian administration, criticism of the regime markedly increased. The military reacted by detaining these critics for indefinite periods and by creating the *Nigerian Security Organisation* (*NSO*). Established in 1976, the NSO was the sole intelligence service for both domestic and international security during its ten-year existence. It was charged with the detection and prevention of any crime against the security of the state, with the protection of classified materials and with carrying out any other security missions assigned by the president. The return of a constitutional government in the Second Republic 1979–83 under Buhari, failed to make any real improvement in the human rights record. The NSO engaged in widespread abuses of due process, including detention without charge and trial, arrests without pretext, and wiretapping. The NSO's performance was bluntly criticised after the 1980 uprisings by the Maitatsine movement. It had penetrated the movement but failed to prevent it from instigating bloody riots. The Maitatsine follow the teachings of Maitatsine Marwa, an Islamic leader from Cameroon whose activities in Nigeria led to his expulsion from Kano in 1960 and a series of bloody uprisings in the 1980s in which more than 4,000 persons are believed to have died.

When Babangida toppled Buhari in August 1985, one of his main arguments was the need to restore civil liberties. The new regime prided itself on being a defender of human rights, and many of Babangida's initial acts justified his human rights posture. He released most of the politicians detained without trial and drastically reduced the jail terms of those already convicted. Fulfilling one of the promises made in his first national address as president, Babangida disbanded the NSO in June 1986 and restructured the security services into three separate organisations under the Office of the Coordinator of National Security.

The National Intelligence Agency (*NIA*) is responsible for foreign intelligence and counter-intelligence.

The State Security Service (*SSS*) is responsible for intelligence and internal security within Nigeria. Although the notorious NSO had been dissolved, the new security establishment continued to have a bad record for human rights abuse with security forces frequently accused of harassment, false arrest and the wide-scale intimidation of the news media. Repression of the political activities of opposition groups – with public meetings arbitrarily cancelled or prevented, including cultural events, academic conferences and human rights meetings – are not uncommon.

Above 11 September 2001: Hijacked United Airlines Flight 175 banks towards the south tower of the World Trade Centre as the north tower burns. There could have been no better illustration of the need for counter-terrorism, nor of the inadequacies of existing US intelligence. Popperfoto

Below 11 September 2001: The WTC seen from Brooklyn Bridge. The flag in the foreground would soon be at half-mast. Popperfoto

Above Crossing the line: Jersey City fire officials and passers-by watch in awe as the collapse of the Twin Towers takes their cross-border colleagues, among many others, 11 September 2001. Popperfoto

Below Osama bin Laden with Ayman al-Zawahiri, an Egyptian linked to the al Queda network, making a news statement to a Karachi newspaper that he had nuclear and chemical weapons and would consider using them in response to US attacks. Bernard Gotfryd/Hulton/Archive by Getty Images

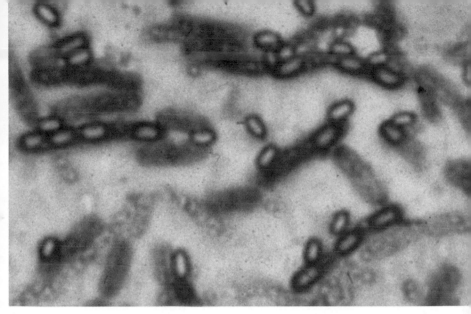

Above Shape of war to come: Anthrax (*Bacillus anthracis*) has a tough protective outer layer that allows the bacteria to survive for decades as spores. Popperfoto

Below 5 December 2001: A US Army scientist opens an anthrax-laden letter sent to the Democratic Senator for Vermont, Patrick Leahy. Subsequent intelligence rumours suggest that the perpetrator of these domestic attacks was allegedly a former US Military insider. Popperfoto

In October 2001, anthrax scares occurred in cities as far afield as Sydney (*left*), Cape Town (*above*) and Liverpool (*below*).
Popperfoto

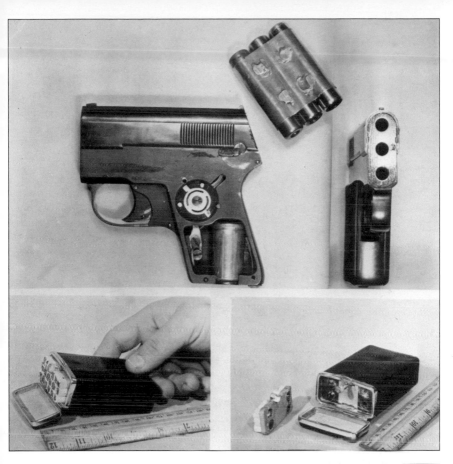

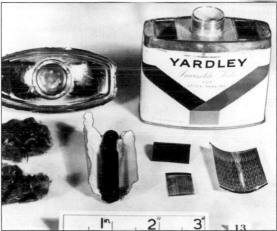

Above Smoking kills! This assassination equipment (found on MVD agent Nicolai Khokhov in West Germany in 1954) seems quaint in our age of anthrax. Yet these implements were chillingly effective, and could fire dum-dum bullets coated with potassium cyanide, with a report no louder than the click of a finger. Popperfoto

Right Equipment used in the Lonsdale Spy Case of the early sixties. Note the microfilm in front of the talc tin, and microfilm reader. Popperfoto

13

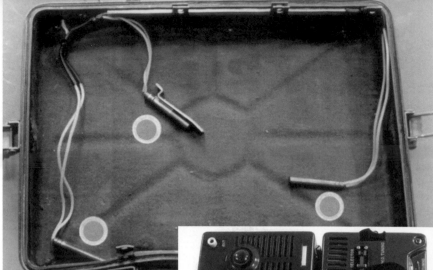

Swiss police were alerted to this Cold War relic in 1999. Buried by a KGB agent in woods near Berne sometime during the 1960s, the suitcase contained spy radio equipment and was rigged to explode. Popperfoto

Left Don't be fooled by the tailoring. Alan Dulles (CIA Director from 1953 to 1961) is the most celebrated Director of US Intelligence in history. Popperfoto

Below The halo of office: William Colby, as CIA Director from 1963 to 1976, fought to keep the Agency's work secret from the House of Representatives' Select Committee on Intelligence. Popperfoto

Left William Casey, Director of Central Intelligence from 1981 to 1987, was implicated in allegations surrounding the Iran-Contra scandal. Popperfoto/UPI

Below From allegations of gun running, to the school run: Lt. Colonel Oliver North, pictured here with his daughters in 1986, is now a successful radio chat show host. Popperfoto

Above If the cap fits. John Poindexter (*centre*), pictured here with his wife Linda and attorney in April 1990 after being found guilty of five felony charges relating to the Iran-Contra scandal, became Crisis Manager of the US government's Information Awareness Office. Popperfoto

Right Fully accessorized. Aldrich Ames and his wife Maria Rosario leave court in Alexandria, Virginia in March 1994. It is estimated that Ames' espionage on behalf of the KGB and later Russia allegedly led to the deaths of up to seven Western agents. Like disgraced FBI agent Richard Hanssen, who when not spying for the Russians would invite his best friend to watch him and his wife having sex via CCTV at his Virginia home, Ames represents a new breed of US traitor, motivated not by ideology but by greed. Popperfoto

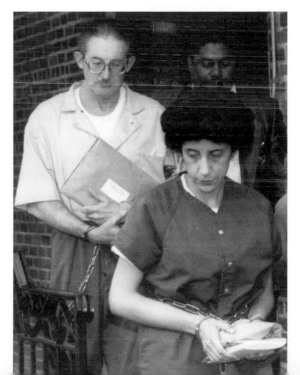

Old School Ties: Guy Burgess, the famous KGB mole (*left*), had once visited Moscow with Tom Driberg. Donald Maclean (*below, fourth from left*), pictured here with unsuspecting colleagues when he was First Secretary to the British Embassy in Washington, fled with Burgess upon exposure in 1955. Popperfoto

The Third Man: Pictured in November 1955, Kim Philby (*above, far right*) denies to the assembled gentlemen of the press that he tipped off diplomats Burgess and Maclean, who were about to be arrested as Soviet spies. A proletarian Philby (*below, left*) walks past a Moscow queue in 1968, a long way from drinks at the Reform Club. Anthony Blunt (*below, right*), in addition to his treasonous work as a double agent, could list tricking the Canadian government into buying fake and looted paintings among his activities, according to the *Daily Telegraph* Popperfoto

Does your mother know? George Blake, former British Vice-Consul in Seoul, pictured with his mother in 1953, after three years in a North Korean internment camp where he had been 'turned' as a Soviet agent. Popperfoto

Dying by the sword: Admiral William Canaris (*above*), Germany's Chief of Counter-Espionage from 1935 to 1944, aided the German resistance to Hitler, but viewed assassination as treason. For his pains, he was hanged naked at Flossenburg before jeering SS officers. Lavrenti Beria (*right*), Stalin's lackey and head of the NKVD, also executed, was untroubled by such moral dilemmas. Popperfoto

Some surprising security assets: Sir Richard Burton (*right*), roué, scholar of erotica, adventurer and gentleman spy. 'Lucky' Luciano (*below, left*), seen here living up to his nickname, was given his freedom in 1945 in recognition of Mafia help given to America's OSS during the invasion of fascist Italy. Alexander Korda (*below, right*) whose company, London Films, operated as an SIS front for many years.

Popperfoto

Literary spies: Graham Greene (*right*) – pictured here (*far right*) at the Brandenburg Gate in 1963 – was an SIS officer stationed in Africa during WW2, while Dennis Wheatley (*below, left*) worked within the super-secret London Controlling Section disinformation department. Perhaps the arts of espionage and storytelling require similar liberties to be taken with the truth. Actor Anthony Quayle (*below, right*) meanwhile, had worked for Britain's SOE. Popperfoto

The Architecture of Intelligence: Secure parking area and discreet personnel access, MI5 HQ, Millbank, London (*left*). SIS HQ, Vauxhall Cross, London (*below*). Sunlight catches a dish at the joint UK GCHQ/US NSA listening station at CSOS Morwenstow, north Cornwall, UK (*bottom*). Before 11 September 2001, it was widely believed that such installations had drastically reduced the need for buccaneering field officers of the old style. Richard M Bennett

The Defence Intelligence Agency (DIA) is responsible for internal military security and for external defence-related intelligence operations.

Federal Investigation and Intelligence Bureau (FIIB): in mid-1989 the National Police Force was reorganised to replace the Directorate of Intelligence and Investigation with a new nationwide domestic security force organised into three directorates for operations, administration and logistics.

NIGHTCRAWLER A talent spotter who prowls bars and nightclubs looking for government employees, military personnel etc. who can be compromised using booze, drugs or sex.

NKVD Soviet intelligence and security service and a predecessor of the KGB.

NMJIC National Military Joint Intelligence Centre (Pentagon's 24-hour intelligence watch).

NOC Non-official cover.

NOFORN Derived from 'NO FOREIGN NATIONALS', a US security restriction that prevents classified documents being seen or given to an allied security service.

NORWAY Norway in the forefront of the Cold War maintained a highly efficient internal security service known as the *NMI National Intelligence Service* and a number of highly important Cold War SIGINT bases, some of which were operated in conjunction with the NSA. These were at Borhaug, Rauske/Vetan, Jessheim, Kirkenes, Randaberg, Skage/Namdalen, Vadso, Vardo and Viksjofellet. In addition the airbase at Bodo was regularly used for U-2 spy flights and naval facilities were used as forward support bases for submarine based ELINT missions to the Arctic Ocean and Barents Sea areas where they monitored the main Soviet Northern Fleet bases and nuclear missile armed Submarine facilities.

NOTIONAL AGENT Fictitious agent or mole, usually part of a disinformation campaign.

NRO National Reconnaissance Office. The Satellite Intelligence agency of the USA.

NSA National Security Agency. The SIGINT agency of the USA.

NSC National Security Council (USA also commonly refers to the NSC staff).

NSTL National Security Threat List (a road map for the redirection of FBI counter-intelligence resources especially pertaining to industrial espionage).

NUGGET British intelligence term for money, political asylum or sexual services used as a 'bait' for a potential defector.

NURSEMAID Soviet term used to describe a security official who travelled with a delegation on visits to the West in order to prevent defections.

O

ODESSA A secret organisation that enabled prominent Nazis to escape the consequences of their actions during WWII. Both British and US Intelligence may well have penetrated Odessa and used it to cover the escape of 'useful' Nazi German Scientists and Intelligence Officers from either vengeful Jewish and later Israeli assassination teams or from Soviet 'snatch squads' in the confusion of the immediate postwar years.

OGPU Soviet intelligence and security from 1923 until 1934.

OKHRANA Intelligence and security service under the Russian Czars 1881–1917.

OLDFIELD, Sir Maurice (1915–81) If it hadn't been for the onset of WWII, Oldfield would almost certainly have embarked on an academic career in medieval history. Instead, having joined the Army, he was transferred to the Intelligence corps. He rose from a corporal to the rank of Colonel during service in Egypt and Beirut. Such was his intellectual reputation that he was recruited by SIS and served in the London HQ, in the Far East and in Washington as liaison Officer to the CIA. Promoted to Deputy Director he went on to become a highly successful, much liked and respected Director or 'C' of the SIS (MI6) from 1973 to 1978.

During his period as head of SIS, the Provisional IRA made at least two assassination attempts against Oldfield and, though he loathed so-called 'dirty tricks', he was realistic enough to accept that occasionally there was no effective alternative, and therefore Oldfield learned to use them sparingly, but to great effect. This, the IRA were to later find out to their cost. Recalled from retirement in 1979 to handle a delicate joint intelligence operation in N Ireland, apparently MI5 decided to expose his latent homosexuality anonymously to the media. This was done as much to settle old scores with SIS dating back to 'turf-wars' between the two British organisations over control of security operations in Ulster, as for any genuine security risk. Oldfield, a much saddened man and by now quite ill with cancer, quickly retired from government service in 1980 to return to his family home in Derbyshire and died the following year.

ONE TIME PAD (OTP)   Sheets of paper or silk printed with random five-number group ciphers to be used to encode and decode enciphered messages.

ONI   US Office of Naval Intelligence.

OPEN SOURCE – OSINT   Open Source Intelligence (unclassified sources; sometimes OSCINT).

OPERATIONAL INTELLIGENCE (OPINTEL)   Intelligence used in the planning of operations in a given region or theatre of war.

OPERATIONS COURSE   The elite 18-week course all CIA case officers take at the beginning of their careers.

OPERATIVE   An intelligence officer or agent operating in the field.

OPRICHNIKI, THE   Russia's first political or secret police founded by Ivan the Terrible in 1565. The power of the Oprichniki was as absolute as it was savage and unjust; whole regions were terrorised and in one instance most of the inhabitants of Novgorod were massacred in a 35-day orgy of cruelty in 1570. Tsar (Czar) Ivan came to fear their power and having allowed the Oprichniki a seven-year reign of terror disbanded them in 1572. The most important leaders were executed and many of the rest dispossessed of their estates.

OPSEC   Operations Security – maintaining secrecy and avoiding surveillance.

ORCHESTRA   A Russian term, believed to have been coined by Lenin, referring to the creation of a network of potential long-term agents under deep cover in a foreign country.

ORDER OF BATTLE – ORBAT   Intelligence describing the unit identity, strength, command structure and disposition of an opponent's military forces.

OSS   Office of Strategic Services (WWII forerunner of CIA).

OTS   The Office of Technical Service formerly the Technical Services Division, the CIA's technical arm for the Clandestine Service. Develops and deploys technical tradecraft equipment needed for clandestine and covert operations.

OVERT INTELLIGENCE   Information collected openly from public or open sources such as the news media. Also known as OSINT.

OWVL   One-way-voice-link; shortwave radio link used to transmit pre-recorded enciphered messages to an operative.

P

PADDING   Additional words added to the beginning and ending of a coded message to confuse enemy decryption efforts.

PAKISTAN   *The Directorate for Inter-Services Intelligence (ISI)*: established in 1948 as a military intelligence service, it was expanded into a foreign intelligence and internal security service in the early 1950s. The ISI is responsible for the co-ordination of intelligence functions of the three military services; surveillance of military personnel, foreigners, the media, politically active segments of Pakistani society, diplomats of other countries accredited to Pakistan and Pakistani diplomats serving outside the country, in addition to the interception and monitoring of communications and the conduct of covert offensive operations. Its most contentious activities have involved its overt support for the Taliban in Afghanistan and its wide-scale involvement with Muslim separatist groups in Kashmir, though this deteriorated markedly during 1997–2001 as differences began to surface over the ISI and its open support for both the Taliban and the Kashmiri terrorists.

The ISI has a considerable amount of autonomy and has for many years been answerable to neither the military nor the political leadership of Pakistan. The result is that there has been no real supervision of the ISI and corruption, narcotics and abuse of civil rights have become endemic. Drug money is used by the ISI to finance its support of the Taliban and this will probably continue covertly even though the regime in Afghanistan collapsed in December 2001. The Taliban is largely a Pakistani religious movement and very much the creature of the ISI. It also provides the finances for the proxy war against India in both the Punjab and Kashmir. CIA provided ISI a large quantity of espionage equipment along with training and access to certain intelligence sources. Initially Pakistani intelligence was modelled along British lines, but subsequently the CIA became the main overseas influence, with improved intelligence methods.

The ISI has its HQ in Islamabad. It is reportedly organised into seven divisions:

● *Joint Intelligence X (JIX)* – serves as the secretariat which co-ordinates and provides administrative support to the other ISI wings and field organisations; it also prepares intelligence estimates and threat assessments;

● *Joint Intelligence Bureau (JIB)* – responsible for political intelligence, the most powerful component of the organisation during the late 1980s; the JIB consists of three subsections, with one subsection devoted to operations against India;
● *Joint Counter-Intelligence Bureau (JCIB)* – responsible for field surveillance of Pakistani diplomats stationed abroad, as well as for conducting intelligence operations in the Middle East, SE Asia, China, Afghanistan and the Muslim republics of the former Soviet Union;
● *Joint Intelligence/North (JIN)* – responsible for Jammu and Kashmir operations, including infiltration, exfiltration, propaganda and other clandestine operations;
● *Joint Intelligence Miscellaneous (JIM)* – conducts espionage in foreign countries, including offensive intelligence operations;
● *Joint Signal Intelligence Bureau (JSIB)* – which includes Deputy Directors for Wireless, Monitoring and Photos, operates a chain of signals intelligence collection stations along the border with India, including the major site at Parachinar, and provides communication support to militants operating in Kashmir;
● *Joint Intelligence Technical*

In addition to these main elements, ISI also includes a separate nuclear section and a chemical warfare section.

A major part of the ISI's importance derives from the fact that the agency is charged with managing covert operations outside Pakistan – whether in Afghanistan, Kashmir, or farther afield. The ISI supplies weapons, training, advice and planning assistance to terrorists in Punjab and Kashmir, as well as the separatist movements in the NE frontier areas of India. This backfired badly on 13 December 2001 when a group of Pakistan trained and armed Kasmiri terrorists from the Jaish-e-Mohammed and Lashkar-e-Taiba attacked the Indian Parliament building in New Delhi. It appeared that they had been trained at the ISI camp in Muzzafarabad in Pakistan-controlled Kashmir.

The ISI is heavily engaged in covertly supporting the Kashmiri Mujahideen in their fight against the Indian authorities in Kashmir. Although all groups reportedly receive arms and training from Pakistan, the pro-Pakistani groups are reputed to be favoured by the Directorate of Inter-Services Intelligence. As of May 2001 there are at least four major militant organisations, and a number of smaller ones operating in Kashmir. They are roughly divided between those who support independence and those who support accession to Pakistan. The oldest and most widely known militant organisation, the Jammu and Kashmir Liberation Front (JKLF), has spearheaded the movement for an independent Kashmir.

ISI is said to have intensified its activities in the southern Indian States of Hyderabad, Bangalore, Cochin, Kojhikode, Bhatkal and Gulbarga. In Andhra Pradesh the Ittehadul Musalmeen and the Hijbul Mujahideen are claimed to be involved in subversive activities promoted by ISI. And Koyalapattinam, a village in Tamil Nadu, is said to be the common centre of operations of ISI and the Liberation Tigers.

Throughout the Cold War and the Soviet occupation of Afghanistan, relations between the USA and Pakistan were very close. The Soviet invasion of Afghanistan made Pakistan a country of paramount geostrategic importance. In a matter of days, the USA declared Pakistan a 'frontline state' against Soviet aggression and offered to reopen aid and military assistance deliveries. The ISI trained about 83,000 Afghan Mujahideen between 1983 to 1997 and dispatched them to Afghanistan. Pakistan paid a price for its activities. Afghan and Soviet forces conducted raids against Mujahidin bases inside Pakistan and carried out a campaign of terror bombings and sabotage in Pakistan's cities, guided by Afghan intelligence agents, causing hundreds of casualties. In 1987 some 90 per cent of the 777 terrorist incidents recorded worldwide took place in Pakistan.

Intelligence Bureau: the IB monitors politicians, political activists, suspected terrorists, and suspected foreign intelligence agents and keeps a close watch on political operatives from countries it considers hostile to Pakistan's interests, and it is responsible for harassing domestic opposition parties. The IB commonly resorts to wiretapping, communications interception and mail opening.

Military Intelligence: activities include operations in Sindh against Indian intelligence operatives. This organisation, implicated in arrests of innocent people, monitors the activities of the leaders of political opposition groups. The MI, though responsible for security and counter-intelligence operations within the Army, co-operates closely with ISI on a whole range of overseas and terrorist operations.

PAKISTAN, SPECIAL FORCES The present SSG (Special Service Group), effectively the enlarged 19th Baluch, has been based at its HQ at Cherat, near Attock City for more than 45 years. In March 1964 a joint CIA Covert Action and US Special Forces training team helped set up the new SF Airborne school at Peshawar; all members of the 19th Baluch have to be airborne-qualified and the training included both basic and jumpmaster courses. The SSG now has some 24 Companies, each of which has specialised units in desert, mountain, ranger, underwater warfare and intelligence-gathering operations.

In 1970 a genuine counter-terrorist capability was added, with the role being given to the independent Musa company, formed in the same year originally as a combat swimmer unit. The Musa company has gone on to become a dedicated counter-terrorism unit and from 1981 onwards has received training by SAS advisers. A wide range of skills is now considered necessary including heliborne insertion, combat shooting, parachute techniques including HAHO (High Altitude-High Opening) and HALO (High Altitude-Low Opening). It has a wide range of weapons available for use including standard army issue and such as black-market 9mm Israeli UZI and German MP5 sub-machine guns, US M16A1 automatic rifles and PSG1 sniper rifles. The SSG has conducted deep penetration operations within India and disputed areas of Kashmir, helped train Sri Lanka Army Commandos for operations against the Tamil Tiger insurgents, conducted covert intelligence missions in Afghanistan on behalf of the Taliban and provides air-marshals for airliners carrying VIPs. Indeed, one of its most notable operations to date was the successful rescue of hostages during the storming of a hijacked civil airliner at Lahore airport in September 1981. It is presently organised into three Special Forces Battalions each of four companies, with two based at the Cherat HQ and one on operations along the borders with India or at strategic locations such as nuclear research facilities or the Terbella Dam. In addition there are a further 12 independent Special Forces companies, including the enlarged MUSA company, now providing Pakistan with in theory an extensive dedicated genuine counter-terrorism capability. However, suspicion abounds that these units are used as much to teach the techniques of terrorism as to actually counter them.

PARTY PIECE   A successful MI5 'Black-Bag Operation' in 1955 which, after illegally breaking into the Mayfair home of a British Communist Party official, succeeded in copying a list of some 55,000 files containing the activities, names and addresses of Party members.

PATTERN   The behaviour and daily routine of an operative that makes his identity unique.

PAVEMENT ARTIST Intelligence term for a tail or skilled street surveillance.

PDB President's Daily Brief – intelligence and analysis on current threats or conflicts.

PENKOVSKY, Oleg (1919–63)   From 1945 to 1948, he attended the Frunze Military Academy in Moscow and was then assigned to the GRU military intelligence. Penkovsky's first espionage assignment was in Ankara where, in 1955, he served as a military attaché in the Soviet Embassy. He spied on Turkish military installations, as well as those of the US in Turkey. The following year he returned to Russia and studied military engineering. The GRU considered him to be one of their most reliable officers who had always carried out instructions efficiently.

Penkovsky claimed to be disillusioned with Communism and its aim to dominate the world. In 1961, Penkovsky led a Soviet trade delegation to London, but his real mission was to operate a GRU spy network. When British businessman Wynne arrived in Moscow to arrange the Soviet delegation's visit Penkovsky told him that he must meet senior Western intelligence officers once he arrived in London. Wynne managed to set up this meeting, which occurred almost immediately after the Soviet delegation arrived. Penkovsky told the SIS officers that he wanted to help the West and after convincing them that he was sincere, his offer was accepted. He was to be a double agent, pretending to conduct Soviet espionage while sending reports to the West. In 1961 and 1962, Penkovsky proved to be a major source of secret information for the West. He passed along to both the CIA and SIS intelligence relating to the Soviet Union's overall military aims, plans and espionage operations around the world. Identifying scores of Soviet agents, armaments, missile systems and even giving details on Soviet satellites. Penkovsky handed over more than 5,000 photographs during an 18-month period.

The manner in which Penkovsky delivered information to SIS when he was in Moscow was prosaic but effective. He would sit on a bench in the Tsventnoy Boulevard alongside Mrs Ruari Chisholm, the wife of Penkovsky's SIS control in Moscow. Penkovsy would then simply hand a box of chocolates containing the microfilm to the Chisholm children. Later, after the Chisholms were returned to London in 1962, SIS Officer Gervase Cowell and his wife Pamela played a similar role. Penkovsky, using the Western codename ALEX, took great quantities of top-secret documents each night and photographed them in his small flat overlooking the Moscow River, using a Minox camera provided by the SIS. Sometimes, Penkovsky would meet Wynne and simply hand him dozens of rolls of film.

The information Penkovsky provided on Soviet ballistic missiles is reported to have been of vital importance to President Kennedy during the Cuban Missile Crisis. However, the KGB slowly came to realise that a highly positioned Soviet official was feeding intelligence to the West. Penkovsky was arrested having finally been compromised by film of his meetings with the Chisholm family, George Blake having warned the KGB that Ruari Chisholm was an SIS Officer. His 'cut-out' Wynne was seized in Budapest and later returned to Britain after a show trial and a short period in a Soviet prison. Penkovsky was tried in May 1963 and was convicted both of treason and espionage. Penkovsky is believed to have been shot by firing squad a few days later. The real problem with the whole Penkovsky saga revolved around the suspicion aroused by the knowledge that the KGB had indeed suspected Penkovsky for months before his arrest, but for reasons as yet unknown he was allowed to continue passing intelligence to the West. Was Penkovsky a triple agent, i.e. ultimately loyal to Moscow and his reported execution mere disinformation or did the KGB, well aware of his connection with SIS following a tip-off from Blake, use Penkovsky to plant misleading information on the CIA and SIS?

PELTON, Ronald (1942–)   Former National Security Agency low-level communications specialist for 14 years before leaving in 1980, intelligence analyst Ronald Pelton was arrested in 1985 and accused of selling secrets to the Soviets. He was convicted in 1986 of two counts of espionage and one count of conspiracy and sentenced to three concurrent life sentences. By the time of his arrest, he was deeply in debt and had already resigned from the NSA. The special US Navy-NSA programme OPERATION IVY BELLS, a top secret compromised by Pelton, consisted of a series of recorders placed by US nuclear submarines on to an undersea communication cable linking the Soviet naval bases of Vladivostok and Petropavlovsk. The take from the programme provided the only unencrypted intercepts of Soviet military command messages. It provided high-grade intelligence from technological information to command procedures, to operational patterns, to typical location of units, to plans, to a basis for cryptologic analysis and much more. When the programme was betrayed, the US intelligence community was in the midst of a multi-billion-dollar effort to turn it into an online system that would have given the US unambiguous warning of any Soviet military move or plan. It was priceless. In the event of war, American lives would have depended on it. To protect the importance of the intelligence he betrayed, Pelton's true activities were not revealed even at his trial and in 1986 he was sentenced to life in prison.

PERSONAL MEETING A clandestine meeting between two operatives, always the most desirable but more risky form of communication.

PETRIE, Sir David (1879–1961) A Scot, educated at Aberdeen University, Petrie served in the Indian Police (1900–36) and had at one time been Assistant Director of Criminal Intelligence to the Government of India, finally rising to the post of Director of the Intelligence Bureau. In 1940 he was appointed head of MI5 in succession to Sir Vernon Kell. MI5 underwent a great deal of reorganisation at this time with constant changes of personnel that made life far from easy for the new chief. Petrie brought in various experts to improve agent running, communications and even administration. This not only made MI5 somewhat more effective, but also helped to establish closer links with SIS. He retired in 1946.

PFIAB President's Foreign Intelligence Advisory Board (USA).

PHILBY, 'Kim' Harold Adrian Russel (1912–88) Philby went up to Trinity College, Cambridge in 1929 and in the next five years set the foundations for a lifetime of espionage and treachery. Philby and his friends were deeply committed to Communism, and Cambridge had Communists aplenty with Roy Pascal and Maurice Dobb to name but two. Others like John Cornford helped recruit Michael Straight, Donald Maclean, Guy Burgess and Philby, who were all thought to be good candidates as NKVD moles. Philby went on to become a journalist, employed by politically moderate publications, as a cover for his Communist beliefs. When the Spanish Civil War broke out in 1936, Philby became a correspondent for the *London General Press* to cover the war. Philby was really being sent to Spain by the Soviets to spy on General Franco's fascist Falangists rebelling against the Republic. Philby's credentials had been enhanced by openly supporting the right-wing Anglo-German Fellowship, attending formal dinners that raised funds for Nazi groups and where swastikas were prominently displayed on the long dinner tables.

Philby was back in England by the outbreak of war between Britain and Germany in 1939 and was posted to the British Expeditionary

Force in France as a seasoned war correspondent. When France fell in June 1940 Philby, despite his previous membership of the Anglo-German Fellowship, was on good terms with the Secret Intelligence Service. Philby, with the approval of his NKVD controller, had put SIS officers in touch with the Soviet network operated by Sandor Rado in Switzerland which resulted in the SIS receiving valuable information on the German military. This must be counted as one of Philby's major contributions to SIS and the British war effort. Philby would later join SOE (Special Operations Executive), the sabotage and subversion organisation that had been formed in 1940 from a number of different paramilitary sections including Section D of SIS. At first, Philby and his Soviet controller thought this would be an excellent opportunity to obtain information on underground movements where future Soviet agents could be recruited. He was not to be sent into the field, however, because he had already been identified by the Abwehr through his membership in the Anglo-German Fellowship. Philby transferred to SIS and soon established himself as one of the 'bright young men' working in the Iberian section of the counter-intelligence directorate. Eventually he would be offered the prized position of establishing a dedicated anti-Communist desk inside SIS which must have delighted his Soviet NKVD control, Anatoli Lebedev, the replacement for Boris Krotov, who had long directed Philby's activities.

Directorate Five of SIS had its offices at No. 14 Ryder Street in West London, one floor below that of the OSS. Philby in his new position became a close colleague of Allen Dulles. One of the detailed reports Philby provided for SIS was the complete background on a NKVD spy named Boris Krotov, who had operated in England for much of the 1930s, thereby chronicling the espionage career of a very senior Soviet officer who had been the control for Philby, Burgess and Maclean, among many others. After the war, Philby, seen as SIS's foremost authority, was selected to go to Turkey in February 1947 to report on possible Soviet intelligence activities that might one day threaten Britain's Middle East oil interests. Yuri Feoktislov, a Soviet intelligence officer who had operated for a quarter of a century in the region became Philby's local control. Philby was soon faced with an immediate threat when Konstantin Volkov, the Russian consul-general in Turkey, contacted British intelligence officers, offering to defect with the names of Soviet agents in Istanbul. Philby quickly took over Volkov's case, contacted his controller and then stalled the plan until SMERSH officers were able to seize the would-be defector and rush him back to the Soviet Union where he was liquidated. Philby's double game accelerated in Istanbul. As part of his FO duties, he regularly met with nationalist leaders attempting to wrest back control of Albania from the Communists who had seized the country in 1945. Through these contacts, he was able to learn about the planned nationalist raids into Albania. He passed this information to Lebedev and when the nationalists crossed into Albania the Communists were waiting for them, killing or capturing scores of the rebels. When the CIA later planned a covert invasion of Albania, Philby obtained advanced information on this operation and passed it along to the Soviets who destroyed the Anglo-American mission. Philby, however continued to be considered one of the most effective officers in SIS and a potential future Chief. In 1949, he was sent to Washington as the first secretary to the British ambassador and the SIS liaison to the CIA. Guy Burgess arrived in Washington a year later and he worked closely with Philby, providing top-level data on NATO and nuclear research to the Soviets. By 1951, however, Burgess began to go to pieces and was also by then an alcoholic; his drunken behaviour soon caused him to be recalled to London and posed the first embarrassing chink in Philby's armour.

Anthony Blunt was soon to inform Philby that MI5 was about to have Donald Maclean arrested. Philby quickly notified Burgess. Guy Burgess panicked and fled Britain with Maclean creating the first serious security doubts about his friend Philby. Burgess and Maclean held a press conference in Moscow on 12 February 1956 in which they attacked Western democracies as corrupt and oppressive, the reasons they gave for their decision to defect. When public questions were asked about the role he may have played in the Burgess and Maclean affair, Philby chose to resign 'in disgust' at the accusations. However his many friends and colleagues within SIS refused to accept that he was anything other than a 'grossly wronged' and honourable member of the service. Philby in truth merely took a 'holiday' and was re-employed by SIS in a lesser role. Finally damning evidence of Philby's guilt was presented to SIS and corroborated by both the CIA and the Soviet defector Golytsin. Philby was presented with the evidence by Nicholas Elliot, a friend from SIS who flew out to Beirut to confront him. On 23 January 1963, having been given a few hours to 'consider his position', Philby boarded the Polish cargo ship *Dalmatova* which promptly sailed from Beirut for the Russian Black Sea port of Odessa. The composure of Philby's response to the evidence and his well-organised defection suggest a degree of warning, but no hard evidence is available as to its possible nature. Philby was comprehensively debriefed for many months in Kuybishev on the Volga, a thousand miles from his friends

Burgess and Maclean, and, by the time he finally reached Moscow, Burgess had died of an alcohol-induced heart attack at age 52.

Philby would became a KGB Major General in Moscow, sleep with Maclean's wife and generally lead a fairly dissolute life. He served his Soviet masters well, though he often felt that he wasn't really trusted or fully appreciated. 'To betray you must first belong,' he stated a few months before his death in May 1988. 'I never belonged.' Philby then added: 'I want to be buried in the Soviet Union, in this country, which I have considered to be my own since the 1930s.' His last wish was honoured to the full.

PHOENIX, OPERATION   US intelligence operation which ran from 1967 to 1971 to identify and eliminate the Vietcong apparatus in S Vietnam. Under the overall direction of the CIA, the US Army, S Vietnamese Central Intelligence Organisation (CIO) and secret police captured over 28,000 and probably killed in excess of 30,000 other purported Communists, though the CIA claim a lower figure of 20,500 deaths.

PHOTOGRAPHIC INTELLIGENCE, PHOTINT   Photographic intelligence; renamed IMINT or image intelligence. Usually involving high-altitude reconnaissance using spy satellites or aircraft.

PIPELINER   An intelligence or case officer who has been designated for an assignment to a station such as Moscow and is undergoing specialised tradecraft training.

PIANIST   Western intelligence term for a clandestine radio operator.

PIANO   Western intelligence term for a clandestine radio set.

PLAUSIBLE DENIAL   When first used it described a way to plan, organise and conduct clandestine operations, and in particular US Covert Action. It allowed for the 'plausible' denial of any official US support or involvement. The concept later evolved into the accepted method used by US high officials and their subordinates to discuss potential or actual clandestine operations by not using precise language and thus not revealing authorisation or involvement. It was considered vital not to record the spoken or written word in any way that if later publicly exposed would prove embarrassing or politically damaging.

An example of where this concept failed is the shooting down of a USAF Lockheed U-2 high-altitude spy plane over the former USSR on 1 May 1960. The 'plausible denial' was that the aircraft was on a weather-monitoring flight and had flown off-course. The cover story quickly broke down when the Soviet Premier Nikita Khrushchev revealed that the pilot, Gary Powers, had been captured, and had admitted to the true purpose of his mission.

PLAY BACK False information provided to an enemy while attempting to obtain accurate information by impersonating a captured spy or by using a turned spy in clandestine radio communications. The British used this in their XX Cross System in WWII and the Germans called it the 'Radio Game'.

PLUMBAT, OPERATION Israeli Mossad operation in 1968, undertaken to steal some 200 tons of uranium for the Israeli nuclear weapons programme. A German registered merchant vessel, the *Scheersberg*, arrived in Rotterdam in November 1968 and took on a new crew. The vessel sailed to Antwerp where it loaded the uranium bought from the Belgian Société Générale des Mineraux for delivery to Italy. The ship however, was to offload the cargo to an Israeli freighter between Cyprus and Turkey, which sailed to Haifa with the Israeli commandos who had posed as crewmen on the German freighter.

PLUMBING (PLUMBERS) The work undertaken to prepare a facility or office for a major operation, such as the planting of 'bugs', such work is undertaken by 'Plumbers'.

PNG Persona Non Grata – diplomatic expulsion usually following the flagrant breach of local laws, morality or being exposed as a spy.

POACHER British intelligence term for an enemy spy who is in the area of an ongoing operation.

POLITICAL INTELLIGENCE Information related to a foreign nation or a movement's internal operations that could prove of assistance to one's own government in deciding future policy.

POLLARD, Jonathan Jay (1943–) Jonathan Pollard, who worked for the Naval Criminal Investigative Service and its Anti-Terrorism Alert Centre was arrested in 1985 and later jailed for spying for Israel. Although he was allegedly paid well for his information, he said that the real reason he had become a spy was because of his Jewish ancestry and sympathy for Israel. Secrets he revealed include details about Libya and the Palestinian Liberation Organisation in Tunisia. Pollard illegally provided to Israel mostly what they had officially received from the CIA prior to the US government's anger over Israel's bombing of Iraq's Osirak nuclear reactor. Another agent may have been at work within the US military, since Pollard indicated the Israelis' requested data of which he had no knowledge. His co-operation later provided CIA officials with valuable information about his Israeli handlers.

POPOV, DUSKO (CODENAMED TRICYCLE) (1912–81) Dusan 'Dusko' Popov was a Yugoslav and a voluntary double agent ostensibly working for the German Abwehr, but actually controlled by MI5. In 1941 the Germans sent him to the USA, officially to gather information on the US Navy base at Pearl Harbor on behalf of their Japanese allies. FBI Director J. Edgar Hoover, however, violently disliked the British-controlled double agent and refused to co-operate in the operation. As a result the potential significance of the German Intelligence gathering on behalf of Japan in the months prior to their attack on Pearl Harbor was overlooked.

PORTLAND SPIES (PORTLAND SPY RING) During the 1950s the British Admiralty's Underwater Weapons Establishment at Portland, Dorset in S England was considered to be at the leading edge of research into the underwater detection, tracking and targeting of submarines. To the Soviet intelligence services this base was therefore a prime target for espionage and a network of at least five agents was created to obtain its secrets.

The true scale of this operation only came to light, however, when the Central Intelligence Agency received a series of letters signed 'Sniper' from a source later identified, following his defection to the US in 1960, as a disaffected Polish UB (Intelligence Service) Officer, Michael Golienewski. 'Sniper' claimed that the Soviets had a spy within the British Admiralty and this information was quickly passed on to the British security service, MI5. Unable to find a likely suspect in the Admiralty, MI5 transferred their attention to the ultra-secret Portland facility.

The internal security investigation eventually led to Harry Houghton, a clerk at Portland who had previously worked for the naval attaché in the Warsaw Embassy. Surveillance of Houghton showed that he regularly met a man later identified only by his cover name Gordon Lonsdale, the assumed name for deep cover GRU 'illegal' Conan Trofimovich Molody. Houghton's mistress, Ethel 'Bunny' Gee, also worked at Portland and was therefore placed under surveillance. Lonsdale had managed to recruit two reasonably low-level agents within the Portland base by playing on Haughton's bitterness at his failure to achieve promotion and by the provision of money to ease the financial pressures put on him by Ethel Gee's greed. Analysts still occasionally question whether Haughton or Gee alone would have had access to secrets sufficient to warrant the size of the Soviet commitment to this operation. Lonsdale was trailed under MI5 OPERATION LAST ACT to a large bungalow in Ruislip, London occupied by Peter and Helen Kroger, later identified as Morris and Lona Cohen, long-term deep-cover KGB officers. The Krogers were put under close surveillance in November 1960. On 7 January 1961 detectives from the Metropolitan Police Special Branch arrested Houghton, Gee and Lonsdale as they met to pass stolen documents. The Krogers were arrested at the same time, and when their home was searched over a nine-day period by MI5 security officers a vast array of espionage equipment, including hidden shortwave radios, one-time pads, codebooks and photographic copying gear, was uncovered. The innocent-looking bungalow in a quiet W London suburb was in fact the spy ring's communications centre.

The members of the Portland Spy Ring were tried on espionage charges at the Old Bailey, starting in March 1961. Their sentences highlighted the importance attached to this massive breach of security; Houghton and Gee both received 15 years. Lonsdale was to receive 25 years, but was exchanged in 1964 for MI6 agent Greville Wynn. The Krogers were sentenced to 20 years, serving only eight years, however, before they were exchanged for several British citizens held by the Soviets on 24 October 1969.

In the security inquests that followed, both the Admiralty and MI5 received justified criticism, the first for lax security and the latter for having failed to uncover an important espionage operation until they received the help of the CIA and information from a Soviet defector.

POSITIVE VETTING British term for a comprehensive Security Check.

PRIME, Geoffrey (1938–) Prime attended a technical school before joining the RAF, where he took a Russian language course and was posted to West Berlin. Lonely and with a deep sense of political confusion, Prime daydreamed about the Soviet Union, mistakenly believing that the regime represented the oppressed peoples of the world. Prime suddenly made a decision to work for the Soviets. He made contact with the KGB by simply going to a Soviet checkpoint in Berlin and handing a note to a Russian officer. Two KGB agents contacted him a short time later. Knowing that Prime's enlistment was about to run out after 12 years in the RAF the Soviets encouraged him to use his training to get a job with British codebreaking organisation GCHQ. Prime did exactly that, obtaining a job at a GCHQ Language

Centre in September 1968, where he translated electronic communications intercepts and then sent them on for analysis at the Cheltenham HQ. Taking a vacation to West Berlin, Prime slipped into East Berlin where he underwent more espionage training and was given a complete spy kit, which was contained in the false bottom of a briefcase. Inside were invisible inks and specially prepared writing pads on which he was to record his secret messages. He was also given £400 to be used in the purchase of a shortwave radio and a tape recorder. Once back in England, he went to work photographing GCHQ secrets which he sent on to his control in East Berlin in the form of microdots. He also made contact with his handlers through shortwave broadcasts in coded messages made up of figures and numbers in groups of five increments. Meanwhile, Prime rose in stature at GCHQ, becoming a highly regarded translator and processor of SIGINT.

He was transferred to GCHQ, Cheltenham in 1975, and was asked to work on intelligence information provided by the Rhyolite spy satellites, a CIA operation producing intelligence for the UKUSA network. So sophisticated were the spy satellites that they could monitor all forms of phone conversations and electronic messages inside the Soviet Union. The CIA, through TRW, manufacturers of the satellite, had almost perfected an even more sophisticated satellite, ARGUS, about to go into operation. Prime contacted his KGB control with this news and, at their request, flew to Vienna to confer with them. The KGB agents gave Prime a small sum of money for confirming information they had already received from two young Americans working at TRW. What Prime's control wanted now was the actual information being delivered by these satellites. Prime delivered and quickly, particularly since he now had access to almost all of the information the satellites were producing after being promoted to a section chief at GCHQ. When he learned that Boyce and Lee had been caught in America and sent to prison, Prime became nervous and seriously thought about accepting the Soviet offer to defect. He stayed on at GCHQ, nevertheless. When he suddenly resigned his post, he remembered to take a further 500 secret documents with him out of the GCHQ offices before leaving.

Prime was working as a taxi driver in Cheltenham when he was arrested on charges of sexually molesting young girls. His wife, Rhona, now felt it her patriotic duty to inform security officials that her husband was a spy. Prime was charged with violating the Official Secrets Act (OSA) and tried in November 1982. He was sentenced to 35 years in prison for espionage and three years for his sexual offences.

Senior officials of both the NSA and CIA went to London to confer with British intelligence and establish methods by which the agencies could better screen those involved with espionage data. Among other procedures, both agreed that all of those involved would be given lie-detector tests before being exposed to sensitive information.

PRIVACY Privacy is a fundamental human right. It underpins human dignity and other values such as freedom of association and freedom of speech. It has become one of the most important human rights issues of the modern age. It is protected in the Universal Declaration of Human Rights, the International Covenant on Civil and Political Rights, and in many other international and regional human rights treaties. Nearly every country in the world includes a right of privacy in its constitution, though in many cases the rules are openly and widely flouted by governments. At a minimum, these provisions should include rights of inviolability of the home and secrecy of communications. Most recently written constitutions in the more democratic societies include specific rights to access and control of one's personal information. In many of the countries where privacy is not explicitly recognised in the constitution, the law courts have attempted to include that right within other legal provisions.

However, advances in technology and a dimming awareness of the misuse that can be made of the invasion of personal privacy to dictate an individual's actions or infringe their human rights has enabled many national intelligence, security and police services to simply pay lip service to individual rights of privacy, while introducing increasingly invasive surveillance of every aspect of the individual's private and business affairs. The ease with which CCTV has proliferated throughout the developed world on the unproven argument that it has an effective role to play in crime prevention should be taken as a warning that 'Big Brother' has finally arrived and that the death of privacy and the individual's right to go about their life free from unwarranted government surveillance, CCTV and other monitoring devices is at hand.

PROBER An operative assigned to test border controls before an exfiltration is mounted.

PRODUCT The final result of an intelligence operation or espionage effort.

PROFILE All the aspects of an operative's or a target's physical or individual persona.

PROFUMO AFFAIR Though it was named after the War Minister John Profumo, this affair really revolved around Dr Stephen Ward, society osteopath to the rich and famous from Winston Churchill to Douglas Fairbanks Jr and a host of other celebrities. Confidant of Prince Philip and close friend of Viscount 'Bill' Astor, Ward was an immensely charming and gifted man. However, he was far less gifted when it came to choosing his friends. His ability as a portrait artist was such that he had been allowed to draw numerous celebrities including Stanley Spencer, A.P. Herbert, Douglas Fairbanks Jr, Churchill, Lord Shawcross, and Prof. Bernard Lovell. Many members of the British Royal Family would also sit for Ward including the Duchess of Kent, Ward's close friends Lord Snowdon and Prince Philip, and Princess Margaret. Indeed his work would later be bought up by a well-known art historian and disappear for ever, avoiding further embarrassment to Buckingham Palace.

In the early 1960s Ward rented Spring Cottage on Lord Astor's estate and celebrities, politicians and statesmen of the time were more than happy to spend days or weekends as his guests there but nearly all of them abandoned him when he needed their support. Ward, however, had entered a rather seedy world of promiscuity and private parties run by the likes of David, Marquis of Milford Haven and the cousin of Prince Philip. These often developed into full-blown orgies lasting over an extended weekend, with participants as varied as the photographer Baron and American superstar, Bing Crosby.

For months, rumours had circulated about the private life of John Dennis Profumo, Secretary of State for war and the 'object of his passion'. Educated at Harrow and Oxford, he was a quintessential high Tory who had achieved cabinet rank after serving in a number of junior posts. He was married to the film star Valerie Hobson and moved effortlessly in the highest of society. In the more deferential spirit of the 1950s, the rumours may have been dismissed. In the early 1960s, however, the rumours flowered and the young woman was soon named. Christine Keeler, unlike Profumo, had had an extremely undistinguished life: she had left home at 16 after an unhappy childhood and gravitated to London where she found work of a sort at Murray's cabaret club.

There she met and befriended another showgirl, Marilyn 'Mandy' Rice-Davies. Soon, both young women had drifted into the cosmopolitan and exciting circle that surrounded Dr Stephen Ward. Both young women were to become notorious players in Ward's celebrity sexual circus centred on his Wimpole Mews flat, equipped with two-way mirrors, Lord Astor's country mansion of Cliveden or weekends at Spring Cottage, parties and other rather more dubious social events. Soon, Keeler, Rice-Davies and numerous other girls in Ward's 'Harem' were sleeping around London and the home counties with publicly well-known figures, many of whom have successfully kept their anonymity. It was at Cliveden that John Profumo was introduced to Keeler. A brief but passionate affair ensued and tongues began to wag. Even then, it might have been brushed under the carpet in the time-honoured English way, but Profumo made a fundamental error: he lied to the House of Commons. In March 1963 he stated that there was 'no impropriety whatever' in his relationship with Keeler. Ten weeks later he appeared before MPs again to say 'with deep remorse' that he had misled the House, and would resign.

What brought Profumo down even more than his deceit of the Commons was the startling revelation that Keeler had also been having sex with Yevgeny 'Eugene' Ivanov, the naval attaché at the Soviet embassy and probable GRU intelligence officer. It was that detail which captured world attention, notably in the USA, where the FBI compiled a detailed report called OPERATION BOWTIE. J. Edgar Hoover was fully aware that the Ward circle included many extremely well-known Americans and girls such as Suzy Chang and Mariella Novotny who had been bedded by President John F. Kennedy. In fact, Novotny's lovers also included Malcolm X and the Rolling Stones guitarist, Brian Jones.

In Britain, Profumo's disgrace naturally caused a huge sensation, inflated by the establishment's crude and cruel attempts to find scapegoats for its own embarrassment. As usual, official wrath was turned on those least able to defend themselves. Stephen Ward was effectively set up in a totally disgraceful way by the British establishment and, to the lasting dishonour of all those involved, abandoned by the rich and famous who had so willingly and so often accepted his hospitality and his girls' favours. Ward was prosecuted on trumped-up charges of living on 'immoral earnings'. On the last day of his trial, he killed himself with an overdose of sleeping tablets. Keeler was also tried and imprisoned on related charges. Rice-Davies escaped prosecution, while several of the other girls who were kept out of the limelight by the prosecution died unexpectedly young over the next few years.

Stephen Ward's downfall was a highly convenient bit of luck for the disgraced ex-Minister for War, John Profumo. Focusing attention, as it did, on the sordid details of the lives of two pretty but extraordinarily silly girls, Ward's trial displaced from public awareness the fact that Profumo had lied to Parliament about his private life and prevented serious investigation of the real security aspects of the affair. Profumo's career in politics ended but he was awarded the CBE in 1975. Following Ward's trial and tragic death he devoted his time to charitable work. Less than two months after Ward's death, an official report was produced by Lord Denning, Master of the Rolls. He criticised the Government for failing to deal with the affair more quickly, but concluded that national security had not been compromised and privately both Denning and the Government pushed the blame on to the shoulders of Sir Roger Hollis, Director General of MI5. He was held responsible for not having warned his political masters of the possible security repercussions of the Minister of War sharing a whore with a Soviet Intelligence Officer. The Profumo affair was no passing sensation. It all but brought down the Macmillan Government and it almost certainly finished Macmillan himself as Prime Minister. In October 1963, less than a month after publication of the Denning Report, Macmillan resigned citing ill health.

The Security aspects of the affair have never been entirely or satisfactorily explained, but it is known that MI5 ran a brothel in Church Street in Kensington throughout much of the 1950s and early 1960s for the use of visiting dignitaries, diplomats and intelligence officers. For those too important to visit such an establishment, certain discreet gentlemen were called upon to provide young female or male company directly to the VIP hotel bedroom; Dr Stephen Ward was probably one of those 'gentlemen'. He certainly had the right social connections, the girls and indeed he had an MI5 controller, Keith Wagstaffe (cover-name 'Woods'). John Profumo stumbled upon a joint MI5–SIS honey-trap operation designed to persuade Ivanov, the Soviet Naval Attaché and probable spy to defect. Indeed, Sir Colin Coote, Editor of the *Daily Telegraph* and a former officer in the Secret Intelligence Service, was responsible for introducing Ward to Ivanov at the behest of his old service.

A senior MI5 officer involved in the operation said that it was a pity that Ward's true role had not been revealed at the time of his trial. 'I think that everyone involved did feel sorry about Ward and the final outcome.' Ward, he added, was a patriot working for his country. 'Nowhere in the Denning Report does it say that Ward was acting under our [MI5] instructions; that is very unfortunate.'

To cover up the risk of international humiliation and political and security embarrassment, someone had to be sacrificed. That someone was the unfortunate and very loyal Dr Stephen Ward.

PROPRIETARY COMPANY   CIA term for a commercial asset or front company, such as AIR AMERICA.

PROVOCATION   A harassing act or procedure designed to flush out surveillance.

PROVOCATEUR   An operative sent to incite a target group to action for purposes of entrapping or embarrassing them.

PURPLE   US codename for Japanese diplomatic cipher machine of 1930s and 40s.

Q

Q CLEARANCE   US Security clearance necessary for access to restricted nuclear data or weapon material.

QUEEN ANNE'S GATE   21 Queen Anne's Gate, in a fashionable area of London, was the official residence of the Head of SIS (MI6) from around 1923 to 1966. It backed on to the main HQ, Broadway Buildings, and was connected by a short tunnel.

QUESTIONABLE ACTIVITIES   The list of possibly illegal or embarrassing activities compiled throughout the CIA during the Senate investigations. These were delivered to Congress by DCI Colby.

R

RADAR INTELLIGENCE (RADINT)   Intelligence gained from Radar, increasingly seen as a sub-part of Imagery Intelligence (IMINT).

RAFTER   One of the most important electronic security operations of the Cold War era. Carried out by MI5 from 1958 onwards, it was tasked to determine whether the KGB were able to track the A4 department 'Watchers' or surveillance teams following suspected Soviet intelligence operatives around London, from within the Soviet Embassy.

RAVEN   A male agent employed to seduce either males or females in a sexual entrapment operation or sexpionage.

RDT   (Rapid Deployment Teams) FBI Counter-Terrorist or Hostage Rescue Units ready for overseas deployment.

RECONNAISSANCE   Observation mission undertaken to acquire, by various means, information about a target of intelligence interest.

REDL, Col. Alfred (1864–1913)   Few men were more powerful in the old Austro-Hungarian empire than Colonel Alfred Redl, chief of military counter-intelligence (Kundschaftsstelle). Outwardly he appeared to his superiors to be the model spymaster and fanatically loyal to Emperor Franz Joseph. Inwardly, he was a shrewd and calculating person, whose secret homosexuality was insatiable and with a definite lust for money. For these two reasons he became his country's arch traitor in the years leading up to WWI.

In 1900 Redl joined Austria's military counter-intelligence corps. By the following year Redl had become chief of counter-intelligence in the Vienna military region. Fascinated with espionage since his childhood, Redl immediately began modernising Austrian intelligence techniques. He introduced photography and fingerprinting into his agency and the 'Third Degree' method of interrogation of suspected spies, having blinding lights flood the faces of those being questioned.

Redl had already begun to supply Imperial Russia with information to fund his extravagant lifestyle and his numerous lovers. Now as chief of counter-intelligence he was to expose a number of low-grade Austrian spies whose names had been passed to him by the Russian

Okhrana in order to protect his own treachery. He became director of all espionage for Austria in 1907 and by 1909 was conferring with his German counterpart, Walther Nicolai, head of the Kaiser's intelligence operations. From these new contacts Redl was able to piece together substantial secret information about German forces and this, too, he sold to the Russians.

In 1912 Redl was again promoted, made chief of staff to General Giesl who commanded an army corps in Prague which allowed him to supply the Russians and indeed French and Italian intelligence with further information on the Austrian forces. However, his luck couldn't run for ever and in 1913 an Austrian counter-intelligence officer, Ronge, discovered evidence of Redl's treachery. Ronge immediately notified his superior, General August Urbanski von Ostromiecz. Later that night Ronge and three of his most trusted officers went to Redl's hotel and entered his suite unannounced. Redl confessed quite quickly and asked permission to die like an officer. He was handed a Browning revolver. Ronge and his aides went to an all-night cafe waiting tensely for several hours, sending a police detective to Redl's suite every half-hour to see if Redl was dead. Each time the detective went to the suite, he found Redl still alive. However at 5 a.m., he found Redl crumpled in front of a full-length mirror. He had placed all of the lamps in his room about him, undressed and while looking at his naked body, fired a bullet into his brain.

RE-DOUBLED AGENT A double agent whose activities are discovered and is turned again by his original service.

REILLY, Sidney George (1874–1925) Sidney Reilly has been falsely glamorised as one of Britain's great secret agents who, it was claimed, 'wielded more power, authority and influence than any other spy.' He was also a professional assassin, expert at 'poisoning, stabbing, shooting, and throttling'. Energetic, unpredictable, self-confident and decidedly ruthless, Reilly loved money, women and power. He possessed, it was reported, 'eleven passports and a wife to go with each of them'.

Born in Odessa, Russia on 24 March 1874, Reilly was the bastard son of a rich Jewish landowner and contractor in Russian-occupied Poland and the wife of a Czarist officer. Though he used his father's name, Rosenblum, he had no official name. Shortly before the Russo-Japanese War broke out in 1904, Reilly travelled to England and in 1909 managed to become a 'freelance' agent of Cumming's Foreign Section of the new Secret Service Bureau. The future SIS chief apparently came to admire Reilly but still maintained certain reservations, saying that he was 'a man of indomitable courage, a genius as an agent but a sinister man who I could never bring myself wholly to trust'. Reilly was a busy and, by all accounts, effective field agent for what had now become the Secret Intelligence Service throughout the 1914–16 period. However, he came into his own with the Bolshevik Revolution in 1917, travelling widely under a number of disguises in both the Red Army and counter-revolutionary White Army areas of Russia during 1917–18.

Reilly was believed to have been involved in at least one failed attempt on Lenin's life, including, according to a secret French intelligence report, an occasion on which 'Reilly and a group of Lettish Soldiers were to storm a meeting of the All Russian Congress of Soviets at the Bolshoi Threatre. At a given signal the soldiers would seal the exits and a group led by Reilly, gun in hand, would jump onto the stage, seize Lenin, Trotsky and the other leaders. All would then be shot on the spot!'

Escaping capture on a number of occasions, Reilly finally managed to return to England where he immediately lobbied Cumming to have the British Foreign Office use him to continue the fight against Bolshevism. He was convinced, he said, that he was the one man to bring down Lenin's regime. The Foreign Office was disinclined to add to their muster a man as flamboyant and uncontrollable as Reilly. He stayed on with SIS, an occasional agent but never employed as an officer. In 1919, Reilly allied himself with Boris Savinkov, a conniving, clever anti-Communist terrorist. Reilly, however, failed to achieve anything of importance either personally or on behalf of his anti-Bolshevik friends over the next few years. Financially ruined and in increasing ill health, Reilly returned to London where he found it almost impossible to raise money for a further expedition to Russia. He had already borrowed heavily from all of his former friends in the SIS and no longer had a useful relationship with British intelligence. Cumming was dead and the new chief, Admiral Hugh Sinclair, believed Reilly was little more than a seedy adventurer. In March 1925, Reilly admitted in a letter to Ernest Boyce, his fellow spy in Russia that 'my own affairs ... as you know, are in a hellish state'. He added with a tinge of self-pity: 'I was fifty-one yesterday and I want to do something worthwhile, while I can.'

Boyce, who was then the SIS chief in Helsinki, wrote to Reilly to tell him that he had been in contact with representatives of the Paris Trust. In reality this was a Communist disinformation and entrapment operation which had already successfully lured Savinkov back to his death in Russia, a fact unknown to Boyce or Reilly. Boyce, however, was convinced that the Trust was extremely powerful and had the contacts, money and secret forces to bring about a radical change in Russia. Through him, Reilly came to meet several of the MUCR representatives, agreeing to go to Russia to confer with the Trust's leading council members. Like Savinkov before him, Reilly was easily hoodwinked. He crossed the Finnish border on 25 September 1925, and was taken to a villa outside Moscow two days later to meet with council members who were really OGPU agents.

Reilly was interrogated and then told that the death sentence imposed upon him 'in absentia' in 1918 would now be carried out. The once nerveless spy panicked. He wrote a desperate note to OGPU chief Dzerzhinsky, according to later Soviet accounts, in which he begged for his life in exchange for priceless information he could provide Soviet intelligence. Reilly's note read: 'After prolonged deliberation, I express willingness to give you complete and open acknowledgement and information on matters of interest to the OGPU concerning the organisation and personnel of the British Intelligence Service. And, so far as I know it, similar information on American intelligence and likewise on Russian émigrés with whom I have had business.' Dzerzhinsky did not respond. Sometime in November 1925, Sidney George Reilly was placed before a villa wall outside of Moscow and executed by a firing squad, his body being later dumped into an unmarked grave.

That Reilly was involved in a direct SIS plot to assassinate Lenin has become clear from a close study of official papers, some of which are still retained by SIS. The embarrassment this caused to the head of SIS in 1998, Sir David Spedding led him to campaign for such documents to remain secret. In 1918 Reilly was sent to Russia as a freelance SIS agent; once there he concocted a plan to murder the Soviet leader. Captain George Hill, Chief of SIS in Russia in a secret CX report to Mansfield Cumming in London, made it clear that both he and Ernest Boyce, SIS station chief in Moscow, were involved in the failed assassination. He commented that 'Boyce had apparently considered the plan risky, but agreed that it was worth trying and that failure of the plan would drop entirely on Reilly's neck.'

That the British Liberal Government of Lloyd George nearly became responsible for the assassination of the Soviet Leader or leadership through the good offices of its own intelligence service is, to say the least, a startling revelation. It also once again highlights that the truth about the world of espionage and clandestine operations is often stranger than fiction.

REPRO   Making a false document.

RESIDENT   The KGB/SVR chief of station in any foreign location.

RESIDENTURA   The KGB/SVR station usually located in their embassy in a foreign capital.

RICHELIEU, Cardinal Armand-Jean Du Plessis (1585–1642) Paris-born Armand-Jean Du Plessis Richelieu was a junior member of the French aristocracy. After entering the clergy, he became Bishop of Lucon in 1607. Politically ambitious, he gained the favour of Marie de Medici, mother of King Louis XIII, who brought him to court and influenced his appointment as Secretary of State for Foreign Affairs in 1616. Though he fell from favour, Richelieu regained his political stature when he was made a cardinal of the Catholic Church in 1622. Two years later he became Prime Minister under Louis XIII, a post he tenaciously held until his dying day. From the day of his appointment, Richelieu began to establish his own espionage network, which he funded from government coffers, an enormous treasure chest that allowed him to put thousands on his payroll. In addition to spying on the nobility to determine plots against the crown, Richelieu's agents spied on his foremost enemies at court, those resentful of his powerful position and who intrigued to have him replaced.

Such was the conspiracy headed by the queen mother and some of her supporters who feared that the very man they had promoted to the position of prime minister was now so powerful that he might usurp the throne. They plotted to have Richelieu replaced. Having learned of this from his spies, the Cardinal burst into a palace meeting where his fate was being discussed. He confronted the conspirators and suavely persuaded the King that he should keep his post for the benefit and safety of France. Louis XIII kept him on and never again was Richelieu's authority seriously challenged. Richelieu's top agent was a Capuchin friar, François Leclerc du Tremblay who travelled to the smaller states of the Holy Roman Empire to spread discontent against Ferdinand II, the Hapsburg emperor. Throughout the Thirty Years' War (1618–48), Richelieu's agents were able to undermine the military might of Austria, then France's greatest political rival. A master at double-dealing, Richelieu maintained relations with Austria while secretly backing Gustavus Adolphus of Sweden to invade the Hapsburg Empire in a war that so weakened Austria that France emerged as the strongest empire in Europe. Tremblay was the instrument by which Richelieu was able to remove Austria's greatest general, Albrecht von Wallenstein, from the active list in 1630. Tremblay had wormed his way into the confidence of Ferdinand II, convincing the monarch that Wallenstein's abilities were overrated. When Adolphus's armies gobbled up many Austrian provinces, Ferdinand returned Wallenstein to his position but by then it was too late to recover the lost lands. Almost all French teachers of dance or fencing who went abroad were invariably Richelieu's handpicked spies, working in the courts of other kings and countries, relaying information to Richelieu through a network made up of tens of thousands of spies. This vast army of agents remained in place and continued to work for France even after the death of the 'Gray Eminence', as Richelieu was called. He was replaced by an equally cunning spymaster Cardinal Mazarin, who removed Tremblay as his chief aide with Ondedei, the Bishop of Fréjus.

RIMINGTON, Dame Stella (1935–)   The first woman to become Director General of MI5. Educated at Edinburgh University and Liverpool University. After joining MI5 full-time in 1969, Rimington worked in all the main fields of the Service's responsibilities, counter-subversion, counter-espionage and counter-terrorism. In charge of 'counter-subversion' F Branch in 1983, Rimington surveilled Patricia Hewitt and Harriet Harman, then running the National Council for Civil Liberties. The Campaign for Nuclear Disarmament and the miners who were striking in an attempt to stop pit closures were all MI5 targets, but Rimington claims only those within them who wanted to bring down Thatcher's government. What is slightly difficult to see is how MI5's 'clear thinkers' were able to tell these categories apart, until they had all been thoroughly burgled, infiltrated and bugged.

One of its most damaging MI5 fiascos of recent times came in 1982. Michael Bettaney, a former agent-runner in N Ireland, was by then serving in the MI5's K4 section, which carried out surveillance on Soviet bloc espionage in Britain. An unstable alcoholic, he was caught trying to tell the KGB about his colleagues' operations. In prison, awaiting trial, he managed to give the IRA the names of most of the intelligence officers and agents in N Ireland. Two years earlier, one of Bettaney's top agents, an IRA infiltrator, met Rimington in London and warned her of Bettaney's volatility and drinking. It would appear that Rimington took no serious action as Bettaney's access to secrets was not restricted. When, however, Bettaney was arrested, Rimington escaped criticism.

When groups such as Islamic Jihad were attacking non-Israeli targets in the wake of Israel's invasion of the Lebanon in 1982, a small unit known as G7 was established as a 'joint section' by MI5 and the Secret Intelligence Service, MI6. The Islamic fundamentalist groups, though based abroad (normally SIS territory), had supporters and an infrastructure in Britain, the province of MI5. Osama bin Laden's Al-Qa'ida network is typical of this pattern, the fax claiming responsibility for the attacks on US embassies in 1998 came from a shop in N London. Against the protests of G7's staff, Rimington disbanded it in 1994. The consequence, intelligence sources say, was that some known and previously monitored operatives disappeared from view: 'When it became clear just how great the threat posed by bin Laden was, we were in a difficult position. Scrapping G7 was a foolish move. Instead of having a cadre of experienced case officers, we were virtually starting from scratch.'

Rimington's memoirs fail to mention in any detail the defection to Britain in 1992 of Vasili Mitrokhin, the former KGB chief archivist who arrived with vast files containing details of almost 70 years of Soviet espionage against the West. This was unquestionably the most important event in counter-espionage during Rimington's period as Director. Mitrokhin's book, co-written with Professor Christopher Andrew, led to the prosecution of Michael Smith, the Soviet agent who worked for Thorn EMI. In 1999, Mitrokhin's book also triggered the exposure of Melita Norwood, the octogenarian former low-level Soviet agent.

Rimington became Director General of MI5 in 1992 and led the Service's counter-espionage work in the closing days of the Cold War. As Director General, it is alleged, she took a dim view of former officers if they disclosed events from the distant past, citing the Official Secrets Act. A distinguished former ambassador to Moscow, who had been at MI5 earlier in his career, was even ordered not to appear on *Desert Island Discs*. However, her attitude was to change dramatically when it came to her own memoirs. Rimington claims to have transformed a sexist male bastion into one of political correctness. This account is bitterly disputed by some of her female colleagues, who say they remember a woman principally devoted to her own personal advancement, who did little to foster other women's careers. While probably more than half of MI5's staff are women, there are still very few in senior grades. Rimington's genius lay in her understanding of 'office politics'. She claims to have helped foster a new style of MI5 officer, quite different from when she first entered the service. The modern version was younger, well travelled, spoke foreign languages. The new breed are committee orientated, comfortable with ministers and above all, safe. In other words, Rimington had rid MI5 of its experienced but difficult old Intelligence and Security officers and replaced them with politically correct Civil Service clones. To quote a journalist, 'Suave, non-sexist, good at presentation, but not very effective at preventing murderous atrocities'.

RIVET JOINT   Codename for ELINT operations during the Cold War using converted KC135 Stratotankers redesignated as the RC-135. These aircraft were to provide the US intelligence community with highly specialised electronic surveillance platforms. The USAF RC-135V/W RIVET JOINT 'RJ' aircraft are equipped with an extensive array of sophisticated intelligence gathering equipment allowing intelligence specialists to monitor the electronic activity of potential or actual adversaries. The aircraft are sometimes called 'hogs' due to the extended 'hog nose' and 'hog cheeks'. RIVET JOINT has been widely used in the Desert Storm operations, Bosnia, Kosovo, Afghanistan and the increasing number of surveillance missions required by the War on Terrorism. Somalia,Yemen and many other potential target countries in the Middle East and SE Asia are regularly monitored by the RC-135. China, N Korea and at present, to a lesser extent, Russia are still prime targets for regular surveillance flights. Using automated and manual equipment, electronic and intelligence specialists can precisely locate, record and analyse much of what is being done in the electromagnetic spectrum.

There are at least 15 RIVET JOINT aircraft available by 2002 which are now able to conduct extensive ELINT and COMINT intercept operations against targets at ranges of up to 240 kms. The other main capabilities of these aircraft include providing indications about the location and intentions of enemy forces and warnings of threatening activity. Broadcasting high priority combat advisory and imminent threat warnings that can be sent direct to US aircraft danger and operating both data and voice links to provide target info to US ground based air defence radar and missile systems. The RIVET JOINT aircraft operated by the 55th Wing, Offutt Air Force Base, Nebraska, provide direct, near real-time reconnaissance information and electronic warfare support to theatre commanders and combat forces. In support of the 55th, the 95th Reconnaissance Squadron operates additional surveillance missions out of RAF Mildenhall in Britain. The 488th Intelligence Squadron provides the intelligence personnel who actually operate the advanced electronic monitoring and interception equipment which is packed tightly into most of these large aircraft's fuselage. RIVET JOINT (RC-135V/W) is often described by the USAF as an 'air refuelable, theatre asset with a nationally tasked priority'. It therefore can collect, actually analyse, report and even exploit intercepted enemy transmissions from a wide variety of sources. In most conflicts it will deploy to the theatre of operations with other airborne Electronic Warfare elements of the USAF Tactical Air Command such as the AWACS, and the Joint STARS. Importantly all the different airborne elements are connected both by datalinks and voice as required. The aircraft has secure UHF, VHF, HF, and SATCOM communications. Refined intelligence data can be transferred from RIVET JOINT to AWACS through the Tactical Digital Information Link TADIL/A or into intelligence channels via satellite and the Tactical Information Broadcast Service (TIBS), which provides nearly real-time theatre information to the intelligence community and to the commanders of military forces in the combat zone.

ROBERTSON, Lt. Col. Thomas Argyll 'TAR' (1909–94) TAR was the architect of the 'Double Cross' system and one of the most successful intelligence operations of the century. As a counter-espionage officer in MI5, TAR uncovered the activities of Arthur Owens, a notoriously slippery Welshman supplying information to the Abwehr. He was arrested and agreed to work for MI5 (codename SNOW) and continue sending misleading information to the Germans. As the deception gained momentum, more of SNOW's friends were recruited as double agents. By December, TAR had some 12 Nazi spies under his control, including two in Sweden. January 1941 saw a special sub-committee set up under J.C. Masterman, one of TAR's subordinates, to co-ordinate what would now became the Twenty or XX or Double Cross Committee. Still under the control of TAR as head of MI5's 1(a) section of B Division, it ran more than 40 double agents.

TAR had originally joined MI5 years before the war through his friendship with John Kell, the son of the Head of the Security service. After the war, TAR, unhappy with the atmosphere in the new HQ at Leconfield House in Curzon Street and the leadership of Sir Percy Sillitoe, transferred to GCHQ to head their internal security branch, first at Eastcote in London and then at the new Cheltenham HQ.

ROLL-OUT A surreptitious technique of rolling out the contents of a letter without opening it. It can be done with two knitting needles or a split chopstick.

ROLLED UP When the operation goes bad and the agent is compromised.

ROMANIA *Romanian Intelligence Service* (*SRI*) Founded in March 1990, the SRI is now the main domestic intelligence and internal security service and strangely the only Romanian secret service under parliamentary scrutiny. However, many observers consider that the successor organisations of the Communist political police continue to use at least some of their predecessor's dubious methods to try to exert extensive control over the population.

From the outset SRI was depicted as the President's 'personal security service' and the history of SRI, plagued by dissent and purges, appears to be rooted in the continuation under a new name of the Communist-era secret service. In March 1994 it was reported that only one-third of approximately 15,000 Securitate officers had been offered employment in the new organisation, but since then the number has increased. The internal organisation of the SRI remains obscure, but Division C is responsible for the protection of the national wealth, and Division A is responsible for the protection of the constitutional order.

Securitate – Departamentul Securitatii Statului – Department of State Security: the Securitate was the hated and feared secret political police force of the Communist Party. It remained largely shrouded in secrecy, but an increasing number of defections from their ranks shed some light on their composition and activities. The Securitate was responsible for guarding the internal security of the Ceausescu regime and suppressing any unrest, disturbance or dissident group that criticised or dared to challenge it. The Securitate succeeded in repressing most organised opposition to the regime for many years through illegal imprisonment, imaginative and appallingly original torture methods, multiple and systematic rape of both prisoners and celebrities, including well-known young female members of the world-famous Romanian Gymnastic team. The widespread use of murder and the assassination of dissidents abroad removed many natural leaders of the opposition. Finally, however, the spontaneous outbursts of discontent with Ceausescu's 'cult of personality', economic austerity policy, treatment of ethnic minorities, anti-religious campaigns and lack of respect for internationally recognised civil and human rights occurred with increasing frequency after the mid-1970s, and ultimately led to the overthrow of the regime.

The *Directorate for Investigations* had agents and informants placed in virtually every echelon of the party and government, as well as among the public, to report on the dissident activities and opinions of ordinary citizens. It carried out illegal entries into public offices and private homes and interrogated and arrested people opposed to Ceausescu's rule. Its agents frequently used force to make dissidents provide information on their compatriots and their activities. *General Directorate for Technical Operations (Directia Generala de Tehnica Operativa (DGTO))* was an integral part of the Securitate's activities. Established with the assistance of the KGB in the mid-1950s, the DGTO monitored all voice and electronic communications in the country. The DGTO intercepted all telephone, telegraph and telex communications coming into and going out of the country. It secretly implanted microphones in public buildings and private residences to record ordinary conversations among citizens. *Directorate for Counter-Espionage* conducted surveillance against all foreigners to monitor their contacts with Romanians. *Directorate IV* was responsible for similar counter-espionage functions within the armed forces and its primary mission was identifying and neutralising Soviet penetrations. *Directorate V and the Directorate for Internal Security* focused mainly on members of the party and government. *Directorate V* provided protective services and physical security for Romanian officials. With more than 1,000 agents, the *Directorate for Internal Security* concentrated on ruthlessly rooting out disloyalty to Ceausescu within the PCR hierarchy, the Council of Ministers, and the Securitate itself. It was a small-version Securitate in itself, with independent surveillance, mail censorship and telephone monitoring capabilities.

SIE Foreign Intelligence Service – DSOI Operative Surveillance and Intelligence Directorate: the first new secret service to be built on the ruins of the old regime was the Foreign Intelligence Service, set up on 18 January 1990. Most observers tend to see the present organisations as the natural successors to the Securitate, the notorious political police of the Communist era. Official denials of any connection between the new agency and their infamous predecessor have not been able to dispel the suspicion that they are splinter organisations of the former Securitate, resuscitated under new names and with specialised functions.

The *DIE (Departamentul de Informatii Externe; Department of External Information)* was Romania's primary foreign intelligence organisation. It worked closely with the Ministry of Interior, the Securitate. The defection of the DIE deputy director, Lieutenant General Ion Pacepa, in 1978 revealed considerable information on its activities abroad for the first time, precipitated a major purge of personnel from the DIE, and contributed to the cooling of relations between Romania and the USA in the 1980s. The DIE was formed with Soviet assistance in the mid-1950s. Until the early 1960s Romania sent its intelligence officers to attend a two-year KGB training course in espionage tradecraft near Moscow. In 1964 the DIE curtailed co-operation with the KGB and established a DIE training centre in Brosteni, Suceava judet. The *Directorate for Operations* conducted clandestine intelligence collection and other activities outside Romania. Its officers operated under cover throughout the world, collecting political, economic and technical intelligence for analysis by the Directorate for Foreign Intelligence.

Brigade SD personnel were assigned primarily to Western countries to conduct technological espionage. Within the Directorate for Operations, the *Emigré Brigade* had intelligence officers who contacted and worked among the 600,000 Romanian émigrés living in the USA, France and W Germany. Playing on Romanian nationalism, they encouraged former Romanian citizens to co-operate with the DIE in obtaining Western high technology. *Service D* conducted covert operations, including the dissemination of forgeries and disinformation, to promote Romanian national interests and foreign policies. Service Z of the Directorate for Operations reportedly maintained ties to non-state entities including guerrilla movements, terrorist groups, and international organised crime.

The Directorate for Technical Equipment was responsible for designing or obtaining specialised espionage equipment required by the DIE. It was reportedly involved in equipping some Romanian TIR trucks to conduct espionage operations in W Europe. The DIE's *National Center for Enciphered Communications* had the mission of protecting Romanian government and party communications from Western and Soviet electronic monitoring. In 1989 the ministries of national defence, interior, foreign affairs, and foreign trade relied on the centre's encryption systems in their daily operations at home and abroad. It is also responsible for the overall COMSEC and SIGINT targeting and policy of the Romanian Army's *Counter-Intelligence Directorate Special Telecommunications Service (STS)*.

ROOM 40 At the outbreak of WWI, the German military began transmitting coded messages that were structured in a cipher unknown to British intelligence. Admiral Henry Oliver quickly assembled a group of cryptologists under the direction of code expert Alfred Ewing. A month after Ewing and his cipher analysts went to work on the German code, Reginald Hall replaced Oliver. Hall moved Ewing's group into Room 40 of the Admiralty Building.

Aiding the cryptologists were three important and unexpected events, the first in 1914, being the sinking of a German cruiser by Russian warships. A surviving German sailor was picked up by the Russians and on him was found a copy of the German naval codebook, which the Russians turned over to British intelligence. That same year a chest was retrieved from a sunken German submarine by a British trawler. It contained a copy of the German naval attaché codebook which was used by Germany's Foreign Office when sending messages to its embassies throughout the world.

In 1915 Wilhelm Wassmuss, the German consul in Persia or Iran, fled his consulate in Bushire so hastily to escape British troops that he left behind a trunk containing a copy of the German diplomatic code. Armed with these priceless intelligence gems, Room 40 was able to decipher virtually all of Germany's top codes by applying variations to the original. However, the greatest triumph of Hall and the codebreakers of Room 40 occurred in 1917 when they broke the notorious 'Zimmermann Telegram'. Germany had blatantly offered Mexico large spoils if the Mexican Government would go to war against the US. More than any single event, the revelation of this German plan by British intelligence helped to bring the US into WWI, the deciding factor in favour of the Allies. Room 40 also reported in 1918 that the sailors in the German Navy had mutinied and this hastened the Kaiser's abdication and the armistice in 1919.

ROOSEVELT, Kermit 'Kim' (1916–2000) President Theodore Roosevelt would no doubt have been proud of his grandson, Kermit. He carried on the family tradition of 'speaking softly and carrying a big stick'. As head of the CIA's Middle East Division in 1953, 'Kim' was to mastermind the overthrow of Iran's nationalist leader, Mohammed Mossadeqh. After Mossadeqh was released from a three-year jail sentence, Roosevelt is reported to have persuaded the Shah to grant the deposed ex-Prime Minister a generous pension, which he received till he died in 1967.

After Harvard, he joined the OSS in WWII. Staying in intelligence after 1945, he had become a senior CIA officer by 1950. He acted as a frequent intermediary with the Egyptian Army Officers who overthrew King Farouk. He tried to persuade both John Foster Dulles and Allen Dulles not to pursue such a violently anti-Communist policy in the Middle East. The disregard of such advice led directly to President Nasser's infuriated nationalisation of the Suez Canal and of course to the disastrous response of Britain and France in 1956.

After Roosevelt retired from the CIA he was commissioned to write a history of the OSS and also turned down an offer from the CIA to repeat his Iranian operation, but this time in Guatemala.

The other 'Kim', Philby, wrote of Roosevelt 'I first met Kim Roosevelt in Washington where he was in charge of [Frank] Wisner's Middle East department. Oddly enough, I dubbed him the "Quiet American" five years before Graham Greene wrote his book. He was a courteous, soft-spoken Easterner with impeccable social connections, well educated rather than intellectual, pleasant and unassuming as host and guest. In fact the last person you would expect to be up to his neck in dirty tricks.' A fitting epitaph for a master of the 'Shadow War'.

ROSENBERG, Julius (1918–53) **and Ethel** (1915–53)   One of the most celebrated espionage cases in US history was that of Julius and Ethel Rosenberg. Though the Rosenberg case is hotly debated to this day, there can be little doubt that they were Soviet spies and had helped to steal nuclear secrets for Moscow. The debate hinges on whether or not the amount of secrets they helped to steal warranted their executions.

The Rosenbergs were only exposed after the arrest and confession of the British physicist Klaus Fuchs in 1949. It was Fuchs's evidence that led to the arrest of Harry Gold, David Greenglass and Morton Sobell, all members of the Soviet Atomic Bomb Spy ring operating in the USA. Greenglass and his wife Ruth, both members of the US Communist Party, implicated their fellow party members Ethel and Julius Rosenberg. It would seem in retrospect that the Rosenbergs' importance to the spy ring, and particularly that of Ethel, was somewhat exaggerated and that other US traitors never exposed played far more important roles in the theft of nuclear secrets. The hysteria that surrounded their trial and execution was very much a symptom of the paranoia brought about by the cold war.

ROTHSCHILD, Lord (Nathaniel Mayer Victor) (1910–90)   The startling accusation against Rothschild is that he, not John Cairncross, is the 'Fifth Man'. According to Roland Perry's book *The Fifth Man* (1994) he is the dominant member of the Cambridge Spy Ring, not Philby, Blunt, Burgess or Maclean and is possibly the most important Soviet spy of all. Soviet intelligence officer, Yuri Modin, commented, 'Just as the Three Musketeers were four, so the Cambridge five were six.'

Rothschild was the British head of the famous banking dynasty which, apart from prolific achievements in art, science, wine and charity, had shaped recent history by such acts as the financing of the British army at the Battle of Waterloo and the purchasing of the Suez Canal for Great Britain and Prime Minister Disraeli. He was on intimate terms with many of the most senior members of the intelligence and security services Guy Liddell, Roger Hollis, Dick White, Stewart Menzies, Maurice Oldfield, Robert Vansittart, the Permanent Under-Secretary of State in the Foreign Office and many others.

It is largely accepted among MI5 officers that during the 1945–63 period, the Soviets were receiving vital information which enabled them to thwart British operations run against the Soviet Embassy and the Intelligence Service. MI5 had apparently been penetrated by someone. The inference was always that it had to be an insider. However, one of the leading Soviet double agents working for SIS (MI6), Oleg Gordievsky, who defected to Britain in 1985, denied that the Soviets had anyone of importance on the inside of M15 in the contentious years from around 1950 to 1963.

Rothschild had been in MI5 during WWII and had been awarded a medal for outstanding bravery for defusing a new type of German explosive munitions. The argument is that he was recruited for the Soviet cause in prewar years by playing on his undoubted commitment to a future homeland for the Jews and his anti-Nazi beliefs. Later the fact that he had spied for the Soviets would have been used to blackmail him into continuing to do so, long after it became obvious that Jews were little better treated in the USSR than in Nazi Germany. Fear of publicity was to be perhaps the driving force behind his supposed treachery and his later involvement in the Spycatcher affair.

In 1958, Rothschild's fostering of Peter Wright turned quickly to patronage on the basis that they were scientists who understood each other. Wright could have been an easy prey for the sophisticated peer. Although talented, Wright was not Oxbridge educated and therefore an outsider in a service which was run by the old school ties. For the first time in his professional life, Wright felt wanted, understood and appreciated. In this atmosphere, Wright may have spilled everything of importance in his section of MI5. Rothschild offered help. He was in the oil group Shell overseeing scientific development. He seconded staff to MI5. Wright told him about every piece of espionage technology under development. Rothschild offered ideas of his own and actually devised some new technology himself. He made introductions to heads of major British organisations like the AWRE (Atomic Weapons Research Establishment), which led to further expansion of MI5's R&D.

Later when Wright was deeply involved in 'mole' hunting there were two Soviet codenames which in particular interested him: DAVID and ROSA. The messages decoded indicated that they had worked together, most likely as a married couple. The Soviet defector Golitsyn asked for the files of all MI5 officers who had been working for British Intelligence at the time of the Venona traffic. He studied the files and after a week asked Wright to come and see him in Brighton. Golitsyn pointed to two files on the desk in the study. 'I've discovered DAVID and ROSA,' he said 'My methodology has uncovered them.' Wright knew the names on the files well. They belonged to Victor and Tess Rothschild, both of whom had served in MI5. Wright told him not to be absurd, Rothschild, he informed the Russian, was one of the best friends this Service ever had. Golitsyn, however, was emphatic.

Fortunately for Rothschild, his close companion and confidant, Wright had been the one informed and there was no further investigation. Golitsyn had earlier informed Wright about a file marked 'Technics' in a safe at the Moscow Centre. It was basically a file on all the MI5 technical operations which Wright and his team had initiated. This proved to him that a mole had indeed been spying directly upon him and his activities. Wright never discussed with Golitsyn what he had told Rothschild. If he had, the Russian would have realised that his 'methodology' might have been accurate. According to an MI5 source, Rothschild was later fed information, which ended up 'in the wrong place'. However, just as Philby had survived for so long, because his colleagues and the establishment simply couldn't accept his treachery, so the argument goes, Rothschild's charmed life continued.

Later, when Rothschild feared that journalists might link him to his close friend Anthony Blunt, he put a by now retired Wright and journalist Chapman Pincher in touch. The resulting series of collaborative books, *Their Trade is Treachery* and *Too Secret Too Long*, neatly deflected suspicion on to Roger Hollis and away from Rothschild. Wright's own book *Spycatcher* would later reinforce the image that Hollis was the damaging 'mole'. Rothschild, apparently quite alarmed about being implicated, begged Wright to 'write down every single point he could recall of the ways Rothschild had helped MI5'. 'Things are starting to get rough,' he added. Rothschild also secretly channelled cash to Wright via a Swiss bank.

Rothschild was thought by many to be more loyal to his Jewish heritage than anything English. According to both CIA and Mossad sources, Rothschild was very useful to the Israelis in 'mending fences' with some neighbours in the Middle East after the disruption of the Six-Day conflict. For instance, he called on his old friend the Shah of Iran and suggested several 'crop breeding' ventures, which had been perfected in Israel and elsewhere. Some were adapted in Iran. To many observers Rothschild may have been an unwilling Soviet asset after the war until 1963, but there can be no doubt that he would have willingly spied for Israel. In fact Philby claims that on leaving MI5 in 1947, Rothschild had seized or copied all the six by four file cards listing known or supposed Soviet agents in Europe and elsewhere. These, Philby believed, were later used by the Israeli Intelligence service, Mossad, to identify and possibly 'turn' a number of important Soviet assets.

Rothschild must have certainly come under suspicion for it is believed that he was investigated and interviewed no less than 11 times by MI5, and when in 1986 he wrote a very public letter avowing his innocence, Mrs Thatcher's response was the famously terse 'we have no evidence he was ever a Soviet agent'. As a clearance it was less than fulsome, although, when Rothschild died in 1990, Thatcher attended the memorial. The publication of *The Fifth Man* was greeted in dignified silence by Rothschild's family.

Rothschild's role in MI5 and within the scientific community is considerable, his role with Shell and later as Head of Prime Minister Edward Heath's 'Think Tank' in the early 1970s makes him an important player in postwar history. If eventually sufficient information becomes available to prove beyond doubt Roland Perry's belief in his treachery, then Rothschild will certainly have created history for himself, as the most important Soviet spy in history.

RPV Remotely Piloted Vehicle such as drone or UAV which is being increasingly used by the CIA, MOSSAD and a host of other countries' intelligence and military services for relatively low cost unmanned IMINT surveillance of battlefields and sensitive areas. The most advanced RPV can give a virtually real-time image of the target.

RSHA Reich Sicherheits Hauptamt – Reich Main Security Office. The RSHA was a department in the Reich Ministry of the Interior. The Head of RSHA bore the title of Chief of the Security Police and SD and effectively controlled the GESTAPO, KRIPO (Criminal Police service) and the SD. The central offices of the GESTAPO and SD were co-ordinated in 1936 with the appointment of Reinhard Heydrich, the head of the SD, as chief of the Security Police. The central offices of all three services were then brought together in one main office, the RSHA in 1939. After Heydrich had been assassinated by a British-sponsored Czech underground group in January 1943, the RSHA was headed by Ernst Kaltenbrunner.

Amt I of the RSHA handled personnel for the three agencies. Subsection A2 handled personnel matters of the GESTAPO, A3 handled personnel matters of the KRIPO, and A4 handled personnel matters of the SD.

- *Amt II* handled organisation, administration and law for the three agencies.
- *Amt IIII* (SD) was charged with investigation into all aspects of German life.
- *Amt IV* (Gestapon) was charged with the elimination of political opposition and dissent.
- *Amt V* (KRIPO) was charged with combating criminals. Subsection VD, the criminological institute for the SIPO, handled matters of identification, chemical and biological investigations, and technical research.
- *Amt VI* was concerned with foreign political intelligence and contained subsections dealing with W Europe, Russia and Japan, Anglo-American sphere and central Europe. It contained a special section dealing with sabotage.
- *Amt VII* handled ideological research against enemies such as Freemasonry, Judaism, non-Jewish religious groups, Marxism, Socialists and Liberalism.

RUSSIA KGB: Spetsnaz forces were assigned to storm the Russian Federal Parliament building early on 21 August 1991 and seize key leadership personnel, including the Russian Federal leader Boris Yeltsin. Units assigned this mission included the Al'fa (Alpha) counter-terrorist group subordinate to the KGB's Seventh Main Directorate (Surveillance), and commanded by Hero of the Soviet Union, General Major Viktor Karpukhin. Another KGB unit was from the KGB's First Chief Directorate (Foreign Operations) and intended principally for operations abroad. The commanders on the scene decided not to execute the plan and some Alpha subgroup commanders and personnel publicly refused to take part in the action. Vladimir Kryuchkov, KGB Director and one of the leaders of the coup, was arrested. The next day, a reformer, Vadim Bakatin, was appointed in Kryuchkov's place. On 24 October 1991 Mikhail Gorbachev signed a decree abolishing the KGB. The old-style Communist coup against Gorbachev failed, but it led directly to ultimate collapse of the Soviet Union and Gorbachev's resignation.

SVR *Sluzhba Vneshney Razvedki Rossii* or *Russian Foreign Intelligence Service*: the KGB or Committee for State Security was dissolved along with the USSR in late 1991. However, most of its assets and activities have continued to operate in the guise of several new organisations.

First Chief Directorate of the KGB which had been responsible for foreign intelligence survived virtually intact after its name was changed to the Central Intelligence Service – Centralnaya Sluzhbza Razvedkyin or CSR in October 1991. It became the SVR in 1993 and was downsized by about 35 per cent soon afterwards. Like its predecessors, it is responsible for political, economic, scientific, and technical information, and relies on HUMINT, SIGINT and open source analysis for producing intelligence. The majority of SVR case officers operate under diplomatic cover from Russian embassies, consulates and trade establishments around the world.

The Main HQ are situated in the massive 1st Chief Directorates building on the Moscow ring-road. The SVR is presently composed of three separate Directorates, and three Services: *Directorate S* which is responsible for 'illegals' throughout the world; *Directorate T* responsible for the collection of scientific and technological intelligence; and *Directorate K* which carries out infiltration of foreign intelligence and security services and exercises surveillance over Russian citizens abroad. *Service I* which analyses and distributes intelligence collected by SVR foreign intelligence officers and agents, publishes a daily current events summaries for the Politburo, and strategic intelligence assessments; *Service A* which is responsible for planning and implementing active measures; and *Service R* which evaluates SVR operations abroad.

The operational core of the SVR are the 11 geographical departments, which supervise officers assigned to residencies abroad. These officers, or *rezidenty*, operate under legal cover, engaging in intelligence collection, espionage and active measures. In addition the SVR frequently use journalistic cover and indeed many SVR intelligence officers consider this the most useful 'legends' particularly for long-term operations. One of the fastest areas of growth is co-operation with foreign intelligence services, particularly India and the countries of the old Soviet Central Asia. However, since the events of 11 September a new spirit of co-operation has existed, at least temporarily, between Russia and in particular the CIA and SIS. President Putin is well aware that Russia has a major Muslim insurgency in Chechnya and growing problems elsewhere in the Southern and Central Asian regions. Russia expects to benefit greatly from a distancing of Western support for groups formally classed as separatists or even freedom fighters, and now increasingly condemned as Islamic terrorists. The

SVR and FAPSI in particular hope to gain access to advanced techniques and a greater understanding of the hi-technology used by the CIA and NSA by this formal, if temporary, co-operation.

Other aspects of the new dialogue included multi-service meetings to discuss the problems of enforcing the non-proliferation of weapons of mass destruction, the illicit trade in conventional arms, the drugs trade, organised crime and money laundering. The SVR has also reportedly concluded formal agreements with the intelligence services of several former Soviet republics, including Azerbaijan and Belarus, which cover both intelligence and internal security, and in effect make these services into local departments of the SVR. The agreement on intelligence co-operation between Russia and China signed in Beijing at the end of the summer of 1992 partly restored the good relations which were cut off by the dramatic split between the two Communist parties in 1959. This secret treaty covered the activities of GRU and SVR which are now co-operating with the Chinese MSS as well as the People's Liberation Army's Military Intelligence Directorate. It is understood that further agreements to share intelligence between Russia and China were signed in early 2002.

Russia's new found role as a partner in the worldwide War on Terrorism has created a dramatic new emphasis of covert or paramilitary capability. The Spetsnaz unit *Vympel* or 'Banner' is the main combat unit of the SVR (Foreign Intelligence Service). Originally developed in 1981 as a Covert Action unit to conduct infiltration, sabotage and intelligence missions in enemy territory, Vympel subsequently evolved into a Counter Terrorist (CT) unit. By 1987 the unit had expanded to a staff of over 500. Following the dissolution of the Soviet Union in 1991 the unit was transferred to the Main Administration for the Protection of the Russian Federation (GUO), along with Spetsgruppa 'A', and in 1993 the unit was again transferred to MVD. After many original members left, Vympel was disbanded. The SVR then formed a new unit, *Vega*, but this was subsquently renamed *Vympel*. This unit was re-equipped in 2002 to take on a more active covert action role.

The head of the SVR press office announced that the SVR missions abroad were being cut by 50 per cent, that 'the Russian intelligence staff is now being reduced both in the centre and abroad, throughout the world', including the USA, Sweden, Germany and Italy. Cynics pointed out that the reductions in the USA had something to do with the transfer of staff to the Ukrainian and Belorussian delegations in the UN and associated organisations which were becoming independent, while the reductions in Germany included the closure of the 14 former KGB liaison offices in the old GDR and the counter-intelligence personnel of the Soviet Western Group of Forces returning to Russia.

There was to be no real surplus of operational personnel because many of the disillusioned officers 'defected' to private companies and Russia had to establish new intelligence stations and networks in all the former Warsaw Pact countries and newly independent former Soviet republics. Poland, the Czech Republic and Hungary quickly became intelligence targets as important as any European member of NATO. In fact they were even more so, because they were geographically closer to Russia and offered many recruitment possibilities. Never enthusiastically pro-Moscow, Romania was on the opposing side in the Trans-Dnestr conflict, while both Slovakia and Bulgaria, historically close to Russia's heart, saw less and less benefit from maintaining close relations with Moscow. The Russian intelligence teams in former E Europe were known to the local services and in many cases had to be replaced by fresh faces. The three Baltic states considered their Soviet period as an undeserved disaster and wanted to become members of international organisations which could help them to join the West economically, culturally and even militarily.

The SVR sees the CIS nations and especially the Central Asian republics as a priority area for Russia. Moscow has frequently expressed its unhappiness at losing control over the region. The more so, as by mid 2002 the USA had established a semi-permanent military presence in at least four of the former Soviet Republics. Its present economic situation does not permit it to return there as a superpower, nor of course compete with the US intelligence and military machine. Russia does, however, cherish its geographic position and the historical and ethnic links in the region. Russia is very definitely worried about creeping Islamic extremism in the region and co-operation with both China and India are high on their agenda, as is the importance of maintaining a foothold in the new, post-Taliban Afghanistan. The SVR fear hostile intelligence and foreign military influence using countries in the region to become outposts for anti-Russian operations. Despite the new-found level of co-operation with the USA, Russia has complained about the CIA stationing twenty or more officers in each of the CIS capitals.

The SVR has been trying to encourage a number of the CIS countries to fill the vacuum in their security structures. The intelligence vacuum left in all former Soviet republics was far greater than the weaknesses in their security structures and the SVR, often in competition with the

CIA, is attempting to rebuild Russian influence with the often badly organised and chronically underfunded republican intelligence services. When it came to co-operation between the Russians and the individual special services of the CIS in the early 1990s, the SVR had the advantage of knowing the area and the people they were negotiating with. This quickly changed after the generation of the old 'apparatchiks', still ruling in most of Russia's southern neighbours, was replaced. The disadvantages then facing the SVR were those of a political fluid situation in Government, diverging economic and security interests, lack of funds and slow restructuring of special services.

The first agreement on the basic principles of co-operation between the intelligence services of the CIS was signed in Alma-Ata on 5 April 1992 by representatives of the intelligence services of Armenia, Belarus, Kazakhstan, Kyrgyzstan, Moldova, Russia, Tajikistan, Turkmenistan and Ukraine. The signing parties pledged not to spy on one another and to co-operate and assist each other with the training of personnel. SVR co-operation with its CIS counterparts aims at preserving a single security area, and organising with CIS members a regular exchange of information on foreign countries' plans to weaken the CIS or to provoke confrontation between its members. In 1995 12 CIS states signed an agreement in Tbilisi on co-operation on combating organised crime, international terrorism and drug business. All the nation signatories to the agreement, with the exception of the Ukraine have largely agreed to co-ordinate their foreign activities with the SVR.

Throughout the Cold War the USA was, quite naturally, regarded by the KGB as the main opponent. The terminology used by the staff of the Russian intelligence services may have changed but the USA still is and will remain their main object of interest, despite the events of 11 September 2001. The USA is the only country with the economic strength to be able to project its military power worldwide and to support an awesome intelligence-gathering capability. The USA is NATO's senior partner and the Gulf War and the events in Yugoslavia and Afghanistan have only emphasised the unipolar nature of the new world. The CIA are also very active in former Soviet republics in 2002 and the Russians, in particular the SVR and the military, are getting distinctly edgy about US long-term intentions in Russia's oil-rich backyard. The USA has regularly accused Russia of intensifying its intelligence efforts and it seems certain that this will continue as the need for industrial and technological intelligence for Russia's ailing economy and military infrastructure grows. Russia's increasing interest in combating international terrorism and drug trafficking makes the

UK, Germany, Israel and France the most interesting potential security partners. Contacts between the CSR and SIS were established in 1991 in Oslo. But relations were damaged by British rejection of the first candidate for the official CSR post in London, General Gurgenov, who was accused of helping Saddam Hussein during the Gulf War. After the death of General Gurgenov and a series of delicate negotiations, a new Rezident was accepted by London.

Because of the reported reduction in the number of SVR intelligence officers, the Russians will have to place increasing emphasis on gaining information through technical intelligence disciplines and open source analysis. Although the opportunity to collect HUMINT had expanded as a result of the relaxation of the old Cold War security precautions focused on Russia, the upsurge in tight new controls to combat terrorism is bound to have a knock-on effect on SVR operations. HUMINT is likely to be more carefully targeted to gain information not readily available through technical intelligence collection or through open source exploitation. The Russians have always relied on open source information and will continue to obtain intelligence by analysing public data in comparison with intelligence derived through classified sources. The KGB used a variety of research and political institutes for the analysis of open source data and it is worth noticing that the SVR has managed to maintain the vast majority of these and are likely to be performing exactly the same roles as they did under the Soviet Union.

Presidential Security Service (*Prezidentskaya Sluzhba Bezopasnosti* – *Russian Presidential Security Service, PSB*), formerly an element of the 9th Chief Directorate of the KGB, was established as an independent government agency in December 1993 to provide security for Russian top officials and the guards for the Kremlin.

Federal'naya Sluzhba Bezopasnosti (*The Federal Security Service* – *FSB*): when the KGB was disbanded in 1991, the internal security functions previously performed by the Second, Third and Fifth Chief Directorates and the Seventh Directorates were taken over by a new Ministry of Security. It retained the Lubyanka HQ in Moscow. The Ministry was disbanded in December 1993 and replaced by the Federal'naya Sluzhba Kontr-razvedky or FSK, the Federal Counter-Intelligence Service, subsequently redesignated the Federal Security Service or FSB.

In May 1997 the President signed an order for the reorganisation of the FSB. Accordingly, the FSB now has several major departments which were introduced to replace the existing 34 directorates and services. These are the *Investigations Directorate*. In 1992 the FSB

Investigations Directorate was abolished, but in 1995 it was re-established. The unit takes an active part in combating illegal trafficking in weapons and drugs, corruption, and crimes in the sphere of the economy and organised crime. It currently has more than 1,000 ongoing cases under investigation. *The Directorate for Economic Counter-Intelligence* is gaining in importance as the FSB seeks to prevent the leakage of information from Russia's slowly emerging hi-tech industry. *The Military Counter-Intelligence Directorate,* a large component of the FSB Counter-Intelligence Department, along with the security organs in the troops is directly subordinate to the Russian Federation FSB. The Directorate works in the Russian Armed Forces to counter the efforts of foreign intelligence agencies to acquire Russian State and military secrets. *The Military Counter-Intelligence Directorate* is responsible for security within individual military units. The situation in Chechnya involved the Directorate in establishing the whereabouts of Russian servicemen and civilians seized by gunmen and securing their release, often by resorting to the use of heavily armed Hostage Rescue Units. *The Directorate 'T' Anti-terrorism Directorate*, which includes the *FSB Anti-terrorist Centre*, is a special unit, formed in 1995, that encompasses FSB combat and operational counter-terrorist units. In 2001 the Centre responded to more than 500 alerts and perhaps as many as 150 special or actual combat-operation. This includes actions directed against organised criminal groups engaged in illegal arms or drugs trafficking.

Another of Russia's premier counter-terrorist groups, *Alpha,* is now assigned to the FSB *Operational Reconnaissance Directorate*, after changes imposed following Alpha's rather ambiguous role in the failed August 1991 Soviet coup. Alpha comprises a main group of 250 personnel based in Moscow as well as smaller detachments in Yekaterinburg, Krasnodar and Khabarovsk. It appears that the Russian armed forces did not intend a full-scale intervention in Chechnya. An operation led by the Federal Counter-Intelligence Agency (FSK), and secretly supported by Russian Army military contingents enlisted from divisions near Moscow, supported opposition forces operating in Chechnya. These forces, led by Provisional Council leader Umar Avturkhanov, clashed with Dudayev's forces with the intention of either defeating him or at the very least, capturing the capital. But the opposition attack on Grozny on 26 and 27 November 1994 was a catastrophe, and by 1 December it was clear that the opposition would be unable to oust Dudayev. Subsequently Alpha's mid-June 1995 attempt to storm the Budennovsk hospital and free hundreds of hostages seized by Chechen guerrillas also ended unsuccessfully, with the result that the Russian Army found itself involved in a long-running and bloody conflict.

FAPSI (*Federal'naya Agenstvo Pravitel'stvennoy Svayazi i Informatsii* or *Federal Agency for Government Communications & Information, The Administration of Information Resources (AIR) at the Presidential Office*) was formed from the KGB Eighth (Encoding) Chief Directorate and 16th Directorate, the Decoding and Radio Interception Service, and the Government Communications Directorate of the KGB in 1991 and replaced in turn by FAPSI on 19 February 1993.

Unlike the NSA, FAPSI operates both overseas and domestically and is authorised to engage in commercial operations, leasing radio frequency bands and government communications lines to both domestic and foreign companies. Russian law normally prohibits government organisations from engaging in commercial activities or to combine their main responsibilities with business undertakings. However, FAPSI is somewhat exceptional in this regard and, like the CIA and NSA, now has a number of commercial 'front' companies. Both Simaco and Roskomtekh were founded by FAPSI to help with the acquisition of suitable advanced technology from abroad.

FAPSI is organised into the *First Main Government Communications Directorate,* which is responsible for maintaining the government information system and telecommunication lines. The FAPSI also controls the Presidential Communications System that provides the special communications and automatic telephone exchanges for some 2,500 Presidential and administration connections. Although it is not formally authorised to monitor domestic voice traffic, it does in fact do so and on a massive scale.

FAPSI is empowered to monitor and register all electronic financial and securities transactions and to monitor other electronic communications, including private Internet access. *Scientific-Technical Centre* software and hardware products for data protection include Verba, a cryptographic system to protect commercial information and an all-purpose protected subscribers' centre; and identification support hardware. *Atlas Scientific-Technical Centre* is concerned with document management, archives and related information systems. *Russian Academy of Cryptography* is a major scientific academy involved into research on both codemaking and codebreaking and which includes elements of the old KGB 8th Chief Directorate tasked with communications and cryptography. *Financial-Economic Administration FEU* includes the Economic Administration. *Security Service* ensures the security regime and is based on the old KGB 12th Department responsible mainly for eavesdropping on Government and Party officials, the guarding of premises, the protection of electronic intelligence, absorbing elements of the old KGB 16th Directorate and conducting communications interception, while the *Security Service 4th Department* is engaged in physical protection. FAPSI also co-ordinates information warfare for ministries, agencies and services and is the only organisation capable of defending the comparable Russian structures.

FAPSI provides the Russian Strategic Nuclear Forces with communications channels and a cryptographic element. This could suggest that some of the Ministry of Defence Signals Troops and signals facilities were transferred to FAPSI's command or that the MOD system was deliberately allowed to decay so that the agency was 'forced' to create a parallel modern communications infrastructure.

During the first Chechen conflict FAPSI set up a communications post in Mozdok and later at Severnyy airport. FAPSI took part in the Chechen conflict, bridging the communications gap between units from various services, establishing links between civilian officials and Moscow, and together with the Army signals units listening to the Chechens' communication lines. The Chechens were not able to intercept FAPSI messages but the MVD communications system was vulnerable. During the first Chechen conflict FAPSI, like all other services involved, had their own separate commands. When it abandoned Groznyy it left its satellite communications centre in workable condition. The centre was taken over for use by the Chechens, but as every message had to be relayed through Moscow the Russians were able to monitor the traffic. In December 1997 when the attack of a Chechen group destroyed the communications system in the town of Buynaksk (Dagestan), FAPSI was able to rig up a field communications centre within hours after the attack. FAPSI had also acquired the new 'Terek' mobile communications centres, installed in a BT80 armoured vehicle, the Terek assures secure telephone and radio communications.

Russia continues to maintain one of the most sophisticated communications interception programmes in the world. The GRU's Sixth Directorate uses over twenty different types of aircraft, a fleet of some thirty intelligence collection vessels, satellites, and ground stations to collect SIGINT. Together with FAPSI, the GRU operates SIGINT collection facilities in over sixty embassies, consulates, trade legations, and residences throughout the world. The location of a number of Russian diplomatic facilities in the USA would provide Russian SIGINT collectors with access to sensitive information. Russian collection activities could derive sensitive information on government policies from monitoring government activities in the Washington, DC area, and sensitive financial and trade information using Russian facilities located in New York, San Francisco and Seattle. The location of microwave towers and cellular communication repeaters in the vicinity of Russian diplomatic facilities in these cities increases the potential damage from collection activities. In the past, vans from the Soviet Mission to the United Nations were observed in the vicinity of the GE Americom satellite ground station in Vernon Valley, NJ, and vans from the San Francisco consulate were observed in the vicinity of AT&T microwave towers in N California. In both cases, the vans appeared to be conducting SIGINT monitoring at these facilities. While these two agencies operate large ground collection facilities within the territory of the Commonwealth of Independent States, the facilities at Cam Ranh Bay in Vietnam and at Lourdes in Cuba, in operation since 1964, are both scheduled to close.

The Russians have probably also continued the Soviet practice of using covert mobile collection platforms. During the Cold War, the Russians frequently used tractor-trailers, and other vehicles with concealed SIGINT collection equipment to gather intelligence in W Europe. Western intelligence officials estimate that the Soviets conducted over 7,000 covert vehicular SIGINT operations in NATO countries annually. During these operations, the Soviets gathered electronic order of battle (EOB) data, monitored exercise communications, conducted direction-finding operations, and calibrated Soviet SIGINT satellites to determine geo-location accuracies. The Soviets also allegedly used clandestine collection vans located in Mexico to monitor activities at White Sands Missile Range in New Mexico and Vandenberg Air Force Base, California. Vans operating from Tijuana, Mexico reportedly were able to monitor all of Southern California and Western Arizona. There have also been reports that Aeroflot aircraft and clandestine collection vehicles have been used to collect SIGINT data inside the continental USA.

As part of the old Soviet space programme, the first Soviet SIGINT satellite to be launched was the Cosmos 189 ELINT satellite in 1967. Over the next 24 years, the Soviets placed over 200 SIGINT satellites into orbit. The GRU is tasked with operating Russian ELINT satellites. ELINT satellites use active and passive techniques to detect specific targets and they complement the data provided by imaging satellites and assist in developing a more complete picture of an adversary's forces or intentions. These satellites are designed to track and geo-locate radio and radar emanations of ships at sea, mobile air defence radars, fixed strategic early warning radars, and other military emitters for the purpose of identification, location and signals analysis. The data can then be used for targeting, offensive and defensive engagement planning and countermeasure development. Collection activities are managed by the *Satellite Intelligence Directorate*, and data analysis is performed by the Decrypting Service of the Sixth Directorate. Currently, there is no evidence of the existence of a Russian COMINT satellite, however, it is likely that the Russians could develop such a system if they had the finances.

GRU (Glavnoye Razvedyvatelnoye Upravlenie – Russian Military Intelligence): the GRU and the Ministry of Defence supported Gorbachev against the August 1991 coup and unlike the KGB, the GRU survived the aftermath of the coup largely intact. The GRU is responsible for providing strategic, operational, and tactical intelligence for the Russian armed forces. The GRU remains a cohesive, highly efficient and very professional Military Intelligence service and arguably the most effective of Russia's foreign espionage agencies, despite the widespread budgetary and organisational difficulties it faces. The HQ of the GRU is located near Moscow at the Khodinka Airfield. The GRU HQ itself is nicknamed 'The Aquarium'.

Structurally, the GRU remains largely unchanged from the Soviet era and is organised into 12 main directorates:

- *First Directorate* – for HUMINT resources and organised into regional and country sections;
- *Second Directorate* – for strategic intelligence includes a number of Directions responsible for operational intelligence collection and dissemination in the Western Hemisphere including the First Direction controls tactical level reconnaissance; Second Direction manages agent recruitment and the development of agent networks in or adjacent to areas of wartime responsibility; Third Direction is responsible for *spetsnaz* operations within target countries; Fourth [Information] Direction is responsible for intelligence collection management and analysis; Fifth Direction is responsible for SIGINT and ELINT; Sixth Direction special purpose or osnazovtsi signals troops are responsible for special signals; and the Seventh Direction is responsible for ciphers and communications security;
- *Third Directorate* – includes a number of Directions responsible for operational intelligence collection and dissemination in Asia;
- *Fourth Directorate* – includes a number of Directions responsible for

operational intelligence collection and dissemination in Africa and the Middle East;

- *Fifth Directorate* – manages operational intelligence, and intelligence organisations within fronts, fleets and military districts; in the army, all of the chiefs of the military district intelligence fall under the command of the Fifth Directorate head. And fleet intelligence officers (Naval Staff Second Directorate Chiefs) are under the control of naval intelligence, which in turn falls under the Fifth Directorate of the GRU;
- *Sixth Directorate* – responsible for electronic intelligence; this includes clandestine collection from embassies in foreign states, as well as Electronic Intelligence Regiments which are directly subordinated to the Sixth Directorate, which also controls the activities of electronic intelligence assets which are organic to land, sea and air combatant forces;
- *Cosmic Intelligence Directorate* – responsible for space-based intelligence collection; it includes activities at launch sites, a variety of research institutes, and a central co-ordinating facility;
- *Fleet Intelligence* – the Chief of Fleet Intelligence, an office held by a Vice Admiral, is a Deputy of the GRU Director, although operational tasking and co-ordination is conducted through the Fifth Directorate; Fleet Intelligence consists of five Directorates: Northern Fleet, Pacific Fleet, Black Sea Fleet, Baltic Fleet Intelligence Directorates and the Fleet Cosmic Intelligence Directorate, responsible for space-based ocean surveillance and the *Space Intelligence Directorate* which is responsible for the development, manufacture, launch and operation of Russian space-based reconnaissance systems; the directorate is located at Vatutinki, 50 kms SW of Moscow; it operates its own cosmodromes, several research institutes, supporting mission ground centres and a centralised computer processing facility.

The staff of each military district, group of forces and fleet also includes an intelligence directorate Razvedyvatelnoye Upravlenie RU, which is subordinated to the GRU. In turn, lower echelons, such as an Army or Flotilla are also supported by an Intelligence Department RO. Within ground forces armies, each division includes a reconnaissance battalion, which includes scout and electronic intelligence elements.

From Cheka to the SVR: the Bolshevik regime created a police system that proved to be far more effective than the tsarist version. It swept away the tsarist police, so despised by Russians of all political persuasions, along with other tsarist institutions, and replaced it with a political police of considerably greater dimensions, both in the scope of its authority and in the severity of its methods. However lofty their initial goals were, the Bolsheviks forcibly imposed their rule on the people. They constituted a dictatorship of a minority that had to establish a powerful political police apparatus to preserve its domination.

The first Soviet political police, created in December 1917, was *the All-Russian Extraordinary Commission for Combating Counterrevolution and Sabotage (Vserossiiskaia chrezvychainaia komissiia po bor'be s kontrrevoliutsiei i sabotazhem–VChK; also known as the Vecheka or the Cheka)*. The Vecheka was very much an ad hoc organisation, whose powers gradually grew in response to various emergencies and threats to Soviet rule. No formal legislation establishing the Vecheka was ever enacted. It was to serve as an organ of preliminary investigation, but the crimes it was to uncover were not defined, and the procedures for handling cases were not set forth. This situation was the result of the extralegal character of the Vecheka, which was conceived not as a permanent state institution but as a temporary organ for waging war against 'class enemies'. Given its militant role and supra-legal status, it is not surprising that the Vecheka, which was headed by Feliks E. Dzerzhinsky, acquired powers of summary justice as the threat of counterrevolution and foreign intervention grew. After an attempt was made on Lenin's life in August 1918, the Vecheka unleashed its violence on a wide scale – the so-called Red Terror – which continued until 1920 and caused thousands to lose their lives.

The end of the Civil War (1918–21), the demobilisation of the Red Army, and the introduction of the New Economic Policy (NEP) in 1921 brought about a changed atmosphere that seemed incompatible with a terrorist political police. Lenin himself spoke of the need for a reform of the political police, and in early 1922 the Vecheka was abolished and its functions transferred to the *State Political Directorate (Gosudarstvennoe politicheskoe upravlenie – GPU)*. When the Soviet Union was formed in December 1922, the GPU was raised to the level of a federal agency, designated *the Unified State Political Directorate (Ob'edinennoe gosudarstvennoe politicheskoe upravlenie – OGPU)*, and attached to the Council of People's Commissars. On paper it appeared that the powers of the political police had been reduced significantly. Indeed, police operations during the NEP period were considerably less violent, and the staff and budget of the political police were reduced. Initially, the OGPU was subject to definite procedural requirements regarding arrests and was not given the powers of summary justice that its predecessor had. But the legal constraints on the OGPU were gradually removed, and its authority grew throughout the 1920s.

The OGPU was drawn into the party struggles between Stalin and his opponents and was also enlisted in the drive to collectivise the peasantry by force, beginning in late 1929, an operation that resulted in the death of upwards of 5 million people.

In July 1934, the OGPU was transformed into the *Main Directorate for State Security (Glavnoe upravlenie gosudarstvennoi bezopasnosti – GUGB)* and integrated into *the People's Commissariat of Internal Affairs (Narodnyi komissariat vnutrennykh del – NKVD)*, which had been given all-union status earlier that year. The functions of the security police and those of the internal affairs apparatus, which controlled the regular police and the militia, were thus united in one agency. The NKVD was a powerful organisation. In addition to controlling the security police and the regular police, it was in charge of border and internal troops, fire brigades, convoy troops, and, after 1934, the entire penal system, including regular prisons and forced labour camps, or the Gulag.

During the period 1934–40, the NKVD took charge of numerous economic enterprises that employed forced labour, such as gold mining, major construction projects, and other industrial activity. In addition, the Special Board, attached to the NKVD, operated outside the legal codes and was empowered to impose on persons deemed 'socially dangerous' sentences of exile, deportation or confinement in labour camps. The Special Board soon became one of the chief instruments of Stalin's purges. Stalin's domination over the party was not absolute at this time, however. Dissatisfaction with his policies continued to be manifested by some party members, and elements existed within the leadership that might have opposed any attempt to use police terror against the party. Among Stalin's potential challengers was Sergei Kirov, chief of the Leningrad party apparatus. Conveniently for Stalin, Kirov was assassinated by a disgruntled ex-party member in December 1934. This provided Stalin with the pretext for launching an assault against the party. Although Stalin proceeded cautiously, the turning point had been reached, and the terror machinery was in place. From 1936 to 1938, the NKVD arrested and executed millions of party members, government officials, and ordinary citizens. The military also came under assault. Much of the officer corps was wiped out in 1937–38, leaving the country ill prepared for WWII. The era in which the NKVD, with Stalin's approval, terrorised Soviet citizens became known in the West as the Great Terror.

The war years brought further opportunities for the political police, under the control of Lavrenty Beria, to expand its authority. The NKVD assumed a number of additional economic functions that made use of the expanding labour camp population. The NKVD also broadened its presence in the Red Army, where it conducted extensive surveillance of the troops. Towards the end of the war, the political police moved into areas formerly under German occupation to arrest those suspected of sympathy for the Nazis. They also suppressed nationalist movements in the Estonian, Latvian, Lithuanian and western Ukrainian republics. Beria himself steadily gained power and authority during this period. In early 1946, when he was made a full member of the Politburo and a deputy chairman of the Council of Ministers (the new name for the Council of People's Commissars), he relinquished his NKVD post, but he apparently retained some control over the police through his protégés in that organisation. In March 1953, following Stalin's death, Beria became chief of the MVD, which amalgamated the regular police and the security police into one organisation. Some three months later, he made an unsuccessful bid for power and was arrested by his Kremlin colleagues, including Khrushchev. The 'Beria affair' and the shake-up in the Kremlin that followed his arrest had far-reaching consequences for the role of the police in Soviet society. The party leadership not only arrested and later executed Beria and several of his allies in the MVD but also took measures to place the political police under its firm control. These events led directly to the establishment of the KGB.

The KGB participated in the foreign policy decision-making process at the highest level because its chief was a member of the Politburo. At the same time, it influenced the formulation of foreign policy at a lower level as an executor of that policy, a provider of information did, and a generator of ideas, solutions, and alternatives. It played a leading role in the suppression of the Hungarian uprising in 1956 and the appalling abuse of human rights in Budapest. Its role throughout E Europe was repressive and ultimately self-defeating. Thus, for example, when the Kremlin decided to invade Czechoslovakia in 1968, KGB chief Andropov, who was an expert on E Europe and had a direct line of intelligence from Czechoslovakia, presumably influenced the decision-making process significantly. Furthermore, the KGB, as the main provider of intelligence to the leadership, was in a position to influence decision making by screening and interpreting the information. The KGB probably favoured the invasion because of the threat posed by a possible spillover of unrest into the Soviet Union. Also, efforts by

Czechoslovak reformers to reorganise their security police jeopardised KGB operations in Czechoslovakia. Considerable evidence showed that the KGB, in order to bolster the pro-interventionist position, used intelligence and covert action to produce proof of counter-revolution in Czechoslovakia. Andropov did not always favour military intervention as a solution to international problems, however. Other considerations, such as the Soviet Union's international image, no doubt affected his views on the 1979 invasion of Afghanistan (which he reportedly did not favour) and the 1980–81 Polish crisis (where he was probably among those who opposed an invasion).

Both these crises occurred at a time when the KGB was trying to mobilise W European public opinion against plans by the North Atlantic Treaty Organisation (NATO) to introduce intermediate-range missiles in Europe. Chebrikov did not have Andropov's foreign policy expertise when he took over as head of the KGB in 1982, but his admission to the Politburo gave him a voice in foreign policy at the highest level. In addition, many Western experts believe that the KGB chairman served on the Defence Council, an important collegial decision-making body that provided top-level co- ordination for defence-related activities of the Soviet government. Chebrikov's numerous trips to E Europe after he became head of the KGB indicated that he was personally involved in KGB operations beyond Soviet borders, and his forceful advocacy of Soviet 'counter-propaganda' efforts abroad implied a commitment to a strong foreign policy role for the KGB. Kryuchkov, who became head of the KGB in 1988, had been extensively involved in foreign operations as the chief of the First Chief Directorate of the KGB.

The fascinating background of the only Soviet or Russian Intelligence service to remain intact from its inception, the GRU began with its establishment by the Commissar for War Leon Trotsky on 21 October 1918 as the Registered Directorate of the Workers & Peasants Red Army. It was soon informally titled the GRU, though not officially until the reorganisation of June 1942.

Individual Soviet Army and Front Commands had their own intelligence gathering capability and the new organisation's main task was to co-ordinate their activities and ensure that intelligence was properly analysed and distributed within the Central Staff. While it had to ensure the continuing loyalty of the Army, unlike the CHEKA and its successor agencies, the GRU has not been concerned with general internal security duties. The most notable exceptions being its use against NKVD officials during the purges of 1937–39 and again in 1953 against the MVD who were at that time responsible for internal security.

The existence of two major intelligence organisations running in parallel within the Soviet Union led to unnecessary duplication of effort on occasion, but overall the Soviets preferred more rather than less intelligence gain and have continued with the policy right up to the present day. In addition the Communist party could of course play off the two services against each other.

The GRU itself has suffered purges, the first being in November 1920 when Lenin ordered the execution of hundreds of intelligence officers for providing misleading information on the Polish campaign. The GRU quickly re-established itself and in the major Red Army reorganisation of 1926 finally put military intelligence on a firmer footing as the Fourth Bureau of the Red Army's General Staff. During the period of the 1930s the GRU could not escape the spy paranoia that swept the Soviet Union and many of its Senior Personnel fell victim, along with the rank and file, and those recalled from overseas positions. A notable victim being former GRU Chief Ya K. Berzin who before his recall had virtually commanded the Republican forces during the Spanish Civil War. Berzin was executed on 29 July 1938 along with scores of Senior military Officers slaughtered during a three-day period. It was a temporary nadir for the GRU, for they lost control of their own operations for a short while as Yezov, the head of the NKVD actually took command of Military Intelligence. Shortly afterwards he was to disappear into the cellars of the Lubyanka and the GRU once again resurfaced in 1940 under General F.I. Golikov, closely following the debacle of the 1939–40 war with Finland.

The GRU had quietly managed to keep control of their networks of foreign agents even during the purges and the worst of the horrors of the Yezovschina. They were able to give warning of OPERATION BARBAROSSA, the German invasion of the Soviet Union on the eve of 22 June 1941, but Stalin ignored their intelligence at great cost to the Russian people. During the autumn of 1941, the GRU was divided into an Overseas Operations bureau reporting directly to Stalin via a newly established Chief of Intelligence Directorate of the Supreme High Command. The strategic and operational military intelligence bureaux remained the province of the GRU and the Soviet General Staff. The disarray of the first year of the Great Patriotic War very largely disrupted the GRU's ability to provide effective intelligence on the German forces. By considerable restructuring and with great tenacity the GRU had yet again re-established itself as a highly effective intelligence service in time to play a leading part in the destruction of the German 6th Army under Von Paulas at the Battle of Stalingrad. For many this was the seminal turning of the tide in WWII and, with the penetration of the German High Command by the GRU (OPERATION DORA/Lucy Spy Ring), Soviet military intelligence was able to claim considerable credit for the final victory. The GRU controlled other highly successful overseas espionage networks including those responsible for the theft of Atomic secrets via Canada (OPERATION ZARIA) and those run by Richard Sorge in the Far East.

In the postwar years the GRU managed to avoid many of the problems faced by the NKVD and its successors, with the exception of 1947–51 when Stalin removed intelligence gathering from the Army and the NKVD/MGB and placed it under the control of a new organisation known as the KI (Komitet Informatsii). The GRU were able to withdraw from the arrangement by June 1948 and continued to run numerous successful operations abroad. Throughout the Cold War the GRU conducted Strategic and Military Intelligence operations around the world and were mainly responsible for the Soviet Union's highly successful acquisition of Western scientific secrets. The GRU has often been notably more professional than the KGB, running its agents with greater security and with far fewer being subsequently exposed. Indeed even today a scaled down, but largely intact organisation has more resources available to it than the KGB's successor.

The most important element of the KGB from an espionage view was the First Chief Directorate, which was responsible for all international Soviet clandestine activities, apart from military intelligence collection by the GRU and political initiatives of the Communist Party itself. In the final years of its existence it was organised thus:

- *Illegals Directorate (Directorate S)* – recruited, trained and managed KGB officers assigned to foreign countries under false identities. Most of the staff of the Directorate have either served as illegals, or have served abroad under diplomatic cover.
- *Scientific and Technical Directorate (Directorate T)* – created from the former Department 10 in 1963 to intensify the acquisition of Western strategic, military and industrial technology. By 1972 Directorate T had an HQ staff of several hundred officers subdivided into four Departments in addition to specialists stationed at major Soviet embassies around the world. The Directorate's operations were co-ordinated with the scientific and technical collection activities of other KGB elements, and with the State Scientific and Technical Committee (GNTK).
- *Planning and Analysis Directorate (Directorate I)* – established in 1969

to review past operations as a guide to improving future initiatives, although in practice it was said to function more as a dumping-ground for ageing or inept officers.

- *Information Service (Special Service I)* – responsible for the correlation and dissemination of routine intelligence collected by the First Chief Directorate, apart from technical intelligence collected and processed by Directorate T. Other related responsibilities included publication of a weekly intelligence summary for Party leaders, briefing officers prior to foreign assignment, conducting special studies at Central Committee direction. The products of the Information Service did not consist of the finished product, but rather of raw reports that were provided to senior leaders who drew their own conclusions.

- *Counter-Intelligence Service (Special Service II)* – tasked with countering foreign intelligence agencies, including penetrating foreign security, intelligence and counter-intelligence services to undermine their effectiveness in countering the activities of the KGB. Special Service II was also responsible for the security officers tasked with monitoring Soviet civilians stationed abroad, including Soviet nationals working as correspondents, trade representatives, Aeroflot clerks or any other capacity.

- *Disinformation Department (Department A)* – responsible for clandestine initiatives and campaigns to influence foreign governments and publics, as well to shape perceptions of individuals and groups hostile to Soviet interests. The majority of the Department's activities were implemented by other KGB elements, or other Soviet organisations.

- *Executive Action Department (Department V)* – responsible for 'wet affairs' (mokrie dela) – murders, kidnappings, and sabotage – which involve bloodshed. Previously known as the 13th Department or Line F, the Department was enlarged and redesignated in 1969, and tasked with sabotaging critical infrastructure to immobilise Western countries during a future crisis. The Department employed officers stationed in Soviet embassies, illegals stationed abroad and the services of professional assassins.

The operational core of the First Chief Directorate lay in its geographical departments, which were responsible for the majority of the KGB enterprises abroad. The duties of this department included the staff of KGB 'legal' Residencies in Soviet embassies, operating under legal cover while engaged in intelligence collection, espionage, and active measures, as well as KGB illegals. They also managed operations initiated through international Communist-front organisations, as well as other agent of influence operations.

- *1st Department* – USA and Canada;
- *2nd Department* – Latin America;
- *3rd Department* – UK, Australia, New Zealand and Scandinavia;
- *4th Department* – Federal Republic of Germany, Austria;
- *5th Department* – France, Italy, Spain, the Netherlands, Belgium, Luxembourg and Ireland;
- *6th Department* – China, N Vietnam, N Korea;
- *7th Department* – Japan, India, Indonesia, the Philippines and the rest of Asia;
- *8th Department* – Arab nations, Yugoslavia, Turkey, Greece, Iran, Afghanistan and Albania;
- *9th Department* – English-speaking nations of Africa;
- *10th Department* – French-speaking nations of Africa;
- *11th Department* – formerly known as the Advisers Department, conducted liaison with counterpart services in Cuba and E European countries;
- *12th Department* – Cover Organs, provided KGB personnel with cover jobs in other Soviet institutions, as diplomats, journalists, tourists or delegates to conferences;
- *13th Department* – provided secure communications with Residencies, officers and agents in the field;
- *14th Department* – supplied forged passports and other documents, invisible writing materials, incapacitating chemicals and other technical devices required in Foreign Directorate operations; specialists in Soviet embassies monitored local communications and provided technical assistance to the Residency;
- *15th Department* – maintained the operational files and archives of the First Chief Directorate;
- *16th Department* – performed routine personnel functions and recruited prospective staff officers for the First Chief Directorate; many officer candidates were recruited from the Institutes of International Affairs and Eastern Languages in Moscow.

RUSSIA, SPECIAL FORCES *SPETSNAZ* (*Chasti Spetsial'nogo Naznacheniya*): following the creation of a Russian Ministry of Defence in April 1992 the Spetsnaz came under the full control of the GRU. The Spetsnaz are organised into a number of Brigades of around 1,000 men and are attached to both Army and Naval Commands throughout Russia.

Trained in Special Operations and Counter-Insurgency these units are now assigned to the GRU even in wartime. During the Soviet period operational control of the Spetsnaz was firmly in the hands of the KGB, who used these tough and highly motivated Special Forces in the invasions of Czechoslovakia in 1968 and Afghanistan in 1979. They were assigned by the KGB to storm the Russian Parliament building early on 21 August 1991 with the intention of arresting Boris Yeltsin.

Virtually every military district (MD) was assigned one Spetsnaz brigade of 900–2,000 *spetsnazovtsi*. Each Brigade includes an HQ, a signal battalion, support units and battalions (*otriadi*) of variable composition, ranging from fewer than 200 to over 2,000 soldiers. As of mid-1992, GRU special-operations groups remained trained to operate in 3–7-man groups for intelligence gathering and covert action missions in enemy rear areas. They are likely to be assigned missions in ethnic conflict areas, as well. They play a prominent role in the new Russian mobile force now being planned which will be made up of airmobile, naval infantry, para-commando and transport aviation.

Operational control of the Spetsnaz units has remained with the GRU (Military Intelligence) since its formation in WWII. With the exception of an 8th Spetsnaz Brigade raised in 1996 by the MVD (Interior Ministry) especially for service in Chechniya, the other seven brigades continue to be closely involved in an intelligence support role as well as special operations. A wide range of domestic and foreign weapons, explosives and communications equipment is now available to these units, including 5.45mm AKS74 automatic rifles, 5.45mm PRI automatic pistols and such specialist weapons as the NR2 a combined combat knife with a blade that incorporates a short 7.62mm barrel fired by clipping the scabbard and knife together to give some stability.

A more dedicated Counter-Terrorist and Hostage Rescue force is provided by Al'fa or 'special group A'; this was set up originally in 1974 by the then KGB's seventh directorate and was inspired by the British SAS and the US Delta force. It is this force that attacked the Dar-ul-aman Palace in Kabul and murdered the Afghan President Hafizullah Amin and his family on 27 December 1979 right at the start of the Soviet invasion of that nation.

Currently the Al'fa group is controlled by the FSB or Federal security Service which replaced the KGB in 1992 and has an HQ and one operational group in Moscow and three groups in St Petersburg, Murmansk and Vladivostok. It is without doubt the Russian unit nearest in technical ability and organisation to the specialist counter-terrorist groups currently operated by the major Western nations.

S

SAFE HOUSE A dwelling place or hideout unknown to the adversary. A building considered safe for use by operatives as a base of operations or a building used for interrogations or hiding a defector.

SALON KITTY Salon Kitty was a high-class bordello established in a mansion in the Giesebrechtstrasse in the fashionable west-end of Berlin, rented and controlled by the Intelligence Service. It had nine bedrooms, all of which concealed microphones connected to a monitoring system in the basement. Important diplomats such as Count Ciano of Italy were among its visitors. It was run by a Madame Kitty, who, after the war, revealed something of what went on there. She said that not all the girls who worked there were professional prostitutes. Schellenberg claimed of the young society women, who volunteered for this service as a patriotic duty, that 'quite a few ladies from the upper crust of German Society were only too willing to serve their country in this manner'. Salon Kitty was successfully used to obtain large amounts of diplomatic secrets, even though von Ribbentrop, the Foreign Minister, was kept in the dark about its purpose. The establishment was controlled by Schellenberg, head of AMT VI counter-espionage service. The Salon was occasionally used by leading Nazis including Reinhard Heydrich (1904–42) who, of course, had the microphones turned off.

SANCTIFICATION Blackmail for the purposes of extracting political favours from a targeted victim, often using information on sexual, perversion or criminal activities for leverage.

SANCTION Intelligence agency approval for a killing or assassination either for revenge or active countermeasures.

SANITISE To delete specific material or revise a report of document to prevent the identification of intelligence sources and collection methods and to falsify information sources to cover up a mishandled operation.

SATELLITES, SPY The Central Intelligence Agency (CIA) commissioned a report from Rand Corporation on space-based reconnaissance for delivery in 1954. It outlined two different approaches to space reconnaissance. One envisioned a satellite that used a television camera to obtain images, which were then stored by a video tape recorder to be read back when the satellite was in view of a ground station. The other approach was to take photographs in orbit, develop the film in the satellite, and then scan the film for transmission back to a ground station.

The USAF issued a request for proposals for a spy satellite system in early 1955, with the specification loosely based on the Rand study. RCA, Martin, and Lockheed's Missile Systems Division in Palo Alto submitted proposals. The USAF awarded a contract for what was designated Air Force Weapon System 117 (WS-117L) to Lockheed on 29 October 1956. For launch vehicles for WS-117L satellites, Lockheed engineers looked to the Thor intermediate-range ballistic missile (IRBM) and bigger Atlas intercontinental ballistic missile (ICBM), both then in development and expected to be available later in the decade. A second reconnaissance system also evolved out of the original WS-117L programme: an infrared observation satellite system known as MIDAS which apparently means 'Missile Infrared Defence Alarm System' and was intended to detect enemy missile launches or bomber flights from stationary geosynchronous orbit. MIDAS eventually led to the modern Defence Support Program (DSP) early warning satellites.

The Soviet Union was working towards its own space-based surveillance systems and in August 1957 successfully test-flew their R-7 ICBM or SS-6, while the US suffered a series of humiliating public failures of ICBM test flights. On 4 October 1957, the Soviets put the first artificial Earth satellite, Sputnik I, into orbit with an R-7. When the US Navy attempted to launch the first American satellite, Vanguard I, in December 1957, the Vanguard booster blew up on the pad in an impressive fireball.

Sputniks I and II were effectively only cosmetic launches designed to humiliate the US, who were working slowly towards deploying much more advanced technologies. Ground-based intelligence gained by the CIA clearly showed that the Sputnik launches were effectively R-7 test flights, that the R-7 was still in a relatively early phase of testing, and that the Soviet ICBM programme had its share of problems. The Soviet lead in missiles appeared to be little more than an enormous bluff. As one observer put it, Soviet Premier Khruschev was trying to 'defend his country with his mouth'.

The bluff was successful. Eisenhower received USAF intelligence reports that the USSR would have a hundred ICBMs in 1959 and a thousand by 1961. In fact they would have only a few dozen operational and though the President had intelligence data from the CIA, particularly U-2 reconnaissance imagery that tended to suggest a lower figure than that pressed by the USAF, the obvious risks were such that President Eisenhower could do little dampen the agitation in Congress.

The CIA and the USAF both wanted to control space reconnaissance. The CIA were to triumph in 1958 and Richard Bissell of the CIA, who had been a driving force behind the U-2 programme, was also put in charge of the space reconnaissance effort. In principle, Bissell would have to co-ordinate his decisions with an Air Force general, but in practice the USAF would be responsible for building the boosters and launching the satellites, while the CIA ran the show. The WS-117L programme gained top priority, and was redesignated to conceal it. The space reconnaissance effort, now focusing on the film-return system under the CIA, was hidden in plain sight, disguised as the USAF *Discoverer* scientific satellite programme. The actual programme would have a different name: *Corona*.

The *Corona Film-Return Satellites* were to orbit the Earth over the poles three times and then discard a film capsule. The key to the satellite was the sophisticated *Agena* upper stage, built by Lockheed. While most satellites of the time used simple spin stabilisation, the *Agena* provided 'three-axis' stabilisation in orbit, a more difficult prospect. This meant that the satellite could be oriented into any position and stay there, a necessity for keeping a camera aligned on a target.

The actual payload was a panoramic camera developed by Itek, with much in common with the WS-461L cameras. The Itek camera scanned across the line of flight over a 70-degree arc, recording the image on 70 millimeter film provided by Eastman Kodak. The camera was built using a rotating drum that exposed the film from one side to the other, laying down the image in a swath.

The scan was slightly staggered from one side to the other to compensate for the motion of the spacecraft. Best resolution of this early camera was no better than about 11 metres (35 feet), but later generations would provide better resolution.

The film was fed to a re-entry capsule that was to be ejected after the images had been obtained. The capsule, or 'bucket' as it would eventually be known, included a thruster maneuvering system, a solid-fuel deorbiting rocket, a telemetry system and beacon to allow it to be tracked, a recovery parachute controlled by a timer system, and a battery to power its electronics.

The bucket's ablative external heat shield allowed it to survive the heat of re-entry. The bucket had a salt plug that would dissolve after about 24 hours in the water to ensure that the bucket would sink if it were not recovered in a timely fashion. Once the parachute was deployed, the capsule was to be snagged by a transport aircraft trailing a harness system. Originally, C-119 Boxcars were used, but were later replaced in the task by the versatile C-130 Hercules. The USAF recovery group, the 6594 Test Wing, operated out of Hawaii.

On 10 August 1960, *Discoverer XIII* underwent its first successful launch after a large number of failures: it orbited and discarded its re-entry capsule on 12 August. Attempts to snag the capsule in the air failed, but a helicopter recovered it from the sea about 480 kms (300 miles) NW of Hawaii.

Discoverer XIV followed on 18 August 1960 and was the first fully operational system. The satellite worked superbly and sent back its film capsule, which was snatched from the air as planned.

Discoverer XIV returned 1.5 million square miles' worth of imagery. A fifth of the Soviet Union had been imaged. Intelligence photo interpreters were 'flabbergasted' at the gain.

The new high quality reconnaissance information provided by *Corona* led to sharply reduced estimates of Soviet missile capabilities. Image analysis showed that the Soviets, rather than having hundreds of ICBMs available to attack the USA, had no more than 25, a number that was later reduced to six. At the time, the US had 28 operational Atlas ICBMs, and finally the USA had been able to confirm that there was indeed, no missile gap.

When the US government finally released classified documents relating to *Corona* in 1995, a retired major general of Soviet Strategic Rocket Forces named Anatoly Bolyatko participated in the release ceremony. Recounting Khrushchev's 1959 boast that Soviet ICBMs were in mass production, Bolyatko commented: 'But 100 per cent of those ICBMs were junk.' He said that when an ICBM launch was performed for senior officials, 'we would prepare four rockets for launch so that maybe one of them would get off successfully'.

By this time, US space reconnaissance was under the control of an entirely new government agency: the National Reconnaissance Office (NRO) was established in late 1960.

The Eisenhower administration wanted to make sure that infighting and rivalries over space reconnaissance were kept to a minimum, that control of space reconnaissance was provided by civilians rather than the military, and that the tightest secrecy was maintained. The NRO has controlled US space reconnaissance activities since that time.

Despite the intense secrecy, the Soviets were not fooled. They issued complaints about satellite over-flights, made threats to destroy the satellites and did eventually build decoys in an attempt to fool spy satellites including an inflatable submarine that reconnaissance cameras observed had the unfortunate habit of bending whenever the wind blew. Reconnaissance satellites did not provide the information about the movement of Soviet nuclear-armed missiles into Cuba in 1962 that led to the Cuban Missile Crisis in October of that year. Imagery proving the presence of those weapons was provided by U-2 reconnaissance aircraft and additional *Corona* satellites were launched to determine the state of Soviet alert.

The NRO space imaging reconnaissance systems became known by KH (Key Hole) code numbers, along with programme names and the original *Corona* satellites up to early 1962 had designations KH-1 through KH-3. More advanced *Corona* missions were to follow as the first *KH-4 Advanced Film-Return Satellites* were launched in early 1962 and incorporated two panoramic cameras. The cameras were oriented at an angle of 30 degrees from each other front and back to allow them take stereo images.

These satellites were intended for observations of specific targets. As the USA moved toward a deterrent force based on ICBMs rather than manned bombers, precise target locations were required to permit accurate programming of the missiles' inertial navigation systems. Unfortunately, maps of Soviet targets were very crude, in some cases with target errors of almost 50 kms (30 miles).

The KH-5 system, codenamed ARGON, was first launched in the spring of 1962 and was designed to provide target mapping information using a wide-angle snapshot camera, with each image covering 550kms by 550kms (300 x 300 nautical miles). With these images, target planners were able to determine target locations initially to within 300 metres (1,000 feet) and later to less than half that distance. The first successful launch of a KH-4A stereo imaging satellite with two film return capsules was in early 1964. This was followed by the bigger KH-4B stereo imaging satellite also with two film return capsules and was launched by the more powerful Thrust-Augmented Thor booster in September 1967.

The *KH-6 Lanyard* – a high resolution system that was capable of making out details as small as 60cm (2 feet) – was designed and had a single panoramic camera that could tilt front and back to generate stereo image pairs during its over-flight. It was put into orbit on 31 July 1963 and operated for 32 hours. However, it was immediately replaced by the bigger *KH-7 Gambit* system also launched for the first time in July 1963. The KH-7 launches continued into 1967 when they were replaced by the still bigger and better *KH-8 Gambit*, which had to be launched on a Titan 3B. It was followed in turn by the *KH-9A Hexagon* and *KH-9B Big Bird* satellites beginning in 1971, which were much larger than earlier reconnaissance satellites and had four film-return capsules.

The *Corona* series of film-return suffered the major drawback of not being real-time systems. It simply took too long to recover, develop and assess the images to allow fast-changing events to be monitored. This limitation was highlighted by the Soviet invasion of Czechoslovakia in 1968, when images showing Soviet forces massing for the attack were unavailable until after the invasion had occurred. The CIA wanted a more sophisticated imaging system, based on an image-intensifying television camera tube. The first *KH-11 Electronic Imaging Satellite* was put into orbit in 1976 and transmitted high-resolution reconnaissance imagery to ground stations through relay satellites. The KH-11 series are very large spacecraft and have been continuously improved and remain the backbone of the US imaging reconnaissance capability, their associated programme names include *Kennan* and *Crystal*.

Two KH-11 satellites with infrared as well as optical imaging capabilities are generally in orbit at all times with a lifetime of six to eight years. As with earlier imaging satellites, they operate in low altitude, near-polar 'Sun synchronous' orbits. In a Sun synchronous orbit, the spacecraft always passes over the same region at the same times of day, allowing image interpreters to spot changes in shadows. Resolution is estimated at 15cm (6in) or better. The information is directly relayed to ground stations through data relay satellites, most of them operating in geosynchronous orbit. A geosynchronous orbit has an altitude of 36,000km (22,300 miles) above the equator, where a satellite takes 24 hours to orbit the Earth and so hangs in a stationary position in the sky.

KH-11 (Key Hole) satellites are still limited by darkness and bad weather. In December 1988, the US space shuttle *Atlantis* placed the first *Indigo Radar Satellites* satellite into orbit and now known as *Lacrosse*, provided all-weather round-the-clock radar coverage of target areas, presumably at a lower resolution than that offered by imaging satellites. Believed to be conceptually similar to the Magellan Venus Radar Mapping spacecraft, which used a synthetic aperture radar (SAR) to map the surface of Venus through the planet's solid cloud cover. A SAR takes radar readings as its platform moves over a target, and assimilates all the information obtained into a detailed image. *Lacrosse* radar resolution is variously estimated at 1 to 3 metres, possibly using different radar modes, and information is sent back to the spacecraft's masters by the TDRSS satellite constellation.

SIGINT involves listening in to communications (COMINT), missile telemetry (TELINT), radar emissions (RADINT), and other electronic systems (ELINT). Early US SIGINT satellites launched in 1962 were limited, uncomplicated relays that simply transferred signals to ground stations for analysis.

Early SIGINT satellites were believed to use antennas that unfolded like an umbrella, similar to those used on TDRSS. The latest generation of geosynchronous SIGINT satellites have very large antennas, on the order of 100m (110 yards) in diameter.

These satellites cover the full spectrum of SIGINT missions. The geosynchronous satellites have been given cover-names such as RHYOLITE, AQUACADE, CHALET, VORTEX, MAGNUM, MENTOR, TRUMPET, ORION, MERCURY and DOUBLE MAGNUM, Molniya orbiters JUMPSEAT and CANYON. Early SIGINT satellites were believed to use antennas that unfolded like an umbrella, similar to those used on TDRSS. The latest generation of geosynchronous SIGINT satellites have very large antennas, on the order of 100 metres (110 yards) in diameter

The space reconnaissance assets put into orbit by the NRO are ideal strategic information platforms, however the deficiencies in the US reconnaissance satellite capability were strongly revealed during the Gulf War in 1991. Senior Battlefield commanders bitterly complained about the failure of the reconnaissance apparatus to provide timely and useful information. In response to the complaints, the NRO established an Operational Support Office (OSO) to improve co-operation with the military.

OSO proved its value in distributing intelligence data quickly during the Afghanistan air campaign in late 2001 and the continuing air attacks on Iraq in 2002. New communications systems are in development that will allow intelligence information to be transferred in real-time from orbit directly to ground forces in the front line and aircraft actually in a combat zone.

With only a handful of high-value reconnaissance satellites in orbit, the opportunities for deception is considerable and the time between over-flights can be used to move whole units or ready a missile launcher. Similarly, when India detonated a number of nuclear weapons in 1998, their work schedules were designed to deceive satellite over-flights and were thus able to surprise the world with the tests.

The NRO is now readying the Future Imagery Architecture (FIA) series of satellites, which will be about half the size and cost of the KH-11 satellites, but twice as capable. The smaller size will also allow use of smaller and cheaper boosters and the NRO expects to orbit enough imaging satellites to obtain a threefold improvement in target revisit times in 2003 or 2004, with the full constellation in operation sometime after 2005. Defence Advanced Research Projects Agency (DARPA) has investigated advanced technologies including the concept of a low Earth orbit constellation of light-satellites named *Starlite* and intended as having SAR with moving target indicator (MTI) capability and would interface with other tactical reconnaissance assets, such as the J-STARS battlefield reconnaissance aircraft. Starlite spacecraft would be cheap enough to be launched in quantity or for specific missions, and could be replaced easily if an adversary acquired the capability to disable or destroy satellites in low Earth orbit.

SOVIET SPACE-BASED INTELLIGENCE CAPABILITY

The Soviets were working on a space reconnaissance capability in parallel with the American effort, with the task initially assigned in 1956 to the First Experimental Design Bureau (OKB-1) under Sergei Korolyev. The early film capsule satellite versions of the manned *Vostok* systems were renamed *Zenit* and were built in several versions, the short duration *Zenit-2*, the first operational flight was in October 1963, under the cover designation of *Cosmos-20* and the long duration *ZENIT-4 and 6*. Once the Soviets had an operational space reconnaissance capability, they dropped their objections to American space over-flights of the USSR. The greatly improved *Yantar* series of imaging reconnaissance satellites were introduced in 1974, and increasingly replaced the *Zenit* series, the last of which were launched in 1992. The *Yantar* satellites carried multiple film-return capsules and were eventually capable of operating for months. The *Yantar* technology was used as a basis for Soviet electro-optical satellites, the first of which was put into orbit in 1982. *Yantar* also led to another satellite system that has both electro-optic observation capabilities and film-return capsules. The Soviets were not capable of launching low-Earth orbit ferret satellites until 1967. They did not launch a geosynchronous SIGINT satellite until 1985, eventually forming constellations of *Tselina*-class satellites. Beginning in 1970, the USSR launched a series of RORSAT or radar ocean reconnaissance satellites that were equipped with a powerful radar powered by a nuclear reactor, to observe NATO fleet movements. In principle, when a RORSAT's useful life was over, its nuclear fuel was supposed to be boosted into a high orbit where it could remain indefinitely while the fuel decayed to a harmless state.

In practice, there were a few accidents, most spectacularly with Cosmos 954, a RORSAT that fell into Canada in 1978, strewing a trail of radioactive debris behind it. The RORSAT programme was ended in 1988, after 33 launches. While the Soviets pursued new technological developments in space reconnaissance during the 1980s, an impoverished Russia simply does not have the resources to pursue such efforts. At present, Russia is making do with film-return systems and has a few remaining.

SIGINT SATELLITES

China launched their first imaging reconnaissance satellite in 1975; some 20 such spacecraft have now been successfully launched. All of these spacecraft were film-return systems and are known as Fanhui Shi Weixing or 'Return Type Satellite'. The Chinese are developing a radar imaging satellite and genuine SIGINT platforms.

France in co-operation with Spain and Italy, developed the *Helios-1* space reconnaissance satellite system, derived from the French SPOT Earth-resource observation satellite. *Helios-1* was launched in July 1995 and is an electronic imaging system with 1.5m resolution. It was used to assess air-strike damage during the Kosovo air campaign. An improved *Helios-2* is set for launching in 2003.

Israel launched the *Offeq 1* reconnaissance satellite in 1988, which was experimental spacecraft intended to help them develop a space capability, and also apparently built with S African help. It is the beginning of a major space-based effort and the *Offeq* series has been joined by new improved satellites in 2002 and 2003.

India has developed and launched their Polar Satellite Launch Vehicle (PSLV) and is developing a genuine SIGINT satellite and launcher capability and probably with a degree of co-operation with Israel.

Russia is now, among others, offering former military ballistic missile systems as relatively inexpensive space launchers combined with new and highly advanced Western technology. This will make commercial space-based surveillance information and imagery readily available to a whole range of countries who would not normally have access to such high grade or potentially virtually real-time satellite imagery. This will greatly reduce the automatic advantage the USA has so far enjoyed in conflict situations and may produce unexpected results in the new battlefields of the 21st century.

SAUDI ARABIA *al Istakhbarah al-'Amah General Intelligence Service (GIS)* is responsible for internal security protection of the Royal Family; not only their physical safety, but also of their 'reputations' and privacy, counter-terrorism, surveillance operations against Saudi dissidents abroad, counter-sabotage within the oil industry as well as external intelligence concentrating on Iraq and Iran. Insiders have complained that as much time is spent covering up the latest incident of embarrassing behaviour by the younger members of the ruling elite than is spent gathering vital intelligence on national threats. Vast sums have been spent on ensuring that it has the best available communication monitoring, bugging and surveillance equipment available. It is supposed to have a close relationship with the CIA, but in reality have their own agenda which, when it coincides with Western interests, co-operation is possible, otherwise Saudi and in particular, Saudi Royal family interests are paramount. Both the Ministry of the Interior and National Guard have small intelligence sections again dedicated to the protection of the Royal Family and internal security. The Saudi SIGINT service has its HQ in Riyadh and its main internal electronics monitoring facility for telephone tapping and bugging operations. The two main SIGINT listening sites are at Araz and Khafji.

SAUDI ARABIA, SPECIAL FORCES The Special Security Force was established in 1971 and gained its counter-terrorist and hostage rescue role in 1979. The SSF has some 3,500 personnel organised into eight battalions and independent company-sized units and receives regular training from the French GIGN and German GSG9. However, the best such unit in Saudi Arabia is probably the 100-man Special Warfare unit made up entirely of volunteers from within National Guard. Armed with 5.56mm M16A1 automatic rifles, 9mm MP5 sub-machine guns and M700 sniper rifles they were given special training by the French GIGN before launching the successful operation to retake the Great Mosque in Mecca, seized by radical Muslim terrorists in 1979.

The Airborne Brigade controls a further three dedicated Special Force Companies. These units are made up of volunteers, who are fully trained parachutists. Their initial training period includes six months of basic fitness and combat skills, then a further six months developing a range of advanced techniques in all aspects of special operations.

Parachute training including HALO and HAHO, heliborne insertion, combat shooting, desert survival and warfare, close quarter battle, hostage rescue, long-range reconnaissance and patrol or LRRP. Specialist explosive disposal training is also given in dealing with potential sabotage within the petro-chemical industry. These units regularly train with US Delta force and SEAL personnel and are posted abroad on courses with the German GSG9 and French GIGN.

There is very close co-operation with the CIA and US Special Forces based in Saudi Arabia. Since the end of the Gulf War with Iraq, US military bases have been the target of numerous terrorist attacks by among others, Osama bin Laden's group, and prevention of further such outrages is high on the list of priorities for the Saudi Special Forces. The threat of extremist Islamic terrorist activities spreading both to the migrant worker community, and to the indigenous population is of continuing grave concern to the authorities, and the security and special forces in particular. The weapons available for use by these units are the pick of the world's arms, and a wide range has been purchased, but the most popular are the 5.56mm M16A1 automatic rifles, Steyr AUG automatic rifles and 9mm MP5 sub-machine guns, PSG-1 Sniper Rifles and the M203 grenade launchers. A number of specially converted UH60 helicopters are available for Special Forces' use, and have been of considerable value in operations along the disputed desert frontiers to the south and in the north along the border with Iraq.

SCALP HUNTERS British term for intelligence officers who specialise in defections and in differentiating genuine defectors from fakes and plants.

SCIENTIFIC INTELLIGENCE To obtain information providing an early warning of important modifications or new developments in weapons and methods employed by a potential or actual hostile nation.

SCIF Sensitive Compartmented Information Facility.

SDR Surveillance detection run; a route designed to disrupt or flush out counter-surveillance without alerting them to the operative's purpose.

SD SICHERHEITSDIENST (German Security Police) The SD was the intelligence service of the Nazi Party during the years preceding their takeover of the German State and increased their power and influence thereafter. It developed such an important espionage system and network of agents under Reinhard Heydrich that in 1934, just a few weeks before the bloody purge of the SA, Rudolf Hess added the all-embracing role of counter-intelligence and counter political subversion to its portfolio. The task of the SD was to obtain secret information concerning the actual and potential enemies of the Nazi leadership so that appropriate action could be taken to destroy or neutralise opposition. To accomplish this task, the SD created an organisation of agents and informants operating out of various SD regional offices established throughout the Reich, and later in conjunction with the Gestapo and Kripo, the Criminal Police throughout the occupied territories. The organisation consisted of several hundred full-time agents whose work was supplemented by several thousand part-time informants. The SD investigated the loyalty and reliability of State officials, evaluating them by their complete devotion to Nazi ideology and to Hitler. The SD, through its vast network of local informants, spied upon the German people in every aspect of their daily lives, whether economic, recreational, social, political or religious.

SECRET WRITING Any tradecraft technique employing invisible messages hidden in or on innocuous materials usually sent through the mails to accommodation addresses. This includes invisible inks and microdots among many other variations.

SECURITY Measures taken by a military unit, an activity or installation to protect itself against all acts designed to, or that may, impair its effectiveness. With respect to classified matter, it is the condition that prevents unauthorised persons from having access to official information that is safeguarded in the interests of national security.

11 SEPTEMBER 2001 (9/11) The events of that September morning were simply appalling, but the resulting abandonment of long-held civil rights and the ready acceptance by the individual and the news media of draconian new security and surveillance measures, many of which have little or no value in fighting international terrorism, pose a far worse threat; the undermining of democracy and the loss of freedom itself.

Few governments will be willing to quickly reintroduce access to official records and statistics or to dismantle the 'handy' new controls; it is far too tempting to maintain such capabilities long after their usefulness has passed. To ensure individual civil and human rights, democracy must be re-asserted by the electorate at the first opportunity as governments and their intelligence and security apparatus have a vested interest in maintaining the new status quo. The true cost of the Al Qa'ida outrage of 9/11 may be far more wide ranging and damaging to democracy than fighting a war against terrorism, and the world could well be living with the effects long after Osama bin Laden has been consigned to history.

SERBIA-MONTENEGRO Federal Republic of Yugoslavia (FRY)

SID Sluzba Informaitvna u Dokumenti – Information and Documentation Service: SID is the organisation within the Federal Ministry for Foreign Affairs responsible for gathering intelligence overseas. Its principal role is the production of secret intelligence in support of Serbian security, defence, foreign and economic policies.

KOS Kontraobavesajna Sluzba – Counter-Intelligence Service: after the end of WWII KOS was organised into complicated networks of intelligence officers, security experts and what effectively became assassination units. Their role was to uncover and eliminate prominent members of émigré organisations, political opposition groups and ethnic separatist movements. KOS, which was glorified for its work as Tito's private intelligence network during the war, escaped serious reorganisation and remained one of the most conservative services in the world. Until the beginning of the Balkan wars in the 1990s and the break-up of the old Yugoslav federation foreign intelligence and internal security remained largely in the hands of ethnic Serbian Officers.

In late 1991 KOS attempted to place surveillance teams of federal security officers undercover of training schemes at various security centres in Bosnia. These mainly Serbian officers were not welcome in Bosnia, except at the Banja Luka CSB or Security Service Centre. There were similar and unsuccessful attempts to install KOS agents, such as Fikret Muslimovic, in the Bosnia-Herzegovina section of SDB or State Security, leadership in early 1992. During 1992–94 a major conflict emerged between the SDB and military services, with the goal of limiting the influence of the intelligence service of the Army of Yugoslavia, particularly the Counter-Intelligence Service. As early as 1993, there had been an attempt to prosecute the head of KOS General Aleksandar Vasiljevic and a group of his closest assistants on manufactured charges by Lieutenant Colonel Nedeljko Boskovic, one of Milosevic's most trusted allies. The process failed when the President of the Higher Military Court in Belgrade rejected the accusations as unfounded. But Vasiljevic was still removed by the head of the General Staff General Zivota Panic, and a much less capable officer, Boskovic, was appointed to his post. Within a few months, Boskovic was in turn replaced by a friend of the Milosevic, Colonel-General Aleksandar Dimitrijevic by which time the war in Bosnia-Herzegovina was well under way.

SDB Sluzba drzavne bezbednosti – State Security Service: internal security forces were instrumental in establishing and maintaining the Communist-controlled Yugoslav state after WWII. They were responsible for identifying and prosecuting Ustase leaders and others who collaborated with occupying German and Italian forces during WWII. But alleged collaboration became a pretext for reprisals against political opponents such as the Cetnici and others who did not support Tito's Partisans. Many, including Cetnik leader Draza Mihajlovic and Croatian Roman Catholic archbishop Stepinac, were executed or imprisoned after summary trials.

After the break in relations with the Soviet Union in 1948, the Yugoslav government feared that the Soviet Union might find or create a group within Yugoslavia to request Soviet intervention to assist it in 'preserving socialism'. The Yugoslav security agency investigated more than 50,000 alleged 'Cominformists' or pro-Soviet party members, who were subsequently purged from the party. Several thousand were eventually jailed, either without trials or after show trials. They were interned in political prisons at Goli Otok in the Adriatic, Sremska Mitrovica in Vojvodina, and Stara Gradiska in Bosnia. Others were subjected to administrative punishment or petty harassment, while those considered just too dangerous or unrepentant 'disappeared'.

SETTING UP   Framing or trapping an individual by covert means. Includes sexual entrapment by male (Ravens) or female (Swallows) of diplomatic, intelligence or commercial targets.

SHAMROCK   The most ambitious US use of domestic intelligence gathering largely carried out by the armed forces, in particular the Army Security Agency (ASA). The ASA established all pervasive coverage of commercial and private telegrams with arrangements made with Western Union Telegraph Co, ITT Communications and RCA Communications to access all overseas cable traffic with eventually hard copies of each and every overseas telegram each of the companies handled being provided to military analysts.

SHAYLER, David (1965–)   David Shayler joined MI5 as part of a recruitment drive in the early 90s to attract a new breed of non-public school, non-Oxbridge graduates who would shake up the moribund service. With the end of the Cold War, it was felt that MI5 had to shift the emphasis of its operations towards the very real threat from the IRA, Islamic fundamentalists and hostile regimes in the Middle East. A cryptic advert appeared in national newspapers in 1991 showing three empty chairs, with the catchline 'Godot Isn't Coming'. It read: 'If you have already achieved plenty, but now find yourself marking time, stuck in a rut and unable to progress, then it's time to act.'

According to Shayler, he and other officers of his generation soon became disillusioned with intelligence work. Most of it seemed to involve shuffling papers and getting official clearance for the endless MI5 phone taps on ordinary individuals. He became appalled by the level of surveillance of tiny extreme left groups, while the intelligence service was unable to stop terrorist acts by the IRA such as the bombings at Bishopsgate and Canary Wharf. Most seriously he was convinced that MI5 and SIS (MI6) agents often acted outside the rule of law, knowing they were unlikely to be punished. After raising his concerns with senior officers he, like many of his colleagues, left around the time the Labour government came to power in 1997, pledging to make the intelligence services more accountable. He worked for G Branch, dealing with international terrorism, C Branch, where government officials' backgrounds are checked and T Branch – targeting terrorism in N Ireland. Deskbound and increasingly unhappy with his employer, Shayler quit his job in 1997. He took his concerns about the UK's secret services to Mail on Sunday journalist Nick Fielding.

Shayler's revelations about MI5, and its sister espionage service SIS (MI6), range from the general to the embarrassingly specific. In August 1997, the Mail on Sunday published his allegations that MI5 was riven with incompetence and inefficiency. He also 'blew the whistle' on alleged surveillance operations on such 'subversives' as Jack Straw, and Peter Mandelson – now both government high-flyers. Ex-Beatle John Lennon, UB40 and punk band the Sex Pistols were also investigated by MI5, said Shayler. Further allegations have followed, suggesting that a bungling MI5 failed to stop the bomb attack on Israel's London embassy in 1994 and the IRA's 1993 Bishopsgate bombing, which killed one person.

In August 1998, Shayler renewed his attacks on the secret services, alleging that SIS (MI6) had invested in a plot to assassinate Libyan leader Colonel Gaddafi. Even before the publication of the original allegations, Shayler decided it would be prudent to leave the UK temporarily. Shayler's partner, former MI5 agent Annie Machon, returned to the UK to test the waters in September 1997. She was arrested, but never charged. His supporters, who include Richard Tomlinson, a former SIS (MI6) agent who also turned whistleblower, would claim that he has 'set in motion an unstoppable momentum towards real reform of the intelligence services'.

Robin Cook, the UK Foreign Secretary, on the other hand, described claims about the Gaddafi plot as 'pure fantasy'. However, the *Sunday Times* report of 13 February 2000 was titled, intriguingly, 'Revealed: Cook misled public over Libya Plot'. David Shayler's response was that he had been largely vindicated over the existence of a Gaddafi assassination plot. Although the report does not absolutely confirm that SIS (MI6) paid an agent to assassinate Colonel Gaddafi, it does confirm that MI6 had an agent who had prior information about the plans of a group of army plotters who had decided either to arrest or kill Gaddafi as part of a coup in February–March 1996.

'The report contradicts Foreign Secretary Robin Cook's assertion that the Gaddafi Plot was "pure fantasy". The report was sent to the FO's PUSD, the permanent under-secretary's department, which directly advises the Foreign Secretary. The Foreign Office therefore clearly knew that MI6 knew of advanced plans to stage a coup in which Gaddafi would be arrested or killed at exactly the time I was talking about. In that position, to say that the Plot was "pure fantasy" was a dereliction of duty, if not a downright lie.'

An SIS (MI6) document posted on the Internet appeared to confirm there had been a plot to kill the Libyan leader in early 1996. The suspicion that David Shayler has highlighted serious malpractice by both the intelligence and security services is perhaps given added weight by the lengths to which the British Government and his ex-employers seems to be prepared to go to silence him.

SHEEP DIPPING US Intelligence term for camouflaging or disguising the true identity of equipment or individuals especially of military assets used in clandestine activities.

SHOE Russian Intelligence service term for a passport.

SHOE MAKER Russian intelligence term for a forger, particularly of fake passports.

SHOPPED British Intelligence term for an agent or individual who has been deliberately exposed to a hostile security service, occasionally for assassination rather than arrest.

SHOPWORN GOODS   Information offered by a defector or potential defector that is old, outdated or unrelated to the needs. of the intelligence service to which it is being offered.

SIGINT   (Signals Intelligence) Derived from the interception, processing and analysis of communications, electronic emissions or telemetry. Complementary to the worldwide ECHELON system and because of the nature of the sites, the SIGINT networks have remained largely unknown. The secrecy attached to it by the UK and its allies in WWII, particularly codebreaking operations, carried over into the Cold War with the fear that revelations about methods and successes would lead to an adversary changing codes and ciphers. The sudden inability to read an enemy's messages at a crucial time could have truly disastrous results and had to be avoided at all costs. Another aspect of WWII that carried over into the Cold War era was the close co-operation between five countries: the USA, the UK, Canada, Australia and New Zealand, formalised with the UKUSA Security Agreement of 1948.

Over the last 50 years, computer-based encryption has made codebreaking far more difficult and often impossible. At the same time, the interception of unencrypted commercial communications and other electronic signals, particularly radar emanations and missile telemetry, has grown dramatically in importance. This expanded role for signals intelligence was made evident in the construction and operation of a vast network of ground stations spread across the world, ELINT aircraft equipped with intercept antenna and the introduction of advanced electronic surveillance satellites. To some considerable extent this effort was matched by the Soviet Union and later by Communist China.

The attempts at maintaining the secrecy surrounding the use of SIGINT continued when the National Security Agency, established in 1952, was only officially acknowledged in 1957, while the British network based on GCHQ, inheritor of Bletchley Park's wartime codebreaking success, was only to become publicly known in the 1980s. This followed a serious spy scandal and an ill-judged political decision by the Thatcher Government to ban trade unions from the Cheltenham HQ and from its worldwide network of listening stations run by the Composite Signals Organisation.

For years, what were known to be US-operated signals intelligence stations have been officially described as facilities engaged in the research of 'electronic phenomena' or the 'rapid-relay of communications'. It took the US over 20 years after the Soviet Union obtained detailed information on a US signals intelligence satellite even to acknowledge the existence of such satellites.

There are several dozen radio interception stations run by the UKUSA allies and located throughout the world. Many developed in the early years of the Cold War and, before satellite communications became widespread in the 1980s, were the main ground signals intelligence stations targeting Soviet communications. Some stations were also used against regional targets.

Most of this network of stations target long-range high frequency (HF) radio. A powerful HF radio transmitter can transmit right around the world, which is why HF radio has been a major means of international communications and is still widely used by military forces and by ships and aircraft. Other stations target short-range communications – very high frequency and ultra high frequency radio (VHF and UHF) – which, among other things, are used extensively for tactical military communications within a country.

SIGNAL SITE   A prearranged fixed location – usually a public place – where an agent or intelligence officer can place a predetermined mark in order to alert the other to operational activities. The mark made at the signal site – such as chalk marking or a piece of tape – may let one of the parties know, for example, that the dead drop has been loaded.

SILLETOE, Sir Percy (1888–1962)   Director-General of MI5 (1946–53). A civilian police officer and Chief Constable of Kent (1945–46) he was chosen as a clean pair of hands when the Labour government appointed him over the heads of experienced MI5 officers. Never accepted by the Security Service as a whole, his tenure was something of an irrelevance with his Deputy, Guy Liddell, basically in charge of running the organisation, until eventually Liddell came under suspicion as a possible security risk. Sillitoe was to prove incapable of bringing forward the fundamental changes needed to make the security service far less introspective and withdrawn and more responsive to the needs of a modern society.

SILVER BULLET   The special disguise and deception tradecraft techniques developed under Moscow rules to help the CIA penetrate the KGB's security perimeter in Moscow.

SINCLAIR, Admiral Sir Hugh 'Quex' (1873–1939)   Sinclair joined the Naval Intelligence Department during WWI and succeeded Admiral 'Blinker' Hall as Director of Naval Intelligence in 1919. He was appointed the second Head or 'C' of SIS (MI6) in 1923, following the death of Cumming. Not a professional secret service officer, Sinclair was rather out of his depth at times, but he struggled to maintain the semblance of an effective intelligence service in the face of constant cost-cutting throughout the 1920s and 30s.

A conscientious and caring man, he still managed to lay the groundwork for some of the service's greatest successes, notably the decision to prepare for the expansion of the codebreaking department GC&CS and the purchase of facilities later to be known as Station X at Bletchley Park. However, it must be said that he was not strong enough to deal with the behaviour of some of his more wilful senior officers, such as Claude Dansey and Valentine Vivians. Their constant disagreements and Dansey's creation of the parallel Z section created dissension within an already muddled organisation and did little for the overall effectiveness of SIS or staff morale.

SINGAPORE *ISD Internal Security Department*: a combined intelligence and police force, it largely recruits from the Civilian Police. This unit, as the name implies, deals with the internal security of Singapore. It is responsible for internal security, counter-terrorism, organised crime and narcotics crime.

SID Security & Intelligence Division is the main overseas intelligence-gathering service, recruiting mainly from the Diplomatic Service and the Military. For many years Singapore was the Far Eastern HQ for Britain's SIS and this service still maintains a close relationship with SID.

This unit is highly secretive, responsible for the gathering and assessment of intelligence on potential external threats. Most Singapore embassies or consulates overseas have at least one officer from this unit attached with them. It works closely with other government security departments and with public sectors including the Ministry of Foreign Affairs, Ministry of Defence, Singapore Airlines, Singapore Tourism Board, some of which are used as a front for their undercover duties.

SID is in overall control of the Kranji Signals Intelligence complex (KR2) on the Johore straits in N Singapore. Opened by GCHQ/CSO and the Australian DSD as a joint station to replace Chai Keng in 1971, it soon became largely a DSD base with a CSO SLO. Australia handed the base over to the SIGINT department of SID in February 1974. A DSD SLO remained for some time afterwards. Kranji has since been greatly expanded and is now a highly sophisticated centre with direct links to the Echelon network, but importantly, taking Australia's recent complaints into account, a distinct national agenda of its own.

SIS   Secret (Special) Intelligence Service (British MI6).

SITREP   Situation report sent in to HQ during an operation or crisis.

SLAMMER   US intelligence project for obtaining first-hand information from US citizens in prison for espionage activities, their responses being recorded to provide greater understanding of the motives and psychological make-up of traitors.

SLEEPER   A deep penetration agent placed in the target country, but who does not engage in espionage activities until activated many years later and only when promotion to a sensitive position or change of work provides the right opportunity. Term used by KGB and indeed Western Intelligence Services until replaced by the use of the less specific 'Mole'.

SMERSH   Ever since the Bolshevik revolution of 1917, a specialist division of Soviet intelligence has been responsible for seeking out and blackmailing, kidnapping or killing anyone who opposed the Communist regime, especially defecting Russians or Russians opposing the regime who live abroad. Non-Russians who have proved to be particularly antagonistic to the Soviets have also been selected for action by SMERSH, a phrase meaning 'Death to Spies!' or Smert Shpionam. SMERSH was actually the Ninth Division of the KGB. Though the title SMERSH ceased to be used by the KGB after 1948, the organisation continues to exist and was organised into five main sections:

1. The *first section* worked inside the Red Army dealing with dissident soldiers and summarily executing them.
2. The *second section* of SMERSH collected information and, during wartime, was responsible for dropping agents behind enemy lines.
3. The *third section* was responsible for collating and disseminating information and planning operations.
4. The *fourth section* investigated suspects and has the authority to make arrests.
5. The *fifth section* was made up of three-man tribunals of high-ranking soviet officers who hear cases and pass judgment. All sentences by the tribunals were final and, if execution is ordered, it is carried out immediately.

SMERSH (later called Department V of the First Chief Directorate, which is hidden inside the internal security department of the Army, also called CUKR) is responsible for ruthlessly murdering tens of thousands of people in the last eight decades.

The most celebrated SMERSH assassination was that of Leon Trotsky, who had led the Bolshevik revolution of October 1917 in Russia with Vladimir Ilich Ulyanov Lenin. He had been exiled from Russia in 1929 by his nemesis, Joseph Stalin, but had conducted an intense propaganda campaign against the Russian dictator. Stalin had ordered Trotsky murdered. Trotsky had moved to Mexico in 1937 and by 1940 he was living with his wife, Natalya, in Coyoacan, a suburb of Mexico City. The agency was not made public until the defection of KGB Captain Nicolia Khokhlov in W Germany in 1954. Khokhlov himself was a SMERSH agent sent to murder Igor Georgi Okolovich on orders from Premier Nikita Khrushchev. Okolovich was a staunch opponent to the Communists, a leader in NTS, an anti-Soviet émigré organisation headquartered in Frankfurt. SMERSH tactics remained unchanged over the years. Despite defecting killers in their ranks, the agency developed a number of particularly vicious methods of murder, undoubtedly to allow their assassins less chance of being identified and apprehended.

One victim of these new murder weapons was Horst Schwirkmann, a skilled West German technician working in the West German Embassy in Moscow. Schwirkmann was a debugging expert who 'swept' his embassy clean of KGB listening devices. When unearthing a listening device he fed into its microphone a high voltage that undoubtedly sent a terrific shock into the ears of KGB listeners. Schwirkmann discovered and dismantled a sophisticated electronic device, which had been secreted in the embassy's decoding room, one which immediately broadcast to the KGB all messages being typed before they were automatically ciphered. The newly developed device allowed the Soviets to break West German diplomatic codes by comparing ciphered messages with those picked up in the clear. KGB officials ordered SMERSH to kill Schwirkmann and he was injected with nitrogen mustard gas in the buttocks by an agent as he moved through a crowd of tourists at the Zagorsk monastery outside Moscow in 1964. The stricken technician was rushed to the US Embassy, Moscow, where a full-scale medical clinic was maintained. He survived, but only after a painful recuperation period.

SMERSH made an unsuccessful attempt to murder Boris Korczak, a suspected Polish double agent living in Virginia and reportedly working for the CIA. He was jabbed in the back by a sharp instrument wielded by an unidentified passerby. He developed a high fever and was delirious for three days, but he recovered.

Later, at the request of the Bulgarian Intelligence Service, Vladimir Kostov, a Bulgarian living in exile in Paris, was attacked by SMERSH agents but he, too, survived. Georgi Markov, who received the same treatment, was not as fortunate. A well-respected Bulgarian journalist who lived in exile in Britain; Markov detested the Soviets and said so in broadcasts over the BBC World Service and Radio Free Europe. He described in detail how the Communist regimes in Bulgaria and elsewhere practised terror and murder. The Bulgarian block nation had become the most oppressive of all the Soviet-dominated countries. In September 1978, while Georgi Markov stood waiting for a bus on Waterloo Bridge he was jabbed in the thigh with the pointed end of an umbrella. Hours later Markov lay dying. The umbrella had actually fired a pinhead platinum pellet into Markov's leg, containing ricin; a poison made from castor oil plant. Within hours Markov developed a high fever and died of heart failure. SMERSH had believed it had developed the ultimate murder weapon with the use of ricin. The poison is almost undetectable and invariably leads to cardiovascular collapse, a condition that any unsuspecting doctor would simply attribute to a common heart attack.

Although it is claimed that SMERSH was disbanded with the collapse of Communism in Russia, the agency almost certainly still exists in some form, if only for use in Chechnya and against organised criminals and terrorists

SNIE   Special National Intelligence Estimate (fast-track NIE).

SOAP   Nickname for the so-called truth drug Sodium Pentathol usually known for short as 'so-pe'.

SOE (Special Operations Executive)   The SOE came into being after the fall of France, on 16 July 1940, when a British intelligence committee in London organised Special Operations Executive 'to co-ordinate all action by way of subversion and sabotage against the enemy overseas'. SOE's first chief was Dr Hugh Dalton, Minister of Economic Warfare, who had been told by Prime Minister Winston Churchill to 'set Europe ablaze'.

Organised resistance to the Nazis occupying European countries was already to some extent in place. SOE's job was to finance, supply and direct operations and supplement the resistance groups with SOE agents expert in espionage, as well as electronics, explosives and communications technicians. Fortunately for SOE, it had a number of brilliant officers who understood well the conduct of irregular warfare and guerrilla action, such as J.C.F. Holland, Colin Gubbins, George Taylor, Bickham Sweet-Escott, Harold Perkins and Maurice Buckmaster.

SOE worked very closely with the OSS during WWII and its director, William Donovan and his equally brilliant deputy Allen Dulles. Most of the agents working in SOE were not military officers but mountain-climbers, explorers, linguists, geographers, yachtsmen, secretaries, housewives, adventurers of all kinds, who felt it their patriotic duty to help defeat the Nazis in any way possible. SOE agents served in all of the Nazi-occupied countries, from Poland to Scandinavia, from France to Belgium and Holland, from Italy and to Yugoslavia and Greece. SOE spies could also be found in N Africa and in the Pacific islands of the Far East, in China, Burma, Thailand, everywhere the Allies were fighting the Axis powers.

There is no doubt that SOE was instrumental in making the Allied landings in France a success and that the organisation not only supplied but stimulated the resistance movements throughout Europe until the Allied armies were able once again to free those countries. Most SOE officers were wartime volunteers, not professional espionage agents, and most of them were motivated by patriotism.

SIS, and Colonel Dansey in particular, often complained bitterly about the 'cowboy' approach of SOE to security, planning and some of its wilder operations. However on the whole, SOE contributed greatly to the war effort and indeed many of its personnel; attitudes and projects were to be incorporated into SIS when SOE was disbanded after the end of the war.

SOG Special Operations Group; the CIA/SOG was in the Directorate of Operations. The Special Operations Group of the Department of Defence had a similar paramilitary mission but there was no connection between the two.

SORGE, Richard (1895–1944) He moved from Russia to Germany and during WWI served in the German Army, afterwards studying in Berlin, Kiel and Hamburg. He also secretly joined the German Communist Party (KPD), spent 1924–27 in Moscow. Moved to the USA in 1928 and started working for the Soviet military intelligence service, the GRU using his cover as a teacher. He was in Britain in 1928, in Shanghai in 1930 and finally moved to Japan in September 1933 as a journalist working for the 'Frankfurter Zeitung'. While operating in the Far East, Sorge was to be allotted the intelligence codenames

JOHNSON in China and RAMSEY in Japan. Sorge's network of carefully selected agents included Hozumi Ozaki who was an adviser to the Prime Minister, allowing him to obtain high-quality political information about Japan's foreign policy. He also posed as a loyal Nazi and worked as an espionage agent for the German embassy in Japan. This enabled him to obtain information about Germany's intentions towards the Soviet Union and its developing relationship with Japan.

Sorge was able to give Stalin advance warning about the Anti-Comintern Pact in 1936, the German–Japanese Pact in 1940 and probably Japan's attack on Pearl Harbor in 1941. His greatest achievement was to inform the Soviet Union of OPERATION BARBAROSSA as early as December, 1940.

Despite the efforts of Sorge, Stalin did not believe that Germany would attack at that time and did not take the necessary action. As Leonard Trepper, the head of Red Orchestra, later pointed out: 'The generalissimo preferred to trust his political instinct rather than the secret reports piled up on his desk. Convinced that he had signed an eternal pact of friendship with Germany, he sucked on the pipe of peace.' At the end of August 1941, Sorge was able to tell Stalin that Japan would not attack the Soviet Union that year. This was vitally important information that allowed the Soviet Army to move many of its military units based in the Far East to prop up its crumbling front line against the invading German forces in Europe. In October 1941 Sorge and Ozaki were arrested in Tokyo; their network had been discovered accidentally during a routine Japanese counter-espionage operation.

Held in prison for three years, he was finally hanged on 7 November 1944. He received a posthumous 'Hero of the Soviet Union' award.

SOSUS (Sound Surveillance System) US Navy seafloor acoustic detection system for detecting Submarines. The first undersea detectors were operational by 1951. Eventually the USN had arrays in various parts of the Atlantic and Pacific oceans as well as such specific areas as the Straits of Gibraltar and off North Cape of Norway.

SOURCE Any person who furnishes intelligence information either with or without the knowledge that the information is being used for intelligence purposes. In this context, a controlled source is the employment or under the control of the intelligence activity and knows the information is to be used for intelligence purposes.

SOUTH AFRICA *S African Secret Service (SASS)*, Arcadia Building, Cnr Festival and Arcadia Streets, Hatfield, Pretoria, 0083: the SASS is responsible for foreign intelligence. It has sections for Counter-Intelligence and Internal Security. *The Intelligence Division* gathers, correlates and evaluates foreign military intelligence. It is also responsible for counter-intelligence measures within the National Defence Force.

SDMI Subdivision Military Intelligence: the aim of Subdivision Military Intelligence is to establish and define possible military threats against the RSA and the S African region. It includes the *Counter-Intelligence Investigations Department* which is responsible for the monitoring of extremist organisations.

The three independent services have now been amalgamated into the *National Intelligence Agency* (*NIA*), which deals with domestic intelligence. The old National Intelligence Service, and the former intelligence services of Transkei, Bophuthatswana and Venda, the services of the African National Congress and the Pan African Congress were integrated to form the new NIA.

The current status of the former GCHQ SIGINT and Maritime Surveillance base at Silvermine near the naval base of Simonstown is uncertain, though the British maintained a discreet presence there long after it had officially passed into S African hands, despite the anti-apartheid sanctions.

SPAIN *CNI* (*Centro Nacional de Inteligencia – National Intelligence Centre; formerly CESID: Centro Superior de Informacion de la Defensa – Higher Defence Intelligence Centre*) was created in 1977 to replace the intelligence organisations of the Franco period. These had included the Political-Social Brigade, a special branch of the plainclothes corps and the SDPG or Intelligence Service of the Civil Guard. With their files on every part of the rural and urban population, these bodies carried on the close surveillance, political intimidation and massive human rights abuse on behalf of the Franco years. His internal security services had become a byword for torture, illegal imprisonment, murder and the disappearance of the regime's opponents. The abuses and horror of the treatment of combatants and civilians alike in the Civil War (1936–39) are almost unparalleled in modern history.

The principal operating units of the CESID are the domestic intelligence; foreign intelligence; counter-intelligence; economics and technology (primarily industrial espionage); and operational support (principally application of devices for surveillance and eavesdropping). Considerable emphasis in external intelligence was allotted to N Africa and to the security of Ceuta and Melilla. Liaison was maintained with a number of intelligence services of N African and Middle Eastern nations, as well as with the Israeli agency, Mossad. Interception of ship transmissions in the strait area was another focus of activity. Domestic intelligence centred on exposure of plots against the government, monitoring activities of unrecognised political parties and counter-terrorism.

Although CESID was the senior agency, it did not have a firmly established co-ordinating function over other intelligence bodies. These included the General HQ of Information of the Ministry of Defence; the second sections of the army, the air force, and the navy staffs; and the Civil Guard Information Service, dedicated to criminal and terrorist intelligence. Considerable rivalry and overlapping of missions characterised the entire intelligence system. CESID, in particular, was reported to be seeking to gain exclusive jurisdiction over police foreign intelligence activities.

Beginning in late 1983, a right-wing force, the Anti-terrorist Liberation Group (Grupo Antiterrorista de Liberacion – GAL), began a campaign of revenge killings and bombings among suspected ETA terrorists, chiefly in France, where GAL was widely believed to be linked to the Civil Guard. At the same time, an offshoot of ETA-M, Spain Commando, targeted members of the Civil Guard and the armed forces in Madrid, where such attacks, which gained maximum publicity for the movement, had been on the rise. Continued allegations surfaced of involvement by the previous Gonzalez administration in GAL, which murdered 27 people between 1983 and 1987. This secret organisation was reportedly composed of security officers and contract gunmen with links to organised crime. GAL staged kidnappings and shootings of alleged terrorist ringleaders. A judicial crisis ensued when links between police and the anti-terrorists were revealed in the press. An aggressive judge believed the investigation should be pursued to high levels of the Spanish government. It is believed GAL had links to the highest ministerial levels, including a former Minister of the Interior, the commanding officer of the security forces, and the most senior government representative in the Basque region. Judicial investigations into these allegations proceeded through 1997 but did not turn up any significant new evidence. These investigations could lead to trials of former senior officials on GAL-related charges.

In 2001, CESID was renamed the Centro Nacional de Inteligencia (CNI) or National Intelligence Centre.

Dirección General de Administración de la Seguridad – State Security

Secretariat: the transition from Franco's dictatorship to a system of parliamentary democracy was accompanied by a major effort to bring the forces of law and order and the justice system into harmony with the new political era. The police were stripped of most of their military characteristics. The Civil Guard, which maintained order in rural areas and in smaller communities, retained many of its military features, but both the Civil Guard and the police were placed under civilian leadership. Once dedicated to repressing all evidence of opposition to the Franco regime, the police and the Civil Guard were expected to tolerate forms of conduct previously banned and to protect individual rights conferred by the 1978 Constitution and by subsequent legislation. Members of the Civil Guard continued to be implicated in cases of mistreatment and brutality in the campaign against Basque terrorism.

Spain also maintains a network of secret SIGINT listening bases, including those of Pico de las Nieves on Gran Canaria, Manzanares, Playa de Pals and Rota.

SPAIN, SPECIAL FORCES   The BOEL (Special Operations Legion Battalion) is based at Almería, near Granada in southern Spain. This unit is trained and equipped to the highest standards expected of the Spanish Legion. It would operate in wartime in a long-range reconnaissance and patrol (LRRP) role. In addition this unit has specialist intelligence gathering, mountain warfare and sabotage and demolitions squads, and along with the 3rd and 4th Tercio (Legion Regiment-sized units) is committed to the rapid reaction force.

The GOE-11 (Grupo Operaciones Especiales) was formed in 1978 and based just outside Madrid. It is an effective Special Forces formation, largely based on the British SAS, and is a highly trained unit that covers most of the techniques common to similar units, such as HALO (High Altitude-Low Opening), airborne insertion, mountain and desert warfare and survival techniques. In addition, combat swimming, combat shooting, marksmanship, hostage rescue, anti-hijacking, prisoner interrogation, prisoner-of-war rescue, intelligence and clandestine operations behind enemy lines play a part in their overall operational capability. The GOE has access to a wide range of domestic and foreign weapons, including Israeli 9mm miniUzi, German 9mm MP5 sub-machine guns, PSG1 sniper rifles, 5.56mm M16A1 automatic rifles as well as those of standard army issue. A ready action squad is kept on a 30 minute alert at all times. This regular unit is further supported by the GOE-111 and 1V, which are both reserve units and play a similar role to that of the British SAS 21st and 23rd Territorial Regiments to the Regular 22nd.

In addition the Spanish Army also has a much more secretive force, the Special Intervention Unit, which was only created in February 1982. And this, just two years after a Special Training Center had been established in August 1980 for the selection of personnel for a then unnamed formation.

The Special Intervention Unit is company sized, with all personnel parachute and commando trained and with a physical condition well above the norm, capable of passing a series of rigorous and intensive training programmes, and proficient in all forms of special operations techniques, armed and unarmed combat in all terrains and weather conditions. The soldiers of the Special Intervention unit, wearing their all-black uniforms, have created an elite counter-terrorist force now known to be responsible for the rescue of terrorist-hostage Jose Antonio Ortega Lara, and the destruction of ETA's Bizkaia commando unit during 1997 alone.

SPECIAL BRANCH Originally only of the Metropolitan Police in London. Starting off as the Special Irish Branch, it quickly became the prime counter-espionage and counter-terrorist service until relegated to the executive arm of the Security Service (later MI5) after that organisation's creation in 1909. Today all British regional police forces have their own Special Branch, though national policy and standards for these individual forces are still set by the Metropolitan Police Special Branch and its more modern offshoot, the Counter-Terrorist Branch.

SPECIAL TASKS Russian term for assassination, kidnapping, murder and sabotage operations.

SPEDDING, Sir David (1943–2001) Spedding became the new head of the Secret Intelligence Service (MI6) in March 1994 and held the post until 1999. He took over from the Sir Colin McColl in September 1994. He was the youngest man appointed to the job and the 11th to hold the post since SIS was founded in 1909. He was also the first officer to lead the service since the 1920s who had not made his mark as a Soviet specialist and only the second to be publicly named by the government as SIS chief.

After receiving a degree in medieval history from Oxford University's Hertford College, where one of his tutors was a 'talent-spotter' for SIS, in 1967 he was recruited by SIS and sent to Lebanon, where he studied Arabic at the Foreign Office's Middle East Centre for Arabic Studies,

Shemlan in Beirut – which was widely regarded as a spy school. He then became a Middle East specialist, or what some British officials referred to as a member of the Camel Corps. He then joined the Beirut Embassy as a second secretary, where he became familiar with various Palestinian figures and organisations until he was named by Kim Philby in 1971. Following Philby's disclosure he was transferred to Santiago, Chile, where his 1972–74 posting coincided with the CIA-backed overthrow of the Socialist Government of President Salvador Allende by the right-wing military dictator, General Pinochet.

Sir David then served in Britain before returning to the Middle East in 1978 as Embassy First Secretary and SIS station chief in Abu Dhabi. Between 1981 and 1983 he was at the Foreign and Commonwealth Office in London. He served as counsellor in Amman (1983–86), a period when Jordan was acting as a conduit to supply Iraq with western arms. He became a leading British player in forming Middle East policy during the Iraq–Iran war. It was there that he was credited, along with the Jordanian security forces and in mysterious circumstances, with saving the life of Queen Elizabeth II during a visit to Jordan. He returned to London in 1986 where he took responsibility for Middle East affairs. Later as head of the Middle East section's covert intelligence operations during the Gulf War, and finally as director of requirements and production and assistant SIS chief, the official deputy of 'C', Sir David managed to contain public damage and established a working relationship with parliamentary committees.

He was also in charge of a joint operational section that liaised with the Security Service, MI5. In 1992 he became director of operations for MI6. Sir David also maintained some traditions as old as the service itself. He continued to write his official memos in green ink (the only member of SIS allowed to use that colour) and to sign them 'C', as had every chief of the service. The use of a single initial to indicate the Secret Service chief was made famous by Ian Fleming in his novels about his British spy, James '007' Bond, whose chief was always identified as 'M'. This was because the service and its former officers guarded the 'C' usage. Fleming may have chosen 'M' as his label because, during Fleming's years involved with SIS, his chief, or 'C', was Sir Stewart Menzies. In the late 1990s, Sir David invited Dame Judi Dench, the actress who played 'M' in recent James Bond films, to lunch at SIS HQ after the actress voiced her curiosity about Sir David.

His years as 'C' saw the service turning its gaze from the Cold War to devoting its attentions to fighting international terrorism and drug smuggling, and in preventing the spread of nuclear, chemical and biological weapons. Sir David was also part of the effort to bring SIS into modern times despite controversy. He helped organise and execute the move of the service's HQ from Century House to a new facility on the Thames River south bank at Vauxhall Cross that drew criticism as being too high profile for a clandestine service.

Upon learning of the death of Sir David, who was knighted in 1996, British Foreign Secretary Jack Straw called him a 'determined and effective leader of a service whose contribution to Britain's security and well-being has to be unsung, but is nonetheless substantial'.

SPONSOR Term for an intelligence service, which provides the finance and controls an operation carried out by a friendly intelligence service or freelance agents.

SPOOK Generic and popular term for a spy.

SPY/SPIES Any member(s) of an intelligence agency, security service or other organisation engaged in covert intelligence-gathering activities on behalf of another country.

SPY SWAP The arranged exchange of agents and intelligence officers who have been caught and then imprisoned by a hostile nation. The U-2 pilot Gary Powers, imprisoned in the Soviet Union (Russia) and swapped for convicted Soviet Spy Rudolf Abel held by the USA, on 10 February 1962 is a perfect example.

SR-71 SENIOR CROWN Hypersonic USAF reconnaissance aircraft, mothballed in 1990 and resurrected 1993–98, was originally developed for the USAF as reconnaissance aircraft more than thirty years ago. SR-71s are still the world's fastest and highest-flying production aircraft. The aircraft can fly more than 2,200 mph (Mach 3+ or more than three times the speed of sound) and at altitudes of over 85,000 feet. For its reconnaissance mission, the aircraft was outfitted with an advanced synthetic aperture radar system ASARS-I, an optical bar camera and a technical objective camera wet film system.

Like the U-2, the SR-71 was designed by a team of Lockheed personnel led by Clarence 'Kelly' Johnson, at that time vice president of the company's Advanced Development Projects, known as the 'Skunk Works'. The first version, a CIA reconnaissance aircraft that first flew in April 1962, was called the A-11. A USAF reconnaissance variant, called the SR-71, was first flown in 1964 and has a design which includes the leading and trailing edges being made of high-temperature fibreglass-asbestos laminates to reduce the radar signature. Its existence was made public by President Lyndon Johnson on 29 February 1964, when he announced that an A-11 had flown at sustained speeds of over 2,000 mph during tests at Edwards, Calif.

Development of the SR-71s from the A-11 design, as strategic reconnaissance aircraft, began in February 1963. First flight of a SR-71 was on 22 December 1964. The YF-12s were experimental long-range interceptor versions of the same airframe and were first displayed publicly at Edwards on 30 September 1964. The Blackbird weighs about 34 tons empty and can carry another 20 tons of special JP-7 jet fuel for about two hours of flight time in its fuselage and wing tanks. In flight, the fuel is redistributed automatically to maintain the plane's centre of gravity and load specifications. The Blackbird was designed to expand during flight, so it is notorious for leaking fuel when on the ground.

The airframes are built almost entirely of titanium and titanium alloys to withstand heat generated by sustained Mach 3 flight and are coated with a special radar-absorbing black paint. This helps dissipate the intense frictional heat resulting from flight through the atmosphere at faster than three times the speed of sound. It also gives the plane its distinctive 'Blackbird' nickname. The Blackbird, for all attempts otherwise, actually had quite a large radar signature according to the FAA.

STAFF AGENT A CIA staff officer without access to CIA secure facilities or classified communications.

STAGE MANAGEMENT A vital component to a deception operation, managing the operational stage so that all conditions and contingencies are considered; the point of view of the hostile forces, the casual observers, the physical and cultural environment etc.

STASI Formerly, East German secret police and foreign intelligence service.

STATION A CIA base of field operations usually in a foreign location.

STEPPED-ON Deliberate interference with radio traffic.

STERILISE To remove material used in a clandestine operation which may compromise the sponsoring service.

STIBER, William (1818–82?) A lawyer who under King Frederick William of Prussia revolutionised intelligence activities in Europe. Later dismissed, Stiber reorganised the Tsar of Russia's secret police (1858–63). However Stiber continued to spy for Prussia and on behalf of Count von Bismarck created networks within both Austria and France.

STRINGER   A low-level agent who passes on useful information only when the opportunity arises.

STROLLER   An agent operating with a walkie-talkie or wired-up for a covert street surveillance operation.

SUBMARINE   The US Navy (USN) will upgrade its submarine fleet with new intelligence-gathering systems to help the boats fulfil their increasing surveillance and reconnaissance role in littoral operations, according to USN director of submarine warfare Rear Adm Malcolm Fages. A recent Joint Chiefs of Staff study concluded that the current high operating tempo will require 68 submarines by 2015, a dramatic reversal from a planned reduction to 50. It also found that most of the rising deployments are for intelligence, surveillance and reconnaissance (ISR) missions.

The US Navy believes the insertion of new digital technologies, antennas with greater sensitivity and intelligence collection systems can provide dramatic improvements and that one promising way to outfit the fleet with improved intelligence-gathering capabilities is to utilise unmanned undersea vehicles (UUVs). The Boeing-developed Long-range Mine Reconnaissance System is considered the first step towards developing a reconfigurable UUV that can be outfitted with different payloads. These include remotely piloted submersibles that can release masts or antennas to gather intelligence; track and trail enemy submarines and serve as key nodes in a future undersea integrated sensor network.

USN Submarines on ELINT missions in the Barents Sea believe that the giant Russian Submarine *Kursk* was lost following two onboard torpedo explosions, the second of them catastrophic on 12 August 2001. The information comes from sonar tapes and other information analysed at the US National Maritime Intelligence Centre and that had been recorded by the nuclear submarine USS *Memphis*, one of two USN submarines monitoring the Russian naval exercises. In addition to the two submarines, the US Navy had a surface ship, the USS *Loyal*, in the Barents Sea as part of its monitoring operation.

The USS *Memphis* docked in Bergen, Norway, on 18 August, six days after the *Kursk* sank, allowing the American submarine to unload its recordings, which were then flown to the US for examination.

The US submarines were also able to monitor the Russian fleet's transmissions in the minutes and hours following the disaster and gained vast amounts of useful material as Communications Security COMSEC was abandoned in the frantic attempts to discover the fate of the *Kursk*. The US Navy refuses to say just how close their submarines were to the *Kursk* at the time of the disaster. US rules of engagement restrict snooping vessels from going within five miles of their targets. Nevertheless, the two US submarines were close enough to the *Kursk* to feel the underwater impact of the fatal blast, though without suffering any damage. There is no evidence on the US Navy's sonar recordings of the 'tapping' from within the *Kursk*, which was reported by the Russians as late as two days after the sinking.

The new submarine, the USS *Jimmy Carter*, will be the US Navy's premier underwater intelligence platform when it finally puts to sea in 2005. The state-of-the-art submarine will be capable of inserting teams of Navy SEALs into trouble spots around the globe, launching camera-equipped airborne drones while underwater and relaying real-time images to shore and silently tracking the fleets of nations such as Russia, China and N Korea and engaging in other 'special ops' missions that the Pentagon won't even hint at. The USS *Jimmy Carter* is presently undergoing almost $900 million in modifications at a shipyard in Groton, Connecticut and this includes adding over a 100 feet to its length so it can carry, among other things, 50 SEALs and a special operations command centre. New manoeuvring devices are being added to its bow and stern that will allow it to hover for hours in a fixed position underwater. Also being installed will be a special hull opening, known as a 'wasp waist', that will allow the sub to deploy and recover special payloads such as a submersible craft capable of carrying eight commandos. An upgraded radio room and high-tech communications, combat and sonar systems are being added and, according to some reports, the submarine may also be equipped with a special claw that can lift such things as enemy missiles or torpedoes off the ocean floor without being detected. The submarine will have tremendous capabilities and the US Navy has said little about the *Jimmy Carter*'s modification or its future mission. It will also be one of the newest attack subs in the fleet, capable of speeds up to 25 knots while submerged and able to operate at depths of more than 800 feet.

The *Jimmy Carter* will operate from one of the US Navy's most modern Submarine bases at Bangor, home of the USS *Parche*, currently the most advanced ELINT submarine. The USS *Parche* has been involved in a vast number of espionage operations including on one occasion almost being caught while trying to change the recording tapes on a tap that had been fitted to a Soviet undersea cable in the Barents Sea, but managed to escape the Soviet hunter-killers.

US Naval underwater surveillance missions have been conducted since the beginning of the Cold War and on occasion the USS *Lampon* trailed a new Soviet Yankee Class submarine for a record 47 days, with daily updates provided to then President Nixon. Others were used to tap underwater communication cables used by the Soviet Union in the Barents Sea and the Sea of Okhotsk near the Soviets' Pacific fleet HQ in Vladivostok.

The initial codename for the use of specially equipped attack submarines to conduct electronic warfare missions against the Communist bloc was *Holystone*. Although no US submarines were actually lost on such intelligence missions, there were a number of close calls, particularly the experience of the USS *Swordfish*. This vessel was covertly monitoring a Soviet naval exercise in the Northwest Pacific during 1963, when it was detected after light glinted off the periscope. The USS *Swordfish* was to spend the best part of 48 hours under depth charge attack by Soviet ASW vessels. However, even this proved to be of value to the United States as the *Swordfish* was able to monitor many of the communications between the Soviet warships.

In mid-November 1969 a Sturgeon-class submarine, the USS *Gato,* collided with a Soviet submarine it was monitoring in the White Sea. Fortunately neither vessel was fatally damaged. However, the nuclear submarine USS *Scorpion* lost off the Azores on 22 May 1968 was on passage back to its base at Norfolk, Virginia after completing a *Holystone* intelligence mission. Part of the reason for the blanket secrecy that surrounded the loss of this vessel was the initial and unfounded fear among certain analysts that the USS *Scorpion* had been tracked down and sunk by a Soviet hunterkiller submarine.

While the US Navy has reduced its spy missions against Russia by about 90 per cent since the Cold War, there are plenty of other targets including China, N Korea and Iran. The US surveillance submarines can eavesdrop, track deployments of other navies, monitor missile and torpedo tests conducted by other countries and deploy Navy SEALs. One particular area of tension that is constantly monitored by US submarines is the Taiwan Straits and the risk of a Chinese seaborne invasion, but as one submariner commented, 'We can track what they are doing. Our subs could run up the Yangtze River if they had to.'

SUCKING DRY   Russian term for the prolonged debriefing of an agent following an operation.

SUN TZU (*c.*555–*c.*496 BC)   Early 4th-century BC Chinese general and contemporary of Confucius who developed a considerable understanding of the essential value of good intelligence in war. Wrote the classic *The Art of War* (*Ping-fa*) *c.*510 BC, the earliest known treatise on intelligence in war which is still required reading in military colleges throughout the modern world.

SURREPTITIOUS ENTRY UNIT   A unit in the CIA's Technical Services whose speciality was opening locks and gaining access to secure facilities in support of audio operations.

SVR   (Sluzhba Vneshney Razvedki Rossii or Russian Foreign Intelligence Service) The Russian Federation's successor to the KGB's first chief directorate.

SWEEPER   Term for an electronic-technician who examines or 'sweeps' an office or facility to determine whether the building has been 'bugged'.

SWALLOW   Russian intelligence term for a female agent used for sexual entrapment in a 'Honey Trap' operation.

SWEDEN *MUST* (*Militära Underrättelse och Säkerhetstjänsten – Military Intelligence and Security Agency*) and *SÄPO Säkerhetspolisen – Security Police*: Sweden has a large intelligence community and maintained a less than neutral stand throughout the Cold War. Both the British SIS and the CIA had over-large stations in Stockholm for many years.

During WWII a veritable intelligence war was fought out between the SOE, OSS and the German intelligence services. Up until October 1942, the *Combined Intelligence Bureau*, under its then chief Col. Aldercreutz had been rather pro-Nazi. Fortunately, the head of Foreign Intelligence, the *Interception Service* was under the command of the pro-British Col. Bjoernstierna. This service was to provide invaluable intelligence to SIS by monitoring the German cable and teleprinter traffic between Berlin and its friends in Sweden, but even more importantly the German High Command's communication cables to its forces in occupied Norway passed through Swedish waters. The Swedish Interception Service was able to 'tap' these cables on Britain's behalf.

FRA Försvarets Radio Anstalt – Defence Radio Institution: responsible for SIGINT. It also operates modified Gulfstream ELINT aircraft over the East Sea and the take is shared, though not officially, with the NSA. Its HQ is at Lovon, with listening sites at Karlskrona and Musko.

SÄPO SÄkerhets Polisen – Security Police: counter-intelligence and counter-terrorist organisation.

IB Informations Byrån – Information Bureau: internal security force and responsible for monitoring political dissidents.

SWITZERLAND *Bureau Ha Intelligence* Agency: Switzerland's main Military Intelligence service was established by Brigadier Roger Masson in 1937 and was organised into Bureau D, covering Germany; Bureau F, covering France; and Bureau I, covering Italy. With Masson's agreement, Captain Hans Hausamann formed and privately financed what would become the Burea Ha.

Operating out of a villa on Lake Lucerne, the Bureau Ha would successfully penetrate Nazi Germany and acquire considerable intelligence on its political and military intentions for the duration of the war. Among a number of important spy networks was the one run by Captain Thomas Sedlacek whose information was supplied to the British and US intelligence services. Masson also recruited Rudolf Roessler who, though he was probably used to pass ULTRA information to the Soviet Union, also provided good intelligence from within occupied Europe for both the Swiss and the British SIS.

Switzerland provided a relatively safe espionage centre within a German dominated continent and became the temporary home for a considerable selection of British, US and Soviet intelligence services for most of the war.

Still very conscious of maintaining its neutrality, Switzerland has maintained a considerable internal security and SIGINT capability under the *BUPO Bundesamt fur Polizei* or Federal Security Police and the *UNA Untergruppe Nachrichtendienst und Abwehr* or Ministry of Defence counter-intelligence and security service.

SYRIA *GSD General Security Directorate – Idarat al-Amn al-'Amm*: the GSD is the main civilian intelligence service in Syria. It is divided into three branches. The *Internal Security Division* is responsible for internal surveillance of the population in general, a duty which clearly overlaps with that of the PSI. The other two divisions of the GSD are *External Security*, a foreign intelligence service and the *Palestine Division*, which monitors the activities of Palestinian groups in Syria and Lebanon.

Military Intelligence – Shu'bat al-Mukhabarat al-'Askariyya: Syria's military intelligence service, headquartered at the Defence Ministry complex in Damascus, is formally responsible for the usual range of military surveillance operations and planning. In addition, it is responsible for providing military and logistical support to Palestinian, Lebanese and Turkish extremist groups, monitoring and often assassinating political dissidents abroad and co-ordinating the activities of Syrian and Lebanese military forces stationed in Lebanon.

Air Force Intelligence – Idarat al-Mukhabarat al-Jawiyya: despite its name, this intelligence service is not primarily concerned with providing information to the air force. Its evolution into Syria's most secretive and fearsome intelligence service has a great deal to do with the fact that Hafez Assad was once commander of Syria's air force. After he assumed power in 1970, Assad turned to this intelligence service, dominated by men he knew well and in most cases had appointed himself, to undertake sensitive domestic and international operations. For nearly 30 years, the service was commanded by Maj. Gen. Muhammad al-Khouli, a trusted adviser whose office was adjacent to Assad's in the presidential palace.

On the domestic level, Syrian air force intelligence has frequently spearheaded operations against Islamic opposition elements in the country. It played a leading role in the regime's suppression of Muslim Brotherhood revolt during the 1970s and early 80s. More recently, air force intelligence agents reportedly led the nationwide manhunt for members of the Islamic Liberation Party (Hizb al-Tahrir) in December 1999.

Air force intelligence has also been central to the regime's sponsorship of international terrorism. Its agents, frequently stationed abroad in Syrian embassies and in branch offices of Syria's national airline, have directly co-ordinated dozens of terrorist operations. The most well-documented example was the attempted bombing of an Israeli airliner at London's Heathrow airport in April 1986. The subsequent investigation revealed that the primary culprit, Nizar Hindawi, who had duped an unsuspecting woman into carrying explosives onto the aircraft, was operating in co-ordination with Haitham Sayid, the deputy chief of Syrian air force intelligence at that time. As a result of this fiasco, an international warrant for Sayid's arrest was issued and Britain broke diplomatic ties with Syria (they were restored four years later when Syria joined the allied coalition against Iraq).

GID General Intelligence Directorate: this is the current incarnation of civil intelligence. It was established in its present form in 1971. It controls the civil police, the border guards and has primary responsibility for maintaining surveillance over the Ba'ath Party, the civilian bureaucracy and the general populace. *PSD Political Security*

Directorate Idarat al-Amn al-Siyasi is the branch of the GID that handles political intelligence and security, as opposed to criminal and civil policing. It is divided into the *Internal Security Department* and the *External Security Department* (*ESD*) which is divided into three units: Arab Affairs, Refugee Affairs and Zionist and Jewish Affairs. The PSD is responsible for detecting signs of organised political activity that run counter to the interests of the regime. This involves surveillance of suspected political dissidents, as well as the activities of foreigners residing in the country and their interaction with locals. The PSD also monitors all print and audiovisual media.

MI Military Intelligence: the Deuxième Bureau that preceded MI was a powerful political actor. MI, established in 1969, is now probably the dominant intelligence agency in Syria. In Lebanon, MI appears to control not only the military and security situation but also Syrian political policy. MI controls the Military Police, who provide security for elements of the ruling elite, and the Office of the Chief of Reconnaissance, which is probably responsible for strategic and tactical military intelligence collection, collation and analysis. MI's main role is to ensure the loyalty of the military. It is also responsible for carrying out unconventional warfare operations.

SYRIA, SPECIAL FORCES The counter-terrorist capability is provided by one of the Special Forces Regiments, and believed to be known as Al Saiqa. This unit is trained in a whole range of special operation techniques: combat shooting, hostage rescue, anti-hijacking, intelligence gathering, clandestine operations and long range reconnaissance and patrol. In addition Al Saiqa has trained in recent years with the Spetsnaz in Russia and is also believed to have a small number of ex-East Germans and non-Israeli Jews attached to its operations section. It is known to have operated covertly with some success within the Lebanon, Jordan, the Palestinian areas on the West Bank of the Jordan and on a very few occasions, within Israel itself. It has the pick of standard issue arms from the Syrian Army, but also has access to foreign weapons acquired, often on the black market. So that it is not unusual to see US 5.56mm M16A1 automatic rifles, Israeli 9mm UZI, Italian 9mm Beretta BM12 and German MP5K silenced submachine guns being used for clandestine operations.

T

TACTICAL INTELLIGENCE Intelligence for planning and conducting tactical operations at the small unit level.

TAIWAN *The National Security Bureau* was established on 1 March 1955, falling directly under the National Defence Council (NDC). In 1967 the NSB became a subsidiary of the new National Security Council (NSC). The National Security Bureau was feared by the people, like the police force in the Japanese occupation era. Its HQ, located at 110 Yangteh Boulevard of Yang Ming Mountain, a suburb of Taipei, was referred to as the 'Mystical 110', where no visitor or reporter was admitted and photography was forbidden except from outside the gate.

The NSB is responsible for monitoring the latest developments in the international community, mainland China and within Taiwan, collecting and assessing intelligence of strategic importance to national security. The Bureau is authorised to integrate, co-ordinate and support national security-related intelligence operations conducted by various functional services within the intelligence and law enforcement community. Effectively it can act as a Joint Intelligence Organisation.

The NSB now has six divisions: *International Intelligence, China, Internal Security, Strategic Intelligence Analysis, Scientific and Technological Intelligence* and *Telecommunications Security*. It also has control of codebreaking, interception and monitoring facilities. The NSB also runs the *Coordination Meeting for National Security Intelligence (CMNSI)*. It runs a number of major SIGINT sites including forward listening bases on the offshore islands of Quemoy and Matsu, and indeed a major complex in conjunction with the NSA and the German BND at the J3 SIGINT HQ at Shu Lin Kuo.

TAIWAN, SPECIAL FORCES The Taiwanese Special Forces are trained for the eventuality of clandestine intelligence operations on the mainland of China. In the event of a serious deterioration in relations between the two states it would be vitally important for the Taiwan Forces to have a greater understanding of Chinese activities. Information on the overall capabilities and large-scale military movements can often be gathered successfully by either SIGINT (signals intelligence) or from satellite surveillance. However, the insertion of deep cover units from the offshore islands Kinmen (Quemoy) or Matsu, or by the Taiwanese Navy, would certainly be within their known ability and would play a vital part in obtaining the sensitive information needed to predict Chinese intentions. Taiwanese Special Forces are also known to have stocks of suitable documents, uniforms and standard Chinese weapons to equip such units, either to gather intelligence or to carry out a spoiling attack with sabotage operations against Chinese forces preparing for an assault on Taiwan or the offshore island garrisons.

In this context, it should be noted that the only other major Special Forces units are the Long Range Amphibious Reconnaissance Commandos trained for pathfinder operations, as para-commando, in underwater warfare and in the beach reconnaissance and sabotage role against enemy bridgeheads. This unit, though not strictly part of the Army, is very similar to the USMC Recon (Reconnaissance) and receives regular training at USMC bases. The remaining Special Forces formation of note is the Para-Frogman Assault Unit which is very similar in training, equipment, organisation and operational techniques to the US SEALs. This unit can parachute into the sea in full scuba gear, and carry out underwater reconnaissance or sabotage missions against Chinese coastal positions or warships. Both these units also have a distinct anti-terrorist role.

TALENT SPOTTER Person, place or thing against which intelligence operations are directed. Performs personal reconnaissance for recruiters.

TARGET Person, service or facility against which intelligence operations are directed.

TARGET OF OPPORTUNITY Person, service or facility that becomes available as a target for intelligence operations unexpectedly.

TASK FORCE 157 (US Naval Intelligence) During the 1970s TF157 was involved in a variety of intelligence operations including providing top-secret secure communications for Henry Kissinger's clandestine trip to Communist China in 1971 through to monitoring ports and airports.

TAXI British intelligence term for a 'jacksie' or a homosexual member of a sexual entrapment operation. Now most are called 'Ladies', 'Sisters' or even 'Swallows', using these terms in a bi-sexual way.

TECHINT Technical intelligence (umbrella term for the technical INTs: IMINT, SIGINT and MASINT). Sometimes TECHINT refers to a specific sub-specialty of intelligence, the hands-on scientific evaluation of documents and foreign equipment that has been obtained by the USA.

TELEPHONE TAPPING Britain, as an example, has long had a comprehensive ability to monitor private and commercial telephone calls. As early as the 1950s there was a small Metropolitan Police tapping centre in Petty France with about 30 available lines; this moved to the Duke of York Barracks in Chelsea with 300 lines in the 1960s. A second was opened at 8/14 Douglas Street, just behind 60 Vauxhall Bridge Road, which was the SIS London Station. A centralised Tapping Centre was later established at 93 Ebury Bridge Road by 1971 with over 1000 lines. This was run by the Post Office and known as OPERATION TINKERBELL. To avoid problems with the public and the Trade Unions the main Tapping Centres have constantly moved, to Chantry House as Network Services Department, then to Camelford House on the Albert Embankment not far from the present SIS HQ and by 1984 to the top floor of BT's former HQ at 2-12 Gresham Street in London. These are just a few of the sites used by the Post Office, British Telecommunications, the Police and Security Services to make sure that there's no such thing as a private phone call. In Ulster the Army used the top floor of Churchill House in Belfast, while there is a joint BT-GCHQ Research Centre at Martlesham Heath near Ipswich, which spends a vast budget on developing, among other items, advanced 'bugging and tapping' equipment. Because of the huge advances in telecommunications, most tapping today can be carried out at national monitoring centres such as BT's Broggyntyn Hall in Oswestry.

TELINT Telemetry intelligence (part of MASINT; intercepted telemetry from foreign missile tests).

TEMPEST 'Transcient ElectroMagnetic Pulse Emanation Standard'. Codename for activities related to van Eck monitoring, and technology to defend against such monitoring. TEMPEST is a short name referring to investigations and studies of compromising emanations (CE). Compromising emanations are defined as unintentional intelligence-bearing signals which, if intercepted and analysed, disclose the national security information transmitted, received, handled or otherwise processed by any information-processing equipment.

Compromising emanations consist of electrical or acoustical energy unintentionally emitted by any of a great number of sources within equipment/systems which process national security information. This energy may relate to the original message or information being processed in such a way that it can lead to recovery of the plain text. Laboratory and field tests have established that such CE can be propagated through space and along nearby conductors. The interception/propagation ranges and analysis of such emanations are affected by a variety of factors, e.g. the functional design of the information processing equipment; system/equipment installation; and environmental conditions related to physical security and ambient noise. The term 'compromising emanations' rather than 'radiation' is used because the compromising signals can, and do, exist in several forms such as magnetic and/or electric field radiation, line conduction or acoustic emissions.

Which means that with the right equipment 'they' can read what you type, read, send or receive, from the radiation your computer gives off. 'They' can be outside your office or home, in a van across the road or a passive monitor could be installed covertly. So install van Eck and acoustic screens and encrypt everything you do and hope everyone else does the same. Alternatively use pen and paper.

TERRORISM, INTERNATIONAL The terrorist groups in the period 1920–30 were in truth mainly anarchist in origin and tended towards the insular with only a limited knowledge of or involvement with other similar groups. What outside influence there was tended to be State orientated as in the Soviet Union's largely unsuccessful attempt to sway such groups towards having a Communist 'agenda'. A thorough search of available Soviet Intelligence archives, the comprehensive works of Dr Chris Andrews and other academics specialising in the prewar period and indeed, close scrutiny of FBI/MI5 'records' all fail to show a genuine international involvement by state-sponsored terrorism or verifiable links between disparate groupings.

During the period 1930–40, there was a distinct change, the Soviet Union became more fearful and paranoiac and indeed began to see 'stirring up trouble at home' as a potentially useful way to deflect the capitalist nations from taking too close an interest in Mother Russia. However, the OGPU/NKVD and even the military GRU tended to look towards political action, involvement with trades unions/strikes/labour unrest and support for rebel groups, rather than towards arming terrorists.

True socialist revolutionaries, particularly those prone to terrorism, often got the cold shoulder from Stalin and indeed sometimes ended up in the cellars of the Lubyanka. The Fascist States of Germany, Italy, Spain and some E European proto-Fascist regimes would support unrest or a suitably right-wing rebellion, but again, had no interest in supporting the 'loose canon' of Terrorism. The exception being to use terrorism against ethnic Germans to provide an excuse for an invasion, examples being the Sudentenland and Poland. Italy and Spain were to use state-sponsored terrorist groups to settle scores, but again most acts of terrorism during the 1930s were committed by deranged individuals or anarchist groups. The IRA during the period 1920–40, having fought a disastrous semi-conventional war against the combined British and Irish Free State forces and which ended with over 15,000 IRA men in Irish prison-camps, was reduced to a mere political rump for a number of years. The traditional Republican suspicion of foreigners was ever present and has continued to hamper the IRA's attempts to broaden its connections with other similar groups ever since. Weapons, money and public support were in extremely short supply, while the then strong Catholic background of many of the surviving IRA leaders precluded any serious attempt to seek aid from the Soviet Union, though it is highly doubtful whether any would have been available.

The foundations of the modern Terrorist International was very definitely laid during WWII when both the British SOE (Special Operations Executive) and the US OSS (Office of Strategic Services) found a ready audience among the freedom fighters/resistance groups that sprang up all over a German-occupied Europe. And indeed, later still in the immediate postwar period, after the Red Armies had conquered E Europe. While in the Far East similar support would be given to any and all anti-Japanese armed organisations with scant regard to what those groups would do with the arms and training once the war was over. SOE and OSS were to take often very highly motivated and politically orientated groups, train them in covert activities, the use of weapons and explosives, the techniques of assassination and sabotage, of clandestine political organisation, in fact, the West primed the terrorist pump. From the training camps in Britain and Canada, and the resistance groups throughout Europe and Asia sprang not only many of the leaders of the postwar world, but also the founders of international terrorism. There is a mass of evidence highlighting the international links between Terrorist groups since 1950 and notable examples must include the following.

The LTTE (Liberation Tigers of Tamil Eelam) or Tamil Tigers and the *PLOTE (People's Liberation Organisation of Tamil Eelam)* both maintain considerable overseas links. The LTTE through its offices in London were connected to both ETA in Spain and the PKK in Iraq, indeed a number of the Stinger shoulder-launched anti-aircraft missiles supplied by the CIA to the Kurds for use against Iraqi Mi-24 helicopter gunships, have been recovered by the Sri Lankan Army from LTTE forces in recent years. The PLOTE, also like the LTTE, a Marxist organisation, admitted to being partly trained by the PFLP of George Habbash at its camps in the Lebanon and Libya.

The Tupamaros in Uruguay started in 1962 as a rural guerrilla force; it was soon to come under the influence of the Argentinian terrorist group *ERP (Ejercito Revolucionarie del Pueblo)* and was quickly to become a serious threat within the cities of Uruguay, notable for holding captive the then British Ambassador Geoffrey Jackson. By 1985 it had also established links with one of Colombia's terrorist groups, *M19*, who, like FARC, were heavily involved with the drugs trade.

ASALA or the Armenian Secret Army for the Liberation of Armenia was formed in 1975 and very soon became a part of the international terrorist community. FATAH were to provide its initial base, training, weapons and funds. In the Lebanon a new Marxist-Leninist group known as the *FARL (Fractions Armies Revolutionaires Libanaises)* was founded around the area of Qubayet and Andaqat by the Christian community. ASALA and FARL soon came under the influence of George Habbash and his *Peoples Front for the Liberation of Palestine (PFLP)*. Habbash was also both a Christian and a Marxist and used these new groups to widen his power base, bridging the gap between the Middle East and Europe. The *FARL* are known to have carried out operations in Europe on behalf of the PFLP, in particular in France where they had connections with '*Action Directe*' and in Italy with the 'Red Brigade'.

This latter group spread the connection through to the *Baader-Meinhof* group in W Germany, the Japanese Red Army and to Black September. Black September also had connections with both Wilfred Boese, leader of the 'German Revolutionary Cells' who had provided them with considerable assistance during the planning stages for the attack on the Munich Olympics and of course Carlos 'the Jackal'. Carlos, or Ilich Ramirez Sanchez, the son of a Venezuelan Communist millionaire, was originally recruited by the Cuban DGI in 1964, received training both at specialist revolutionary warfare camps in the Soviet Union and in 1966, at the Lumumba University in Moscow. This was basically a 'University of Terrorism', 90 per cent staffed by the KGB, and it was to provide a new breed of 'radical terrorists' committed to the ruthless pursuit of terrorism with little ideology and no compunction about taking life. Carlos went on to join the PFLP in Jordan, helping the Japanese Red Army occupy the French embassy in the Hague in September 1974, before going on to his more famous exploits and becoming the 'Osama bin Laden' of his day.

The Provisional IRA inherited the Republican isolationist attitude and with the exception of a close relationship built with *ETA*, Basques, who like the Irish could be considered as acceptable members of the Celtic community, few international links were established beyond that of obtaining a regular supply of arms. This led them to commercial deals with Czech companies and to seek aid from Libya, but their only serious attempt at establishing an international link with another terrorist group failed to produce more than a few deliveries.

Yasser Arafat's *Fatah* provided arms on a reasonable scale in 1976–77, but Israeli Intelligence soon got wind of this activity and a number of subsequent shipments were intercepted. The Provisionals' successes during the period 1970–90 attracted terrorist interest and approaches were made by groups in Nicaragua, Grenada and S Africa, but were to be rebuffed with the offer of moral support only. The Provisionals carefully avoided any association with the student revolutionaries of the *Baader-Meinhof, Red Brigade* or similar. The IRA regarded these groups as self-indulgent middle-class nihilists, while their attempts to forge a closer relationship with Middle Eastern groups foundered on a total lack of understanding of the Irish situation by Arafat and Habbash. Apparently Arafat thought the IRA was a secret arm of the Irish Government at one point.

The appearance of the 'breakaway' *Real IRA* in 1997 has blown away Irish Republican isolationism; a full-blown partnership in the international terrorist movement is the aim of the new group. They were quickly to build upon and expand the relationship with *ETA*, establish new arms routes and provide training in bomb-making to both Croat and Serbian terrorists, and indeed to right-wing groups in the Baltic, particularly with *the Kajtselite* in Estonia.

Offering too, those same skills in return for money and very probably drugs, for this latter is fast becoming the currency of international terrorism, the *FARC,* the *PKK* and many other such groups now either trade drugs or protect those who do.

The presence of three 'former' Provisional IRA men in Colombia recently may suggest various interesting scenarios: has the Provisional IRA decided to follow suit and expand its international links? Are these men actually members of the Real IRA? Or are the Real IRA and the Provisionals merely two 'wings' of the same organisation?

The Saudi multi-millionaire Osama bin Laden has brought a new type of terrorism to the world based on ethnic hatred alone. A man with all the privileges of the 'playboy' has chosen instead to use his vast wealth to create an international, some would say multinational, terrorist organisation and launched effectively a *fatwa* on Israel and all its allies. With a network of bases in Sudan and Afghanistan and an unknown number of connections to Islamic Jihad groups in the Lebanon, Palestinian West Bank, Libya, Bosnia, Kosovo, Albania, probably Egypt and possibly both Malaysia and Indonesia. bin Laden uses his wealth and influence to create a level of 'franchise-terrorism' where you buy results by employing other terrorist groups to bomb and kill on your behalf.

However the actions of his *Islamic Front*, an international network of at least 12 terrorist groups including *Al-Qa'ida,* on 11 September 2001 went beyond anything previously imaginable. The response around the world has seen an unprecedented crackdown on terrorism and forged surprising new alliance. Whether this will prove sufficient to do more than dent extremist behaviour only time will tell. International terrorism is now the club to which every little prejudiced, sectarian or ethnically 'pure' grouping aspires to join. It is now far less idealistic or even political and it will increasingly be based on bigoted nationalistic causes, a perverted view of religion and straightforward racialism. It will become increasingly difficult to distinguish between the multinational terrorist and the multinational criminal gangs, between legitimate business and narcotic money laundering. International terrorism is definitely here to stay.

THURLOE, John (1616–68)   Like his master Oliver Cromwell, John Thurloe was a maverick politician with independent religious beliefs. The son of a clergyman in the Church of England, he joined Cromwell in the Great Rebellion against Charles I in 1642. He studied for the law and took his degree in 1645. In 1651 he was sent to the Netherlands on a special diplomatic mission and was named secretary to the council of state by Cromwell in the following year.

Next to Cromwell, Thurloe was the most powerful man in England, his real position being that of a viceroy. After Cromwell engineered the execution of Charles I, plots and conspiracies beset him by monarchists seeking to place Charles II on the throne. To combat these royalists, Cromwell ordered Thurloe to establish a spy system to identify the plotters. A master at organisation, Thurloe put together the most effective espionage network since the days of Francis Walsingham, spymaster for Queen Elizabeth I. He began a postal censorship programme and hired Oxford mathematician John Wallis to establish a cryptology department, which could break any known code of that day. Within months, Thurloe was actually directing three separate spy networks, a counter-intelligence organisation in England, a spy network throughout Europe and even an espionage ring in the new colonies of America. Thurloe culled his spies from all ranks – scholars and renegades, impoverished aristocrats eager to earn money, arch criminals whom he reprieved in the shadow of the gallows on the promise they would spy for him.

His spies were able to inform him of the sailing schedules of Spanish treasure ships that allowed British warships to intercept them. Other Thurloe agents bribed royalists to betray their plots and fellow conspirators, as was the case when he dismantled the royalist secret society known as the Sealed Knot. (In that case, Thurloe paid Sir Richard Willis a fortune to identify his fellow conspirators.) Charles II was almost kidnapped in one Thurloe-inspired scheme that was upset at the last minute when one of his own men betrayed the plan, a rare exception among Thurloe's legions of spies. The traitor was Sir George Downing, British Resident in Holland. After Cromwell's death, Thurloe served Richard Cromwell but he was imprisoned when Charles II regained the throne in 1660. On the promise that he would obediently serve the king, he was released. Thurloe spent the remainder of his life writing in-depth essays on political problems, although Charles II realised Thurloe's worth as one of the world's greatest spymasters and often consulted with him, almost to the day of John Thurloe's death on 21 February 1668.

TIARA Tactical Intelligence and Related Activities (congressional budget category for military sensor systems like SOSUS and AWACS that are considered by the US military to belong to operations rather than to military intelligence).

TIMED DROP A dead drop that will be retrieved if not picked up by the recipient after a set time period.

TINKERBELL *see* TELEPHONE TAPPING

TOMLINSON, Richard (1963–) Joined SIS (MI6) in 1991. Tomlinson smuggled nuclear secrets out of the new Russia, ran an undercover operation in a besieged Sarajevo and went on to infiltrate and dismantle an organised crime group trying to illegally export chemical capabilities to Iran. However in 1995 an internal dispute led to his leaving the service under a cloud. All attempts to rectify the situation or to get an acceptable explanation failed. Tomlinson was accused of being a 'whistleblower' or worse, and much of the period since he has been alternatively under arrest or on the run. Whatever the truth may turn out to be, Tomlinson's accusations against SIS include illegal acts and could be usefully addressed. The fact that there still appears to be no effective internal or external political oversight of SIS activities is disquieting. That SIS was allowed to pursue Tomlinson without adequately explaining the reasons is quite wrong and simply hiding behind the OSA is not enough to satisfy a genuine democracy.

Tomlinson raised one of the most important elements of his case against SIS by alleging that there was a proposal from within MI6 to assassinate President Milosevic of Serbia. From March 1992 until September 1993 he had worked in the E European controllerate of MI6 under the staff designation of UKA/7. His role was to carry out natural cover operations (undercover as a businessman or journalist etc.) in E Europe. The Balkan War was in its early stages at this time, and so his responsibilities were increasingly directed to this arena. His work thus involved frequent contact with the officer responsible for developing and targeting operations in the Balkans. At the time, this was Nicholas Fishwick, who worked under the staff designation of P4/OPS. They would frequently meet in his office on the 11th floor of Century House to discuss proposed and ongoing operations that SIS was involved in.

Tomlinson alleges that during one such meeting in the summer of 1992 Fishwick casually mentioned a proposal to assassinate President Milosevic of Serbia. Later, Tomlinson claims, he showed him a document from a file that was indeed a proposal to assassinate President Milosevic of Serbia.

The minute was approximately two pages long, and had a yellow minute card attached to it, which signified that it was an accountable document rather than a draft proposal. It was entitled 'The need to assassinate President Milosevic of Serbia'. In the distribution list in the margin were P4 (Head of Balkan operations), SBO1/T (Security officer responsible for E European operations), C/CEE (Controller of E European operations), MODA/SO (the SAS liaison officer attached to MI6) and H/SECT (private secretary to Sir Colin McColl, then Alan Petty).

The first page of the document was a political 'justification' for assassinating President Milosevic – basically that there was evidence that Milosevic was providing arms and support to President Radovan Karadzic in the breakaway republic of Bosnian Serbia.

The remainder of the document, it is alleged, proposed three methods to assassinate Milosevic. The first method was to train and equip a Serbian paramilitary opposition group to assassinate Milosevic in Serbia. This method would have the advantage of deniability, but the disadvantage that control of the operation would be low and the chances of success unpredictable. The second method was to use the Increment (a small cell of the SAS and SBS which is especially selected and trained to carry out operations exclusively for MI5/SIS) to infiltrate Serbia and attack Milosevic either with a bomb or sniper ambush. Fishwick argued that this plan would be the most reliable, but would be undeniable if it went wrong. The third proposal was to kill Milosevic in a staged car crash, possibly during one of his visits to the ICFY (International Conference on the Former Yugoslavia) in Geneva, Switzerland. There was even a suggestion about how this could be done, such as by disorientating Milosevic's chauffeur using a blinding strobe light as the cavalcade passed through one of Geneva's motorway tunnels.

Tomlinson had little doubt about the intentions of SIS to carry out the operation should circumstances permit and has therefore pressed the British Government to take action against the intelligence officer, even if only to show other SIS (MI6) officers that they should not assume that they could plan murders and carry out other illegal acts with impunity.

TOSSES (hand, vehicular) A tradecraft technique for emplacing drops by tossing them while on the move. Usually only carried out in an emergency or when known to be under a degree of surveillance.

TRADECRAFT The methods used by the intelligence community to carry out clandestine operations. Hanssen used his knowledge of tradecraft to take precautions against capture, according to the FBI affidavit. Tradecraft is any technique or trick that substantiates a view of the work as a skilled occupation or craft. There are a large number of individual tradecraft terms used by the intelligence services and many are listed in this book.

TRAFFIC ANALYSIS A form of SIGINT in which the volume of traffic intercepted is studied to try and determine identifiable patterns. Does not require the intercepted traffic to be deciphered.

TRAVIS, Commander Sir Edward Wilfrid (1888–1956) Served as one of Admiral of the Fleet Sir John Jellicoe's Staff Officers (1914–16),

joined Naval Intelligence Divisions Room 40 Cryptographic centre
(1916) and later moved to GC&CS when that organisation was
established in 1919. Served as Alaistair Dennison's Deputy at Bletchley
Park (1939–42), becoming the Deputy Director at BP while Dennison
was moved sideways and back to London as Deputy Director in charge
of Diplomatic codes. When Dennison finally retired through ill health
in 1944 Travis became the Director of GC&CS, though it had
unofficially been renamed GCHQ by then. Travis would remain as
Director until his retirement in 1952. Four years later, on 18 April
1956, Sir Edward died after an operation. He had played a leading part
in Britain's most secret and most important battle, a battle for which his
King awarded him a knighthood. France made him a Chevalier de la
Legion d'honneur, the Italians made him an Officer of the Crown of
Italy and the US President his grateful nation's highest civilian award,
the Medal of Merit. Yet he would remain as much of an enigma in death
as he had chosen to be in life.

TREPPER, Leopold (Grand Chef, Jean Gilbert) (1904–82)   During
the days of the Red Orchestra (Rote Kapelle), the Communist underground in Nazi-occupied Europe in WWII, Leopold Trepper
emerged as an extraordinary intelligence officer known for his ability
to take the initiative without waiting for directives from The Centre
in Moscow. He was known as the 'Grand Chef', and his ability to
escape the clutches of the Nazis, as well as his own Communist
Party inquisitors, was nothing less than phenomenal. Trepper
migrated from Poland to Palestine in 1926, working on a kibbutz, a
communal farm, but this satisfied him less than Communist plotting
and intrigues. He worked against the British, then controlling
Palestine, and was expelled after being identified as a Communist
agent in 1928. Going to France, Trepper worked for Rabcors, an
illegal political organisation that was broken up by French intelligence in 1932. Trepper escaped to Moscow where he became a full-
fledged NKVD spy, moving between Paris and Moscow for the next
six years. Trepper survived the Stalinist purges of 1937 and 1938 by
convincing The Centre of his loyalty to the Soviets. He went on to
run Soviet Red Orchestra espionage networks in German-occupied
Europe, proving his ability on numerous occasions. However he was
eventually compromised and arrested by the Abwehr. Trepper
betrayed most of his contacts to save his life. The Germans intended
him to continue in contact with Soviet intelligence, but Trepper
guessed the NKVD would soon see through his 'playback'

information and when they demanded some specific top secret information, the Germans refused. The NKVD finally realised that Trepper had been turned.

By June 1943, Trepper was living under 'house-arrest' in a private dwelling in Paris. Eventually he managed to escape from his guards and went into hiding. Trepper emerged with the French resistance after the liberation of Paris in 1944. He flew to Moscow in Stalin's personal plane but instead of receiving a hero's welcome, he was thrown into a cell in the Lubyanka Prison. Trepper defended his position, even claiming that he had tricked the Germans and had remained loyal. He claimed to have contacted the Communist underground in Paris and informed them that he was a prisoner and that he was sending misinformation to The Centre at the direction of the Abwehr. Providing a number of signed statements he had tricked out of a number of French Communists that he had, indeed, made contact with while a prisoner and had told them of his double agent's role, he continued to keep himself away from the firing squad. However, Trepper was kept in prison until four years after Stalin's death, in 1957. He was released and returned to Poland where he rejoined his wife and three sons. In 1967 a violent outbreak of anti-Semitism followed the Six Day War in the Middle East and Trepper decided to emigrate to Israel. The Polish Government, at the instigation of the KGB in Moscow, refused permission. An international storm of protest then enveloped the Polish government, who finally relented and let Trepper and many other Jews leave for Israel. Leopold Trepper and his family settled in Jerusalem in 1974. He died there in 1982.

TRIPLE AGENT An agent who serves three separate intelligence services simultaneously.

TROFIMOFF, George (1931–) Retired Army Reserve Colonel Trofimoff was born in Germany to Russian émigrés and became a naturalised US citizen in 1951. He enlisted in the US Army in 1948 at age 17 and was commissioned five years later. He enlisted in Army Reserves in the 1950s and retired as colonel in 1987. He then became a civilian employee of the Army. On 14 June 2000, George Trofimoff was charged with spying for the Soviet Union and Russia for 25 years. Trofimoff allegedly sold classified material to the KGB while serving as the civilian chief of the US Army Element of the Nuremburg Joint Interrogation Centre in Federal Germany from 1969 to 1994. He retired from his Army civilian job in 1995. The FBI and prosecutors said that Trofimoff was paid $250,000 over the course of his spy career, and was awarded the Order of the Red Banner, the Soviet award presented for 'bravery and self-sacrifice in the defence of the socialist homeland'.

According to the indictment, 'Trofimoff was recruited into the KGB by a boyhood friend, Igor Vladimirovich Susemihl, a Russian Orthodox priest who served as the Archbishop of Vienna and Austria and temporary Archbishop of Baden and Bavaria. Trofimoff allegedly took documents from his work and photographed them, passing the film on to Susemihl and other KGB officers during meetings in Austria. The indictment also notes eight meetings between Trofimoff and KGB officers, naming the KGB agents in three instances.' A former KGB general has described Trofimoff as one of the Soviet Union's top spies during the 1970s.

TRUST, THE   Long-running (1918–24) and successful Soviet deception operation to snare anti-Bolshevik White Russian agents and its Western supporters. Notable victims included Sidney Reilly the freelance British SIS agent.

TURING, Alan (1912–54)   Alan Turing graduated from Cambridge in 1934. A mathematical genius, Turing was fascinated by the idea of computers and wrote reports on their capabilities as early as 1936. In WWII, Turing worked at the Government Code and Cypher School (GC&CS) at Bletchley Park, 50 miles N of London. Turing, Gordon Welchman and their gifted superior Dillwyn Knox studied a captured ENIGMA machine used by the Germans to encrypt their unbreakable codes and provided by Polish intelligence. They built a duplicate machine that allowed them to crack the German codes and were thus able to supply the Allies with decoded messages passing between members of the German High Command, an incredible intellectual achievement that helped to shorten the war by a matter of years.

When German cryptographers constructed a machine even more sophisticated and advanced than ENIGMA, Knox, Turing, Welchman and others were able to duplicate it and responded with their own creation, Colossus. This was the world's first programmed electronic digital computer, one which quickly analysed and deciphered a large number of German codes. Unfortunately, Turing never lived to see the blossoming of the computer age, much of it due to his own invention and creativity. After being threatened with exposure as a homosexual by police officers investigating a complaint about his personal behaviour, Turing coated an apple with prussic acid and died soon after eating it.

He was only 42 at the time. Due to intolerance and official bigotry, Britain had lost one of the few true geniuses of the 20th century.

TURKEY   *MIT (Teskilat-I Mahsusa – Special Organisation)*: the MIT has its origins in the establishment of an intelligence service on 5 August 1914 by Enver Pasha. It was reorganised after Turkey's defeat in WWII in late 1918 under the name of *Karakol Cemiyeti (Police Guild)*. This new organisation carried out many important missions during the National Liberation War through providing arms to paramilitary groups and small armed groups fighting against the occupation forces in Anatolia and also through providing supplies and equipment to the national forces. When Istanbul was occupied on 16 March 1920, its activities had come to an end with the arrest of its members. On 6 January 1926, Ataturk finally established a modern intelligence organisation with the creation of the MAH (*Milli Emniyet Hizmeti – National Security Service*). It combined overseas intelligence-gathering activites and counter-espionage within Turkey with secret police duties, as well as counter-subversion operations against ethnic minorites including the Kurds and Armenians.

Colonel Oberst Walter Nikolai, a Polish-originated officer who had guided Germany's intelligence activities during WWI, was called on to undertake that duty. On 6 January the first intelligence organisation of the Republic of Turkey was established under the name of *MAH (Milli Emniyet Hizmeti – National Security Service)*.

MAH was to remain Turkey's premier intelligence service till 1965, when, in a purely cosmetic reorganisation, its name was changed to *MIT (Milli Istihbarat Teskilati   National Intelligence Organisation)*. Its present structure includes External Intelligence with sections devoted in particular to Greece, Cyprus, Russia, Kurdish insurrection and Iraq, Internal Security and Counter Terrorism and Organised Crime. It maintains a large network of SIGINT sites, many of which were of vital importance during the Cold War. These included Agri, Antalya, Ediene, Izmir and Kars, the joint NSA bases at Adana and Diyarbakir and the GCHQ base at Sinop. The emphasis in Turkey's SIGINT programme has moved away from Russia to concentrate on Iraq and Greece.

TURKEY, SPECIAL FORCES   The main counter-terrorist unit is the OIKB or National Police Jandarma Commandos, presently organised into three Special Force companies. They are trained in anti-terrorist operations, hostage rescue and anti-hijacking, as well as riot control. Members of this unit receive extensive training at the Jandarma Security establishment at Foca near Izmir from selected Army instructors. Operational control in peacetime is with the Ministry of Interior, but in wartime it passes to the control of the Turkish Military Intelligence. Its personnel have seen regular action against such extremist groups as the left-wing TPLA or Turkish People's Liberation Army, Armenian rebels and Kurdish Insurgents.

TURNED AGENT   An agent or intelligence officer 'turned' into a double agent.

U

U-2 A ground-breaking and brilliant concept and still operational in one form or another, but in particular as the TR-1. The U-2 provides continuous day or night, high-altitude, all-weather, stand-off surveillance of an area in direct support of US and allied ground and air forces. It also provides critical intelligence to decision-makers through all phases of a conflict or provides peacetime indications and warnings, crises, low-intensity conflict and large-scale hostilities.

The product of a remarkable collaboration between the Central Intelligence Agency, the US Air Force and the Lockheed Corporation in particular, the U-2 collected intelligence that revolutionised American intelligence analysis of the Soviet threat. The Lockheed 'Skunkworks' CL-282 aircraft was approved for production by the CIA, under the code-name AQUATONE, with Richard M. Bissell as the CIA programme manager. President Dwight D. Eisenhower authorised OPERATION OVERFLIGHT, the covert reconnaissance missions over the Soviet Union, after they had flatly rejected the US Open Skies plan, which would have allowed aircraft from both countries to openly overfly each other's territory.

An unusual single-engine aircraft with sailplane-like wings, it was the product of a team headed by Clarence L. 'Kelly' Johnson at Lockheed's 'Skunk Works' in Burbank, CA. The U-2 made its first flight in August 1955, with famed Lockheed test pilot Tony LeVier at the controls and began operational service in 1956.

Members of a unit innocuously designated 2nd Weather Reconnaissance Squadron (Provisional), began to arrive at Adana Air Base in Turkey in August 1956. The extremely sensitive nature of the mission dictated the construction of a secure compound within the base, which did not yet have a perimeter fence. Detachment 10-10 under the Turkey Cover Plan arrived to support a new operation, PROJECT TL-10. The Air Force provided the squadron commander and logistical support, while the Central Intelligence Agency provided the operations officer, pilots, and mission planners. The unit's mission, contrary to its name, had nothing to do with weather. It flew U-2 aircraft at extremely high altitudes to gather photographic imagery and electronic signals for intelligence purposes. The main target of these flights was the Soviet Union.

The US intelligence community came to rely heavily on this information to assess Soviet technological advances. However, the Soviet Union was not the sole objective of the operation. For instance, in September 1956, CIA pilot Francis Gary Powers flew over the E Mediterranean to determine the position of British and French warships taking part with Israel in the invasion of Egypt following the nationalisation of the Suez Canal. Other surveillance flights followed to gather data on the military forces of Syria, Iraq, Saudi Arabia, Lebanon and Yemen.

By the end of 1957, Adana AB, renamed Incirlik AB on 28 February 1958 had become the main U-2 operating location for missions over Soviet ballistic missile sites. These dangerous overflights by Detachment 10-10 usually involved operating from forward airfields at Lahore and Peshawar in Pakistan as well. For every mission that penetrated Soviet airspace, there was at least one surveillance flight along the border to divert Soviet air defence attention from the intruder. These diversionary flights typically departed Adana AB travelling over Van (in E Turkey), Iran, and the S Caspian Sea to the Pakistan–Afghanistan border; they returned along a similar route. These periphery missions usually collected communications and electronic signals instead of photographic imagery.

These flights were to discover the existence of the Soviet 8K38 (NATO codenamed SS3 SHYSTER) and 8K63 (SS4 SANDAL) medium-range ballistic missile (MRBM) sites at Kapustin Yar. The same unit was responsible for gaining evidence of the Soviet Union's first intercontinental ballistic missiles (ICBM), the 8K78 (SS6 SAPWOOD) being tested at the future Cosmodrome space launching facility at Tyuratam. The SS6 SAPWOOD, a crude though powerful missile, was the basis of the space booster responsible for the world's first successful satellite launch of SPUTNIK-1 in 1957, the first successful manned launch VOSTOK-1 with Cosmonaut Yuri Gagarin in 1961 and most of the earlier launches of the Soviet intelligence satellite programme.

The U-2 operation continued at the base for several years in the utmost secrecy, until 1 May 1960. On that morning Gary Powers, then a veteran of 27 missions, took off from Peshawar destined for Bødo, Norway. He was to overfly and photograph two major intercontinental ballistic missile test sites in the Soviet Union en route, one at Sverdlovsk, the other at Plesetsk, which were both protected by heavy anti-aircraft missile concentrations. While on the photo run at 67,000 feet over Sverdlovsk, the Soviets launched a volley of 14 V750VK (SA-2 GUIDELINE) surface-to-air missiles at Powers's aircraft. Although the V750 could not achieve the same altitude as the U-2, the aircraft disintegrated in the shock waves caused by the exploding missiles. Soviet authorities subsequently arrested Powers after he successfully ejected from the plane, and held him on espionage charges for nearly two years. The Turkish, Pakistani and Norwegian governments claimed to have no knowledge of the American U-2 overflights, and shortly afterwards all U-2s and support personnel quietly returned to the USA.

On 15 October 1962, Maj. Richard S. Heyser piloted a U-2 over Cuba to obtain the first photos of Soviet offensive missile sites. Maj. Rudolph Anderson, Jr was killed on a similar mission on 27 October 1962, when his U-2 was shot down. Since these embarrassing incidents the USAF and CIA have changed the mission profiles to allow the regular use of the valuable U-2 without placing it in direct danger. This was greatly helped by the introduction of improved technology, the advanced SR-71 Blackbird aircraft and the greater reliance placed on satellite platforms.

The Taiwan Air Force has also made considerable use of some nine or ten U-2 aircraft for surveillance missions deep into mainland China since around 1961, often with mission responsibility shared with the USA. At least five have been shot down by the Communist Chinese air defences.

US Air Force U-2s have been used for various missions, with primary operations originating out of Air Force Plant 42 in Palmdale and Beale Air Force Base, both in California, and RAF Alconbury, UK. Beale AFB also serves as the U-2's Home station with a full compliment of flight line support, training and depot facilities for up to 16 aircraft normally on-station. CIA U-2 aircraft also flew from the 3rd WRS(P) base at Atsugi in Japan and from Bodo in Norway, Kadena on Okinawa and Eielson AB in Alaska. The missions included Electronic (ELINT) and Photographic (PHOTINT/IMINT) and those involved in 'sniffing' as part of the High Altitude Sampling Program (HASP) to monitor worldwide fallout radiation levels from nuclear weapons tests.

The US Air Force plans to keep the U-2 in service to the year 2020 with a wide variety of upgrades and technological improvements. Thse include a reprogrammable Radar Warning Receiver and Jammer capable of detecting and defeating modern threats, cockpit modifications to improve pilot situational awareness, and airframe Infra-Red (I/R) signature reduction. These modifications will greatly increase U-2 survivability and flexibility in future combat environments. The U-2 aircraft was designed and fielded as one of the most secret US weapon systems during the height of the Cold War without the help of modern computer design techniques. However, the venerable U-2 aircraft seems set to continue to perform outstandingly in various hot spots around the world for years to come.

UAV Unmanned aerial vehicle (drone, usually used for reconnaissance and surveillance operations).

UKRAINE *SBU (Sluzhba Bespeky Ukrayiny – Main Intelligence Directorate of the Security Service of Ukraine)*: the national replacement for the Soviet Intelligence Service, formed in 1991 with its HQ at 33 Volodymyrska Street, Kiev-34. It very largely inherited the structure, personnel and operations of the local KGB and retains responsibility for the protection of the state, internal security (GUR SBU), external intelligence, SIGINT and relations with foreign intelligence services. The SBU has already benefited from improved co-operation with NATO intelligence services and in particular the CIA. However, the Russian SVR is believed to have thoroughly penetrated both the SBU and the Defence Ministry and the Western intelligence community will no doubt be taking that fully into account when considering just how much sensitive information or equipment to share with the Ukrainian SBU.

GUR SBU: established within the HQ of the Security Service of Ukraine on 28 December 1991, it carries out counter-intelligence and internal security activities. Combating international organised crime, in particular terrorism, drugs trafficking and arms smuggling priorities for the GUR.

UNITED KINGDOM Britain has a complicated and rather bureaucratic political control over its intelligence and security community and one that tends to apply itself to long-term targets and strategic intelligence programmes, but has little real influence on the behaviour and operations of SIS or MI5. Not so much 'oversight' as 'blindsight'. Despite the cosmetic changes of recent years and their formal establishment as legal government organisations, there is still little true accountability for their actions or a valid test of their overall efficiency. This myriad of organisations include the following:

Ministerial Committee on the Intelligence Services: in their day-to-day operations the Intelligence and Security Agencies operate under the immediate control of their respective Heads who are personally responsible to ministers. The Prime Minister is responsible for intelligence and security matters overall and is supported in that capacity by the Secretary of the Cabinet. The Home Secretary is responsible for the Security Service; the Foreign & Commonwealth Secretary for SIS and GCHQ.

PSIS (*Permanent Secretaries' Committee on the Intelligence Services*): ministers are assisted in the oversight of the Agencies by the Permanent Secretaries' Committee on the Intelligence Services (PSIS).

JIC (*Joint Intelligence Committee*): the principal collection agencies for secret intelligence are GCHQ and SIS. The Joint Intelligence Committee (JIC) agrees on the broad intelligence requirements and tasking to be laid upon SIS and GCHQ.

The UK Intelligence Community has four main elements: *SIS* (*the Secret Intelligence Service*) responsible for foreign intelligence and counter-intelligence and still popularly known by its military cover name, MI6; *The Security Service*, responsible for internal security and counter-espionage within both the UK and Commonwealth countries and also still popularly known by its military cover name, MI5; *GCHQ* (*Government Communications HQ*), SIGINT and COMSEC agency; *DIS* (*Defence Intelligence Staff*), responsible for the intelligence and security activities within the UK's armed forces.

SIS (*Secret Intelligence Service – MI6*): the British Admiralty and its Naval Intelligence Department had been largely responsible for Foreign Espionage operations for some years and partly at their insistence a Secret Service Bureau was finally established in 1909. By early 1910 it had been divided into two: a Home Section under the War Office as MO5, much later to become the Security Service (MI5), and a Foreign Section under a Naval Officer, Captain Mansfield Cumming, which would be restored to Admiralty control and continue to be responsible for overseas intelligence gathering. The Foreign Section, soon to be known as the Secret Service, also gained a military cover designation of MO6. The major reorganisation of intelligence and the War Office in 1916 saw the creation of the Directorate of Military Intelligence. MO5 would become MI5, while the Secret Service as it was now known gained a new military covername of MI-1C and became part of the War Office. It also became accountable to the Foreign Office, which largely funded its budget.

The Russian Revolution (1917) provided SIS with some of its more outlandish characters and operations: George Hill; Ernest Boyce; Paul Dukes; Augustus Agar, who sank a Russian Battleship in the Baltic; and Sidney Reilly and his attempt to assassinate Lenin and many of the Communist leadership. Although in the end the operations were a valiant failure, it did create a reputation in Europe that SIS was the most dangerous and efficient intelligence service in the world. SIS was, in part, to survive on that reputation for many years.

Following the end of the war the restructuring of the intelligence community saw the Admiralty and War Office codebreaking sections combined as the Government Code & Cipher School in 1919 still under Admiralty control. However, in 1921, GC&CS became a department of what would now be known as the Secret Intelligence Service and now controlled by the Foreign Office. It also gained a new military covername of MI6. The Security Service remained part of the War Office still as MI5.

During the 1920s and 30s, SIS was to concentrate on the Communist threat, often to the exclusion of the fascist threat from Germany, Italy and Spain or the growing Japanese militarism. Denied a decent budget, SIS attempted to create a second far more secret intelligence network in Europe, the Z section. Its originator Claude Dansey had little difficulty in persuading 'C', Admiral Sinclair, that SIS officers' normal cover abroad, Passport Control Officer at the Embassy, was already well known to all their potential enemies. Although SIS made considerable use of willing journalists and journalistic cover for intelligence officers, this was no substitute for a permanent network. Unfortunately, seven years of operations were thrown away in one stupid incident at Venlo in the Netherlands in 1939. The officers leading the two supposedly separate groups were ordered to meet a representative of an anti-Nazi group, together.

The Germans turned out to be Abwehr officers and captured the SIS officers and within months had rolled up both networks. When Germany finally invaded France and the Low Countries in May 1940, SIS was left without a single valuable network in occupied Europe. Apart from Sweden, Switzerland and Portugal, SIS was blind to continental events. Fortunately for SIS, the new 'C' Stewart Menzies was to make extraordinary use of both his friendship with the Prime Minister, Churchill, and the steady flow of ULTRA decrypts of the German ENIGMA traffic. Without this, SIS may well have been disbanded and replaced by its wartime rival, SOE. As it was by 1944 SIS had still not recovered sufficiently to be a major intelligence source, without the ULTRA material from Bletchley Park. Menzies was a master at using his political and social connections to win time and eventual survival for SIS, indeed so successful was he that in 1946 he persuaded the Labour Government to close down SOE and transfer its best staff and most promising operations to SIS. During this reorganisation

GC&CS became a separate organisation as GCHQ within the Foreign Office, leaving SIS without its major source of intelligence. Apart from changes of personnel, facilities and intelligence targets, SIS has remained under the Foreign Office and retained its name.

The resulting spy scandals of the late 1940s and early 50s saw doubt cast on some of SIS's most respected officers, Philby, Brooman-White, Ellis and others. Menzies retired in 1953, saddened and exhausted by over 37 years in intelligence. His replacement, Maj. General John Sinclair, allowed the service to be further tarnished not only by its inept handling of the Suez crisis, but also by its involvement in the Buster Crabb affair, when a diver disappeared while carrying out surveillance on a Soviet Cruiser in Portsmouth. Sinclair's reward was to be replaced by the head of MI5, Sir Dick White.

In 1973 under the new CSS or 'C', Sir Maurice Oldfield, operations were to be strictly controlled and scrupulous in their adherence to the wishes of the Government. Oldfield's unique style brought a refreshing blast of fresh air through the corridors of Century House, the SIS multi-storey glass and concrete HQ in south London. SIS objectives were also widened to take account of the increasing demand for commercial intelligence, on the USA, Britain's European partners, Japan and the Middle East oil states in particular. A new government organisation, the Overseas Economic Intelligence Committee (OEIC) became a major customer for both SIS and its SIGINT partner GCHQ.

Also during the early 1970s, SIS increasingly became involved in the convoluted politics of N Ireland. During the earliest years of the Ulster conflict, the British Government favoured the use of SIS in N Ireland. On the basis of countering the IRA bombing campaigns in Britain, MI5 pushed for a presence in the North and from 1973 onwards began to build an infrastructure in Ulster. From that time onwards, SIS has played only a minor operational role. However, that has still had a considerable political and intelligence significance. It was Michael Oatley, a senior SIS officer, who acted as Mrs Thatcher's direct link to the republican leadership during the 1981 hunger strike, apparently over the heads of MI5 and the N Ireland Office and later another SIS officer, Frank Steele, established an important dialogue with Gerry Adams. SIS was also involved in later discussions with Sinn Fein representatives on arms decommissioning and ensuring a ceasefire. By the late 1970s, most MI6 agents had been taken over by RUC SB or MI5, and SIS itself had withdrawn from RUC and Army HQ, although it retained an office at Stormont. SIS is thought to have an operational staff of about 25 in Ireland as a whole, split between the Stormont office, an office at Army HQ Lisburn and the British Embassy in Merrion Road, Dublin.

However in 1972, SIS was to be deeply embarrassed by the Littlejohn incident, when two brothers operating as SIS agents in Ireland were arrested for freelance activities including armed bank robberies. They also claimed to have been given a list of leading IRA members to assassinate. SIS emphatically denied any involvement and Oldfield went so far as to call a meeting of SIS staff to assure them that there was absolutely no truth in the allegations. SIS was soon to withdraw from the battle for control of British intelligence operations in the Province and the strong suspicion remains that the Littlejohn affair was somehow set up by the Security Service (MI5) to damage SIS's reputation. Oldfield was to suffer from a Security Service dirty tricks campaign some years later when appointed the Government's Security Coordinator for N Ireland in October 1979. It is widely believed that MI5 informed a number of friendly journalists that Oldfield was a homosexual and that his behaviour was a security risk.

SIS came out of the Falklands War, Gulf War and the Balkans conflicts throughout the 1980s and 90s with an enhanced reputation. Trust in its internal security has been restored by the succession of major Soviet defectors and double agents who were happy to co-operate with the service. The final act of coming out of the Shadows, becoming an 'established' government department and its move to a new high profile HQ at Vauxhall Cross has markedly raised its image. SIS is probably now considered a trendy new employer for well-scrubbed young graduates. Whether of course this new generation of politically correct and computer-literate civil service recruits will prove capable of dealing with the increasingly dangerous and terrorist-dominated intelligence environment of the 21st century is very much open to question.

In response to the threat of international terrorism, the Secret Intelligence Service (MI6) is pressurising the Government to fund the expansion of its Special Operations Directorate and virtually double its recruitment of frontline officers, often from the SAS, for the war against terrorism. The British Cabinet agreed a 15–20% increase in its budget for 2002–2003, allowing the SIS to greatly increase its counter-terrorism section which before 11 September 2001 had only 35 Officers attached to it. There will be a significant new emphasis placed on unarmed combat, weapons training and advanced surveillance techniques. The numbers of Intelligence Officers recuited annually will increase from 20 to 50 or more, however that will also require a further

150–200 support staff. A potential problem for SIS is the high visibility of its headquarters at Vauxhall Cross, and a number of covert facilities are expected to be quickly reactivated around London for Counter-Terrorist Officers.

A historical review of SIS facilities includes their main HQ at:

- Watergate House, 13–15 York Buildings, London 1909–13
- 2 Whitehall Court, London 1913–23
- 1 Melbury Road, London 1923–25
- Broadway Buildings, 54 The Broadway, London 1925–66
- Century House, 100 Westminster Bridge Road, London 1966–95
- Vauxhall Cross, 85 Albert Embankment, London 1995–

At one time or another SIS has had offices scattered all over London and in 'The City'. These are known to include:

- Artillery Mansions, Victoria Street, London – SIS Production Research Dept: 1950s–60s
- Bush House, Aldwych, London – Colonel Dansey's Z Sections based here, 1933–40
- 3 Carlton House Terrace, London – SIS Front Office and recruitment centre, 1950s onwards; may still be used by SIS
- 2 Caxton Street, London – SIS Section D, 1939
- Clarence Terrace, Regents Park, London – SIS-CIA centre for Berlin Tunnel operation in mid 1950s
- Coleherne Court, London – SIS 'safe' house, 1960s
- Glenalmond and Prae Woods, St Albans, north of London – SIS Section V, 1940–43 and Registry, 1940–45
- Queen Anne Mews, London – SIS large underground car park, 1940s–early 1970s
- 21 Queen Anne's Gate, London – official residence of 'C', 1923–66; backed on to Broadway Buildings
- Princes House, Princes Street, London – SIS 'General Craft Centre' Training, late 1940s
- 14 Ryder Street, London – SIS Section V/R5 Counter-Intelligence section, 1943–45; Soviet defectors centre, 1948–71
- 60 Vauxhall Bridge Road, London – SIS London Station, 1950s and 60s
- SIS (MI6) Technical Security Department, Hanslope Park, Buckinghamshire
- SIS (MI6) Training Centre, 296–302 Borough High Street, London
- SIS (MI6) Specialist Training Centre for Covert Operations, Fort

Monkton, old Napoleonic fort on the south coast at Gosport, Hampshire

A historical review of the great changes in SIS organisation charts the growth from the first formal restructuring after SIS came under the control of the Foreign Office:

In 1921 it was made up simply of the G or Geographical Officers and the four Circulating Sections which provided liaison with the *Foreign Office, Military* MI-1C, later MI6, *Naval* NI-1C and *Air* AI-1C from 1929. By the late 1930s this had expanded to ten circulating sections with the original four renamed I, II, III and IV, and Section V Counter Espionage, VI Industrial intelligence, VII Financial intelligence, VIII Communications, IX Ciphers and X Press.

The massive wartime changes and the absorption of SOE resulted in a structure that now included:

Directorate of Production with

- DP1 Controller Northern Area (CAN) Soviet Bloc and Scandinavia
- DP1 Controller Western Area (CWA) Spain, France and N Africa
- DP1 Controller Eastern Area (CEA) Germany, Switzerland and Austria
- DP2 Controller Middle East (CME)
- DP3 Controller Far East (CFE)
- DP4 Controller London Station

Directorate of Requirements (Circulating Sections)

- R1 Political
- R2 Military
- R3 Naval
- R4 Air
- R5 Counter Espionage (combining V & IX)
- R6 Industrial
- R7 Financial
- R8 GCHQ Liaison
- R9 Scientific Intelligence

By 1968 this had been simplified to:

- DP1 W Europe
- DP2 Middle East and Africa
- DP3 Far East and Americas
- DP4 London Station

In 1978–79 the service finally merged the old Requirement and Production Directorates to create a somewhat more streamlined, at least on paper, structure with six major Controllers:

- C1 London Station
- C2 Middle East
- C3 Far East
- C4 Western Hemisphere
- C5 Soviet Bloc
- C6 Africa

The last major restructuring was occasioned by the end of the Cold War and the need to redirect SIS activities more towards Terrorism and Global crime and so by 2001 the overall organisation had had been rationalised into:

- Directorate of Operations with a London Station
- Middle East & Africa
- Far East & Western Hemisphere
- Eastern Europe
- Global Tasks (new in 1994 to tackle crime proliferation and narcotics)
- Operational Support (new in 1994 to support deep cover or covert operation)

SIS has decided, in the wake of the terrorist attacks on 11 September 2001, to strengthen its Special Operations department markedly. It already has 'The Increment', small teams of SAS or SBS who are available to SIS for particularly difficult activities, such as intelligence gathering in S Ireland or Afghanistan.

However, the SIS already directly employs a considerable number of ex-SAS, SBS and 14th Intelligence Detachment of Military Intelligence and is actively seeking up to 100 additional recently retired special forces personnel to expand its own 'Covert Action' capability greatly.

Directors or Chiefs of the Secret Intelligence Service

1.	Capt. Sir Mansfield Smith Cumming	1909–23
2.	Admiral Sir Hugh 'Quex' Sinclair	1923–39
3.	Maj. Gen. Sir Stewart Menzies	1939–52
4.	Maj. Gen. Sir John Sinclair	1952–56
5.	Sir Dick White	1956–68

6.	Sir John Rennie	1968–73
7.	Sir Maurice Oldfield	1973–78
8.	Sir Arthur 'Dickie' Franks	1978–81
9.	Sir Colin Figures	1981–85
10.	Sir Christopher Curwen	1985–89
11.	Sir Colin McColl	1989–94
12.	Sir David Spedding	1994–99
13.	Richard Dearlove	1999–

GCHQ (GOVERNMENT COMMUNICATIONS HQ)

GC&CS (Government Code & Cipher School) was formed on 24 October 1919 and was fully operational by 1 November. It merged the Naval Intelligence Department 25 Room 40 and the War Offices MI-1B codebreaking services under the civil administration of the Admiralty at Watergate House. The British Army formed the Royal Corps of Signals on 5 August 1920 to maintain the so-called 'Army Chain' via the Rhine Army Signals, Egypt Signals, No. 2 Wireless Centre at Sarafand and through to Jubbulpore centre in India. At the same time the Admiralty maintained the most important elements of its wartime network, particularly those stations in the vital strategic centres of Singapore and Hong Kong. In April 1922 it was to be the most significant event in British SIGINT history, the Foreign Office took over responsibility for GC&CS and placed it under the operational control of SIS (MI6). 'C' became the Director of GC&CS, while the day-to-day control rested with the Deputy Director. The new HQ was in a large private house situated on the corner of Queen's Gate and Cromwell Road, which was destroyed by a V-I in August 1944. The Admiralty finally agreed to establish a Naval section within GC&CS in 1924. In an attempt to cope with the tiny budget the government of the day allowed SIS, GC&CS was moved into the 3rd and 4th floors of the Broadway Buildings in 1925.

Another important milestone was reached in 1928 when a 'Y' Committee was formed to co-ordinate the development and activities of the worldwide chain of British service radio interception bases, and in rapid succession the Army opened a section in 1930, while the Admiralty created NID-9 to operate the naval intercept stations in 1932. In 1934 the Air Ministry followed suit with the AI-4 and indeed open its own section within GC&CS in 1936. By now, the clouds of war in Europe were clear to see and a dedicated German section was established in May 1938. During this period the head of SIS Admiral Sinclair had found an alternative wartime site for the codebreakers well away from London. It was widely believed that in the event of a war, the capital would quickly be devastated and such a vital intelligence resource as GC&CS could not be risked. Therefore on 1 August 1939, in anticipation of war being declared, the service sections of GC&CS were able to move into a new operational HQ at Bletchley Park in the quiet Buckinghamshire town of Bletchley. The Diplomatic and Commercial sections followed on 15 August.

The new facilities were to provide an immense opportunity to expand and before many months had passed the ground would be covered in the famous 'Huts'. Bletchley would be known by a variety of designations during the war, BP, Station X and even HMS *Pembroke-V*. In 1939, MI5 formed the civilian RSS or Radio Security Service which would further increase the amount of intercepts flowing into Bletchley. In April 1940 the Commercial section returned to London. Soon GC&CS were to be faced with an internal revolt by many of the brilliant codebreakers and academics, who had swelled the staff at Bletchley to nearly 10,000. Frustrated at what appeared to be damaging, bureaucratic and unnecessary restrictions on the development of the ULTRA material derived from the ENIGMA intercepts, a group of the rebellious 'war service only' personnel went over the heads of their superiors, contacted Churchill and explained the problems they believed were holding up the war effort.

Churchill was to issue his famous 'action this day' instruction and long overdue changes occurred at Bletchley: expansion, extra staff and more relaxed working conditions for staff under huge pressure.

More fundamental was the acceptance that the senior management would have to change if the problems of breaking into the German U-Boat communications were to be solved before the convoy system broke down under the mounting losses.

In January 1942, the joint Committee of Control made up of two SIS and two GC&CS officers was scrapped and GC&CS was split in two following the recommendations of a former Deputy Director of Military Intelligence. Diplomatic and Commercial sections would operate from 7–9 Berkeley Street in London under Denniston as Deputy Director (C), while the Service sections would remain at Bletchley under Edward Travis, previously Denniston's assistant, as Deputy Director (S).

The new structure enabled a vast improvement in the service GC&CS was able to offer and an expansion that led to extra facilities for the new computers and extra staff, mainly Wrens, needed to operate them. Country houses all over the area were to become outstations for the remainder of the war.

New purpose-built facilities followed at Canons Corner in Stanmore and Lime Grove in Eastcote in London. In anticipation of a new threat from Britain's wartime ally, the Soviet Union appearing after the war, GC&CS embarked on a major reorganisation in February 1945. Following the suggestions of Sir Findlater Stewart, RSS was absorbed and within a year GC&CS had gained its full independence from SIS and placed under the direct control of the Foreign Office with the formal designation GCHQ or Government Communications HQ. Many of those who served at Bletchley will confirm that unofficially GCHQ had been used certainly since 1942.

As part of the new and vastly expanded capability to monitor the Soviet Union, the British and US intelligence communities created the UKUSA agreement Treaty in 1946 – together with Canada, Australia and New Zealand (later they were joined by W Germany, Denmark, Norway, Japan and S Korea) to co-ordinate SIGINT worldwide. GCHQ formed the Composite Signals Organisation (CSO) to run its civilian network of intercept stations.

Eventually the CSO would take over control of the various networks run by the armed forces, though not in some cases until the creation of the Ministry of Defence in 1963–64. In 1952 GCHQ moved its operations to Oakley in Cheltenham. As other sections including the Joint Technical Language Service and Communications Security were transferred to GCHQ, it expanded to the Benhall site in Cheltenham as well. GCHQ has played a pivotal role in the British intelligence community and with the wide-scale introduction of Commercial and Intelligence satellites its importance has increased.

GCHQ has operated SIGINT sites in W Germany, Gibraltar, Malta, Cyprus, the Middle East, Ascension Island, Silvermine in S Africa, Singapore and Hong Kong. It co-operates with the similar organisations in the USA, Canada, Australia and New Zealand, while the listening sites in Britain have at one time or another included Blakehall in Wiltshire, Hawklaw, Bower and Brora in Scotland, Cheadle in Staffordshire, Flowerdown in Hampshire, Island Hill and Gilnahirk in Ulster, Culmhead in Somerset, Goonhavern in Cornwall and many more. There is no doubt that GCHQ played a leading part in the Cold War and in conflicts since, including the Gulf War, Kosovo and Afghanistan; indeed it probably produces more than 70 per cent of all the intelligence gathered by the UK.

A historical review of the Signals Intelligence Services main establishments would run to many pages, so it will be sufficient to list its major secret interceptions bases only, these would include its HQs at:

- 15 Watergate House, York Buildings Adelphi, London 1919–22
- Queen's Gate, London 1922–25
- Broadway Buildings, SIS HQ, London 1925–40
- Bletchley Park, Buckinghamshire 1940–45
- Eastcote, Lime Grove, London 1945–52
- Cheltenham, Gloucestershire 1952–

GCHQ has two main sites either side of Cheltenham, one at Benhall and the other at Oakley. Benhall is now the home of a massive new bagel-shaped complex, the size of Wembley stadium. Construction began in 1998 and the intention is to ensure the centre's readiness for the hi-tech national security and intelligence-gathering challenges of the 21st century. It will have one of the largest and most sophisticated computer systems in the world.

In 2002 the Composite Signals Organisation operate SIGINT sites at Irton Moor in Yorkshire, Morwenstow in Cornwall and Ayios Nikaloas in Cyprus. In addition to a number of jointly run stations throughout Britain and the world, mainly with the British Armed Forces, the NSA and the Australian DSD. The London stations include 2–8 Palmer Street and part of the Empress State Building in Earls Court.

Directors of GC&CS (the head of GC&CS was the Deputy Director, as the head of SIS was the official Director)

- Alaistair Denniston 1921–42
- Alaistair Denniston, Deputy Director (C) 1942–44
- Sir Edward Travis, Deputy Director (S) 1942–44
- Sir Edward Travis 1944–46

Directors of GCHQ

- Sir Edward Travis 1946–52
- Sir Eric Jones 1952–60
- Sir Clive Loehnis 1960–65
- Sir Leonard Hooper 1965–73
- Sir Arthur Bonsall 1973–78
- Sir Brian Tovey 1978–83
- Sir Peter Marychurch 1983–89
- Sir John Adye 1989–96
- David Omand 1996–98
- Francis Richards 1998–2003
- David Pepper 2003–

The present structure of GCHQ has two main directorates:

Directorate of Organisation and Establishment with a number of divisions:

C	Overseas Staff
E	Personnel
F	Finance and Supply
G	Management and General
M	Mechanical Engineering
Q	Technical
R	Security

Directorate of SIGINT

H	Crypt analysis
J	Special SIGINT
K	General SIGINT
S/T	Statistical Operations
W	Search Technology
X	Computer Services
Z	Liaison

GCHQ also has the directorates of communications and CESG communications security (COMSEC); a directorate of SIGINT plans and the JSRU Joint Speech Research Unit.

In the late 1980s a new special unit K20 was set up to monitor telephone calls and the activities of radical groups and individuals within the UK. It passes this information to the Joint Intelligence Committee (JIC) in the Cabinet Office.

THE SECURITY SERVICE – MI5

In March 1909, the Prime Minister, Mr Asquith, instructed the Committee of Imperial Defence to consider the dangers from German espionage to British naval ports. In July a sub-Committee recommended the creation of a Secret Service Bureau which should be a separate organisation, but keep in close touch with the Admiralty, the War Office, Home Office as well as the Police, Post Office and Customs authorities.

The Secret Service Bureau began work on 1 October 1909 under the nominal control of MO5, the special section of the Military Operations Directorate that was responsible for enemy aliens. Within months the two senior officers involved had agreed on a division of responsibilities to fulfil the Admiralty's requirement for information about Germany's new navy. By early 1910 this had been formalised into a Home Section under Captain Vernon Kell of the South Staffordshire Regiment and a Foreign Section under Captain Mansfield Cumming of the Royal Navy, which became known as the 'Secret Service'. Between March 1910 and 1914, more than 30 spies were identified by the Home Section, known as MO(T). All were to be arrested upon the outbreak of hostilities, thereby depriving the German Intelligence Service of its network. At the time, the Bureau had a staff of only ten, including Kell ('K') himself.

The Bureau was rapidly mobilised as a branch of the War Office on the outbreak of war in 1914, becoming MO5(G). In January 1916 it became part of a new Directorate of Military Intelligence as MI5. The Foreign section became MI-IC and also took over responsibility for counter-espionage in non-Empire countries. Wartime legislation increased the responsibilities of MI5 to include the co-ordination of government policy concerning aliens; vetting and other security measures at munitions factories. MI5 also began to oversee counter-espionage measures throughout the Empire.

By the end of the war, during which a further 35 spies were identified and arrested, making it virtually impossible for the Germans to maintain any form of espionage network in Britain, MI5 had approximately 850 staff.

After the Bolshevik coup d'état of October 1917, MI5 began to work on the threats from Communist subversion within the Armed Services, and sabotage to military installations. It was to be involved in close surveillance of potential subversives among the Trade Unions, particularly during the General Strike in 1926. It actively pursued a Communist involvement and the spy ring that operated as part of the Soviet trade delegation with offices in London with the All Russia Cooperative Society Ltd (ARCOS). In May 1927 the operation was closed down following a raid by some 150 Metropolitan police and MI5 officers. Problems caused by there being a number of counter-espionage departments with overlapping responsibilities came to a head in the late 1920s. On 15 October 1931 formal responsibility for assessing all threats to the national security of the UK, apart from those posed by Irish terrorists and anarchists, was passed to MI5. It was to absorb both Captain Guy Liddell's Home Office Directorate of Intelligence and Maxwell Knights SIS department. This date marked the formation of the Security Service, although the title MI5 has remained in popular use to this day.

Following Hitler's rise to power, the new Service had to face the threat of subversion from the right wing. Sir Oswald Mosley's British

Union of Fascists was of particular concern, as were the pitched battles between Fascists and Communists in some of the larger cities. However, at the time of the outbreak of WWII, MI5 still was ill equipped for its many tasks, which included counter-espionage; monitoring of enemy aliens and advising on internment. In early 1939 the Service's strength stood at only 30 officers and its surveillance section comprised just six men. Following the disaster of the sinking of the Battleship HMS *Royal Oak* at anchor in Scapa Flow and a number of other incidents all put down to the activities of 'undiscovered Nazi spies', Churchill then First Lord of the Admiralty forced Kell to resign on 25 May 1940. In the turmoil that followed, MI5 was put under the temporary control of a Security Committee under Lord Swinton. To make matters worse, in September 1940 many of its records were destroyed or damaged by a German bomb, which hit the Wormwood Scrubs Prison where the registry had been moved for added safety. In late 1940 the majority of staff were evacuated to Blenheim Palace and in early 1941, Sir David Petrie was appointed the first Director General of the Security Service. He was also finally given the resources to rebuild a substantial organisation. In 1942 MI5 was reorganised and the continuing arguments over responsibilities between MI5, SIS and the newly created SOE were settled, up to a point.

Internment at the outbreak of the war effectively deprived the Germans of most, if not all, of their existing agents. Moreover, when German intelligence records were studied after 1945, it was found that all of the further 200 agents targeted against Britain during the course of the war had been successfully identified and caught. Some of these agents were 'turned' by the Service and became double agents who fed false information to the Germans concerning military and diplomatic strategy throughout the war. This was the famous 'Double Cross' system. This highly effective deception contributed to the success of the Allied Forces landing in Normandy on 'D Day' in June 1944. MI5 had grown from a small ramshackle but dedicated counter-espionage section in 1939 to a vast, efficient and highly effective national security service by 1945. Its reach extended across the old Empire and through offshoots such as SIME in the Middle East as well. The new Labour Government of Clement Atlee, suspicious of an ultra powerful and probably fairly 'conservative' security service imposed an 'honest copper' as its new Chief in 1946, Sir Percy Sillitoe, an ex-Chief Constable of Kent. An inexperienced outsider was not what MI5 desperately needed at the beginning of the Cold War.

MI5 had for some time been focusing on the activities of the

Communist Party of Great Britain which, at its peak in the early 1940s, had 55,000 members. In March 1948 the Prime Minister, Clement Atlee, announced that Communists as well as Fascists were to be excluded from work 'vital to the security of the state'. This was achieved through the setting up of the vetting system under MI5's control. The cases of Philby, Burgess and MacLean, in particular, showed how effective the Soviet Intelligence Service had been before the war in recruiting ideologically motivated spies in Britain.

Active espionage by the Soviets, already considerable during the war, now grew apace. The Atom spies and traitors within MI5, SIS, GCHQ and the Diplomatic Service failed to gain the proper attention of a service lacking leadership and riven with internal dissension.

In 1952 the Prime Minister, Winston Churchill, deputed his personal responsibility for the Security Service to the Home Secretary, Sir David Maxwell Fyfe, who issued a Directive describing the Service's tasks and setting out the role of the Director General. This Directive provided the basis for the Service's work until 1989, when the Security Service Act placed the Service on a statutory footing for the first time. The Security Service now officially became a civilian organisation, though it retained its old military cover-title, MI5.

By the early 1950s, the Service's staff had increased again to about 850. These included some 40 Security Liaison Officers overseas who provided advice and assistance to governments in the Commonwealth and Colonies. In the 1960s, the successful identification of a number of spies – including George Blake, an officer of the Secret Intelligence Service; the Portland spy ring; and John Vassall, an employee at the Admiralty recruited by the KGB in Moscow – illustrated the need for still greater counter-espionage efforts. Lord Denning's report into the Profumo Affair in 1963 revealed publicly for the first time details of the Service's role and responsibilities, but must rank alongside the Warren Commission report on the Kennedy Assassination as one of the most misleading and ineffective reports in history. During the 1960s and 70s MI5 was again plagued by internal doubts about the loyalty of senior officers and the divisive nature of the relationship with SIS in N Ireland. In particular the accusations that a small group of MI5 officers had deliberately set out to blacken and undermine the British Prime Minister, Harold Wilson, created a deep-seated distrust of the 'secret services' that has still not dissipated entirely in certain political circles in 2002.

This period of its history culminated in the mass expulsion from the UK in 1971 of 105 Soviet personnel, which severely weakened KGB and GRU intelligence operations in London following the defection of a Soviet intelligence officer.

By the early 1970s, the Service's resources were being redirected from work on subversion into international and Irish terrorism. The Service's counter-terrorist effort had begun in the late 1960s in response to the growing problem of Palestinian terrorism. Major incidents, including the terrorist sieges at the Iranian Embassy in London in 1980 and the Libyan People's Bureau in 1984, tested the Service's developing procedures and links with other agencies. During this period, the Service played a leading role in establishing an effective network for co-operation on terrorism among Western security and intelligence services.

N Ireland was to see a battle for control between SIS and MI5, but eventually victory went to the Security Service. The main terrorist organisations on the Republican side – the Provisional IRA (PIRA), Republican Sinn Fein's 'military wing', which calls itself the 'Continuity IRA', and the Irish National Liberation Army (INLA) – have sought, by violent means, to create a unified republic in the island of Ireland. Although they have been most active in N Ireland, Republican terrorist groups, especially PIRA, have carried their attacks to the British mainland and to the continent of Europe. Foreign nationals as well as British subjects have been killed and injured as a result. British politicians have been killed and on two occasions PIRA has attempted to kill members of the Cabinet: the bombing of the Conservative Party Conference in Brighton in 1984 and the mortar attack on Downing Street in 1991.

N Irish loyalist paramilitary organisations, notably the Ulster Volunteer Force (UVF), the Ulster Defence Association (UDA) and the Loyalist Volunteer Force (LVF), have all been involved in a violent campaign in response to what they claim to regard as the threat posed to the Protestant community in N Ireland by republican terrorism. Much of their activity has been essentially sectarian in character, often resulting in the random murder of Catholics who may have no connections of any kind with republican terrorism. Before the ceasefire declarations in August 1994, loyalist groups were murdering more people than PIRA. Both loyalist and republican groups, especially PIRA, have for some years sought support from outside Ireland to sustain their campaigns of violence. Such support has included the provision of weapons and finance. PIRA's principal supplier during the 1980s was Libya, but the organisation has also acquired weaponry and related equipment via sympathisers in N America and from the arms black market in the Baltic and Balkans in particular.

In 2001 it became clear with the arrest of three suspected PIRA members in Colombia just how closely involved international terrorism and organised crime have become, while the breakaway Real IRA has established itself as a ruthless and less sectarian terrorist movement determined to create international links with ETA and probably Islamic groups.

The Director and Co-ordinator of Intelligence (N Ireland) or DCI (NI) sits on MI5's Board in London and reports directly to the Secretary of State for N Ireland. He also chairs the N Ireland Security Committee attended by representatives of the British Army, RUC and government ministers and sits on the Joint Intelligence Committee in London – he is reported to have easy access to the Prime Minister. A former DCI (NI), the late John Deverell was at one time tipped to become head of MI5 but his career was damaged by revelations concerning the WARD and SCREAM undercover operations in Germany which were designed to establish informers in expatriate Irish communities throughout the world. These operations clearly breached the agreement between the German and British authorities regarding the scope of British intelligence work in Germany. In an embarrassing security leak, *An Phoblacht/Republican News* published documents detailing the two operations and naming Deverell in 1989.

Deverell was to be killed on 2 June 1994 while travelling from N Ireland to a conference at Fort George, Scotland, 25 intelligence personnel and four RAF crew died when their CH47 Chinook helicopter crashed on the Mull of Kintyre. Among the dead were ten members of RUC SB, including the head of SB, two regional heads and the divisional heads of E1, E2, E3, E3A, E3B and E4. Four other MI5 officers also perished in the crash along with a British Army colonel, three Intelligence Corps lieutenant colonels, and five majors. It is widely acknowledged that the crash killed the upper echelons of the intelligence agencies in N Ireland, including key members of the Provincial Executive Committee. MI5's HQ, known as The Department, is based at Stormont, in the parliament building on the fringes of east Belfast. It has two operational bases in Belfast city centre, one at River House in High Street and the other at Churchill House, Victoria Square. The latter is the centre for electronic surveillance, including telephone monitoring, for which MI5 receives assistance from the Government Communications HQ. GCHQ goes under the name of Composite Signals Organisation in the North and Diplomatic Telecommunications Maintenance Service in the South. MI5 also retains offices at Army HQ in Lisburn and at Royal Ulster Constabulary

(RUC) HQ in Dundonald (east Belfast). While in theory the RUC has overall responsibility for counter-terrorism, in practice MI5 is in the stronger position of power and influence over British policy. Its links to RUC Special Branch are via a small network of Security Liaison Officers.

In 1983, Michael Bettaney, a member of the Service who had offered information to the KGB was detected, in part because the KGB in disbelief that he could be a genuine MI5 officer, suspected a set-up and complained to the Security Service about Bettaney's actions. This highlighted once again a lack of security within the Service and indeed they were to be plagued for the next two decades with the constant drip of such accusations. The public exposure of Soviet spies who had been offered immunity from prosecution in return for a confession and co-operation added to the Service's woes. Following a Security Commission inquiry, whose findings were critical of aspects of the Service, Sir Antony Duff was appointed as Director General. He initiated the discussions which laid the foundations for the Service as it exists today, strengthened by the legal status conferred upon it by the Security Service Act 1989.

Major changes in the focus of the Service's work took place in the early 1990s with the end of the Cold War. The threat from subversion had diminished, and the threat from espionage, though it persisted, required less of the Service's effort. International terrorism, however, had not abated. In October 1992 responsibility for leading the intelligence effort against Irish Republican terrorism on the British mainland was transferred to the Service, despite protests from the Police Special Branch who had some 110 years of experience in dealing with this threat.

However, the Security Service was able to draw on the experience it had gained in the 1970s and 80s in running long-term intelligence counter terrorism operations. Between 1992 and April 1998 the Service's work with the police against Irish republican terrorism resulted in 18 convictions for terrorist-related offences. However, Stella Rimington as Director General disbanded a specialist section of G7 responsible for Islamic terrorism in 1994 against the protests of experienced counter-terrorist officers. This was an unbelievably ill-advised action in view of the growth of Hizbollah in the Middle East, the Lockerbie bombing in 1988 and the many obvious portents of the threat that Islamic terrorism would pose.

The new measures introduced since the attacks of 11 September 2001 and the new responsibilities heaped on to the Security Service will mean considerable changes in the Security Services structure and targets. The present Director General retired in October 2002 and his replacement is Eliza Manningham-Buller, formerly Deputy Director-General of the Security Service.

Despite the cosmetic changes in accountability introduced with the 1994 Intelligence and Security Committee established under the Intelligence Services Act, the service stills lacks a true and effective external oversight authority.

ORGANISATION OF MI5 1909–2002

The structure that developed after 1918 and throughout the interwar period was dominated by the Communist threat, subversion and the needs of the Empire. By 1939 this had solidified into an organisation that contained:

- A Division (Registry, Transport and Room O55)
- B Division (Counter-Espionage and Counter-Subversion)
- C Division (Vetting)
- D Division (Liaison with SIS and the Service Departments)
- E Division (Foreign Nationals)
- F Division (The Colonies and Political Parties)

During WWII B Division was to be vastly expanded and eventually included among numerous other extra responsibilities:

- XX Committee (Double Agents)
- Enemy Analysis, Wireless and Mail
- SHAEF Liaison
- RSS (MI8c) Radio Interception
- GPO Telephone Bugging Services

F Division expanded to include SIME (Security Intelligence Middle East), BSC (British Security Coordination) in the USA with SIS and SOE and DSO regional security officers in Gibraltar, Malta, Bermuda, S Africa and so on.

By the height of the Cold War in 1952 and following the transfer of MI5 from the War Ministry to effective Home Office control in the Maxwell Fyfe reforms, its structure had again dramatically changed:

- A Branch – administration
- B Branch – personnel
- C Branch – protective security
- D Branch – counter-espionage

- E Branch – the Commonwealth
- F Branch – political parties and subversion

The organisation of MI5 at the end of the Cold War still showed clearly the influence of a service dedicated to defeating the Communist espionage threat and that of internal political subversion. D Branch was renamed K Branch in 1968 and E Branch was disbanded. The growing threat of terrorism was still perceived as mainly a home-grown Irish problem. The organisation of 1991–92, instigated by Sir Patrick Walker, but which came into effect under Stella Rimington included:

- *A Branch surveillance* (based at Curzon Street House, Mayfair)
  - A1 Operations including:
  - A1A Bugging and break-ins
  - A1B Obtaining confidential personal data from the DHSS, tax, banks etc.
  - A1C Running 'safe houses'
  - A1D Expert locksmiths, safe crackers and carpenters to make good any damage
  - A1E Electronic monitoring, provides the tapes for A2A
  - A2 Technical back-up (surveillance devices)
  - A2A Transcribed tapes
  - A2B Specialist photographs and electronic experts; liaison with GCHQ
  - A4 Direct surveillance – The Watchers, including vehicles
  - A5 Scientific research

- *B Branch personnel* (based at Curzon Street House, Mayfair)
  - B1 Recruitment
  - B2 Personnel management
  - B3 General management services
  - B5 Finance

- *C Branch protective security* (based at Curzon Street House, Mayfair)
  - C1 Security in Whitehall
  - C2 Vetting government contractors
  - C3 Vetting civil servants and Ministers
  - C4 Security against terrorist attacks

- *F Branch domestic surveillance* (based at HQ, in Gower Street)
  - F1 Communist Party (CPGB)
  - F2 Trade Unions including:
  - F2N Trade Union leaders

- ○ F2R Dealing with the media, education, MPs and entertainers
- ○ F3 Non-Irish terrorism
- ○ F4 Agents in the CPGB, Trade Unions and journalism
- ○ F5 Irish terrorism
- ○ F6 Agents in radical groups and terrorist organisations
- ○ F7 Surveillance of political and campaigning groups including anarchists, feminists, pacifists, Black Power, Fascists and nationalists in Scotland and Wales

The roles of F3 & F5 were soon to be transferred to a new T Branch, while F Branch would be renamed G Branch.

- ● *K Branch counter-intelligence* (based at HQ, Gower Street)
  - ○ K1 Potential espionage in government departments
  - ○ K2 Monitors KGB and GRU (Soviet military intelligence)
  - ○ K3 Recruitment of Soviet agents
  - ○ K4 Surveillance of Soviet diplomats, trade delegations etc.
  - ○ K5 Recruitment of E European and Chinese agents
  - ○ K6 Recruitment of other 'hostile' intelligence agents in UK
  - ○ K7 Investigation of penetration of UK security and intelligence agencies including MI5
  - ○ K8 Non-Soviet bloc counter-intelligence

However these were then grouped into two controlling sections:
- ○ *KX Investigative work* which had K1, K2 and K3
- ○ *KY Operations* which had K4, K5, K6, K7 & K8

At one time it was suggested that a K9 section dealt with defectors and unexpected resignations.

- ● *S Branch training and computer systems* (based at Curzon Street, Mayfair)
  - ○ S1 Runs the Joint Computer Bureau linked to other agencies including MI6
  - ○ S2 Registry of files
  - ○ S3 Training
  - ○ S4 Supplies, travel arrangements

- ● *T Branch anti-terrorism* (based at HQ, Gower Street)
  - ○ T1 Irish terrorism
  - ○ T2 Non-Irish terrorism

The latest reorganisation of the Security Service under Sir Stephen Lander has created a structure more suited to a post-Cold War environment and with MI5's new responsibilities for combating organised crime. However the greater emphasis now being placed on counter-terrorism will see the expansion of certain sections of both G and T branches, perhaps the creation of new departments and a shift in personnel and resources into fighting the War on Terrorism.

- *A Branch* still remains largely unchanged as the 'technical' service.
- *B Branch* is administration and training.
- *D Branch* was recreated to combine the much reduced F, K and C branches; it is now responsible for counter-espionage and all non-terrorist threats; organised crime, subversion and arms proliferation.
- *G Branch* covers international terrorism only since the formation of T Branch in October 1992. It has a minimum of nine G sections covering various aspects of the terrorist threat.
- *H Branch* is a new section intended to improve strategic planning, information technology and finance.
- *S Branch* provides support services, though it may have been largely absorbed into A Branch.
- *T Branch* covers domestic terrorism, with the emphasis on Loyalist and Republican groups, but with a small section that monitors both Scotland and Wales.
- *General Intelligence Group* (GI) is made up of some 350–400 officers who can be readily assigned to any security task. All sections are now based at the HQ complex at Thames House on the embankment.

B and H Branch come under the direct control of the DGSS or Director-General of the Security Service, while A, D, G and T Branch are under the DDG (Ops) or Deputy Director-General (Operations). The third senior position of DDG (Admin) was abolished in January 1996, the responsibilities being taken over by the DGSS.

A historical review of major MI5 facilities includes the main headquarter buildings at:

- Winchester House, 21 St James's Square, London – MO5, 1905–Nov 1906
- War Office Main Building – MO5, Nov 1906–1925. Secret Service Bureau formed in 1909 with a Special Intelligence Branch. The Home Section which would remain MO5 until renamed MI5 in 1916.
- 124–126 Cromwell Road, London – 1925–37

- Thames House, Millbank, London. Two floors of the then ICI Building – 1937–40
- 57–58 St James Street, London – 1940–45 (later to become MGM's HQ, Metro House)
- Leconfield House, Curzon Street, Mayfair – 1945–74
- 140 Gower Street, Bloomsbury, London – 1974–94
- Thames House, Millbank, London – both North and South buildings totally rebuilt 1988–93) 1994–
- Euston Tower, 17th Floor, Central London – still the MI5 Communications Centre and also the A4 'Watchers' surveillance base.

Thames House now contains the service registry and in 2001 the Security Service claimed that it currently holds in total about 440,000 files which have been opened at some time since its establishment in 1909. Of these, approximately 35,000 files relate to Service administration, policy and staff, and 10,000 concern subjects and organisations studied by the Service. About 75,000 files relate to people or groups of people who have never been investigated by the Service such as those who have received protective security advice. This leaves about 290,000 files, which relate to individuals who, at some time during the last 90 years may have been the subject of Security Service enquiry or investigation. Of these 290,000 some 10,000 have been reduced to microfilm and placed in a restricted category to which Security Service staff have access only for specific research purposes. A further 230,000 files are closed so that staff may use them where necessary in the course of their current work, but may not make enquiries about the subjects of the files.

Many other buildings have a previous intelligence connection and there is considerable interest in these buildings and their fascinating history:

- 1–8 Barnard Road, Battersea, London – MI5 Surveillance Centre, moved to Euston Tower 1978;
- 7–9 Berkeley Street, Mayfair, London – MI5 Training Centre in 1970s;
- Blenheim Palace, Oxfordshire – safe country retreat from wartime London; housed the Registry and Administration sections 1940–45;
- Bolton Street (probably 29–40) – housed parts of F Branch and Technical Offices until 1994;
- Curzon Street House, 1–4 Curzon Street, Mayfair, London – built with large underground facilities for the Ministry of Aircraft

Production in WWII; these were adapted to hold the MI5 Registry and its computers; housed many departments not transferred to the new HQ at Gower Street when the Service moved out of Leconfield House in 1978;

- Clarence Terrace, Regents Park, London – A4 Watchers Centre in 1950s;
- Cork Street (probably No. 5), London – home for much of C Branch throughout the 1950s and 60s;
- Dolphin Square, London – 308 Hood House was a 'safe house' while 10 Collingwood House was an operations centre; Maxwell Knight's 'B sections', 1924–45;
- 14–17 Great Marlborough Street, London – Legal department and during 1960s housed parts of D Branch; also housed MI5 'Front Office' including Box 500 address;
- 71–72 Grosvenor Street, London (Top Floors) – housed Political File Centre in 1980 and also used for training in the 1980s;
- Horseferry House, Horseferry Road SW1 – extra office space was used here in 1938–40 because of overcrowding at the Thames House building just round the corner;
- Keble College, Oxford – housed Registry overspill from Blenheim Palace;
- Kensington High Street (probably No. 375 Charles House), London – MI5 Phone-tapping Centre;
- 6–7 Kensington Palace Gardens, London – Wartime MI5 Interrogation Centre ('The London Cage');
- 26–28 Mount Row, Mayfair, London – MI5 Computer Centre, moved to Curzon Street House in 1977;
- South Audley Street (probably No. 33), London – covert surveillance office;
- Wormwood Scrubs Prison, London – housed the registry, until a German bombing raid forced them to move to a safer location, and the transport section, 1939–40.

Directors of the Security Service

● Maj. Gen. Sir Vernon Kell	1909–40
● Sir David Petrie	1940–46
● Sir Percy Sillitoe	1946–53
● Sir Dick White	1953–56
● Sir Roger Hollis	1956–65
● Sir Martin Furnivall Jones	1965–72
● Sir Michael Hanley	1972–79

- Sir Howard Smith   1979–81
- Sir John Lewis Jones   1981–85
- Sir Anthony Duff   1985–88
- Sir Patrick Walker   1988–92
- Dame Stella Rimington   1992–96
- Sir Stephen Lander   1996–2002
- Elizabeth Manningham-Buller   2002–

DIS (DEFENCE INTELLIGENCE STAFF)

Each service (Army, Navy, Air Force) have their own intelligence arms; the DIS provides the overall assessment and evaluation. HQ: Old War Office Building, Whitehall, London SW1. It gathers intelligence on 'threats' from surveillance, military attachés in UK embassies, SIGINT from GCHQ and from the US NSA. The three main directorates are:

- Directorate of Management & Support Intelligence
- Directorate of Economic & Logistic Intelligence
- Directorate of Scientific & Technical Intelligence

In addition there are:

- DISC (Defence Intelligence and Security Centre), Chicksands, Shefford, Bedfordshire SG17 5PR; created on 1 October 1996 to integrate all intelligence and most security training into a single tri-service organisation; core functions are to provide training in intelligence and security disciplines, training in conduct after capture, and advice on intelligence and security policy; DISC trains the Armed Forces and other intelligence agencies in intelligence and security disciplines, and conduct after capture;
- JARIC (Joint Air Reconnaissance Intelligence Centre), RAF Brampton, Huntingdon, Cambs PE18 8QL; acts as the Department's centre of excellence for the production of imagery intelligence. Its role is to exploit and analyse imagery from all available sources and produce intelligence products and services to meet the requirements of MOD and the operational Commands. It provides this intelligence to military commanders and the Government, in support of current military operations, defence planning and wider intelligence matters.

The Defence Intelligence Staff can trace its ancestry back to 1946, when the Joint Intelligence Bureau (JIB) was established under the direction of General Keith Strong, General Eisenhower's British wartime Chief of Intelligence. It was created in 1964 by the amalgamation of all three service intelligence staffs and the civilian Joint Intelligence Bureau to form an integrated body able to serve the Ministry of Defence and the Armed Forces and other government departments.

The provision of intelligence support to the Peace Implementation Force (IFOR) in the former Yugoslavia has been allocated a significant proportion of the resources available to the Defence Intelligence Staff (DIS). The DIS runs a full-time Yugoslav Crisis Cell, which can call upon the in-depth expertise of all directorates within the DIS, including military, infrastructure, technical and industries analysts and the embargo-monitoring cell. All assessments are rapidly and securely disseminated to British forces operating as part of the IFOR deployment via the Joint HQ at the same time as they are passed to the Department. Wherever possible and appropriate, they are sent to Allies operating alongside our own forces in the former Yugoslavia, both through the NATO communications system and via the intelligence liaison staffs resident within the DIS itself.

The DIS are also involved in the setting up of the WEU Situation Centre and Intelligence Section. The DIS submits Weekly Intelligence Summaries to the Intelligence Section, supplemented by weekly briefing on the situation in the former Yugoslavia. It has also responded to ad hoc requests from the Section for more detailed briefing on particular areas. The DIS will continue to work with WEU partners to refine current arrangements and to improve the WEU's ability to receive and circulate intelligence.

The British Army runs its own intelligence operation in N Ireland under the name of Northern Ireland Command Military Intelligence (NICMI). Very little is known about NICMI and its organisational structure. On the operational side, it is reputedly made up of staff from the SAS, the Royal Corps of Signals, the Royal Air Force (which pilots helicopter surveillance), 14th Intelligence Company and Field Research Units (or Forward Reconnaissance Units). These units were set up by Commander of Land Forces Major General Glover in 1980. All intelligence from Army sources is stored on the Crucible computer at Lisburn HQ which is maintained by 12th Intelligence and Security Company.

The role of military intelligence has come to light in three recent incidents. The two corporals attacked and killed at the funeral of one of those who in turn had been killed by loyalist Michael Stone's attack on the burial of the three IRA volunteers, shot by the SAS in Gibraltar, were part of the Signals Corps. 14th Intelligence Company killed three men robbing a bookmakers' shop in Belfast's Falls Road in January

1990. While it was claimed they had stumbled across the robbery, other reports suggest that the men were deliberately targeted because the undercover unit thought they had acquired intelligence maps of West Belfast targets while robbing a car outside a bar. More significant is the case of Brian Nelson. Nelson worked for FRU for ten years. During this time he was the intelligence officer for the loyalist group, the Ulster Defence Association. This gave military intelligence direct knowledge of all UDA operations, including killings and the large shipment of arms from S Africa in 1989. Since the Ceasefire and attempts to get the political process under way, the security situation in the Province has somewhat improved. A limited dismantling of surveillance towers began in late 2001. However, much of the security infrastructure will remain in place as well as certain armed elements of both the Republican and Loyalist movements have not yet accepted a cessation of hostilities.

UK, SPECIAL FORCES The British Army were to form what was to become the role model for much of the world's special forces when in 1942 the first Special Air Service unit was created. Although the idea was temporarily abandoned for regular service in 1946, the changing nature of conflict was quickly to prove the value of such highly specialised forces. In 1952, the 22nd Regiment, Special Air Service, was formed as a temporary measure during the Malayan emergency. Based on the operational skills developed by the SAS units in WWII, the 22nd quickly proved itself in operations against the Communist Terrorists and went on to become an established regular unit. The continued need of special forces units in British territories around the world soon became apparent, and the 22nd SAS was to deploy to Oman, Dhofar, Aden, Kuwait and to many other areas in Africa and Asia. High-visibility operations such as the successful storming in May 1980 of the Iranian embassy in London to free 90 hostages held by a group of anti-Government rebels and conducted in the full glare of the world's television cameras has ensured the SAS lasting and largely unwanted fame. The SAS were to be involved in many further clandestine operations, often in support of foreign governments during the next ten years. But some operations that were ultimately to prove unsuccessful during the Gulf War of 1991, failed mainly due to a woeful lack of sufficient and, at times, even basic equipment available to the operational squadrons deployed to Saudi Arabia. Considerable efforts have been made to ensure that the SAS is better funded and equipped for large-scale operations in future.

The 22nd SAS has gone on to acquit itself with honour in innumerable anti-terrorist operations and in Bosnia and Kosovo (1994–2000). However, concern has been expressed that the effectiveness of the 22nd SAS has been reduced by the level high of public interest in this unit. Undermined, too, by the willingness of ex-members of the regiment to write publicly about their experiences and indeed, the overrecruitment of so many Parachute Regiment personnel at the expense of its more traditional, and more technically orientated volunteers from the Engineers, Signals, Intelligence and elite Infantry corps.

However, the SAS were to be quickly deployed in covert intelligence-gathering operations in Afghanistan within a few weeks of the attacks on the USA in September 2001. Several squadrons were deployed in identifying targets for later US bombing raids and went on to lead many of the operations in the Tora Bora mountains in particular. Extraordinarily dangerous fire-fights took place in well-defended cave complexes in the search for Osama bin Laden and his Al-Qa'ida senior commanders.

In the ongoing War on Terrorism, the SAS are sure to be called upon to play a leading role and it is to be hoped that the British Government will ensure that the regular 22nd and the two TA Regiments are now equipped with the very best equipment available, and in sufficient quantities.

Today the 22nd Regiment Special Air Service remains one of the prime anti-terrorist and hostage rescue units in the world. It has its HQ at the Duke of York Barracks in West London, where its Crisis alert unit is based. Its main training base and depot has recently moved to new accommodation just outside the city of Hereford in the western area of England. It is presently organised into five operational units: A Squadron, B Squadron, D Squadron, G (Guards) Squadron and R (Reserve) Squadron, the original C Squadron having been made up of Rhodesian recruits and disbanded in the 1960s. Each Squadron has four operations squads of 16 men each again in turn divided into four four-man specialist units known as the Boat, Air, Mountain and Mobility Troops. Each squadron takes it in turn for a six-month period to act as the 'crisis alert unit', or Counter Revolutionary Warfare (CRW) squadron, sometimes known as the Special Project Team.

It has its own communications support in the form of the 264th (SAS) Signals Squadron, which provides for secure links for operations worldwide.

The 22nd SAS is further strengthened by the addition of two

Territorial units, the 21st (Artists Rifles) Regiment SAS, actually the oldest SAS unit, having been established in 1946 as a reserve unit and which currently recruits highly trained personnel in Southern England. It acts as a mirror unit for the 22nd SAS, as well as emphasising intelligence gathering.

The second territorial unit is the 23rd SAS, which recruits largely in the N of England and Scotland, keeps alive the skills developed by the highly secretive WWII organisation, MI-9 and therefore carries out combat rescue, escape and evasion, prisoner of war rescue or interrogation and clandestine intelligence gathering.

Both the 22nd SAS and the territorial units demand an extraordinary level of physical fitness, stamina and technical ability from its personnel. They are trained in the 'Killing House', Close-Quarter Battle, combat shooting and combat swimming, explosives, sabotage, sniping, heliborne-insertion, desert, mountain, arctic and jungle warfare and survival, languages, camouflage, parachuting using paravanes, HALO (High Altitude-Low Opening) and HAHO (High Altitude-High Opening), hostage rescue, defensive driving, as VIP bodyguards and much more. They have at their disposal a huge range of British and foreign weapons and explosives, including many used by the world's terrorists: 5.56mm M16AI automatic rifles, 5.56mm L85AI (SA80) automatic rifles, 5.56mm G41 sniper rifles, 7.62mm L99A1 sniper rifles, 12.7mm Barrett M82A2, 5.56mm FN Minimi machine guns, Remington 870 combat shotguns,7.62mm L7A1 machine guns and 94mm LAW anti-tank rocket launchers, Milan anti-tank missiles, M203 40mm grenade launchers and Stinger manportable surface-to-air missiles.

The 22nd Regiment SAS will, if properly supported and equipped, and as long as there is a steady stream of the right personnel, remain at the pinnacle of the world's special force units.

UKUSA In 1947 succeeded the 1943 BRUSA agreement in formalising co-operation between British and US SIGINT or Signals Intelligence agencies.

ULTRA WWII codeword for deciphered high-level enemy communications.

UMBRA Overall US codename for the highest-grade SIGINT gathered by the Keyhole KH11,12 & 13 satellites.

UNITED STATES OF AMERICA The USA suffered an intelligence disaster on 11 September 2001 of a magnitude on a par with Pearl

Harbor. In many ways it was far worse: in 1941 the USA did not have a vast global network of intelligence agencies that had been in place for more than fifty years and that was the recipient of simply thousands of millions of dollars of taxpayers' money. That the communications interception network belonging to the giant NSA; the all-pervasive worldwide ECHELON electronic surveillance system; the human intelligence and analytical resources of the CIA; the defence-related intelligence of the DIA; the worldwide spy satellite coverage of the NRO and the crime fighting, anti-terrorist and counter-intelligence expertise of the FBI failed catastrophically to provide adequate warning of, let alone protection from, that terrorist outrage is absolutely stunning in its consequences both for the USA and the world as a whole.

CIA (CENTRAL INTELLIGENCE AGENCY)
Background
The USA has carried on foreign intelligence activities since the days of George Washington, but only since WWII have they been co-ordinated on a government-wide basis. Even before Pearl Harbor, President Franklin D. Roosevelt was concerned about American intelligence deficiencies. He asked New York lawyer William J. Donovan to draft a plan for an intelligence service. The Office of Strategic Services was established in June 1942 with a mandate to collect and analyse strategic information required by the Joint Chiefs of Staff and to conduct special operations not assigned to other agencies. During the war, the OSS supplied policy-makers with essential facts and intelligence estimates and often played an important role in directly aiding military campaigns. But the OSS never received complete jurisdiction over all foreign intelligence activities. In October 1945, the OSS was abolished and its functions transferred to the State and War Departments. But the need for a postwar centralised intelligence system was clearly recognised. Eleven months earlier, Donovan, by then a major general, had submitted to President Roosevelt a proposal calling for the separation of OSS from the Joint Chiefs of Staff with the new organisation having direct Presidential supervision.

Donovan proposed an 'organisation which will procure intelligence both by overt and covert methods and will at the same time provide intelligence guidance, determine national intelligence objectives, and correlate the intelligence material collected by all government agencies'. The military services generally opposed a complete merger. The State Department thought it should supervise all peacetime operations affecting foreign relations, while the FBI supported a system whereby military intelligence worldwide would be handled by the armed services, and all civilian activities would be under FBI's own jurisdiction.

To bring an end to the constant arguments over the future of US Intelligence, President Harry S. Truman established the Central Intelligence Group in January 1946. Truman directed it to co-ordinate existing departmental intelligence, supplementing but not supplanting their services, under the direction of a National Intelligence Authority composed of a Presidential representative and the Secretaries of State, War and Navy. Rear Admiral Sidney W. Souers, USNR, who was the Deputy Chief of Naval Intelligence, was appointed the first Director of Central Intelligence. Twenty months later, the National Intelligence Authority and its operating component, the Central Intelligence Group, were disestablished. The 1947 Act charged the CIA with co-ordinating the nation's intelligence activities and correlating, evaluating and disseminating intelligence, which affects national security. In addition, the Agency was to perform such other duties and functions related to intelligence as the NSC might direct.

In January 1952, the CIA's intelligence functions were grouped under the Directorate for Intelligence (DDI). Its intelligence production components included: the Office of Research and Reports (ORE), which handled economic and geographic intelligence; the Office of Scientific Intelligence (OSI), which engaged in basic scientific research; and the Office of Current Intelligence (OCI), which provided current political research. Collection of overt information was the responsibility of the Office of Operations (NO). The Office of Collection and Dissemination (OCD) engaged in the dissemination of intelligence as well as storage and retrieval of unevaluated intelligence.

Government and military demands for the Agency to provide information on Communist intentions in the Far East and around the world and particularly generated by the Korean War resulted in a massive increase in both its size and intelligence production. Despite the sweeping changes, the fundamental problem of duplication among the Agency and the Departments remained.

The DDI's major effort was independent intelligence production rather than co-ordinated national estimates. The establishment of the office of National Intelligence Programs Evaluation (NIPE) in 1963 was the first major effort by a DCI to ensure consistent contact and co-ordination with the community.

The NIPE staff directed most of its attention to sorting out intelligence requirements through USIB and attempting to develop a national inventory for the community, including budget, personnel and materials. Remarkably, this had never before been done.

The Office of Policy Co-ordination (OPC), renamed the DDP or Directorate of Plans remained self-contained and largely independent of direct control from the DCI. Under Bissell, Wisner, Roosevelt and other Cold War warriors the DPP was the covert action or special operations branch of the CIAS. The DDP staff considered themselves the real cutting edge of American international policy and were to become involved in clandestine wars, coups, subversion and much else, often very successfully as in the return of the Shah to Iran in 1953.

The CIA in the 21st century

The Central Intelligence Agency has been put through a wringer largely of their own making since 11 September 2001 and the reactions of their political masters risk a return to the 'bad old days' before the reforms which began in the mid 1970s. Dissident CIA Officer John Stockwell, an experienced Africa-desk operative, succinctly described the period as being 'In search of enemies'. A time when a gung-ho, try anything and don't get caught attitude prevailed in the corridors of the CIA HQ at Langley. Deniable operations, cut-outs and a contempt for democracy led Director after Director of the CIA simply to mislead the politicians on the 'the Hill' at every opportunity.

Unaccountable operations and even small-scale wars were carried out with either the merest nod from the White House or in complete absence of any form of government control and eventually lead to the undermining of an otherwise responsible Intelligence community and indeed the trust of a large part of the American nation. In actions that had ranged from attempting to supply exploding cigars to the Cuban dictator, Fidel Castro to the CIA's private war in Angola and the involvement with narco-criminals, the drug trade and illegal gun-running of the Iran-Contra Affair, the swash-buckling CIA OSO officers attempted to assassinate or overthrow those Langley considered to be America's enemies.

By the mid 1970s fear of international repercussions had caused the US Government finally to reign in the CIA, not completely, but to a level considered manageable by the administration. New working practices, including the banning of assassination by President Ford's Executive Order 12333 and tighter controls on overseas operations, were quickly followed by the early retirement of a generation of experienced, highly capable but politically unreliable field officers. This led in due course to a crisis in intelligence gathering, a growing reliance on technology and a distancing of the agency from long-term covert operations. Langley's staff soon came to be very largely made up of analysts, clerks and administrators. As one highly experienced former CIA Officer remarked, 'The "company" has very few field officers with mud on their boots any longer, but thousands of card-carrying employees whose grasp of espionage begins and ends with the more lurid spy novel.'

The CIA has failed to understand or prepare to deal adequately with the growth of international terrorism in large part because while re-establishing necessary controls over the wilder excesses of its field operatives, a new generation of politically safe management destroyed much of the agency's human intelligence-gathering capability. Operations to penetrate terrorist groups, hostile foreign governments and organisations takes time, skill, commitment and is strewn with pitfalls and certainly did not fit in with the new risk-avoidance culture of the 1980s and 90s.

Those overseas operations that were carried out were often ill advised and frankly unprofessional. Its long-term attempts to influence or even control events in the Middle East and S Asia were littered with failures. The 'botched' support for the Kurds in N Iraq ended ignominiously with the CIA's operatives quickly high-tailing it across the Turkish border to avoid capture by Saddam Hussein's Republican Guards. The CIA had provided both military aid and training to the young Saudi Islamic militant and dedicated anti-Communist, Osama bin Laden, from the mid 1980s onwards for his Holy War against the Soviet occupation forces in Afghanistan. However, following the Gulf War of 1991, bin Laden switched his militancy towards driving US forces out of his beloved and to many Muslims, sacred homeland. The CIA was to continue to maintain contact with Al-Qa'ida, both directly and through the Pakistan ISI or Inter-Service Intelligence Service until just a few months before the attack on the World Trade Center.

During 1998, the CIA carried out a major covert operation to capture five members of the Egyptian Jihad organisation in Albania and Kosovo and ensure their deportation back to Cairo for trial. At the time the Egyptian Jihad was merging with Osama bin Laden's Al-Qa'ida network and US authorities considered the Tirana cell among the most dangerous terror outfits in Europe. This group had been under construction since around 1992 and was eventually to number at least 30 active members before it was broken up by the CIA. They had created what appeared to have been a classic 'sleeper' cell: a self-sufficient group safely sheltering within a friendly community, simply awaiting a call from its leadership to begin terrorist activities and indeed part of a far bigger and more dangerous Muslim terrorist organisation that has now spread throughout the Balkans and much of W Europe.

The CIA has refused to acknowledge this operation publicly. Privately its officers have described it as one of the most successful counter-terrorism efforts in the annals of the intelligence agency and was one of the first tangible benefits of Bill Clinton's decision to ease restrictions on the CIA's ability to conduct clandestine operations. Although executed swiftly and successfully, the CIA's operations in Albania and Kosovo still had faults. At least two men targeted by the USA eluded capture, while another was shot dead during a gunfight with Albanian security forces. Fatos Klosi, head of SHIK, Albania's intelligence service, acknowledged that some of his agency's actions undertaken on behalf of the CIA, while 'not so justified legally' were undoubtedly necessary. 'They convinced us not to be soft with terrorists,' said Klosi.

In the wake of the events of 11 September, the Bush administration has now largely removed restrictions from the CIA and a rejuvenated Special Operations directorate has finally got its 'hunting licence' back after some 23 years. It is now free to interpret the rules governing foreign assassinations, penetration of organisations that provide a 'clear and present danger' to the USA and to conduct paramilitary activities, on a case by case basis. Carrying the fight to the terrorist will mean teaming up with foreign security services that engage in political repression and pay little heed to human rights. By authorising trial by special military courts for some of the terrorists captured abroad, President Bush has clearly signalled that they are considered to have forfeited any rights to US Civilian-styled justice by their actions.

The days when large-scale covert operations and paramilitary activities could be conducted by the CIA Directorate of Operations, 'The Clandestine Service', with the merest nod of approval from the 40 Committee has returned with a vengeance. The CIA's private armies run by the Special Operations Division conducted insurgencies, staged coups and carried out assassinations in countless countries during the Cold War and though such activities were rejected during the Carter–Stansfield Turner era, the ability to carry out such clandestine and deniable operations against terrorist organisations and their host nations will prove invaluable in any successful 'War on Terrorism'.

America, the CIA and Afghanistan

The USA's tortured involvement with Afghanistan had begun with a lie that was not to be laid for nearly twenty years. In answer to the following question posed to Zbiegniew Brzezinski in 1998: 'The former director of the CIA, Robert Gates, stated in his memoirs, *From the Shadows*, that American intelligence services began to aid the Mujahidin in Afghanistan six months before the Soviet intervention. In this period you were the national security adviser to President Carter. You therefore played a role in this affair. Is that correct?' Brzezinski answered, 'Yes. Now, according to the official version of history, CIA aid to the Mujhadeen began during 1980, that is to say, after the Soviet army invaded Afghanistan, 24 Dec. 1979. But the reality, secretly guarded until now, is completely otherwise: Indeed, it was July 3, 1979 that President Carter signed the first directive for secret aid to the opponents of the pro-Soviet regime in Kabul. And that very day, I wrote a note to the president in which I explained to him that in my opinion this aid was going to induce a Soviet military intervention.'

The original and flawed decision by the Carter administration locked the USA into a relationship with Afghanistan that directly led to the events of 11 September and the declaration of a War against Terrorism, a conflict that US Government officials regularly warn will last a lifetime.

Amid widespread and entirely justified domestic criticism of their failure to gain foreknowledge of the recent terrorist attacks, the US intelligence community are coming under increasing pressure to explain their apparent inability to deal with Islamic extremist activity on American soil. The key debate revolves around the question of whether these incidents were preventable. Leading experts on Western intelligence warn that similar failures are all too likely in the future unless there is fundamental reform within Langley and a major restructuring of CIA activities. Without doubt the terrorist attacks in New York and Washington are concrete proof of very serious shortcomings in the operational methods and intelligence-gathering capabilities of the entire US intelligence community, though they certainly received warnings from the Israeli Mossad and several less obvious sources among the strategic forecasting and corporate intelligence organisations.

There was clear evidence that bin Laden and his Al-Qa'ida network were capable of both planning and executing major acts of terrorism against US targets, notably the provable link with the suicide bombing of the warship, the *USS COLE* in Yemen last year. However, there appears to have been a remarkable reluctance to commit resources to gather reliable intelligence on those suspected of having links, however distant, with Al-Qa'ida or its allies among the Islamic fundamentalist organisations in Algeria, Egypt and elsewhere. As one very well-informed source close to US intelligence commented, 'The main problem is not a lack of information, that comes in all the time, but that we simply don't have sufficient skilled operatives capable of analysing the intelligence we receive in a timely manner and identifying those who pose a real risk to our interests.'

According to some analysts, at the time of the suicide attacks on 11 September, the CIA did not have a single competent speaker of Pushto, the language of the Taliban, on active service. Local intelligence agents on the ground in the 90 per cent of Afghanistan controlled by the Taliban are believed to have been similarly lacking, despite bin Laden's presence on the CIA Counter-Terrorism Centres hit list for a number of years. However, some of the best informed sources have also suggested that previous plans to capture or kill the Al-Qa'ida chief, which were supported by the Russian Government, had been shelved by the White House on the grounds that they might end in humiliating failure and loss of US service personnel. As one source put it: 'Before the latest catastrophe there was a distinct lack of political will to resolve the bin Laden problem and this had a negative impact on wider intelligence operations.'

Despite the indications of a strong financial aspect involved in the failure to develop an efficient covert penetration of Al-Qa'ida and its support network, the fundamental problem remains the political reluctance to take decisive action during the Clinton era. This was combined with a general complacency in Washington towards persistent warnings that the USA itself, as opposed to US facilities and personnel abroad, might be targeted. Given the particular structure of the Al-Qa'ida operational cells, it was very unlikely that a Western intelligence service could penetrate such a group without a considerable investment in both time and money developing the right 'moles'. Their members are often related by blood or tribal origins, so the only practical option would have been to 'turn' one of the existing or prospective members, a highly dangerous, but not an entirely impossible task even given the fanatical devotion such extremists have for their beliefs. Developing a network of native Pushto-speaking informants in Afghanistan itself should have presented less difficulty given the unpopularity of the regime among many ordinary Afghans. That this was not attempted on any reasonable scale, and the evidence certainly suggests that it wasn't, must rate as a very serious error of professional judgement on behalf of the US intelligence community.

However, restoring faith in the intelligence gathering and analytical capabilities of the CIA will be difficult to say the least. In early 2002 there were already signs of a major rift between the Pentagon and the CIA concerning the standard of material being provided to the US Armed Forces in Afghanistan. A jury-rigged and underdeveloped intelligence system was providing little solid information in the hunt for Taliban and Al-Qa'ida leaders. Inexperienced CIA field officers and poor analysis of raw intelligence are slowing the US military's search operations.

The problem of CIA–US military relations surfaced when a Pentagon spokesman openly attacked the fact that poor intelligence had left the US forces 'chasing shadows'. He was essentially admitting the lack of any idea of where the Taliban and Al-Qa'ida leadership were at that time. Even worse, it was an admission of how little confidence the Pentagon has that US intelligence will find them soon. Complaints about 'chasing shadows' are a swipe at all intelligence operatives who have been flooding the Pentagon with unconfirmed reports straight from the mouths of Afghan sources who often have their own agendas and limitations.

The Pentagon's patience may have finally reached its limit after one particular operation in January 2002 to apprehend Mullah Omar. US military forces spent several days doing house-to-house searches in the southern Afghan city of Baghran looking for the Taliban leader or even some of the reported 1,000 loyalist fighters protecting him. But Omar was nowhere to be found, and the reports that followed approached the ridiculous, suggesting that he escaped the area on a motorcycle and took along $1 million in a shoulder bag.

The CIA does not seem to have an efficient, centralised analytic apparatus, one that can distinguish credible intelligence from fantasy. Instead, it appears that some of the raw intelligence is simply being forwarded to the Pentagon, causing a gap in belief that will prove very hard for the CIA to bridge. To some extent this also applies to the NSA and other elements of the US intelligence community who have failed to make up the shortfall in CIA capability.

The CIA was very active in Afghanistan during the Soviet era, not least among the Mujhadeen groups, which at that time included many of the fighters who went on to form Al-Qa'ida. The close relationship built with Osama bin Laden during the years he ran anti-Soviet operations out of the Pakistan capital of Islamabad was to cool dramatically after the 1991 Gulf War and, following a number of outrages against US facilities in Saudi Arabia, East Africa and the Yemen, bin Laden and his Al-Qa'ida network were to become America's Public Enemy Number One. However, as late as July 2001 and despite being a hunted man with a US price on his head, it was even rumoured that Osama bin Laden had been able to travel safely to an American hospital in a Gulf State to receive treatment for a serious kidney problem. While there the DGSE or French Foreign Intelligence Service claimed that the local CIA Chief of Station paid bin Laden a private visit on at least one occasion.

The tragic events of 11 September were cruelly to expose the CIA's shortcomings, its dubious and ongoing connections with international terrorists and importantly destroy a highly sensitive CIA facility at 7 World Trade Center in New York. Operating under Federal Government cover, this vital CIA station had played a leading role in Counter-Intelligence operations against Russia, the turning of foreign diplomats at the United Nations, covert operations under business and diplomatic cover and a major anti-terrorist liaison facility run jointly with the FBI. It was also to throw a shocked agency, demoralised by such a public failure, into disarray. The CIA's management policy of risk avoidance and a disdain for HUMINT and anything that smacked of old-fashioned spying was to be quickly called into question. President Bush has firmly ordered his deskbound intelligence agency back into the field, to end the virtual reliance on electronic intelligence-gathering methods and even gone so far as to partly lift the public ban on assassination of foreign leaders and terrorists. The Central Intelligence Agency is now on a fast learning curve to rediscover the skills of deep-cover penetration, of covert action, that took 35 years to develop, often misused and which were largely thrown away a quarter of a century ago.

The long-term result for the US intelligence community will undoubtedly be a muddled initial response and an eventual, and hopefully, well thought out major reorganisation of the CIA. It will require a veritable 'night of the long knives' as both senior personnel and long cherished policies must be changed if the CIA is to cope with the 21st-century threats of international terrorism, the globalisation of crime and the growth of asymmetrical warfare. A loosening of domestic wiretap restrictions, a willingness to employ spies with 'dirty hands', and even a reconsideration of America's long-standing ban on political assassinations are likely consequences of the 11 September terrorist attacks on the World Trade Center and the Pentagon. Reversing the ban on political assassinations, whether the US is directly or indirectly involved, carries with it the risk that terrorists may choose deliberately to target senior Western political figures for revenge. Or indeed spread their range of targets to include celebrities, movie stars, sports personalities or multinational businessmen. 'Assassination was not a feature of the Cold War,' said Fred Hitz, former Inspector General of the Central Intelligence Agency, 'because each side could see that if you go down that road, where does it end?' though there had been precedents with the British SIS-sponsored assassination of Reinhard Heydrich in 1942 and the aerial ambush and assassination of the Japanese Admiral Yamamoto by the USA.

The invasion and defeat of Iraq in the war of March–April 2003 has been rightly seen as something of a triumph for the newly expanded and restructured CIA. Assassination attempts on the life of Saddam Hussein were made on several occasions largely based on intelligence from CIA teams on the ground inside Baghdad, while the Agency's Special Operations teams operating alongside the US Special Forces were responsible for the widespread disruption of the regime's command, control and communications networks and undoubtedly played a considerable part in America's eventual success. New links are indeed now being forged with many foreign intelligence services throughout the world, though this expansion has also lead to a growing involvement with many groups that had previously been shunned because of their known connections with political or religious extremism and organised crime. However, a significant development has been the intention to create a Joint Counter Terrorist Task Force with the British services which has been seen by many analysts as a major advance in the onging war against Islamic Terrorism.

Technology versus human intelligence

There has been considerable debate over the shift from human intelligence gathering to electronic and satellite methods. In part, such criticism is justified. The sheer volume of communications interception, using systems such as the Echelon monitoring network, largely precludes the quick and effective analysis of those intercepts and further encourages reactive intelligence gathering after an act of terror has taken place. This often involves little more than traditional investigative techniques.

Preventative intelligence, however, requires significantly greater investment, most noticeably in terms of skilled personnel who are capable of interpreting material and deciding which of the many warnings received each day represent a real and credible threat. Rebuilding and enhancing such a vital capability will take time, and that is something the West is running short of. However, few closely involved with the US intelligence community would suggest that anything other than a chronic lack of political will and understanding in the past was one of the real underlying problems behind the lack of an active intelligence ability in place when it was most needed. Perversely, that same community often lacks the understanding, knowledge and even, on occasions, the interest to analyse and assess correctly the enormous amounts of intelligence material received daily. So much intelligence of great value is lost under a veritable blizzard of trash, that the seeds of its fundamental problems are firmly planted in its own successes.

The recent heavy reliance on the technology of signals interception and analysis is likely to be replaced by the altogether more difficult and dangerous business of recruiting and running agents close to the terrorist groups. The CIA will have to deal with and employ some very unsavoury characters if they are to succeed in the war on terrorism in the long run. However, the most immediate problem facing the intelligence community is a shortage of expertise at HQ and credible, knowledgeable agents in the field. Indeed, evidence of how US agencies are rushing to catch up came when FBI Director Robert Mueller publicly solicited résumés from Arabic and Farsi speakers.

Three important aspects of the changes faced by the CIA will be the concentration on Countering Terrorism, an increasing involvement in Domestic surveillance and the use of commercial high technology. The CIA's *Counter-Terrorist Centre* or *CTC* is run from a futuristic communications and threat situation room and its role is far more extensive than merely that of proving liaison with foreign services. It was founded in 1986 in the wake of the hijacking of TWA Flight 847, in which a US Navy diver was killed. The CIA wished to bring under one organisation the analysts from the Directorate of Intelligence, covert case officers from the Directorate of Operations and the Directorate of Science and Technology in order 'to pre-empt, disrupt and defeat terrorists'. The CTC is also home to permanent representatives from a dozen other federal agencies involved in the fight against terrorism, carrying the fusion concept across the federal government. And, perhaps most importantly, the CTC is directly linked to the FBI's Domestic Counter-Terrorism Centre, meaning that the CIA and FBI should share their information freely and openly. However, does the CIA really have the ability to play offence against terrorists? The CTC hasn't been highly successful in penetrating operational terrorist cells and, without changing the 'risk avoidance' culture of the last twenty or so years, is highly unlikely to improve. The CIA has shown a distinct aversion to operating in hostile territory, because the risks are extremely high and the benefits are questionable. 11 September will have caused a considerable rethink of this attitude in the CTC.

The Central Intelligence Agency has been given new freedom to get involved in *domestic surveillance and investigations* in ways that would have been considered unacceptable in 2000. The CIA's intelligence gathering has long been kept as separate as possible from domestic law enforcement, which is bound by strict evidence-gathering rules and legal safeguards protecting the rights of those investigated. Observers may be concerned at the CIA's past history of domestic operations. In the 1960s and 70s, for instance, OPERATION CHAOS included CIA involvement in spying on US citizens including anti-war protesters, black militant groups and even congressmen. President Nixon's White House encouraged these activities, convinced that foreign powers stood behind anti-war radicals. The CIA's domestic involvement damaged its reputation and hindered its operations and it is doubtful if their actions will produce a different result in 2003.

The CIA is actively promoting the involvement of *private industry and specially set-up commercial companies* to ensure its access to advanced technology, particularly in the field of information warfare and electronic surveillance. The Central Intelligence Agency has established a venture capital company, In-Q-It, to nurture high-tech companies, executives and former CIA officials. It has chosen a veteran Silicon Valley software executive, Gilman Louie, to head the effort, which now has an office in Washington and a second office in Silicon Valley.

The reorganisation of the CIA following the collapse of Communism and the end of the Cold War has resulted in an agency built around two support Directorates:

- *The Directorate of Administration* – includes the Office of Communications, Office of Facilities & Security Services, Office of Finances & Logistics, Office of Information technology, Human Resources management, Office of Personnel Security, DCI Centre for Security Evaluation, Centre for Support, Coordination and Office for Training & Education;
- *The Directorate of Science & Technology* which includes Office of Advanced Projects, Office of Development & Engineering, Office of Research & Development.

While the two main directorates are:

- *The Directorate of Intelligence* with the Office of Russia & Europe, Office of Near East & Africa, Office of Asia & Latin America, Office of Trans-national Issues, Council of Intelligence Occupations and Office of Current Intelligence;
- *The Directorate of Operations* with the Counter-Intelligence Centre (CIC), DCI Counter-Intelligence Centre, National HUMINT Requirements Tasking Centre and Counter Terrorism Centre (CTC).

A joint *Clandestine Information Technical Office* is run by the DS&T and the DoO, while a joint *Office of Advanced Analytic Tools* is run by the DS&T and the DoI.

A description and chronology of the CIG and CIA's Senior Management Structure includes here, arguably, the three most influential positions:

Director of Central Intelligence (DCI)

1.	Rear Admiral Sidney W. Souers	January 1946–June 1946
2.	Lt. Gen. Hoyt S. Vandenberg	June 1946–May 1947
3.	Rear Admiral Roscoe H. Hillenkoetter	May 1947–October 1950
4.	Lt. Gen. Walter Bedell Smith	October 1950–February 1953
5.	Allen W. Dulles	February 1953–November 1961
6.	John A. McCone	November 1962–April 1965
7.	V. Admiral William F. Raborn	April 1965–June 1966
8.	Richard M. Helms	June 1966–Feburary 1973
9.	James R. Schlesinger	February 1973–July 1973
10.	Lt. Gen. Vernon A. Walters	July 1973–September 1973 (acting DCI)
11.	William E. Colby	September 1973–January 1976
12.	George H. Bush	January 1976–January 1977
13.	E. Henry Knoche	January 1977–March 1977 (acting DCI)
14.	Admiral Stansfield Turner	March 1977–January 1981
15.	William J. Casey	January 1981–January 1987
16.	Robert M. Gates	December 1986–May 1987 (acting DCI during Casey's illness)
17.	William H. Webster	May 1987–August 1991
18.	Richard J. Kerr	September 1991–November 1991 (acting DCI)
19.	Robert M. Gates	November 1991–January 1993

20. R. James Woolsey   February 1993–January 1995
21. Admiral William Oliver Studeman   January 1995–May 1995
                                                             (Acting DCI)
22. John M. Deutch   May 1995–December 1996
23. George Tenet   December 1996–July 1997
                                                             (Acting DCI) 1997–

NSA (NATIONAL SECURITY AGENCY)

NSA is the nation's cryptologic organisation, tasked with making and breaking codes and ciphers. In addition, NSA is one of the most important centres of foreign language analysis and research and development within the government. NSA is a high-technology organisation, working on the leading edge of advanced communications and data processing. NSA's SIGINT organisation provides an effective, highly structured capability and consists of all the foreign signals collection and processing activities of the USA.

Although codemaking and breaking are ancient practices, modern cryptologic communications intelligence activities in the USA date from the WWI period and radio communications technology. In 1917 and 1918 the US Army created, within the Military Intelligence Division, the Cipher Bureau (MI-8) under Herbert O. Yardley. The MID assisted the radio intelligence units in the American Expeditionary Forces and in 1918 created the Radio Intelligence Service for operations along the Mexican border. While the US Navy had established a modest codebreaking unit, it was also absorbed into Yardley's postwar civilian 'Black Chamber' in 1918.

The US Army and State Department continued to support Yardley until the termination of his 'Black Chamber' in 1929 following the bureaucratic intervention of Stimpson who disliked the interception and reading of 'a gentleman's' communications. The US Army's codebreaking capability was maintained, however, by the small Signal Intelligence Service of the Army Signal Corps under the direction of William F. Friedman. The US Navy re-established a cryptanalytic unit in 1924 as the 'Research Desk' under Commander Laurance F. Safford in the Code and Signal Section, OP-20-G, within the Office of Naval Communications. While emphasis was on the security of US military communications (COMSEC), both organisations developed radio intercept, radio direction finding and processing capabilities prior to WWII; they achieved particular successes against Japanese diplomatic communications. The exploitation success of their respective counterpart service communications had to await the shift of resources until after hostilities commenced. However, wartime successes by the USA and Britain proved the value of COMINT to military and political leaders and, as a result, both service organisation expanded greatly in terms of manpower resources and equipment.

Finally, the potentialities of expanding technical COMINT capabilities of the late 1940s could not always be realised. During the Korean War the quality of strategic intelligence derived from COMINT fell below that which had been provided in WWII. Consumers were disappointed and increasingly critical. By late 1951, AFSA had clashed with the service cryptologic agencies, with consumers, with the CIA, and with the State Department, although not all at one time nor with all on one issue. Despite the intentions, AFSA had in fact become a fourth military cryptologic agency.

On 4 November 1952, Major General Ralph J. Canine, USA, became the first Director, NSA.

The NSA was established on 4 November 1952 as a separate agency responsible directly to the Secretary of Defence. In addition, it was granted SIGINT operational control over the three Service Cryptologic (collection) Agencies (SCAs): the Army Security Agency, Naval Security Group Command, and Air Force Security Service.

In 1957 NSA consolidated its HQ operations at the Fort George G. Meade complex in Maryland. This is dominated by two high-rise buildings completed in 1986 and dedicated by then President Ronald Reagan in a special ceremony. Located midway between the cities of Baltimore, Washington DC, and Annapolis, near the communities of Odenton, Laurel and Columbia, the complex includes an operations building, a technical library and other facilities which house logistics and support activities. Other facilities include:

● Friendship Annex – Airport Square Linthicum, Maryland; connected to Ft. Meade and other Washington area facilities through the Washington Area Wideband System (WAWS), a coaxial cable network established in the mid-1970s;
● National Business Park – Ft. Meade, Maryland;
● Laboratory for Physical Sciences – University of Maryland College Park, where the NSA carries out work in the design and development of specialised chips for national security uses;
● Supercomputer Research Center – Bowie, Maryland.

The NSA is the centre of a global network of electronic interception networks, which include ECHELON, the UKUSA and numerous allied services that share their intelligence take with Fort Meade, and is now organised into the following sections:

The *SIGINT* or foreign intelligence mission of NSA/CSS involves the interception, processing, analysis, and dissemination of information derived from foreign electrical communications and other signals. SIGINT itself is composed of three elements: Communications Intelligence (COMINT), Electronics Intelligence (ELINT), and Telemetry Intelligence (TELINT). COMINT is intelligence information derived from the interception and analysis of foreign communications. ELINT is technical and intelligence information derived from electromagnetic radiations, such as radars. TELINT is technical and intelligence information derived from the interception, processing and analysis of foreign telemetry. The *COMSEC* mission protects US telecommunications and certain other communications from exploitation by foreign intelligence services and from unauthorised disclosure. COMSEC systems are provided by NSA to 18 government departments and agencies, including Defence, State, CIA, and FBI. The predominant user, however, is the Department of Defence. COMSEC is a mission separate from SIGINT, yet the dual SIGINT and COMSEC missions of NSA/CSS do have a symbiotic relationship, and enhance the performance of the other.

Central Security Service components
The Naval Security Group Command is the Navy component of the Central Security Service. The Army CSS component is the Intelligence and Security Command (INSCOM). INSCOM organisations which perform national SIGINT functions are being restructured from conventional OCONUS lines of sight and HF collection mission units into jointly manned organisations, at CONUS locations, with the access to enemy signals provided via remote collection technology and communications linkages.

Directorates and groups
The National Security Agency is believed to be organised into five Directorates, each of which consists of several groups or elements:

- *Operations Directorate* – responsible for SIGINT collection and processing;
- *Technology and Systems Directorate* – develops new technologies for SIGINT collection and processing;
- *Information Systems Security Directorate* – responsible for NSA's communications and information security missions;

- *Plans, Policy and Programs Directorate* – provides staff support and general direction for the Agency;
- *Support Services Directorate* – provides logistical and administrative support activities;
- *A Group – Former Soviet Bloc* – performs worldwide SIGINT operations at fixed sites and with assigned and attached mobile assets to collect against targets in the Former Soviet Bloc; maintains liaison with service CSS components on SIGINT operations of direct interest to this area of responsibility, under the SIGINT OPCON of the DIRNSA or the Chief, Central Security Service (CHCSS); current designation of this Group is uncertain;
- *B Group – Asia* – performs worldwide SIGINT operations at fixed sites and with assigned and attached mobile assets to collect against targets, including China, N Korea, and Vietnam; maintains liaison with service CSS components on SIGINT operations of direct interest to this area of responsibility, under the SIGINT OPCON of the DIRNSA or the Chief Central Security Service (CHCSS); current designation of this Group is uncertain;
- *G Group – Operations* – performs worldwide SIGINT operations at fixed sites and with assigned and attached mobile assets to collect against targets areas not covered by A and B Groups; maintains liaison with service CSS components on SIGINT operations of direct interest to this area of responsibility, under the SIGINT OPCON of the DIRNSA or the Chief, Central Security Service (CHCSS); current designation of this Group is uncertain;
- *K Group – Operations Research* – directs NSA Cryptologic research activities to provide theoretical and other support for all US Communications Security (COMSEC) and SIGINT activities; identity of this Group is tentative;
- *P Group – Production* – NSA's principal element for the production of finished SIGINT (ELINT and COMINT) products in support of other consumers in the intelligence community; provides signals intelligence research, retrieval and dissemination services for NSA programs, associated contractors and other government agencies and contractors;
- *W Group – Space* – implements operational control of space-based sensors; documents, maintains and implements operational requirements, monitors capabilities and co-ordinates activities for sensors; provides resource management for collection, transmission and processing of SIGINT derived from space-based sensors; monitors and performs analysis on sensor operations, system capabilities and

performance; manages technical service support (TSS) contracts to ensure operational support for ground stations; interfaces with NRO on system acquisition; co-ordinates and monitors system testing for space-based sensors, and interfaces with the Air Force Satellite Control Facility (SCF) for operational tasking; also co-ordinates and provides input on future sensor requirements.

Directors of NSA

- Lt. Gen. Ralph J. Canine, USA — November 1952–November 1956
- Lt. Gen. John A. Samford, USAF — November 1956–November 1960
- Vice Adm. Laurence H. Frost, USN — November 1960–June 1962
- Lt. Gen. Gordon A. Blake, USAF — July 1962–May 1965
- Lt. Gen. Marshall S. Carter, USA — June 1965–July 1969
- Vice Adm. Noel A. M. Gaylor, USN — August 1969–July 1972
- Lt. Gen. Samuel C. Phillips, USAF — August 1972–August 1973
- Lt. Gen. Lew Allen, Jr, USAF — August 1973–July 1977
- Vice Adm. Bobby Ray Inman, USN — July 1977–March 1981
- Lt. Gen. Lincoln D. Faurer, USAF — April 1981–April 1985
- Lt. Gen. William E. Odom, USA — May 1985–July 1988
- Vice Adm. William O. Studeman, USN — August 1988–April 1992
- Vice Adm. John M. McConnell, USN — May 1992–January 1996
- Lt. Gen. Kenneth A. Minihan, USAF — February 1996–March 1999
- Lt Gen. Michael V. Hayden, USAF — March 1999–

DIA (DEFENSE INTELLIGENCE AGENCY)

Established on 1 October 1961, the DIA finally provided the USA with one central authority to collate information from and direct the operations of the separate armed forces intelligence departments. The DIA later assumed responsibility for the Defence Attaché System on 1 July 1965.

The first major Agency-wide reorganisation occurred in November 1966 and was undertaken to streamline and improve the reaction time of the military intelligence production elements. An overwhelming number of requirements, particularly those resulting from US involvement in Vietnam, brought about these fundamental changes in internal management. Its HQ is situated within the Pentagon complex.

Analyst attention during 1967 was divided between US operations in Vietnam and other crises around the world. On the one hand, there were OPERATIONS CEDAR FALLS and JUNCTION CITY in SE Asia, plus the stand at Khe Sanh, while on the other, there was the Six-Day War between Egypt and Israel and continuing troubles in Africa, particularly Nigeria. Organisationally, the JCS delineated counter-intelligence responsibilities between the DIA and the Unified and Specified (U&S) Commands. Intelligence requirements reached an all-time high as a result of the 1968 Tet Offensive in Vietnam, N Korea's seizure of the Pueblo, and the Soviet invasion of Czechoslovakia. Resource cutbacks threatened the Agency, and the President's Blue Ribbon Defence Panel proposed structural and managerial changes in the DIA to deal with a situation in which the Agency had 'too many jobs and too many masters.'

The Soviet invasion of Afghanistan, the overthrow of the Iranian monarchy, and the taking of American hostages in the American Embassy in Teheran began a long period of DIA work in these areas. Furthermore, the Vietnamese takeover in Phnom Penh; the China–Vietnam border war; the overthrow of Amin in Uganda; the North–South Yemen dispute; troubles in Pakistan; Libya–Egypt border clashes; the Sandinista takeover in Nicaragua; and the Soviet movement of combat troops to Cuba during the signing of the Strategic Arms Limitations Treaty II – all served to increase intelligence requirements levied on the DIA. The Agency really came of age by focusing on the intelligence needs of field commanders as well as national-level decision-makers and by 1980, the DIA's products grew to include the annual Soviet Military Power. The DIA provided intelligence support to the newly established Rapid Deployment Force during OPERATION BRIGHT STAR, while analysts were preoccupied with Rhodesia (Zimbabwe), Iraq's attempts to seize Iranian oil fields and the resulting war, the assassination of Egyptian President Anwar Sadat, and civil war in El Salvador.

Events in the Middle East occupied the DIA's attention including the Iranian hostage release, the US downing of two Libyan jets over the Gulf of Sidra, two Iranian hijackings, and Iranian air raids on Kuwait. Terrorism, the Strategic Arms Reduction talks, and Intermediate-Range Nuclear Forces talks, a reordering of DoD Human Intelligence (HUMINT) activities, support for warfighting elements, Defence-wide intelligence planning, strengthening the J-2 role, and DIA personnel/career improvements were issues requiring attention during the year.

A significantly larger number of hijackings – notably, of a TWA airliner by radical Shiites and the *Achille Lauro* cruise ship by the PLO

– plus numerous bombings, kidnappings, murders, and other acts of terrorism led to characterising 1985 as the 'Year of the Terrorist'. During 1987 the DIA Persian Gulf working group tracked on a 24-hour basis all developments in the region and provided CENTCOM with an assortment of intelligence products. OPERATION EARNEST WILL and incidents such as the Iraqi rocket attack on the USS *Stark*, the destruction of Iranian oil platforms, and Iranian attacks on Kuwaiti oil tankers were covered in detail.

With Iraq's August 1990 invasion of Kuwait, the DIA immediately launched an extensive, 24-hour intelligence effort that resulted in perhaps one of the finest examples of intelligence support to operational forces in modern times. All phases of the Agency's workforce and more than 2,000 people contributed to OPERATION DESERT SHIELD. Highlighting DIA support to OPERATION DESERT STORM was around-the-clock intelligence monitoring and daily tailored intelligence products dispatched to coalition forces. As a result, it is claimed, no combat commander in history ever had as full and complete a view of his adversary as did US and coalition field commanders during DESERT STORM. The Agency has played a leading role in providing vital and timely intelligence to the campaigns in the Balkans, Somalia, Afghanistan and the Middle East. By 2002 the organisation of the DIA included:

- *Directorate for Intelligence* (J2) – provides intelligence support to the Chairman, JCS; the Office of the Secretary of Defense; and the Director of Central Intelligence;
- *National Military Intelligence Production Centre* (NMIPC) – produces and manages the production of military intelligence throughout the General Defense Intelligence Program (GDIP) community in response to the needs of DOD and non-DOD agencies;
- *National Military Intelligence Collection Centre* (NMICC) – provides centralised management of DOD all-source collection activities and also operates the Defense Attaché System;
- *Central MASINT Office* – an adjunct to the NMICC, and the focus for national and DOD MASINT matters;
- *National Military Intelligence Support Centre* (NMISC) – provides information services to the DIA and the IC. These services include ADP support; systems development and maintenance; communications engineering, operations and maintenance; information systems security; imagery and photo processing; and intelligence reference, publications and printing.

● *Directorate for Scientific and Technical Intelligence* – composed of four analytical divisions:
  ○ *Weapons and Systems Division* – employs professional military and civilian aerospace, electronics and general engineers; they are responsible for analysing all ballistic missile systems, all aerodynamic systems, all naval systems and all ground forces systems;
  ○ *Strategic Defences, Command and Control & Space Division* – employs professional military and civilian aerospace and electronics engineers and general physicists; they are responsible for analysing all foreign strategic defence systems, command and control systems, electronic warfare systems and space systems;
  ○ *Missile and Space Intelligence Centre* – The Army's Missile Intelligence Agency serves as the principal adviser in matters pertaining to the acquisition, production, maintenance, and dissemination of Scientific and Technical Intelligence (S&TI), in Intelligence pertaining to missile and space systems;
  ○ *Global Analysis Division* – as a focal point for analysis, production and co-ordination of intelligence support throughout the Intelligence Community in response to terrorism insurgencies, narcotics interdiction, and other asymmetrical conflict issues.

NRO (NATIONAL RECONNAISSANCE OFFICE)

Created on 25 August 1960 following months of intense controversy between the White House, CIA, the US Air Force and the Department of Defense over the allocation of responsibilities for satellite reconnaissance, by 1961 the Agency and the US Air Force had established a working relationship for overhead reconnaissance systems through a central administrative office, whose director reported to the Secretary of Defense. By informal agreement, the US Air Force provided launchers, bases and the recovery capability for reconnaissance systems, while the Agency was responsible for research, development, contracting, and security.

NRO operations

The NRO is the quintessential expression of the Cold War and one of the outstanding successes. The well over quarter of a trillion dollars spent on the NRO over the past 40 years has been by far the most productive investment by the US intelligence community. Now that the Cold War has ended, the entire national security establishment is confronted with the imperative of restructuring to meet the needs of the novel and profoundly different security environment of a 'Warm

War': terrorism, global narcotics crime and asymmetrical warfare. As the NRO was so uniquely a response to the peculiarities of the Soviet adversary, it may be anticipated that the challenge of its restructuring will be particularly difficult.

The NRO's new permanent HQ is situated in the Westfields Facility Westfields International Centre 14225 Leesburg Highway Fairfax, Virginia. While its main operation facilities include those at Onizuka Air Force Base, Sunnyvale, California which is the primary control facility for NRO intelligence satellite platforms through the Satellite Control Network and the Communications Electronics Evaluation Test Activity or CEETA at Buelah Road, Ft. Belvoir, Virginia is the primary ground station for imaging intelligence satellites, from which imagery is relayed to the National Photographic Interpretation Centre. The Buckley Air National Guard Base, Aurora, Colorado controls high Earth orbit JUMPSEAT and TRUMPET signals intelligence, HERITAGE measurement and signature intelligence, and Satellite Data System data relay satellites from a facility co-located with the Defense Support Program Aerospace Data Facility at Buckley.

FBI (FEDERAL BUREAU OF INVESTIGATION)

A major reorganisation of the FBI is under way in the wake of the terrorist outrages of 11 September 2001 and will involve the wholesale restructuring of the counter-terrorist and domestic surveillance capabilities of the Bureau. The major elements of the first phase of the HQ reorganisation include the creation of four new Executive Assistant Director positions to oversee key FBI functions:

● *Executive Assistant Director for Criminal Investigations* – headed by Ruben Garcia, Jr, 23-year FBI veteran who was formerly Assistant Director of the Criminal Investigative Division;
● *Executive Assistant Director for Counter-terrorism/Counter-Intelligence* – headed by Dale L. Watson, currently Assistant Director for the Counter-terrorism Division; Mr Watson entered the Bureau in 1978 and has served continually in intelligence and counter-terrorism roles since 1982; in 1996, he was named Deputy Chief of the CIA's Counter-terrorist Centre at CIA HQ;
● *Executive Assistant Director for Law Enforcement Services* – headed by 23-year veteran Kathleen L. McChesney; currently Assistant Director of the FBI Training Division;
● *Executive Assistant Director for Administration* – headed by Robert J. Chiaradio, currently an assistant to FBI Director Robert Mueller.

FBI divisions and offices will realign under one of these four Executive Assistant Directors who report through the offices of the Director/Deputy Director. This reorganisation will greatly increase efficiency, accountability and oversight, and most importantly speed of reaction to terrorist incidents.

Two new divisions have also been created to increase emphasis on computer-facilitated crimes and security: the *Cybercrime Division* will address intellectual property investigations, as well as hi-tech and computer crimes; the *Security Division* will be responsible for ensuring the integrity of FBI employees, contractors, visitors, information systems and facilities. The Investigative Services Division has been disbanded and its important responsibilities and assets integrated into the new *Intelligence Office* charged with enhancing analytical and intelligence capabilities, particularly in the critical counter-terrorism and counter-intelligence areas.

The FBI originated from a force of Special Agents created in 1908 by Attorney General Charles Bonaparte during the Presidency of Theodore Roosevelt. Today, most Americans take for granted that the country needs a federal investigative service, but in 1908 the establishment of this kind of agency at a national level was highly controversial. The US Constitution is based on 'federalism': a national government with juris-diction over matters that crossed boundaries, like interstate commerce and foreign affairs, with all other powers reserved to the states. By 1907 the Department of Justice most frequently called upon Secret Service 'operatives' to conduct investigations.

With the April 1917 entry of the USA into WWI during Woodrow Wilson's administration, the Bureau's work was increased again. As a result of the war, the Bureau acquired responsibility for the Espionage, Selective Service and Sabotage Acts. The years from 1921 to 1933 were sometimes called the 'lawless years' because of the levels of organised crime and the public disregard for Prohibition, which made it illegal to sell or import intoxicating beverages.

The FBI also participated in intelligence collection throughout most of its existence. Here the Technical Laboratory played a pioneering role. Its highly skilled and inventive staff co-operated with engineers, scientists, and cryptographers in other agencies to enable the USA to penetrate and sometimes control the flow of information from the belligerents in the Western Hemisphere. Sabotage investigations were another FBI responsibility. In June 1942, a major, yet unsuccessful, attempt at sabotage was made on American soil. Two German submarines let off four saboteurs each at Amagansett, Long Island, and

Ponte Vedra Beach, Florida. These men had been trained by Germany in explosives, chemistry, secret writing, and how to blend into American surroundings. While still in German clothes, the New York group encountered a Coast Guard sentinel patrolling the beach, who ultimately allowed them to pass. However, afraid of capture, saboteur George Dasch turned himself in – and assisted the FBI in locating and arresting the rest of the team. All were tried shortly afterwards by a military tribunal and found guilty. Six who did not co-operate with the US Government were executed a few days later. The others were sentenced to life imprisonment, but were returned to Germany after the war. The swift capture of these Nazi saboteurs helped to allay fear of Axis subversion and bolstered Americans' faith in the FBI.

Even before US entry into the war, the FBI uncovered a major espionage ring. This group, the Frederick Duquesne spy ring, was the largest one discovered up to that time. The FBI was assisted by a loyal American with German relatives who acted as a double agent. For nearly two years the FBI ran a radio station for him, learning what Germany was sending to its spies in the USA while controlling the information that was being transmitted to Germany. The investigation led to the arrest and conviction of 33 spies. War for the USA began on 7 December 1941, when Japanese armed forces attacked ships and facilities at Pearl Harbor, Hawaii. On 7 and 8 December, the FBI arrested previously identified aliens who threatened national security and turned them over to military or immigration authorities.

Separated from Bureau rolls, these Agents, with the help of FBI Legal Attachés, composed the Special Intelligence Service (SIS) in Latin America. Established by President Roosevelt in 1940, the SIS was to provide information on Axis activities in S America and to destroy its intelligence and propaganda networks. Several hundred thousand Germans or German descendants and numerous Japanese lived in S America. They provided pro-Axis pressure and cover for Axis communications facilities. Nevertheless, in every S American country, the SIS was instrumental in bringing about a situation in which, by 1944, continued support for the Nazis became intolerable or impractical.

In April 1945, President Roosevelt died and Vice President Harry Truman took office as President. Before the end of the month, Hitler committed suicide and the German commander in Italy surrendered. Although the May 1945 surrender of Germany ended the war in Europe, war continued in the Pacific until 14 August 1945.

The world that the FBI faced in September 1945 was very different from the world of 1939 when the war began. American isolationism had effectively ended and, economically, the USA had become the world's most powerful nation. The US fear of Communist expansion was not limited to Europe. By 1947, ample evidence existed that pro-Soviet individuals had infiltrated the American Government. In June 1945, the FBI raided the offices of *Amerasia*, a magazine concerned with the Far East, and discovered a large number of classified State Department documents. Several months later the Canadians arrested 22 people for trying to steal atomic secrets. Previously, Americans felt secure behind their monopoly of the atomic bomb. Fear of a Russian bomb now came to dominate American thinking. The Soviets detonated their own bomb in 1949.

Counteracting the Communist threat became a paramount focus of government at all levels, as well as the private sector. While US foreign policy concentrated on defeating Communist expansion abroad, many US citizens sought to defeat the Communist threat at home. The American Communist Party worked through front organisations or influenced other Americans who agreed with their current propaganda ('fellow travellers'). Several factors converged to undermine domestic Communism in the 1950s. Situations like the Soviet defeat of the Hungarian rebellion in 1956 caused many members to abandon the American Communist Party. However, the FBI also played a role in diminishing Party influence.

By 1971, with few exceptions, the most extreme members of the antiwar movement concentrated on more peaceable, yet still radical tactics, such as the clandestine publication of *The Pentagon Papers*. However, the violent Weathermen and its successor groups continued to challenge the FBI into the 1980s. Therefore, the FBI addressed the threats from the militant 'New Left' as it had those from Communists in the 1950s and the KKK in the 1960s. It used both traditional investigative techniques and counter-intelligence programmes or Cointelpro, to counteract domestic terrorism and conduct investigations of individuals and organisations that threatened terrorist violence. Wiretapping and other intrusive techniques were discouraged by Hoover in the mid-1960s and eventually were forbidden completely unless they conformed to the Omnibus Crime Control Act. Hoover formally terminated all 'Cointelpro' operations on 28 April 1971. FBI Director J. Edgar Hoover died on 2 May 1972, just shy of 48 years as the FBI Director. He was 77. The next day his body lay in state in the Rotunda of the Capitol, an honour accorded only 21 other Americans.

Three days after Director Kelley's appointment, top aides in the Nixon Administration resigned amid charges of White House efforts to obstruct justice in the Watergate case. Vice President Spiro T. Agnew resigned in October, following charges of tax evasion. Then, following impeachment hearings that were broadcast over television to the American public throughout 1974, President Nixon resigned on 9 August 1974. Vice President Gerald R. Ford was sworn in as President that same day. In granting an unconditional pardon to ex-President Nixon one month later, he vowed to heal the nation.

Director Kelley similarly sought to restore public trust in the FBI and in law enforcement. He instituted numerous policy changes that targeted the training and selection of FBI and law enforcement leaders, the procedures of investigative intelligence collection, and the prioritising of criminal programmes.

In 1978 Director Kelley resigned and was replaced by former federal Judge William H. Webster. At the time of his appointment, in 1982, following an explosion of terrorist incidents worldwide, Webster made counter-terrorism a fourth national priority. He also expanded FBI efforts in the three others: foreign counter-intelligence, organised crime and white-collar crime.

The FBI solved so many espionage cases during the mid-1980s that the press dubbed 1985 'the year of the spy'. The most serious espionage damage uncovered by the FBI was perpetrated by the John Walker spy ring and by former National Security Agency employee, William Pelton.

In 1984, the FBI acted as lead agency for security of the Los Angeles Olympics. In the course of its efforts to anticipate and prepare for acts of terrorism and street crime, it built important bridges of interaction and co-operation with local, state and other federal agencies, as well as agencies of other countries. It also unveiled the FBI's Hostage Rescue Team as a domestic force capable of responding to complex hostage situations such as tragically occurred in Munich at the 1972 games.

Perhaps as a result of the Bureau's emphasis on combating terrorism, such acts within the USA decreased dramatically during the 1980s. In 1986, Congress had expanded FBI jurisdiction to cover terrorist acts against US citizens outside the US boundaries.

In the summer of 1994, Freeh led a delegation of high-level diplomatic and federal law enforcement officials to meet with senior officials of 11 European nations on international crime issues.

At the outset, Richard Holbrooke, US Ambassador to Germany, declared, 'This is the evolving American foreign policy. Law

Enforcement is at the forefront of our national interest in this part of the world.' Meetings were held with officials of Russia, Germany, the Czech Republic, the Slovak Republic, Hungary, Poland, the Ukraine, Austria, Lithuania, Latvia and Estonia. On 4 July 1994, Director Freeh officially announced the historic opening of an FBI Legal Attaché Office in Moscow, the old seat of Russian Communism. He also mounted aggressive programmes in specific criminal areas. During the years 1993–96, these efforts paid off in successful investigations as diverse as the World Trade Center bombing in New York City and the Archer Daniels Midland international price-fixing conspiracies. In addition, there were the attempted theft of Schering-Plough and Merck pharmaceutical trade secrets and the arrests of Mexican drug trafficker Juan Garcia-Abrego and Russian crime boss Vyacheslav Ivankov.

The new Director of the FBI, Robert Mueller, faces a huge upsurge in both international terrorism and globalised crime. At the same time he has to preside over the largest peacetime reorganisation of the bureau, increased demands for international co-operation and live up to both the political and public expectations of his nation.

The Directors of the FBI and its predecessors

1.	Stanley W. Finch	July 1908–1912
2.	Alexander Bruce Bielaski	April 1912–1919
3.	William E. Allen (Acting)	February 1919–July 1919
4.	William J. Flynn	July 1919–1921
5.	William J. Burns	August 1921–1924
6.	J. Edgar Hoover	May 1924–1972
7.	L. Patrick Gray (Acting)	May 1972–1973
8.	William D. Ruckelshaus (Acting)	April 1973–July 1973
9.	Clarence M. Kelley	July 1973–1978
10.	William H. Webster	February 1978–1987
11.	John E. Otto (Acting)	May 1987–November 1987
12.	William S. Sessions	November. 1987–1993
13.	Floyd I. Clarke (Acting)	July 1993–September 1993
14.	Louis J. Freeh	September 1993–2001
15.	Thomas J. Pickard (Acting)	June 2001–September 2001
16.	Robert S. Mueller	September 2001–

UNITED STATES, SPECIAL FORCES The 1st Special Forces Operational Detachment, otherwise known as Delta Force, is the USA's first dedicated national intervention, counter-revolutionary warfare and Special Operations unit.

Activated in November 1977, it was largely the brainchild of Charles Beckwith, an experienced Special Forces officer who had served with the British 22nd Regiment Special Air Service during the 1960s.

Organised and indeed trained along SAS lines, Delta Force was soon to develop a very distinct ethos and character of its own with the initial intake being from the 10th Special Forces Group (Airborne) at Camp Dawson, WVa. To this were soon to be added a sprinkling of US Army Rangers and volunteers from other Special Forces Groups and in May 1978 the first 73 trainees made it into the newly operational force.

Delta's first major operation would have been the attempted rescue of the hostages held by Iranian militants in the occupied US embassy in Tehran on 25 April 1979. Whatever may be said about the standard of the overall planning and execution of the operation, which has justly deserved severe criticism, it cannot be similarly levelled at Delta's training and planning which was meticulous and would have stood a good chance of success in other circumstances. Delta Force has gone on to be used in Special Force operations as part of OPERATION URGENT FURY, the US invasion of Grenada in 1983 and, during OPERATION JUST CAUSE, the US invasion of Panama in December 1989. Here they successfully carried out OPERATION ACID GAMBIT, the rescue of the US citizen Kurt Muse, being held hostage in the Carcel Modelo Prison. In the Gulf War (1990–91) they were covertly deployed within Iraq itself, tracing and destroying SCUD missile launchers. And as part of Task Force Ranger, the US intervention in Somalia (1992–93), Delta Force were called upon to carry out difficult and dangerous clandestine operations within rebel held areas of the capital Mogadishu. Delta Force has also seen widespread service during the recent Balkan wars (1992–2000), in operations to track down and capture suspected war criminals in Croatia, Bosnia and Kosovo. Delta Force were also to be the first regular troops to see combat in Afghanistan when specialist teams were inserted prior to the beginning of the air campaign in October 2001. In common with other elements of the Special Operations Command, Delta is expected to have a significant role to play in counter-terrorist operations around the world over the next few years.

The Delta Force's HQ is at Fort Bragg, NC and its training is of the very highest standard, providing its personnel with extraordinary levels of physical fitness, mental toughness and motivation. All aspects of modern special forces techniques are practised regularly until they become instinctive: combat shooting, sniping, the 'House of Horror', Delta's own version of the SAS 'Killing House', hostage rescue, anti-hijacking and VIP protection. Other techniques include heliborne insertion, HAHO (High Altitude-High Opening) and HALO (High Altitude-Low Opening) parachuting, unarmed combat, combat swimming, demolition and sabotage, and training to survive and operate effectively in all combat environments, jungle, desert, arctic, mountain, riverine, urban and built-up city areas. It trains and operates regularly with other similar units from around the world, in particular the British SAS, German GSG9, French GIGN and the Israeli Sayeret Matkyal.

It has access to a huge range of high-technology surveillance, electronic warfare, communications and intelligence equipment; it is also provided with the finest logistic, communications and transport back-up possible from the US Army, US Air Force, US Marine Corps and US Navy and other Federal agencies. It liaises very closely with the Central Intelligence Agency and other organisations within the US Government's intelligence community.

The Delta Force has access to a complete arsenal of US and foreign weapons and explosives, favoured arms being the 7.65mm PPK, 9mm P7 and Browning HP automatic pistols, 9mm MP5 and 9mm Uzi sub-machine guns, 5.56mm M16A1 automatic rifles and the CAR-15 carbine version. Remington 40XB sniper rifles, .5 Barrett M82 long-range sniper rifles, H&K 21 machine guns, 7.62mm M60 machine guns, 40mm M79/M203 grenade launchers and an eye-opening array of unusual and exotic weaponry.

The Delta Force provides the USA with a first-rate national intervention anti-terrorist force, but is only part of a much larger Special Forces community.

The US Army has a highly covert unit, the *ISA (Intelligence Support Activity)* which draws its personnel from the US Navy SEALs and the Army's own Special Forces. With some 200 personnel, it is tasked to provide clandestine intelligence for special operations, including pathfinder units and providing guides armed with local knowledge, communication specialists, deep penetration experts, and with a small team of Commandos.

It operates closely with Delta Force, while the US Navy's *SEAL* 6 unit, established in November 1986, actually forms part of the Delta Force. Similar in operation and training to the British Royal Marines' 'Commachio' unit, it is tasked to protect offshore oil installation and other highly classified potential terrorist targets and has developed a close working relationship with both the British SAS and the Royal Marines Special Boat Squadron (SBS). The *US Special Operations Command,* formed in 1980, controls a range of units that include five

Regular and four Reserve Special Forces groups (the Green Berets). These groups provide highly effective elite infantry, more in the style of the French Foreign Legion's specialist 2nd Regiment than that of the British SAS. Created during the Korean War (1950–53), 10th Group (Airborne) was the first unit to be raised by Col. Aaron Bank at Fort Bragg, NC and adopted the Green Beret in honour of the British WWII Commandos.

They have given honourable service in many campaigns, the most famous being Vietnam, and the latest being Colombia where the 'Green Berets' are training the Colombian Army to combat not only the FARC anti-Government Guerrillas, but also their Drug-cartel paymasters.

By 1969 seven such *Special Force Groups* had been formed, the 1st, 3rd, 5th, 6th, 7th and 10th, and although there has been some downsizing there are today four operational groups, 1st HQ at Fort Lewis,Wa, with 1 battalion in Okinawa, 5th HQ at Fort Bragg, NC,7th HQ at Fort Benning, Ga and 10th HQ at Fort Devens, Ma with 1 battalion at Bad Tolz, in Germany. Other units within the Special Operations Command include the *75th Ranger Regiment*, reactivated as 'The Rangers' at Fort Benning, Ga in 1975 with two battalions, a third being raised in 1984 when the official title of the 75th Regiment was actually given.

The Special Operations Aviation Brigade and 160th Aviation Battalion 'The Night Stalkers' equipped with stealth helicopters, the 122nd Special Intelligence Signals Battalion and finally the 4th PSYOP Group (Psychological warfare) with four battalions.

USA, SPIES AND TRAITORS

For many years following the end of WWII, most spies and traitors appeared to have either a British or central European accent; however it has become increasingly obvious that the USA has had more than its fair share of security disasters. Indeed by 2002 a new breed of young Americans began to appear whose rejection of their nation did not revolve around money, sexual blackmail or political beliefs. A dedication to Islamic extremism was claimed by *John Walker* when captured in N Afghanistan in late 2001 while fighting for the Taliban against Special Force soldiers from his homeland. The list of recent US traitors is surprisingly long and includes *George Trofimoff*, a retired Army Reserve colonel, who was accused in 2000 of spying for the Soviet Union and Russia for a quarter of a century. He is the highest-ranking US military officer ever charged with espionage. He allegedly photographed US documents and passed the film to KGB agents, and was later recruited into the KGB.

In 1997 *Earl Pitts*, who was stationed at the FBI Academy in Quantico, Va., was sentenced to 27 years in prison after admitting he spied for Moscow during and after the Cold War. CIA Officer *Harold James Nicholson* was arrested by the FBI in November 1996 and charged with committing espionage on behalf of Russia. Nicholson was arrested at a Washington airport en route to a clandestine meeting in Europe with his Russian intelligence handlers. At the time of his arrest, he was carrying rolls of exposed film which contained Secret and Top Secret information. In March 1997 Nicholson pleaded guilty to the charges and was sentenced to 23 years in prison.

Aldrich H. Ames, a CIA counter-intelligence official, and his wife, Rosario, pleaded guilty in 1994 to spying for the Soviet Union in the most damaging espionage case in US history. Ames passed information to the Soviets from 1985 to 1994, including the identities of US agents. He is blamed for the deaths of at least nine US agents in the Soviet Union, and for disclosing US counter-intelligence techniques. Former CIA officer *Edward Lee Howard* fled the country in 1985 as the FBI investigated allegations that he was spying for the Soviet Union. Howard, accused of disclosing the identities of CIA agents in Moscow, still lives there. Former CIA clerk *Sharon Scranage* pleaded guilty in 1985 to disclosing the names of US agents to her Ghanaian boyfriend. Scranage served the CIA in Ghana. FBI agent *Richard W. Miller*, a Los Angeles agent, was arrested in 1984 on spying charges and sentenced to twenty years in prison. The sentence was reduced to 13 years, and he was released in 1994 after serving only nine years. Former CIA agent *David H. Barnett* pleaded guilty in 1980 to spying for the Soviet Union between 1976 and 1979 while based in Indonesia. The first current or former CIA agent convicted of espionage, Barnett admitted exposing the identities of 30 US agents.

Retired Navy Warrant Officer *John A. Walker Jr.* pleaded guilty in 1985 along with his son, Navy Seaman Michael L. Walker, 22, to charges of spying for the Soviet Union. Walker admitted passing secrets to the Soviets while he was a shipboard communications officer and after his retirement by recruiting his son, brother and a friend to provide fresh information. Walker's brother, Arthur Walker, a retired Navy lieutenant commander, was convicted in 1985 of stealing secret documents from a defence contractor and giving them to John A. Walker Jr. for delivery to the Soviets. Another member of the ring, *Jerry A. Whitworth*, a Navy chief petty officer, was convicted in 1986 of passing secret Navy codes to Walker. Former CIA officer *Edward Lee Howard* fled the country in 1985 as the FBI was investigating him for spying for the Soviet Union. Howard, who is accused of disclosing the identities of CIA agents in Moscow, turned up in the Soviet Union in 1986, where he still lives. He eluded FBI surveillance of his home in Santa Fe, NM, where he worked for the New Mexico Legislature. The CIA withheld from the FBI its suspicions about Howard, who had been fired in 1983 after failing a lie-detector test.

Former National Security Agency employee *Ronald W. Pelton* was convicted in 1986 of selling top-secret signals intelligence information to the Soviet Union. *Jonathan Jay Pollard*, a civilian Navy intelligence analyst, pleaded guilty in 1986 to spying for Israel. He is serving a life sentence, which President Clinton refused to commute despite pleas from the Israeli government, while Foreign Service officer *Felix Bloch* was suspended in 1989 by the State Department after reportedly being monitored by video camera passing a suitcase to a Soviet agent in Paris. Bloch, who was once chargé d'affaires at the US Embassy in Vienna, was not charged with espionage, but was fired in 1990 on the grounds that he lied to investigators.

UNWITTING AGENT An agent or source who provides information without knowing that the ultimate recipient is an intelligence service or without knowing that the recipient is not the service he believes it to be.

V

VASSELL, (William) John (Christopher) (1924–)   He worked as a clerk in the Admiralty offices and was sent as an assistant to the naval attaché at the British Embassy in Moscow in 1954. Soviet Intelligence officers learned that Vassall was an enthusiastic homosexual and quickly compromised him, showing him photos they had taken of him and other homosexuals they had sent to seduce him. Vassall became a Soviet spy in 1955, stealing classified information from the Embassy and passing these to his Soviet handlers. Returning to London in 1956, Vassall was assigned to the highly sensitive Admiralty's Naval Intelligence Division and later both to the office of the Civil Lord of the Admiralty and the Military Branch, where he continued spying for the Soviets. He was paid so well that he was able to rent an apartment in the exclusive Dolphin Square district, one that he furnished with expensive antiques. In meetings with his Soviet controller, Nikolai Borisovich Rodin (alias Korovin) during a period of almost four years Vassall handed over thousands of highly classified documents on British and NATO Naval policy and weapons development. Interestingly, Rodin was also the handler for another British traitor, George Blake.

Vassall was promoted in 1959 to a position of greater security, one that allowed him to steal Admiralty secrets concerning radar, newly developed torpedoes and anti-submarine devices. Further, he provided the Soviets with fleet operational orders and communications, as well as classified publications. When the Portland Spy Case broke and Gordon Lonsdale, Helen and Peter Kroger, Harry Houghton and Ethel Gee were exposed as spies stealing Admiralty secrets, his Soviet controllers ordered Vassall to cease operations only to resume his activities some months later. He was able to secure details of the new Invincible class carriers being built by the British and this information greatly aided the Soviets in the development of their helicopter carriers, Moskva and Leningrad.

In 1962, MI5 finally caught on to Vassall when the British Embassy in Moscow reported that the Soviets were in possession of information that could only have come from the British Admiralty Office in London. Several persons in the office were investigated and the hunt narrowed down to Vassall who was arrested by Special Branch officers. One hundred and seventy-six classified documents were found hidden in a secret drawer in his apartment along with a miniature Praktina document copying camera and a Minox. He was sentenced to serve 18 years in prison but was paroled in 1973. Vassall expressed surprise in later years that, as an obvious homosexual, he was not identified as a potential security risk when he was posted to Moscow in 1954.

There is some reason to believe that the Soviet intelligence service 'burned' Vassall, deliberately exposing him to divert attention from at least one other and far more important 'mole', who would have remained active and probably received promotion within the soon to be formed Ministry of Defence.

VATICAN The Vatican's involvement in clandestine affairs has often been underestimated, no more so than during the closing stages of WWII when Pius the XII had a small department largely devoted to 'obscure' financial affairs and criminal links with the Mafia. It had played no small part with the organised crime bosses in the USA in creating what eventually turned out to be highly embarrassing links between US Intelligence and the Mafia. However, in 1943 and 1944 they proved to be highly useful during the allied invasions of both Sicily and Italy and in the eventual defeat of the powerful Communist movement in postwar Italy.

The role the Vatican was to play in providing safe houses, Papal passports and an escape network for Nazi war criminals is public knowledge. The activities of the Catholic Church in providing 'legends' or new identities for those Nazis both Britain and the USA intelligence services 'needed' to protect from revengeful Jewish hit squads or the Nuremberg War Crimes Trial investigators are far less well known. It is an area of intelligence history, which even in 2002, remains largely shrouded in an embarrassed cloud of mystery.

However, certain senior and rather more liberal Vatican officials were to play a valuable part in running the so-called 'ratlines' that enabled many allied prisoners-of-war to escape from occupied Europe. The British created a secret organisation in Rome under the control of Sam Derry as a part of Norman Crockett's MI9 'escape and evasion' organisation and this remained effectively controlled by SIS from their Broadway intelligence HQ.

The British minister to the Vatican, Sir d'Arcy Osborne, firmly supported Derry's activities and gained the support, in confidence, of

Giovanni Montini. As head of the Vatican's secretariat for international affairs and at the very heart of Pope Pius XII's wartime clandestine affairs bureau, Montini proved a valuable ally. Montini's assistance was in no small way assured by Osborne's assistant at the Vatican, Hugh Montgomery, who helped run the escape lines with Derry.

Montgomery, a devout Catholic, was also the homosexual lover of Giovanni Montini, the future much loved and respected Pope John Paul I. Montini's wartime romance with Montgomery and his evident support for the allies made him detested by right-wing elements in the Vatican. His evident wish to clean up the Vatican's 'complicated' financial dealings, a determination to break its ties with organised crime and modernise the Church, was to gain him yet more enemies.

The suggestions that often surface that his tragic and untimely death so soon after his election as Pope was not a natural one are given added interest by events both preceding and following his death. The 'suicide' under a London bridge of Robert Calvi, a man with close links to the Vatican Bank and the strange case of Cardinal Paul Marchinkus's financial impropriety, the Vatican's chief financial controller, are both among a number of events that have been rumoured to be linked in some way with John Paul I's death.

The British Secret Intelligence Service (MI6) is certain to have had an extensive file on Giovanni Montini from as early as 1944. Indeed Sam Derry, a close friend of Montini's lover, Hugh Montgomery, went on to join SIS as full-time officer after the war, eventually first replacing Norman Crockett as head of MI9 and later working in the Southern European department of the service.

SIS (MI6) would have been able to create a substantial dossier on the future Pope's past activities and those of his close associates, particularly after the absorption of the wartime SOE in 1946 and its close relationship with many of the OSS officers who joined the CIA in 1947, both of which organisations had maintained close relations with both organised crime and the Catholic Church in Italy. It would, indeed is, of considerable interest to discover just how much Western Intelligence Service also knew about the circumstances surrounding the final tragic days of John Paul I.

VELA   US Satellite series developed in early 1960s to detect nuclear explosions.

VENEZUELA   *DISIP Direccion de Sequridad e Inteliqencia Policial*. The Directorate of Intelligence and Prevention Services.

Controlled by the Ministry of Interior, DISIP's nationwide

jurisdiction includes the investigation of crimes involving espionage, subversion, narcotics and arms smuggling. DISIP's paramilitary responsibilities include operations against terrorists and other potentially violent groups, including organised crime. The organisation maintains its headquarters in Caracas, with field offices in principal cities throughout the country. Human rights abuse by the Venezuelan Intelligence services has been widespread and torture not unusual, however it has decreased somewhat in more recent years. The DISIP maintains close contact with the Intelligence services of Colombia, Peru and of course the United States.

DISIP were believed to have been deeply involved in a CIA anti-drug program being run in Venezuela which ended up with a ton of cocaine being illegally shipped into the United States by CIA staff in 1990. The incident admitted in 1993 resulted in one CIA officer resigning and a second being disciplined. US Government officials said that the joint CIA–DISIP force was headed by Gen. Ramon Guillen Davila and that the ranking CIA officer was Mark McFarlin, who had worked with anti-guerrilla forces in El Salvador in the 1980s. The mission had been to infiltrate the Colombian gangs that ship cocaine to the United States. In December 1989, officials of the United States Drug Enforcement Agency said McFarlin and the CIA chief of station in Venezuela, Jim Campbell, met with the drug agency's attaché in Venezuela, Annabelle Grimm, to discuss a proposal to allow hundreds of pounds of cocaine to be shipped to the United States through Venezuela in an operation intended to win the confidence of the Colombian traffickers. Unlike so-called 'controlled shipments' that take place in criminal investigations, shipments that end with arrests and the confiscation of the drugs, these were to be 'uncontrolled shipments', officials of the drug agency said. The cocaine would enter the United States without being seized, so as to allay all suspicion. The idea was to gather as much intelligence as possible on members of the drug gangs. Although a thousand pounds of cocaine was eventually recovered, some two thousand pounds at least was not. The suspicion remains that this was simply another of the numerous occasions on which the CIA was guilty of a deep and sinister involvement in the South American drugs trade.

Military Intelligence Division (MID)
It has intelligence units assigned and deployed in the five geographically defined military regions. Most of its personnel are attached to Military Region One, headquartered in Caracas. While a battalion-sized unit services with each of the other Military Regions;

Two, Three, Four and Five with headquarters in San Cristóbal, Maracaibo, San Fernando and Ciudad Bolívar, respectively.

VENLO INCIDENT   Few other espionage events in WWII proved to be as embarrassing for British intelligence as the 'Venlo Incident' of 1939 in the Netherlands. Not only were two top British Intelligence Officers snared by German intelligence but also their superiors, such as Claude Dansey, deputy chief of SIS under Graham Stewart Menzies, had their reputations seriously damaged.

SIS (MI6) had long searched for a German underground that might be able to overthrow the dictatorship of Adolf Hitler. Two of Dansey's top SIS officers, Captain Sigismund Payne Best from the secret Z organisation and Major R.H. Stevens under traditional and therefore known cover of a PCO or Passport Control Officer at the British Embassy in the Hague, attempted to infiltrate what they thought to be a genuine German resistance movement. Tricked, by a well-prepared German operation conceived by Walter Schlenberg, into accepting a false conspiracy story, the two British officers arrived at about 3.30 p.m. in a large Buick motorcar and were promptly ambushed and seized by the German Security team.

Best and Stevens were held throughout the war and, to varying extents, co-operated with their German captors, though in neither case was this pursued by the British authorities on their return after liberation. The Venlo Incident was a tactical victory for German intelligence, one which cruelly exposed the lack of security within the SIS. Dansey, of course, was the real villain; he had used his top agents like pawns, throwing them away on a madcap scheme. His superior, Menzies, who became chief of SIS a short time later when Hugh Sinclair died, commendably took responsibility for the fiasco at Venlo in order to try to protect the service from further damaging infighting.

VENONA TRANSCRIPTS   Venona is a name that was applied to a set of translations that were made from NKVD and GRU messages that were solved by the Army. The Security Agency started work on this in 1943 and continued until 1980. During that period the translations that were made pertaining to spying were given a covername of Venona. In fact, Venona was the third covername that had been given to these same messages. The Soviet messages were obtained primarily during the war through censorship, which required the cable companies to file copies of all incoming and outgoing messages with the US government, at Arlington Hall, which was the US Army's cryptanalytic organisation. A very large number of messages were sent by the

Soviets between Washington and Moscow in the year 1943 – about 25,000 trade messages alone. The breaking of Venona was a very complicated process that went on, in some sense, throughout the 37 years it was worked on. However, the single most important event occurred when an army Lieutenant, Richard Halleck, in October 1943 took 10,000 messages and sorted them to look for repetitions of text. When he did, he found seven clear cases of a duplicate key. By mid 1944 a similar result had been achieved with Soviet intelligence messages by pairing them with the trade traffic. It was about two years later when Meredith Gardner, the extraordinarily able linguist, began to break out enough of the text of the KGB messages to confirm that it was in fact intelligence related. The list of names of scientists, which Meredith Gardner uncovered by December of 1946, was a key event. It included a large number of American and British scientists who were at Los Alamos.

Klaus Fuchs was tracked down because one of the Venona messages was on the gaseous diffusion process of separating the various kinds of Uranium. The FBI and MI5 were able from the very nature of this message to narrow it down to just a small number of scientists who might have had some involvement and later to Klaus Fuchs alone. The final confirmation of Klaus Fuchs as a spy came when MI5 persuaded him to confess. He described his contact in New York, known only as Raymond and described him physically. The FBI searched through all of its files of pictures. Fuchs looked through these pictures and finally identified Harry Gold. Harry Gold, too, confessed and led them to David Greenglass. Greenglass's confession eventually led to the Rosenbergs.

The British participation in Venona really began in about 1947 and later, when Kim Philby became the SIS intelligence representative in Washington he was briefed on the contents of Venona. He was probably able to monitor the progress in identifying people during a period from 1950. Philby's access to Venona would have been only to the translations, but this would have meant that he would have been able to monitor the exact progress of breaking out names and identifying people as spies, so that he would have known exactly when the US was about to identify somebody, perhaps even just before or just as it happened. Philby could well have seen the codename HOMER and warned Moscow that Donald MacLean was about to be identified or had been identified. The Soviets probably knew about the Venona project from as early as 1945, when a US Army officer named William Weissband was assigned to the Soviet section as a Russian linguistic consultant. Weissman was in fact a GRU agent and had been a Soviet agent on the West Coast, handling a spy in the aircraft industry just before he entered the army.

The Soviet intelligence service would have been most anxious for Philby to discover the amount of intelligence detail and in particular names the US codebreakers were recovering from the Venona traffic. The Venona project exposed a large number of people including at least 130 US citizens identified as being spies for the Soviet Union. There were another 100 names that looked like covernames who might be Americans but were never identified. There were two primary names that were not identified, atomic scientists 'Pers' and 'Kvant'. In addition 'Erie' and 'Huron' also appear to be involved in the atomic programme. There are thousands of such transcripts that were still unbroken when the project was largely abandoned in the early 1980s; many referred to British and European traitors. The true extent of the wartime Soviet espionage campaign against its Western allies is never likely to be fully uncovered or understood.

W

WALKER SPIES (WALKER, John Anthony) (1938–) John Walker worked as a Soviet spy while serving as communications specialist for the US Navy. It is estimated that he helped the Soviet Union gain more than one million messages and compromised US code security. He had already retired as a Navy officer when arrested in 1985. Other members of his ring included his sailor son Michael, his brother Arthur James Walker, who also served in the Navy, and his friend Jerry Alfred Whitworth, who trained in the Navy's satellite communications. Though Walker is thought to have won a high military rank from the Russians, he also became a member of the racist Ku Klux Klan and the ultra anti-Communist John Birch Society.

Walker had begun selling secrets to the Soviets while at Norfolk in 1962 and created a spy ring which by 1968 included at least two other members of the US Navy. Reassigned to San Diego in 1969, Walker was put in charge of the radio school, training recruits in using communications equipment. Since he now had only a limited access to secrets, he was able to supply his Soviet handlers with less substantial secrets and his monthly stipend from the KGB dropped from $4,000 a month to $2,000 a month. Retired in 1975 after twenty years in the navy, Walker had made an estimated $1 million from the Soviets for selling secrets for about 17 years. He was convicted and sent to prison for life. Other members of his spy ring included his son Michael, who received a 20-year sentence; Arthur Walker, who got three life terms; and Jerry Alfred Whitworth, who received 365 years in prison. None of them, except Michael, the most pathetic of them all, expressed any regret for selling out their country.

WALK IN A defector who declares his intentions by walking into an official installation and asking for political asylum or volunteering to work in place.

WALKING THE CAT US intelligence term for retracing the activities of a 'Blown' agent back to the beginning of an operation to see if it is possible to discover how it was compromised.

WALSINGHAM, Sir Francis (1532–90) The son of a Norfolk lawyer in the court of King Henry VIII, Francis Walsingham graduated from Cambridge with a law degree in 1552, spending the next six years on the Continent in protest against the Catholic reign of Queen Mary. While living in Italy he befriended several aristocrats who were furthering the espionage arts of secret writing that had come into existence during the Italian renaissance. He went on to study and master codes and ciphers.

When Queen Elizabeth I assumed the throne, Walsingham returned to England in 1558. He took an active part in the persecution of Catholics and, with the backing of William Cecil, entered Parliament in 1663. Joining the Privy Council in 1573, he was knighted in 1577. Throughout this period Walsingham proved a staunch supporter of Elizabeth and her rigid anti-Catholic policies. The ousted Catholics championed Mary Stuart, Queen of Scotland, in that she promoted the Catholic faith and had an equal claim to the British throne. In jeopardy, Elizabeth offered Mary sanctuary against the Scottish reformers and then betrayed her, imprisoning her. She then plotted with Walsingham, whom she had made her spymaster, to compromise Mary.

A long time earlier, Walsingham had established the most extensive spy network the world had ever seen, placing secret agents throughout Europe, especially in the Catholic courts of Spain, Italy and France, to ferret out Catholic plots against Elizabeth. To that end, he sent the poet Christopher Marlowe to study at a Catholic seminary in Rheims where anti-Elizabeth plots were being hatched. Marlowe later became a celebrated playwright and Walsingham's homosexual lover but he was mysteriously murdered in a tavern brawl, which may have been staged to effect his permanent disappearance. Walsingham had a penchant for using writers as spies. William Fowler, the Scots poet, worked for him at one time or another, as did Matthew Royston.

The insidious Walsingham probably invented many of the so-called plots against Elizabeth. He jailed many innocent persons whom he accused of espionage in order to enhance his image of spy-catcher with his sovereign. One real plot, however, involved Anthony Babington who planned to release Queen Mary from the Tower of London and remove Elizabeth in 1586. Walsingham's spies unearthed the plot and Babington and others paid the price of the plot with their lives. One of Walsingham's most astute and assiduous spies was Anthony Munday who lived in Rome and infiltrated the English College there, exposing many Catholic plots and identifying many anti-Elizabethan spies for his spymaster in London. At home he relied upon John Dee and Thomas Phelippes, both scholars of ancient ciphers and codes, to decode all of Queen Mary's mail which was intercepted by another Walsingham spy,

Gilbert Gifford, who posed as an ardent Catholic and gained Mary's confidence.

Through these men Walsingham built a case against Mary, one which eventually spelled her doom. Mary's correspondence, according to Dee and Gifford, also a cryptographer of sorts, contained secret treasonable statements. One letter of Mary's in particular was used by Walsingham to prove that Mary had been part of the Babington plot and it brought about a death warrant from Elizabeth. It is likely, however, that Walsingham himself, or Dee or Gifford acting under his direction, concocted this forgery, perhaps with Elizabeth's collusion, in order to eliminate Mary. When Elizabeth sent Mary to the block in 1587, King Philip II of Spain became enraged, branding Elizabeth a regicide. The Catholic monarch sought revenge against Elizabeth and began to build a huge armada that would sail to England, invade the island and sweep the English Protestant Queen from her throne. Walsingham, however, sent one of his best spymasters, Anthony Standen, to organise a spy network along the coasts of Spain and France. Standen was able to learn the exact time of sailing and route taken by the Armada and sent this information to Walsingham.

One of Standen's agents was on the staff of the Marquis of Santa Cruz, who had been appointed by Philip as the grand admiral of the Armada. This agent was able to learn the exact number of vessels in the Armada, their captains and crews, the number of troops being conveyed, along with all stores, ammunition and armour to be employed in the invasion. Acting on Standen's information, Elizabeth's fleet intercepted the Armada and destroyed what was left of it after it had been decimated by a powerful hurricane. Though he had given great service to Elizabeth, Walsingham did not find his queen a grateful monarch. After her triumph over Spain and its vanquished Armada, Elizabeth all but ignored her spymaster. Walsingham, whom Elizabeth obviously distrusted as being too powerful and having information that might implicate her in Mary's official 'murder', removed him from office. He died penniless two years later. The many petitions he sent to Elizabeth were returned to him unanswered.

Walsingham's espionage procedures and systems, however, outlived him and were employed by John Thurloe, Oliver Cromwell's exacting spymaster. Walsingham's code expert Thomas Phelippes, upon his spymaster's death, founded and became the proprietor of the first private espionage agency, one that successfully catered to the English gentry. Like Thurloe and Phelippes, countless spymasters to come the world over would owe a debt to the clever, immoral Walsingham.

WATCHCON Watch Condition (military I&W rating system for potential world hotspots).

WATCHERS A member of the Security Service (MI5) A4 Section which conducts surveillance on foreign targets within Britain.

WATCH LIST A list of persons considered of potential interest to an intelligence agency.

WATSON Produced in the USA, Watson is a reasonably advanced system for analysing intelligence data and for listening in on digital communication. An instrument radiates enough for the conversation to be picked up by satellite. Such conversations are then classified by computer and analysed on the basis of the numbers of the transmitting and receiving phones, the location of the transmitting and receiving phones, time of the conversation, language, keywords and voice typing. Once classified and analysed, the conversations are sent to analysts for checking.

Protection against this kind of surveillance is possible only if both the transmitting and receiving instruments are in rooms built on the lines of the Faraday Cage, and if all electrical cables and connections that transmit the signal are buried deep under the ground. If an intelligence service has 'friendly ties' with the local telephone company, not even this kind of protection is safe. Protection against attack by the new digital communication surveillance system, and especially mobile phones, leaves just one option: the battery and any other power source should be completely removed, while the least secure action is to become a subscriber to a mobile telephony network.

Today, all intelligence data collected is incredibly swiftly analysed automatically by the Watson program. For example, in just a few seconds it responds to a single question about a person or event graphically or visually by collating and processing all available data, conversations, financial transactions and presents a complete picture of the user that can be displayed in the form of diagram, map, chain of command, or the like. What Watson can do in a few seconds might take a team of analysts days. The surveillance equipment covers the territory within a certain radius and follows a traveller with a mobile phone and the moment the traveller moves out of range of a surveillance station, he is picked up by another in the next town thanks to the identification code of each phone under surveillance. Surveillance equipment in Croatia operates in the same way as in foreign countries. Surveillance by way of mobile phones even when the instrument is turned off is carried out by the relevant services dialling the number of the mobile phone and then, before dialling the last digit, running a particular code that turns on the microphone. The telephone thus becomes a 'bug' which conveys all sounds up to 15 metres in diameter. This kind of surveillance can be disabled only by removing the battery from the mobile phone.

Watson was originally a Windows-based program written in the early 1990s by Harlequin, Inc. Cambridge, Mass. The software was very popular with intelligence analysts and its improved versions continue to play a leading role in the War on Terrorism.

WEAPONS An intelligence officer does not normally carry a weapon, partly because its discovery by a foreign counter-intelligence or police force would be highly incriminating. Intelligence agencies do however stock and even develop weapons for the use of personnel carrying out specialised duties such as covert action officers, bodyguards and, of course, assassins.

Silenced weapons: although not used as regularly as the writers of the more lurid spy fiction would suggest, these weapons do have a definite role in the work of the modern intelligence agency. Firearms are never totally silent, although they can be made quiet enough not to attract attention. A silencer eliminates most of the sound of the muzzle blast but not, of course, of the weapon's working parts. Latest developments have seen a combination of much improved silencer techniques, partly plastic handguns like the Austrian Glock to cut down the sound of its action and the use of specially developed reduced charge cartridges to greatly reduce any unwanted noise. Such weapons have been regularly used in the past by the Soviet Intelligence Services and in particular the Israeli Mossad, who have their own specialist assassination teams, known as the Kidon. The weapons they use include a specially modified and silenced Beretta model 70, with reduced charge 7.65mm cartridges.

The British SAS in 1945–46 operated special three-man 'Hunter' teams which used captured German and Italian weapons including the popular Beretta, to hunt down and secretly kill German Gestapo and SS personnel responsible for the torture and murder of SAS or SOE officers during WWII. A member of one of these teams, Captain Peter Mason, later served in the Defence Intelligence Staff and became one of the leading experts on special weapons and close combat shooting.

Other weaponry that may be found in the intelligence service armoury includes high-performance and silenced sniper rifles, concealed weapons, dart-firing pistols, crossbows, steel-wired garrottes, 'knuckle-duster' knives, single-shot pistols disguised as a cigarette, gas assassination pens and much more.

The Soviet SMERSH or 'Death to Spies' department of the Intelligence Service developed a whole range of assassination weapons including the gas guns used by KGB officer Bogdan Stashinsky to kill Ukrainian dissidents Lev Rebet in Munich in 1957 and Stefan Bandera in 1959. Both deaths were ascribed to heart attacks until Stashinsky defected to W Germany in 1961 and admitted the murders. The weapon he had used could be concealed in a newspaper and fired the concentrated cyanide gas directly into the victims' faces, killing them almost instantly. To protect himself, the assassin would take a tablet of sodium thiosulphate 30 minutes before the attack and an ampoule of amyl nitrate was then broken and inhaled immediately after the assassination had taken place.

One of the CIA's plans to assassinate Fidel Castro involved the decidedly odd method of impregnating one of Castro's cigars with a deadly botulism bacilli. However, the most effective weapons are those that leave no trace, commonly known as 'Measles', the cause of death being described as 'from natural causes'. This has been the chosen method of a number of major intelligence organisations and the techniques are constantly being perfected.

WET AFFAIR   Soviet/Russian term for an operation that includes a 'killing'.

WET SQUAD   Soviet/Russian term for an assassination team.

WET WORK   Intelligence term for an intelligence operation involving a murder or assassination.

WHITE   Term for an unclassified or acknowledged classified project or for an agent who has not been identified as being involved in intelligence operations.

WHITE, Sir Dick (1906–93)   The only intelligence officer to have headed both the internal Security Service (MI5) (1953–56) and the foreign espionage service, the Secret Intelligence Service (MI6) (1956–68). White joined MI5 in 1936 and worked for SIME or Security Intelligence Middle East, the local cover name for MI5, where he quickly built up a reputation as a considerable talent. Both he and his future MI6 colleague Maurice Oldfield, along with others in the counter-espionage departments, were required to study in great detail the reports on the Gouzenko case in Ottawa produced by Roger Hollis. In consequence, as early as 1946, White was warning his superiors about the SIS Officer Kim Philby. When White took over SIS in 1956 he discovered that his warnings had been ignored. White, though still with no hard proof, was to keep Philby at arm's length until such time as he was able to send Nicholas Elliott out to Beirut in 1961 to confront Philby with new evidence. Philby took the hint and defected.

White, doubtful of the value of over-relying on electronic intelligence, whether gathered by SIGINT or satellites, preferred to develop HUMINT sources. This paid off handsomely during the Cuban Missile Crisis when all that the massive US intelligence community could provide Kennedy with was satellite photos of what the Soviets were doing or had already done, and SIGINT which largely confirmed the photos. SIS had nurtured and pampered Oleg Penkovsky, a temperamental Soviet GRU officer. From this source SIS was able to provide the CIA with information on the lesser threat Soviet missiles actually posed, intelligence on Soviet weaknesses and most importantly, intentions. When the crisis was over, Sir Dick summoned his senior staff at the Broadway HQ to praise them for the 'great feat' SIS had achieved Kennedy is believed to have personally thanked the SIS chief later, much to the chagrin of the CIA and NSA Directors.

It is also important to note that Sir Dick White, an experienced and highly capable counter-espionage officer chose Roger Hollis as his deputy Director at MI5 1953–56 and strongly recommended that Hollis should replace him as head of MI5 when White moved to SIS in 1956. White at SIS and Hollis at MI5 were then to work closely together for another nine years until Hollis retired in 1965. Sir Dick went on record as saying he had complete confidence in Hollis and condemned strongly those who doubted his loyalty to MI5 and the UK.

A highly capable administrator and most importantly, after a series of intelligence disasters, a politically safe pair of hands, on his retirement from SIS in 1968 White was consequently appointed as Intelligence and Security adviser to the Cabinet Office until his final retirement in 1972.

WILSON PLOT (Harold Wilson, British Prime Minister 1964–1970 and 1974–76) This has long been derided by academic researchers, the intelligence community and successive governments, even those formed by what used to be the socialist Labour Party. However, there can be little doubt that, from Harold Wilson's first election victory in 1964 to his surprise resignation in 1976, significant elements within MI5 in particular carried out a determined campaign to undermine his administration and to blacken his reputation. The extended cover-up has been largely successful in that few now remember the events of those troubled years in Britain and fewer still would accept the idea of the talk of coups and bringing down the British Government. Yet the conspirators are believed to have included senior civil servants, members of the opposition political parties, newspaper owners such as Cecil King, MI6 and fairly senior officers of the Security Service, MI5.

The Wilson Plot was ultimately successful too, in that Harold Wilson, the only Prime Minister brave enough to challenge seriously the 'secret state', was eventually destroyed as a politician and died with his reputation undeservedly ruined. The thirty or so MI5 officers involved are believed to include Peter Wright, Barry Russell-Jones and Harry Wharton, one time head of K5. Other names often linked to the 'plot' include Lord Beeching, Lord Rothschild, David Stirling; the founder of the SAS, and George Young; former deputy Chief of the SIS [MI6]. Indeed, the CIA are also understood to have played a part in providing ammunition for the conspirators and are believed to have penetrated the very heart of Wilson's Labour Cabinet as Michael Stewart, the Foreign Secretary, has long been considered to have been an important CIA 'asset' at the time.

WINDOW DRESSING Ancillary materials that are included in a cover story or deception operation to help convince the opposition or other casual observers that what they are observing is genuine.

WISNER, Frank G. (1909–65)   Frank G. Wisner was a Wall Street lawyer and friend of William J. Donovan, head of OSS, who recruited him for espionage work in WWII. John Toulmin, a deputy chief of OSS, appointed him station director in Istanbul in early 1944, where he quickly established a reliable espionage organisation whose tentacles curled into Nazi-occupied countries of SE Europe. Through Wisner's spy network, he was able to provide invaluable information to the US Air Force regarding the Ploesti oilfields in Romania, which were successfully destroyed in a later bombing campaign.

When the OSS was disbanded, Wisner remained in intelligence and after the CIA was established in 1947, became the Assistant Director of Policy Coordination (OPC) with the specific mission of combating covert activities of the NKVD. As head of Special CIA operations, Wisner initiated the Berlin Tunnel operation, later blown by the British traitor, George Blake. He was also responsible for obtaining the 1956 secret speech Premier Nikita Sergeyevich Khrushchev gave in the

Kremlin in which he denounced Joseph Stalin. Wisner was one of the CIA chiefs responsible for the successful coup in Guatemala and the failed coup in Indonesia.

From 1953 to 1959, Wisner was Deputy Director for Plans at the CIA, handling all covert operations and dirty tricks. He worked closely with the CIA's infamous consultant Dr Sidney Gottlieb who concocted bizarre schemes to assassinate Cuban dictator Fidel Castro, such as slipping him poisoned cigars or shooting poison darts into a wet suit Castro was expected to wear when SCUBA diving. Wisner helped direct radio propaganda into Soviet-occupied Hungary in 1956, encouraging the Hungarians to revolt against the Communist Government and its Soviet allies, with appalling consequences for those involved. Hungarian anti-Communist leaders had been promised that US forces would come to their aid once they revolted.

When this did not happen, the Soviet Army brutally crushed the Hungarian revolution, killing tens of thousands of civilians. Wisner had supposedly expected a widespread anti-Communist revolt that would unseat the Soviets from all or most of the Eastern Bloc countries. When the Hungarians were defeated, he went to pieces, suffering the first of many nervous breakdowns, brought on by a severe attack of hepatitis.

A second possible explanation for Wisner's collapse has always been that the CIA had used the Hungarian patriots to trap the Soviet Union into a brutally repressive reaction that would lose them support throughout both the Communist and non-Communist world. And indeed, fatally undermine the Soviet Union's long-term ability to maintain control of E Europe. This later scenario is, of course, exactly what was to occur.

After returning to work, Wisner became the station chief in London but he suffered several more nervous breakdowns. After long periods in the hospital, he resigned from the CIA in 1962. In 1965, tormented by what was described as 'his own inner demons', Wisner, one of the last true Cold War Warriors, killed himself with a shotgun.

WRIGHT, Peter (1916–95) Peter Wright attended Oxford and worked in the Admiralty Research Office during WWII. He was head of scientific research for a private firm before Sir Frederick Brundrett recruited him to MI5 in 1949 as a scientific adviser. He joined MI5 full-time in 1955. Until his retirement as a deputy director (effectively only a departmental head) of MI5, Wright had worked through the Cold War years handling the technical end of British counter-intelligence, including its sophisticated wiretapping devices, direction-finding units and other espionage devices. Obsessed with the threat of Soviet penetration of MI5, Wright began to formulate all sorts of suspicions against his fellow officers, including the Director Sir Roger Hollis. Wright had, not surprisingly, also developed a strong friendship with fellow obsessive and 'mole-hunter' James Jesus Angleton, head of CIA counter-intelligence. Wright and his small team of supporters virtually paralysed MI5 by their tactics and continual accusations. Finally, Wright with no further prospect of promotion resigned in January 1976 to live in Australia.

Following his disenchantment with MI5 after his failure to receive the level of service pension he had expected, Wright was introduced to Chapman Pincher, a writer on security matters with the London *Daily Express*, by a mutual friend, Lord Rothschild, a former senior adviser to Prime Minister Edward Heath's Conservative Government of 1970–74. Wright's book *Spycatcher* quickly raised a political storm. In it he confirmed that an MI5 cabal had run a 'black propaganda' campaign to discredit the Labour Prime Minister Harold Wilson by labelling him a Communist sympathiser. The publication of Wright's revealing autobiography and its exposure of MI5 operations so rattled Conservative Prime Minister Margaret Thatcher that she conducted a two-year campaign to ban the book. In Australia, where Wright had taken up residence as a farmer, the British Government filed a suit to prevent the publication of an Australian edition. Thatcher's efforts succeeded in making it a runaway best seller in the US and elsewhere, with more than a quarter of a million copies sold. Though banned in the UK, its contents soon became well known.

The *Spycatcher* saga was a talking point throughout the world; much less well known however has been the interesting suggestion that Rothschild's primary interest in promoting the book and its subsequent worldwide publicity was simply to direct public and media attention towards Sir Roger Hollis and well away from the real Soviet 'mole', none other than Lord Victor Rothschild himself!

X

XOI Operations Deputy for Intelligence, Surveillance & Reconnaissance (ISR); US Air Force intelligence chief, a 2-star Pentagon-based general.

XX COMMITTEE *see* DOUBLE-CROSS SYSTEM

Y

YAGODA, Genrikh Gregorevich (1891–1938) Joseph Stalin's selection of Genrikh (Henry) Yagoda as the replacement for Vyacheslav Menzhinsky to head the OGPU was one of genocidal expediency. Coarse, uneducated and revelling in his illiteracy, Yagoda was nevertheless ruthlessly energetic in carrying out Stalin's orders. A Polish Jew, he had joined the Communist Revolution of 1917 and had served in the Red Army during the Russian civil war. Vitally he had also won the trust of Joseph Stalin. In 1920, he worked for the Cheka, the successor to the Okhrana, the Czarist secret police. His role model was Felix Dzerzhinsky, the brutal and uncompromising Cheka chief.

Throughout the early 1920s, Yagoda was directing slave labour programmes. In 1926, Dzerzhinsky died of overwork, and was replaced by Menzhinsky who appointed Yagoda to SMERSH, the Ninth Division of the OGPU, the liquidation department that sought out dissident Communists and murdered them. When Menzhinsky introduced Yagoda to his fellow OGPU officers in 1926, he smilingly stated: 'This young man enjoys the full confidence of Comrade Stalin.' He also enjoyed secret orders from his mentor Stalin to murder anyone who appeared to challenge the dictator's authority. He surrounded himself with first hundreds, then thousands of officers loyal to himself while taking over all foreign espionage from Menzhinsky. Eventually he became the director of SMERSH, training and assigning OGPU assassins to murder dissident Communists throughout Europe and particularly those personally critical of Stalin.

Many of Yagoda's victims were poisoned and indeed developing new quick-acting poisons apparently fascinated Yagoda and he maintained a purpose-built laboratory. One of those poisons Yagoda used to murder the independent-minded Menzhinsky in May 1934 and on Stalin's direct orders. The Soviet leader's first directive to Yagoda as the new head of OGPU was to assassinate S.M. Kirov, a member of the Politburo, Stalin's chief lieutenant in Leningrad and one of the founding fathers of Communist Russia. On 1 December 1934, Kirov was shot and killed as he walked down a corridor on the sixth floor of the Smolny Institute. His killer was a young Communist named Leonid V. Nikolaev, who, along with 13 accomplices, was then executed by

firing squad on 29 December 1934, before Nikolaev could reveal
Yagoda's involvement and more importantly, Stalin's. This was the plot
revealed by Nikita Khrushchev in his famous 1956 Kremlin speech
finally denouncing Joseph Stalin.

Stalin then ordered the OGPU deputy director, Nicolai Yezhov, to
arrest and accuse Yagoda of conspiring to murder Kirov and to commit
other crimes against the Soviet State. Yagoda and other 'conspirators'
went on trial in March 1938 and at first Yagoda denied the charges.
During a court recess he was taken to the infamous basement prison of
the OGPU's own Lubianka HQ where among other inducements both
his shoulders were 'grossly dislocated'. Yagoda confessed his guilt to the
court a few hours later. He admitted to poisoning Menzhinsky, plotting
Kirov's murder, killing Maxim Gorky and his son with poison, as well
as wiping out thousands of political victims and all as part of a
conspiracy he hatched with the Western powers such as Germany, to
the amazement of a shocked and saddened Stalin.

Yagoda was imprisoned while Yezhov took over control of the newly
renamed NKVD. Sometime in 1938, again on Stalin's orders, Yagoda
was dragged from his cell and executed by a firing squad. Stalin,
however was soon to find that his replacement, the 'bloody red dwarf'
Yezhov, was even more dangerous not only to lives of the Soviet people,
but to Stalin himself.

YARDLEY, Herbert O. (1889–1958) Yardley obtained a job in
Washington in 1912, working for the State Department as a telegraph
operator. He found the work fascinating. After some four years Yardley
had proved to his own satisfaction, and his superiors' annoyance, that
US codes were hopelessly vulnerable and when the US finally entered
WWI in 1917, he was sent to the War Department and then on to the
US Signal Corps. Here he was given the rank of lieutenant and named
the head of a special bureau dealing with cryptology called MI8
(Military Intelligence, Section 8).

Within months, Yardley's small bureau had broken almost all of the
German diplomatic and Abwehr codes. By August 1918, while battles
still raged along the Western Front, Yardley went to Europe to learn
more about cryptology from the British and French intelligence
agencies. In England, he met Vernon Kell, director of MI5, and Admiral
William Reginald Hall, head of British naval intelligence, whose
celebrated Room 40 operation had broken the coded contents of the
notorious Zimmermann Telegram, a deciding factor for America's entry
into the war against Germany. He also went to France, where he studied

the operations of French cryptology. After attending the Paris Peace Conference in 1919 as chief cryptologist of the American delegation, Yardley was told that his job was at an end. He disagreed, pointing out that America had enemies around the world and the codes of these nations would have to be deciphered so that the US could realise any future threat to its security. He prepared a comprehensive plan to establish a peacetime cryptological bureau and submitted this to the State Department and the Chief of Staff, a report titled *Code and Cipher Investigation and Attack*.

General Marlborough Churchill, head of Army Intelligence, persuaded officials in the State Department to fund an 'unofficial' codebreaking operation. Because of legalities, the State Department insisted that this operation not be located in Washington. Instead, in 1919, Yardley opened up his cryptology bureau in a four-storey New York City brownstone at 141 East 37th Street, just east of Lexington Avenue. Yardley quickly organised a staff of 20 top cryptologists, mostly those who had worked under him at MI8, including Dr Charles Mendelsohn and Victor Weiskopf. One of his most brilliant codebreakers was F. Livesey, who became his assistant. Yardley dubbed the operation the AMERICAN BLACK CHAMBER (after the French Black Chamber, the cryptology division of French intelligence in WWI that he so admired) a name that soon became world famous.

Yardley's group proved to be successful in breaking the difficult codes of the newly formed Cheka, the Bolshevik secret police in Russia, which had supplanted the Czarist secret police, the Okhrana.

The Black Chamber broke the Japanese diplomatic codes in time to allow the US negotiators to operate from a position of strength during the 1921 Washington Naval Conference. In 1924, Yardley's funds were considerably reduced by the State Department, which was then undergoing budget cuts under direct orders from President Calvin Coolidge. In 1928, Henry L. Stimson became Secretary of State. In reviewing the AMERICAN BLACK CHAMBER operation, Stimson dismissed the organisation as non-essential. Stimson, an old-school diplomat, was repelled by espionage and covert operations of any kind. He reportedly told Yardley in a reproachful, stuffy manner, 'Gentlemen do not read each other's mail.' He then ordered the State Department to cease funding Yardley's operation.

Yardley was to suffer greatly, finding his reputation made him unemployable. However, after using up his savings, he succeeded in writing an enormously successful book entitled *The American Black Chamber*. The book earned both a great deal of money and the enmity of Congress, where he was denounced as having given away America's secrets. His career as one of the great cryptologists was finally over.

YEZHOV, Nicolai (1895–1938)   Like his predecessor Yagoda, Nicolai Yezhov was a cold-blooded killer who murdered on Stalin's orders. He had been a zealous Bolshevik who allied himself to Stalin from 1918 onwards. After serving in various capacities within the Cheka, GPU, OGPU, he became, at Stalin's insistence, Yagoda's deputy. After Yagoda had served the dictator's purposes, he summarily dismissed him, sending a telegram to the Politburo on 25 September 1936 which stated: THE IMMEDIATE APPOINTMENT OF COMRADE YEZHOV AS PEOPLE'S COMMISSAR OF INTERNAL AFFAIRS IS UNQUESTIONABLY NECESSARY. YAGODA IS PROVING INCAPABLE OF DEALING WITH THE TROTSKY-ZINOVIEV BLOCK.

Yezhov then conducted a general purge of Yagoda supporters from the OGPU inside the newly renamed NKVD. More than 3,000 officers were summarily executed in 1937. One of the worst of Yagoda's officers, an interrogator named Chertok (Little Devil) did not wait for arrest. He threw himself from the 12th floor balcony of his Lubyanka office while many others simply took their own and their families' lives before they could fall into the hands of Yezhov's torturers.

Before this appalling bloodletting came to an end more than two million Russians, Stalin's political enemies, the officer corps, peasants who had resisted agrarian reform and collectivism and a wide and increasingly arbitrary range of those accused of being 'enemies of the state' had been killed by Yezhov's murder squads. Aiding Yezhov's reign of terror was Lavrenti Beria, a brutal, sadistic policeman from Stalin's own province of Georgia and the future Soviet Premier Nikita Sergeyevich Khrushchev, then the First Party Secretary in Moscow and who would denounce Stalin in 1956 as a mass murderer.

Stalin believed the slaughter of the so-called 'Yezhovschina' required the help of a reliable deputy and suggested his old Bolshevik comrade, Lavrenti Beria. Yezhov certainly knew what that would eventually mean for his own chances of survival, but having no choice, appointed Beria his deputy. Together these two extraordinary characters embarked on a purge of the upper ranks of the Red Army; a near suicidal mistake as it turned out, only three years before the German Army would invade the Soviet Union. More than 35,000 top-ranking Soviet officers were seized and executed on the bogus charge of being collaborators with the Nazis in Germany. Beria arrested Yezhov a short time later. Many of his senior officers were also arrested and murdered by the end of 1938.

It has been suggested that Beria himself confronted Yezhov or the 'bloody red dwarf' as he was often known. He wrapped chicken wire about Yezhov's neck, strangled him and strung him up from a window bar, leaving his carcass to rot for months, showing the decaying corpse to other prisoners in order to intimidate them into making confessions.

Y SERVICE   British Signals interception organisation in WWII feeding the intelligence gathered to GC&CS at Bletchley Park.

Z

ZIMMERMAN TELEGRAM Intercepted message from German Foreign Minister Arthur Zimmerman to the German Ambassador in Mexico City discussing an offer to be made to Mexico of an alliance with Germany in return for a chance to reconquer Texas, New Mexico and Arizona. British Naval Intelligence intercepted and decoded the telegram and in a roundabout way to hide the origins of the decoded message, passed it on to the US Government. The resulting furore played no small part in bringing the USA into WWI.

ZINOVIEV LETTER A forged secret letter from President Grigori Zinoviev to the Communist Party of Great Britain was sent to SIS from one of its agents in the Latvian Capital of Riga. It was part of a campaign organised by White Russians with good contacts among right-wing elements in Britain. It was then 'leaked' by members of the intelligence service and the opposition Conservative Party, to the *Daily Mail*, a major national newspaper. It was published on 25 October 1924 just prior to a General Election. The resulting scandal and publicity may have been partly responsible for costing the Labour Party Government any chance it had of retaining power. That was certainly the intention of the forgers. In 1952, SIS (MI6) allowed documents relating to the scandal to be destroyed, just before the retirement of Sir Stewart Menzies as 'C'. Menzies, a conservative by nature, had admitted to sending a copy of the 'Zinoviev letter' to the *Daily Mail*. The letter to the Foreign Office 'weeders' authorising the destruction of the papers was significantly signed by 'C' himself!

ZOO Western intelligence term for a police station.

Z SECTION OF THE SIS It had always been something of a joke to foreign intelligence services that, while Britain always pretended it did not possess a secret service and never admitted its existence, everyone knew it operated from Passport Control offices around the world. But Colonel Dansey, deputy head of MI6, decided that, with the growing threat of war with Germany, it would be wise to have a separate or parallel network of agents working independently under a non-diplomatic cover, but still reporting to the SIS. This was to be called the Z Section. HQ for Z Section was established at Bush House in London and each member or agent of this network was given a Z number, thus Dansey was Z1, Commander Kenneth Cohen (Royal Navy) Z2 and Z3 was Colonel John Codrington. Many commercial and business firms were used as cover addresses for the section, which soon had agents all over Europe, but it was a project which did not commend itself to many SIS personnel. The big mistake was that Z Section insisted on being as dominant in The Hague as the larger SIS already based there on the principle that a neutral country was an ideal HQ for an intelligence service network. The incident at Venlo, when Major Richard Stevens (MI6) and Captain Payne Best (Z Section) were together lured over the frontier into Germany on 9 November 1939, destroyed both Z Section and the other SIS networks throughout Europe.

ZUBATOV, S.V. (1868–1917)   To counter the revolutionary tide that was beginning to sweep over Czarist Russia at the turn of the century, S.V. Zubatov, police chief of the Okhrana, the Czarist secret police, invented what came to be known as 'police socialism', or 'Zubotovism'. It was an ingenious attempt to pre-empt the politicisation of the workers by tricking them into joining a labour movement actually controlled by the secret police.

Using scores of police spies, Zubatov, in 1901, organised the Society for Mutual Aid for Working Men in the Mechanical Industries. In all major cities, tens of thousands of workers joined the union, not knowing, of course, that it was secretly sponsored by the Okhrana. Those elected to the union leadership were Okhrana spies who made sure that the attitude at these meetings always reflected reverence and loyalty to the Czar. To show that the national union was effective, Zubatov pressured employers to grant small concessions to the workers. Though Zubotov eschewed the support of intellectuals, he was practical enough to realise that without some sort of intellectual representation, his union movement would be suspect. He recruited professors and journalists to support the movement and they dutifully delivered lectures laced with unwavering allegiance to the Czar. Zubatov's successes throughout Russia were phenomenal, but what eventually ruined the plan were the reactions of the very people he sought to protect, the industrialists.

The Ministry of Finance was inundated with demands from industry leaders, both Russian and foreign businessmen financing industries in Russia. They demanded that such government-backed unionism cease at once. Right-wing elements began to attack Zubatov in the press for, by then, he was directly associated with the union movement. He was portrayed as 'a servant of the Jews'. Then, some of his unions went farther than he envisioned and beyond the control of his secret agents. In the summer of 1903, a number of police unions went on strike. This led to Zubatov's dismissal.

He was advised to leave Russia since both the revolutionaries now knew that he was an Okhrana official and would seek revenge. He was also hated by the aristocracy and industrialists for creating a revolutionary state of mind in Russia. Given a large sum of money, Zubatov went into exile but he remained a fervent Czarist. In 1917, Zubatov, on hearing that the Czar had been forced to abdicate, proved his utter allegiance to the Russian autocrat by placing a revolver to his temple and blowing out his brains.

BIBLIOGRAPHY

I was able to draw upon the files and reference library of over one thousand books created by AFI Research during the last thirty years or so, the library of the Royal United Services Institute for Defence Studies in Whitehall and, when necessary, the vast, web-based resources of both ComLinks and Milnet in the United States.

However certain books were of particular value either for checking facts or providing interesting leads and a shortlist of these includes;

THE PUZZLE PALACE James Bamford – Sidgwick & Jackson 1983
SECRET POWER Nicky Hagar – Craig Potton Publishing 1996
THE TIES THAT BIND Richelson & Ball – Allen & Unwin 1985
DEFENDING THE REALM Hollingsworth & Fielding – Andre Deutsch 1999
THE NEW SPIES James Adams – Hutchinson 1994
UK EYES ALPHA Mark Urban – Faber & Faber 1996
THE IRISH WAR Tony Geraghty – Harper Collins 1998
GUARDIANS Curtis Peebles – Ian Allan 1987
DEEP BLACK William F. Burrows – Bantam 1988
THE IMPERFECT SPIES Melman & Raviv – Sidgwick & Jackson 1989
KGB (The inside Story) Andrew & Gordievsky – Hodder & Stoughton 1990
THE GREAT TERROR Robert Conquest – Hutchinson 1990
THE AGENCY John Ranelagh – Sceptre 1988
PLOTS & PARANOIA Bernard Porter – Unwin Hyman 1989
THE COERCIVE STATE Hillyard & Percy - Smith – Fontana 1988
BLACKLIST Hollingsworth & Norton - Taylor – Hogarth Press 1988
BIG BROTHER Simon Davis – Pan 1996

Magazines of particular interest include the excellent subscription-only STATEWATCH published by an independent group of journalists (Statewatch PO Box 1516, London N16 OEW) and
LOBSTER (available from Robin Ramsay at 214 Westbourne Avenue, Hull HU5 3JB)

While websites that consistently publish material that many governments wish to cover up include:
CRYPTOME (jya.com) New York, USA,
SERENDIPITY (serendipity.cia.com.au) Australia,

DRUDGE REPORT (drudgereport.com) USA,
COVERT ACTION (covertaction.org) USA and
INTELBRIEF (lntelbrief.com) Washington DC, USA.

This is but a small selection from the vast resources of information available to those who wish to seek out the truth. There is little excuse for those who choose to remain in ignorance of the facts and accept the misinformation fed them by democratic and totalitarian governments alike.

INDEX

A

Abel, Rudolph 1, 296
Afghanistan *see* wars and
    conflicts
aircraft 2–3; A-11 296–297;
    AWACS 237; C-119
    Boxcars 270; C-130
    Hercules 270; Constellation
    3; EY-8 2; J-Stars 236, 274
    KC135 Stratotankers 236; RC-
    135V/W 'RJ' 236–237;
    SR-71 4, 296–297, 323;
    U-2 1, 4, 30, 86, 100,
    194, 205, 218–219,
    321–324; UAV xi, xii 62;
    YF-12 297
al-Khouli, Muhammed 303
Al-Qa'ida vii, viii 29, 62, 63,
    143, 145, 235, 312, 352,
    357, 359–363
Albania 5, 143, 357–358
Algeria 5, 105
Allende, Salvador 49, 126
Ames, Aldrich 5, 0, 87, 108, 384
Angleton, James 7–8, 59, 102,
    103, 118–119, 175
anti-terrorism *see* terrorism
Argentina 8–9
Attlee, Clement 122, 338, 339
Australia 13–17, 89, 283
Austria 17–18, 229–230
'axis of evil' vii
Azerbaijan 18

B

Baader-Meinhof 310, 311
Bangladesh 134, 137
Belgium 22, 30
Beria, Levrent 22–24, 260, 407
Best, Payne 70, 390, 410
Bettaney, Michael 26–27, 39,
    234, 342
Bielaski, Alexander Bruce 380
bin Laden, Osama vii 29, 62,
    143, 145, 195, 235, 277,
    312, 352, 357, 359–363
Binghams 39, 188
biological warfare vi–vii, viii
Bissell, Richard 10, 20, 30–31,
    74, 269, 321, 356
Blake, George 24–25, 31–33,
    41, 339, 386, 400
Blunt, Anthony 33–34, 39, 41,
    43–44, 82, 127, 187, 193,
    217, 242, 244

BND 24, 34, 113
Bosnia 65, 236, 279–280
Boyce, Ernest 231–232, 325
Brazil 36–38
Bulgaria 249, 288
Burgess, Guy 34, 39, 41–42, 44,
    82, 187, 191, 193, 217,
    339
Bush, President George (Snr) 9,
    76, 150
Bush, President George W vii
    63, 358, 362
Bush, George H W (CIA) 59,
    366

C

Cairncross, John 43–44, 82,
    190, 193, 242
Cambodia, CIA in 11
cameras: Itek 269; Minox 214,
    387; Praktina 387
Cameron, Dr Ewen 74–75
Canada 44–46, 89, 283, 331
Canaris, Wilhelm Franz 1, 47,
    166, 172, 197
Canine, Raph J 368, 371
Carlos 'the Jackal' 310–311
Carter, President Jimmy 47, 63,
    186, 358
Casey, William 47–48, 366
Castillo, Jose Blandon 68
Castro, Fidel, and CIA 10–11,
    19–21, 30, 67, 76, 120,
    356, 398, 401
Ceausescu, Nicolai 238–239
Chechnya 145, 247, 252, 254,
    288
Chile 49–50, 295
China 11, 50–56, 170–171,
    198, 248, 249, 305–306,
    323; surveillance by 2–3,
    53–56, 275; surveillance of
    4, 236, 300
Church Commission 8, 10–11,
    30, 33, 59
Churchill, Sir Winston 128,
    168, 172, 187, 197, 201,
    224, 288, 326, 333, 338,
    339
CIA 4, 7–8, 24, 31, 44, 47–48,
    56–57, 59, 62, 74, 103,
    267–269, 354–367; in
    Afghanistan 61–62; in
    Africa 9–10, 12, 30; in
    Cuba 10–11, 12, 19–21,
    30, 76–77, 356, 398, 401;
    in India 11; in Indo-China

11, 138; in Latin America 3,
    12, 48, 242, 389; in Middle
    East 9–10, 11, 30, 48, 63,
    241, 277, 357, 373, 381
CL-282 321
Clinton, President Bill 9, 385
codes and ciphers 58, 103, 112,
    187, 196, 316, 326, 332,
    367; decryption 25, 31, 35,
    43, 49, 66, 95, 100, 110,
    221–222, 240–241, 283,
    318, 332–333, 390–392,
    405–406
Cointelpro 378
Colby, William 7–8, 33, 58–59,
    77, 160, 228, 366
Colombia 311, 341, 383, 389
communication and surveillance
    systems: ECHELON xi 16,
    89–93, 106, 199, 283;
    MVD 248, 254, 261; NSEI
    65; TADIL/A 237; Terek
    254; TIBS 237
Congo, CIA in 9–10, 12, 30
Costa Rica, CIA in 12
counter-intelligence 7–8, 19, 41,
    48, 187, 229, 234–236,
    237
counter-terrorism: Australia
    14–15; Canada 45; India
    137; Russia 252, 252; UK
    vi; US 381
Croatia 65–66, 280, 396
Crockett, Norman 387, 388
Crowley, Aleister 175–176
Cuba 66–68, 310; CIA in
    10–11, 12, 19–21, 30,
    76–77, 356; Missile Crisis
    21, 99, 191, 271
Cumming, Sir Mansfield Smith
    68–69, 230–232, 325, 331,
    337
Czech Republic 249

D

Dansey, Col Claude 70–71, 289,
    326, 390, 409–410
de Gaulle, Charles 21, 105–106
Dearlove, Richard Billing 71, 332
Dee, John 71–72
Denmark 72–73
Denning, Lord 226, 339
Denniston, Alaistair 316, 333,
    335
Derry, Sam 387–388
disinformation 6, 25, 33, 78,
    119, 184

415

ELITE FORCES: THE WORLD'S MOST FORMIDABLE SECRET ARMIES

Richard M. Bennett, with a Foreword by Barry Davis BEM

The invincible reputation of specialist military units such as the USA's Delta Force, Israel's IDF and of course Britain's SAS has grown steadily in recent years. Thanks to a number of campaigns and successful anti-terror operations, from London's Iranian Embassy siege in 1980 to their crucial role in Afghanistan following 11 September 2001, it's now assumed that special forces are ideal for our world of small, localised conflicts – and especially George W. Bush's war on terror.

With a capacity for fast, covert response that regular battle orders do not have, elite forces represent the future of conflict for governments everywhere. But their operations often raise the issue of democratic accountability, by making it possible for a government to conduct a successful military campaign to completion without reference to a legislature and without a declaration of war. As well as presenting stories of individual heroism, *Elite Forces* takes a look at operations of dubious legality; examines how deserved the reputation of each elite forces unit is; and takes an objective look at what happens when things go wrong, as they have most famously during the Gulf War of 1991, and in America's disastrous intervention in Somalia in 1993.

- Over 500 compelling entries which cut through the myth and the secrecy surrounding modern-day special forces
- Comprehensive overviews of the history, selection and training procedures, and orders of battle, of every major elite fighting force in the world today
- Packed with hair-raising examples of individual heroism, endurance and courage in adversity
- Fully up to date to include the impact of 11 September 2001 on the world of special forces
- Explores the hidden links between elite forces and governments, intelligence organisations and business, and their controversial lack of accountability
- Examines how new technologies have come to the aid of the elite soldier

It is the first book of its kind to examine all aspects of the overlap between elite forces and the hidden worlds of intelligence and counter-terrorism, and takes an objective look at the secret, controversial role of special forces and 'freelancers' in covert, deadly operations around the world. Fully up-to-date, it examines their relevance to the global fallout from 11 September 2001. *Elite Forces* is both a compelling, revealing and occasionally shocking read, and an authoritative and easy-to-use reference resource.

Published in hardback 6 February 2003
1 85227 974 5
£18.99

CONSPIRACY: PLOTS, LIES AND COVER-UPS

Richard M. Bennett, with a Foreword by Gordon Thomas

In recent years, conspiracy theories have been thought to come exclusively from the wilder shores of political observation – implausibly nutty at best and downright dangerous at worst. By definition, however, a conspiracy occurs each time a group of influential people agrees a course of action in private and by extra-democratic means. Conspiring is part of any politician's job description, and any criminal's attempt to pervert the course of justice.

From new information on the usual suspects, like the Bildeberg Group; through covert intelligence involvement with Britain's Wilson government and in the Profumo affair; to Reagan's secret post-Cold-War agenda; and a mooted plot within the current US administration to supersede George W. Bush, Richard M. Bennett, author of *Espionage* and *Elite Forces*, has written a frightening and authoritative reference work detailing modern conspiracy theories, with notes as to the credibility of each. This book will reclaim the concept of conspiracy from UFO-spotters, Holocaust denialists and survivalist obsessives.

- Takes a topical look at how 9/11 has changed the political climate around the world
- Debunks the more ridiculous or racist notions that have given conspiracy theory a bad name
- Reclaims conspiracy theory from the ironic approach of Jon Ronson or Louis Theroux
- Global in scope, and an accessible reference resource

Published in hardback 4 September 2003
1 85227 093 4
£20.00